Mozart *and his* Music

Mozart
and his
Music

by John N. Burk

RANDOM HOUSE, NEW YORK

Contents

Introduction

THE MUSIC of Mozart is often described as the spirit of youth. Indeed it is, but not exclusively so. It could hardly have been otherwise, for he composed from the age of eight until his death at thirty-five, and every one of his many works is at least in some degree a personal communication. The high spirits, the tender heart of the boy and the adolescent give many of the so-called juvenilia a special charm. This fresh exuberance persists even to *The Magic Flute* of his last year. Yet nothing could be more mistaken than to assume that Mozart as a man and as an artist was a sort of perpetual youth. It is true that his youthful spirit was never broken, even when he was burdened with cares in his later years. Then, his music showed every aspect not only of a mature, but of a great universal artist. *The Magic Flute* is young where its subject is young; it has a basically simple style because Mozart, who at last became the subtlest of composers, never forfeited the simplicity which is the very essence of his style. *The Magic Flute* has many elements; with the heavily tragic *Requiem* which he worked upon simultaneously, it is evidence enough of the expanding diversity of its composer, who could grow older and still remain young.

Another point of view finds a kind of finality in the last works, as if Mozart had brought eighteenth-century music to its ultimate degree of refinement, and thereupon obliged the categorists by passing out of the picture neatly before the end of the century. Mozart did belong to his century, and more specifically to late eighteenth-century Vienna, to the extent that his friendly intercourse, his audiences, were closely involved in everything he composed, for the sociable and the musical Mozart are one. There too he found his material, for he always drew directly upon his musical surroundings. How he made his music his own and immeasurably greater than his time no one will explain. Goethe in his conversations with Eckermann spoke of "the daemons that tease and make sport of men by placing among them single figures so alluring that everyone strives after them, and so great that nobody reaches them. . . . Mozart they set up as something unattainable in music, as Shakespeare in poetry." Mozart, he said again, "was altogether in the power of the daemonic spirit of his genius, and acted according to its command." Genius, which will never be properly defined, may be called that quality in a man's work which transcends all accountability. No analyst can pin it down, nor differentiate between a precious jewel of Mozartean melody and a commonplace contemporary tune. What lifts the music of Mozart high and clear above the music around him was not perceived at first. His musical friends were not aware of his greatness, nor do his letters show that he was aware of more than his skill. He simply fulfilled orders as they came. Such vague concepts as "posterity" and "immortality" did not occur to anyone. Too often a man must die before his transcendent qualities will become plain and vivid to the world at large. Mozart had more than enough of them to have embraced the emergence of another century, if he had been spared for a few years more.

His death led to fatalistic speculation. Goethe decided that Mozart's case was like that of Raphael and Byron. He had lived his creative life, spent his vital energy, fulfilled his mission as artist. The essence of his art lay in its youthfulness. Dying in his thirties, he had given his most to the world.

It is a strange assumption. The belief that he had fulfilled his mission at thirty-five is about on a par with the superstition expressed by his father in a letter of February 16, 1778: "Many observant people have prophesied your early death on account of your precocious and reflective expression."

God, having performed a "miracle" in giving Leopold such a son, would duly take him when his mission was performed.

But was his mission performed? There is really nothing final about his latest works. The late Vienna quartets and quintets are his most adventurous music. Who could say that his last three symphonies do not open new horizons? He had everything to live for. His *Magic Flute* was about to win a wide and general public, and would have assured him commissions and at last a living through opera. Thus secured he could have been bolder and more exploratory. The composer who eagerly sought new color possibilities in the clarinet, who was working toward dynamic expansion and delving so boldly into chromaticism, is strangely unrecognizable as a conservative, an "old schooler" at thirty-five.

To take a flight into footless speculation, let us suppose that Mozart had lived as many years as Haydn did, and so survived by some thirty years the century with which he is too often conveniently classified. If he had reached Haydn's age of seventy-seven, he would have outlived Beethoven, Weber and Schubert, witnessed the first flowering of such Romantics as Schumann, Chopin, Mendelssohn, Berlioz. He would have been confronted with the "Eroica" Symphony at the age of forty-eight, and lived to hear the remaining symphonies of Beethoven, the last quartets and piano sonatas. To confound speculation altogether, at seventy-four he could have heard Berlioz' *Fantastic Symphony!*

Since Vienna drew and held Beethoven for precisely the same reason that it drew and held Mozart, it is reasonably certain that the two would have dwelt in Vienna together on a basis of mutual esteem. When Beethoven, at twenty-two, went to Vienna in 1792, a principal purpose was to study with Haydn. If Mozart had not died in the year previous Beethoven would surely have gone to him, for his reverence for Mozart's genius was unbounded. Mozart would surely have been a more sympathetic master for Beethoven than the aging and rather grudging Haydn, and Mozart, younger, more open-minded, more alert to change, would have been a more cordial companion. As Mozart once drew upon Haydn and later influenced him, Beethoven, who drew deeply upon Mozart, might later have influenced Mozart. The two could never have been congenial artists in the way that Mozart and Haydn were congenial artists, for the spontaneous Mozart could hardly have been at ease with the pondering and self-searching Beethoven. Mozart might have been influenced by Beethoven somewhat as Schubert was, while much in Beethoven's "new paths" would have remained alien to his own nature and seemed extravagant. Certainly he would have remained a symphonist rather than a colorist, and would have found Liszt and Berlioz strange company. Schubert, on the other hand, was another spontaneous lyricist, if by comparison a more timid one than Mozart, with a more limited invention, a narrower horizon.

It would be absurd to suppose that Mozart would not have taken quick advantage of the strengthened pianoforte, the coming of valve instruments, new uses for his beloved trombones, a vaster choral writing. The few operas he had time to write dwarfed everything attempted in that field for a half century to follow (not excepting *Fidelio,* which was greater than its method). He might easily have composed two dozen more!

The Life of Mozart

I

Salzburg, Eighteenth Century

THE TRAFFIC of a modern city hardly helps us to conjure up the eighteenth century. Mozart's Vienna, except for an occasional house front, a relic in stone or iron of ancient elegance, one or two suggestions of a rampart, is pretty well obliterated. With Salzburg it is different. The old part of the town keeps its past and in every respect suggests Mozart to a visitor today, as one looks down from the vertical mountain precipice of the Mönchsberg upon its close houses, converging narrow streets and abundance of church domes and steeples. The brightly painted decorations of the churches with all their rococo theatricality seem at one with the simple, cheerful and friendly air of the Salzburgers, at one too with the most amiable and engaging of all composers.

Unfortunately, the Salzburg that now loves, honors and performs Mozart for its own pleasure as well as profit was by no means loved by Mozart in his time. He had never a good word for it. Of individual friends he had many, for he made friends readily, wherever he happened to be. The main trouble with his native town was its musical provinciality. It had no adequate orchestra for Mozart the symphonist, no opera company for the composer who loved opera above everything. The Archbishop Sigismund, who ruled completely the little community, expected the composers in his court to provide Masses for the routine fulfillment of his services. Mozart wrote what was required of him with loving care. They were accepted as routine.

Salzburg was not entirely a musical outpost. It was close

enough to Vienna to reflect the musical ways of that city. The archiepiscopal court made some attempt to live up to its position. Sometimes when a stage production or a service was planned for a special ceremony, good musicians were imported from Vienna or Munich. Mozart in 1776 (he was then twenty) wrote to Padre Martini in Bologna: "We have here two splendid contrapuntists—Signori Haydn and Adlgasser." From Cajetan Adlgasser, the Archbishop's organist, he may have learned something of that instrument, for he was later to succeed him at the post; from Michael Haydn, the younger brother of Joseph and concertmaster at Salzburg from 1762, he learned a great deal. This Haydn, whose influence is unmistakable in some of Mozart's music, was by far the most distinguished permanent composer in Salzburg. Association with individual musicians is well enough. The needs of the young composer who must develop in sufficient musical surroundings, identify himself with the center where his works are produced, is quite another matter. Mozart composed important works in Salzburg, but he based their style on his observations elsewhere. The vital centers for him were to be Milan, Paris, London, Mannheim, Munich, and finally Vienna.

Still, the town that gave Mozart birth was a part of him to some extent, and remained so. With all his wanderings and friendships in high places, his fondness for fine dress, he never became completely urban. His open sociability, his pleasure-loving ways, his fondness for simple company, for wine, for local jokes as often vulgar as not, suggest the *Gemütlichkeit* of the Austrian countryside. On Sundays at Salzburg, a favorite pastime of the Mozarts and their neighbors was something called *Bölzelschiessen,* a game of darts, the target at each meeting humorously inscribed with the shortcomings of one of the players. K. Risbeck in a letter describing Salzburg society at the time, divides its inhabitants into the "country gentlemen who hunt and go to church" and the plain folk who "eat, drink, and pray," with less elegance, and on the last point with more sincerity. The bourgeois class "conduct their love affairs in public; the others in private. All alike live in sensual indulgence."

Just or not, this implies a rigid division. Socially speaking, and by his habits and preferences, Mozart belonged to the lower estate. If taste has anything to do with class, Mozart the musician was of course above them all; from the point of view of the nobility, being a musician put him well down in the scale. Musicians were servants; their place was to entertain their betters. They were professional performers as distinct from those who lived on their inheritance, entertained, hunted, dabbled in the arts, and otherwise gracefully disported themselves. If a musician was invited to the house of a count and countess, he waited to be announced by a lackey. He could expect to be graciously received, but must answer with a *"gnädige Herr."* Musicians in Salzburg were admitted into the few wealthy houses as teachers, as in the case of Mozart's father, or in the pursuit of amateur music making, when Mozart would naturally be sought and expected to play. Such gatherings were on a far more modest scale than in Vienna, where home concerts in the larger houses were elaborate and competitive. It was there and not in Salzburg that Mozart made genuine friendships with titled people.

In Salzburg the disparity was more marked. The players were for the most part countrified, without education or manners. Court officialdom listened to their music but refrained from knowing them. That Mozart's father, Leopold, was better educated, more intelligent than most of his fellows, helped him neither socially nor professionally. That he had a son who was reported from elsewhere to perform remarkable feats on the clavier for a long while won him no special attention or standing at home, nor did the son receive as much attention there as elsewhere.

Wolfgang as a boy heartily enjoyed his friends and their bourgeois pastimes, but his life then and always was confined to musical activities, and as he grew up his need for congenial talent among his friends increased. When he wrote to his father (in 1778) in rather rueful anticipation of his return to Salzburg: "A fellow of mediocre ability will remain always mediocre, whether he travels or not; but one of superior talent (which I cannot deny that I possess) will lose it if he always remains in the same place," this was not vain boasting but a reminder to a father who knew. It was also an urgent truth, clearly perceived by an artist eager to function and wanting only favorable surroundings. As a small boy he was quite content with the village life about him in Salzburg. He continued to love his friends and took part in their gaieties more heartily than his father, for unlike his father he was nothing of a prude. He could fall into the mountain dialect, and sometimes in his travels threw in an exuberant phrase in letters to his sister at home. The occasional earthy humor of his letters, unprintable by modern custom, tends to shock people who form an image of him from the rare and pure elevation of his music. Mozart was pure at heart, and the purist of artists. The letters and the evidence of those who knew him in everyday life show a fundamentally decent but a very down-to-earth person.

The country characters who people his operas and have such a vivid life in the music may well have grown in part from Salzburg types. Perhaps the unnamed girl at home to whom the adolescent Mozart sent veiled messages through his sister was an inspiration for Zerlina. We are told that he loved masquerades and once took the part of a peasant bridegroom—hence Masetto. Then there is Papageno, the country lout, created with native affection. The ties with Salzburg were no doubt closer than Mozart realized or would have cared to admit.

Indeed, Mozart spent a very small part of his life in Salzburg. It served as little more than a stopping place between journeys. From the period of his babyhood until he was nineteen he never lingered there as much as a whole year at one time. It was simply a home base in which the family could take a long breath before another departure. His father brought him up to be a habitual wanderer around Europe, first as a prodigy, and later as a young musician in hope of a court appointment. Every sizable town he visited was musically more stimulating than his own, and he became restless at each of his necessary returns. Treated contemptuously and pointedly ignored by the Archbishop Hieronymus von Colloredo, Sigismund's successor, he became openly rebellious. At last he made a definite break, established himself in Vienna as his ultimate home in 1781, and there through his last ten years reached the fullness of his powers. Vienna never gave him general approbation, and only briefly a proper living. It held his loyalty to the extent that he refused better offers elsewhere. Vienna, the musical center of Europe, compatibly Germanic, harboring the foremost composers of the late century, was the best stimulus for the flood of his music in its most superb development, shut off only by his early death.

II

Salzburg, Eighteenth Century

THE MOZART couple and their two children lived as modestly as their neighbors in a rented flat: the third floor of the house of Lorenz Hagenauer on the Getreidegasse. It was Salzburg's longest street, a mixture of shops and dwellings, but narrow as the rest. The house faced what was once the Löchelplatz, with its fountain, and is a short block from the left bank of the Salzach, a tumultuous mountain stream. This had been the home of Mozart's parents for all of their married life. The stairs are dark and narrow to a modern visitor. The rooms are fair-sized but low-beamed. The kitchen seems cramped and primitive by present-day standards. These were unpretentious quarters in a day when country folk expected little more than adequate food and shelter. Clothes had to last. Among the neighbors there were many parties with games and dancing. Their musical gatherings were mostly in the Mozarts' home. The family included the maid Therese, who had a few coins more than her living.* Very much a part of the family were the pets—the fox terrier and the canary, to whom small Wolfgang sent messages in his first letters on tour—"Fräulein Bimperl" and "Herr Canari," he called them. There is even a reference to a captive grasshopper. The mother was content with this kind of homely living, but the father, while compelled to make the best of

---

* She was taken for granted as a part of the household, was sent greetings from the road, and had not complained when in Frau Mozart's absence her pay was discovered to be more than a year overdue.

it, looked higher. Leopold cultivated elegance and would
have liked to cut a figure in the world. That he never obtained
the first position in the Archbishop's *Kapelle* especially galled
him. His first restlessness, before the career of his son became
all-important, may have been thwarted personal ambition.

Leopold must first occupy our attention, for his absolute
control of the prodigy and the young phenomenal performer
as a subject for exhibition were of course an important part
in the shaping of the young artist. The lives of the father and
son were closely interwoven for more than half of Mozart's
years. Leopold dominated him as parent, as teacher, as man-
ager in every arrangement of the road, allowing him to devote
his entire time to learning, playing and composing. The letters
to and from Salzburg through these years (our main source
of information) could be read as an account of overstimula-
tion, of the subjection of a child to the rigors of travel. The
way he was made to perform ridiculous tricks in ridiculous
costumes sometimes makes the reader wonder, until we behold Wolfgang quite normal as a small boy, happy, affectionate, unspoiled. If "exploitation" means systematic pressure,
inhuman driving for intent of profit, it is not the word to apply
to the father of the first real prodigy in the history of music.
Leopold's entire devotion to the boy and his fundamental
gentleness cannot be questioned. Small Wolfgang never had
to be kept at his music—he could hardly be kept away from
it. Leopold watched and guided him, but never interfered with
him as a composer. The child's incredible aptitude could
adjust to the constant experience of music in court after court.
It made possible his rapid growth as a composer. His perpetual
high spirits, his normal boyishness, are an assurance that all
was well.

Before reproaching Leopold for dragging his child about
Europe, we should look well at the result. There is never the
slightest sign of that abnormal lack of ease with everyday
surroundings so often found in a precocious child wrapped
up in his one subject. Small Wolfgang throve on stimulation,
and derived from it a rounded as well as a speeded development. There can be no real doubt that this early stimulation
had a good deal to do with the special ability which sets him

above all other composers—the ability to produce instantaneously and at any time music perfectly formed which is a
sociable communication "from the heart to the heart." This
Mozart that we know, as first glimpsed in his childhood music,
develops consistently through the traveling years. If Mozart
had stayed quietly at home in Salzburg he would have missed
the knowledge of superior music and musicians. In that day of
little publication a thorough acquaintance with general musical
trends would have been impossible in a small and isolated
center. Salzburg would not have provided him with a live and
growing experience of opera. He would have been expected
to write little more than orthodox church services and an
occasional chamber piece for inept local performance. He
might have lived longer in this more sedentary existence. As
a composer he would certainly have been far more limited.

It must be said at once that Leopold managed the presentation of his son far and wide with skill and diplomacy; also
that he was completely devoted to the boy's fame and future.
The father almost always made a favorable impression upon
those whom he approached on entering a city. He was a musician of attainment and distinction. Indeed he was qualified for
a more exalted position than he held. All music in Salzburg
other than the household variety was that which Archbishop
Sigismund von Schrattenbach controlled. From violinist in the
court orchestra he became assistant *Kapellmeister* in 1762, at
the age of forty-three. Even if he had been granted the first
position, which might have happened if he had not neglected
his duties to build his son's fame elsewhere, the salary would
not much have exceeded the 400 gulden he ultimately drew.*
Leopold composed a quantity of music which was considered
good in its time—liturgical music for the Salzburg services,
chamber music, divertimentos. We have two proofs that he
was an excellent teacher: the one is his son, the other his
book *Search for a Basic Violin Method* (*Versuch eine gründli-
chen Violinschule*). The book is well written and authoritative.

---

* Leopold was worth more, and was aware of it. Encountering
Jommelli, the *Kapellmeister* to the Duke of Württemburg, he wrote
home pointedly that this "Italian" received 4,000. *For comparative
eighteenth-century money values, see* Appendix I.

It is now available in reprint, and is valued as a record of performing practice in his century. His treatise, published in the year of Wolfgang's birth, was his special pride and it fed his personal vanity to know that he was something more than the father of a talented son when he found during his travels that it had been translated into Dutch and French.

In Augsburg, where he was born November 14, 1719, bookbinding had been a craft in his family for three generations. Leopold was studious-minded and looked higher. His father put him in the boys' choir of the Monastery of St. Ulrich in Augsburg, with the thought that he might be led into the ministry. If Leopold himself entertained the thought, it was not for long. A devout believer in God, he was skeptical about the ministers of God. Music absorbed him as he played the organ and learned the violin. He entered the University of Salzburg at eighteen, studied law and did well in it, but music continued as his main pursuit. He entered the Archbishop Sigismund's orchestra as violinist in 1743. He was promoted to assistant *Kapellmeister* when the *Kapellmeister* Johann Ernst Eberlin, whom he respected, died, and when Joseph Franz Lolli, whom he did not respect, succeeded to the post. Leopold's duties when he was at home to perform them, and not off somewhere with his son, consisted in composing the services, training the choirboys and teaching violin. He had points of contact in cultured circles, for he was interested in the arts, well read and a linguist. The latter necessarily: Italian was the court language at Salzburg; Italian, French, Latin were the working materials of every musician. The letters of father and son often drop into passages from those languages in natural reference to what is going on around them.

Leopold was the brains of a family harmonious, united, and without apparent friction. His direction was accepted as natural by his wife and children. His letters show that he was a man of the world, the skeptic who in his dealings seeks the most he can get, and, failing, remains resilient; the cynic ready to stoop—a certain distance—to gain his ends. Wolfgang, who in many ways was the very opposite of his father, was too confiding and too quick to stand on his pride. He was never a man of the world in this sense, although in his later years he had plentiful need to become one. Nor did his interests extend far beyond the world of music and musicians. This was largely due to his training, which, thanks to Leopold, was almost exclusively musical. He never showed a special interest in the abstractions of philosophy, political doctrine or even religion in more than the sense of simple acceptance. Among the arts, his own sufficed. It cannot be said that he was really limited as a composer for that reason. The time was still to come when musicians would be versed in the other arts, widely read, involved in literary concepts. He wasted no time in speculation—he gave himself fully to tones, often meeting texts as they came to him, and shaping them without question to his musical purpose. He was no intellectual. His music was a direct, simple, sensuously agreeable communication, based on the "gallant" style of his day. It was also born of human sympathy and human understanding, at one with his sociable nature, his constant need of friendly intercourse. It was inseparable from this need. He addressed his improvisations to an audience; his chamber works to pupils or colleagues, his opera arias to singers whom he personally knew. He often preferred company to solitude while he composed. As he worked on a score he liked to have friends and lively conversation about him.

His sociable nature would have derived more from his mother than his father. She seems to have been an affectionate and sensible member of the family, active in its parties, but at a disadvantage in being no musician. The colloquialisms, the spelling in her letters are in violent contrast to the literacy of her husband's. Education was then not expected in a country wife of humble origins.

Born Anna Maria Pertl in 1720—and therefore a year younger than her husband—she came from St. Gilgen on the Wolfgang See, near Salzburg. She was the daughter of the *Pfleger* (caretaker) of the convent there. Her own family might have been larger, for she gave birth to seven children. But only two survived. Maria Anna was the fourth, born July 30, 1751, and Wolfgang Amadeus, the seventh, January

27, 1756.* To lose as many as five children was not unknown in those days of sudden epidemics and little knowledge of child care. Leopold's ready submission to "the will of God" when the life of either child was in danger from sudden illness while on tour may well have been the result of these earlier fateful encounters with death. The mother nearly lost her own life when Wolfgang was born. The world might have been deprived of Mozart's music, for several times during his childhood he survived by a slim chance. He was laid low by scarlet fever and later by smallpox, in a period when the world was quite helpless against those diseases. And once during the carnival at Milan, in 1770, a grandstand in which father and son had been supposed to sit collapsed and killed many spectators.

The principal account of Mozart's babyhood and the first manifestations of his extraordinary musical instincts has survived in a letter which Johann André Schachtner, trumpeter in the Salzburg *Kapelle* and a close friend of the family, wrote to Mozart's sister in 1792, after the composer's death, putting down recollections which had remained vivid for more than thirty years. There were frequent gatherings for chamber music in the lodgings on the Getreidegasse, and the clavier† was kept busy, for Nannerl, when she was seven, was started with lessons by her father. Small Wolfgang, then three, was naturally unnoticed until his unmistakable response to the tones about him seized the astonished attention of his father.

Herr Schachtner often played with the baby and found that in every game there had to be music. "When he and I carried his toys from one room to another, the one of us who

---

* The sister was known at home as Marianne, or "Nannerl." Wolfgang's baptismal name was Joannes Chrysostomus Wolfgangus Theophilus. Gottlieb was a German variant, and Amadeus a Latin variant, of Theophilus. To his family he was "Wolfgangerl" or "Wolferl."

† "Clavier" is a general and convenient expression for the stringed keyboard instruments of the period. The harpsichord was often used through Mozart's childhood years although there was a piano in the household and the fainter-toned clavichord too for convenient home purposes. In Augsburg, in 1777, Mozart became enamored of the pianoforte ("forte piano") there produced by Stein, adopted it for use thenceforth when he could, and became its propagandist.

was empty-handed always had to sing a march and play the fiddle. He was always sensitive. He used to ask me over and over again whether I loved him, and when as a joke I would say no, bright tears would fill his eyes, so tender and affectionate was his dear little heart." Leopold has testified to Mozart's affection as a baby. Years later (February 12, 1778), at a moment when he feared that he was losing control of his son, he appealed to him by recalling his babyhood: "Those happy moments are gone when, as a child and as a boy, you would never go to bed without first standing on a chair and singing to me '*Oragna fiagata fa*' [nonsense words] and you would always end by kissing me again and again on the tip of my nose and telling me that when I grew old you would put me in a glass case and protect me from every breath of air, so that you could always have me with you to honor."

Schachtner tells of traits prophetic of extraordinary talent. The little boy was avid to learn whatever was put before him. When shown the beginnings of arithmetic, he covered every surface within his reach with figures. His emotional response was immediate. "He was full of fire; his inclinations were easily swayed. I believe that if he had not been given the advantage of careful guidance, he might have become reckless in evil ways, so susceptible was he to every enticement before he could distinguish the good from the harmful."

Once, says Schachtner, his father discovered him absorbed in writing and asked him what he was doing:

> "Writing a concerto for the clavier," he said. "It will soon be done." "Let me see it." "It's not finished yet." "Never mind, let me see it."
>
> Your father took it from him and showed me a smear of notes, most of them written over ink blots. The little fellow dipped his pen every time down to the bottom of the ink well, so that as soon as it touched the paper a new blot appeared; that did not disturb him in the least. He rubbed the palm of his hand over it and went on writing. At first we laughed at this nonsense, but soon your father began to discern a theme, a note succession, a composition form. He looked more closely, and tears of wonderment and delight came to his eyes. "Look, Herr Schachtner," he said, "how correct and orderly it is. Of course it could never be of any use, for it is so difficult that no

one in the world could play it." Then Wolfgang said: "That is why it is a concerto; it must be practiced. See, this is how it should go." He began to play, but could bring out only enough to show us what he meant by it. He then absolutely believed that playing concertos and performing miracles were one thing.

Once the violinist Wentzl came to the house with some trios he had just written. They were at once played over, Wentzl taking the first violin part, Schachtner the second, Leopold the viola.

Wolfgang begged to be allowed to play the second violin, but your father reproved him for such a silly request, since he had never had the least instruction on the violin. Wolfgang said, "There's no need of lessons to play the second violin part," whereupon his father told him to go away and not interrupt us again. Wolfgang began to cry bitterly, and went away with his little fiddle. I interceded for him to be allowed to play along with me, and at last his father said: "Play with Herr Schachtner then, but not loud enough to be heard, or you shall go away again." So it happened that Mozart played with me. I soon realized with astonishment that I was quite superfluous. I put my instrument quietly down, and looked at your father, who was much moved. And so he played through all the six trios.

III

Munich and Vienna, 1762, 1763

A LESS ADVENTUROUS man than Leopold Mozart might have placidly allowed this little musical family to fit into their surroundings. If his means were limited and their quarters plain, his position was at least secure. The two children had, thanks to his careful efforts, developed a considerable talent. They would later have been accepted in the *Kapelle*. Here prudence counseled. At the same time, something stirred in Leopold's thoughts. There was musical activity in centers larger than Salzburg which could be far more engrossing, and more profitable. The limitations of the Salzburg court, on the other hand, stifled ambition, and Leopold was an ambitious man; his ambition readily turned to his children. It was certainly not usual at that time to carry one's children about Europe as infant prodigies. It implied boldness and imagination on Leopold's part. It also implied ruthlessness. Traveling conditions in those days were hard, diseases were rife and struck children swiftly and terribly. To subject his children to the whims of patrons was the order of the day; these were the only employers. At home it would be the same—or worse. Leopold's aim would be to find a patron more fond of music than his Archbishop—more able and more ready to support music from his treasury.

Leopold first planned his child-exhibiting journeys with a different purpose from that of building his son's career. Wolfgang, just short of six at the beginning of 1762, was a phenomenon to be watched rather than counted upon. Marianne, then ten, he had deliberately pushed. He later revealed his

attitude in referring to the early development of his children:
"Every moment I lose is lost forever." Marianne could then,
but not for long, be shown as a wonder child, a profitable one
who might lead him in her innocence to favorable attention
and a position at one court or another. His first letters describing their travels praise Marianne's prowess. Gradually
Wolfgang becomes the center of his attention. At length Marianne is left at home. Wolfgang becomes the sole object of his
efforts and soon of his life.

What was to settle into a well-organized procedure, constantly repeated and extended, was at first a trial venture.
The first journey lasted three weeks (January 12 to the beginning of February, 1762). For so short a period the presence of the mother was evidently not required. Since Salzburg
was then under the jurisdiction of Bavaria (although a separate episcopal state), Munich was a natural choice. The
children performed on the clavier, or with their father as violinist, before the Elector Maximilian Joseph and his guests,
to the wonderment of all. Particulars are lacking, but Leopold
felt sufficiently encouraged to plan a bolder journey, this time
to the Austrian capital. The whole family set out on September 18, 1762, and approached Vienna by easy stages. They
drove northward to Passau on the Danube and followed the
river to Linz, where they lingered for a fortnight. From there
they took a boat to Manthausen, and on the following day
to Ybbs, where Wolfgang astonished the monks in the monastery by playing the organ. A minute account of this and
the two journeys to follow is given by Leopold in letters to
his landlord in Salzburg, Lorenz Hagenauer. Hagenauer had
lent him money for initial expenses, a debt to be added to the
rent due at home. These obligations the methodical Leopold
was at pains to meet. Consequently, his letters, sent at fairly
regular intervals, carefully list the amounts paid out and
amounts received from patrons. Leopold's letters to his landlord form an almost continuous diary of their travels, the exploits of Wolfgang carefully noted. The landlord, as creditor,
is the natural recipient. Later, when the father and son were
to undertake Italy, he would write an equally faithful and de-

tailed account to his wife at home, warning her several times to preserve the letters carefully. His purpose of ultimately writing a biography of his son is admitted in one of his letters from Vienna. The biography was never written, because his son outlived him (having since gone his own way); but the letters remain the basis of all accounts of Mozart's childhood and early youth.

The journeys of the little family were precarious so far as income was concerned. The gifts which were their only profit often vanished in the costs of coaches, fine costumes to make a proper appearance, food and lodging while they spent idle days waiting for the beckoning nod from the palace or mansion. Leopold's method was to approach whatever titled dignitaries were to be found and to interest them in giving an audience to two remarkable children. The plan seems to have worked from the start. His success at this time, when the prodigy Mozart was still unknown, and also later when the family was warmly befriended on every side, bespeaks the charm and naturalness of the boy, but also the diplomatic astuteness and initial presentability of the father. Even at Passau, their first stop, he penetrated to the Bishop of that diocese, and so won the favorable attention of the Canon Herberstein that the Canon took them with him to Linz, and continued to Vienna, ready to spread "a sensational report." In Linz he somehow persuaded the Landeshauptmann von Schlick to precede him to Vienna with a similar mission. On arriving there, Leopold must have been gratified at the success of his publicity methods. He at once reached the Emperor by way of the imperial paymaster, and received forthwith a hundred ducats and an appointment. This was a handsome sum and a good beginning from every point of view. "At Schönbrunn," Leopold writes on October 16, "their Majesties received us with such extraordinary graciousness that when I describe it, people will not believe me. Suffice it to say that Wolferl jumped upon the lap of the Empress [Maria Theresa], put his arms around her neck and kissed her heartily."

The royal family was disarmed at once by the ready friendliness of the boy. Nissen* relates that "He was especially devoted to the Archduchess Marie Antoinette [two months older than himself]. Once, when he fell on the polished floor, she lifted him from the ground and consoled him, while one of her sisters stood by: 'You are good' said Wolfgang, 'I will marry you.' 'Why?' 'From gratitude' he answered; 'she was good to me, but her sister stood by and did nothing.' " "He is as intimate with everyone," wrote Leopold, "especially with the courtiers, as if he had known them all his life."

The Empress Maria Theresa had long prided herself on her voice, and had sung at private opera performances. Her daughters, the two archduchesses, were taking singing lessons, for it was the ambition of royalty to take part in palace functions. All were charmed with the boy, and by the time they had put him through his exploits, the afternoon session had lasted from three to six. The Emperor called him a "little magician" (*kleine Hexenmeister*), and had a cloth put over his hands as he played. Whether this was the invention of the monarch or the father does not appear; at any rate, Leopold was to use it as a regular trick in the future. Wolfgang was not in the least awed by the spacious, high-ceilinged, utter magnificence of Schönbrunn, or by the exalted degree of his hosts. The only rank that interested him was musical rank. He knew and had played at home the music of Georg Christoph Wagenseil, at that time the best of Vienna's clavecinists, and the teacher of the Empress. He asked for Herr Wagenseil and played one of his concertos while the composer turned the pages. Wolfgang was presented with an outfit that had been made for the Archduke Maximilian, "of fine lilac cloth trimmed with double-width gold braid," which would have been set off by a dress wig and buckled shoes. Nannerl was honored with a hand-down—from the Archduchess Marie Caroline, who was just her age—a white brocaded taffeta with the semblance of a bodice surrounding her eleven-year-old waist.

The news of the sensation which the wonder boy from Salzburg had made at court spread instantaneously through

---

* Georg Nicolaus von Nissen married Mozart's widow, and from her account and Marianne's wrote Mozart's first biography.

Vienna. The list of chancellors, princes, counts and countesses who received them is formidable. A passage from the letter of October 19, 1762 shows this:

> Today we were at the French Ambassador's. Tomorrow we are invited to Count Harrach's from four to six. . . . On every occasion we are fetched by a servant in the nobleman's carriage and are brought home again. From six or half past six to nine we are to perform for six ducats at a big concert which a certain rich nobleman is giving and at which the greatest virtuosos now in Vienna are going to perform. The nobles send us their invitations four, five, six or eight days in advance, in order not to miss us. For instance, the chief Postmaster, Count Paar, has already engaged us for next Monday. Wolferl now gets enough driving, for he goes out at least twice a day. Once we drove out at half past two to a place where we stayed until a quarter to four. Count Hardegg then fetched us in his carriage and we drove full gallop to a lady's house where we remained until half past five. Thence Count Kaunitz sent to fetch us and we stayed with him until about nine.

This was strenuous going. Further musical experiences in the great capital must surely have made their impression on the young Wolfgang, if he was taken to the opera and concert performances mentioned by his father and given at hours when boys of six are supposed to be in bed.

At this point came the first of the setbacks which were to worry the parents at intervals. "Wolferl" developed red spots and a temperature. It was scarlet fever. "Black powder,"* the inevitable remedy, was brought forth. A bungling doctor only increased their alarm. The delay meant postponements with continuing expenses through four weeks of anxiety. Leopold ordered six masses to be divided between two of Salzburg's churches. He must not be too quickly condemned for subjecting his children to epidemics in various cities. At that very moment there was smallpox at home. Now prospective patrons must not be approached too boldly. "In Vienna," wrote Leopold, "the nobility are afraid of pockmarks and all kinds of rash."

Leopold delayed the return home by a journey to Press-

---

* Elsewhere referred to as *pulvis epilepsis niger*. It is a laxative.

burg in Hungary, in pursuance of an invitation, having entreated his employer in Salzburg, "his Grace my worthy and holy Father Confessor," to extend his leave beyond the Christmas season. Leopold timed a letter to his landlord to assure a fire in the "front stove" on their arrival, which took place on January 5, 1763.

The father's continuing account of their travels shows that he was more anxious to make the most of every opportunity than to protect his children from undue fatigue and from being exhibited like trained animals. Wolfgang especially was subjected to what we must call the indignity of being shown off as a marvel before the idle curiosity of any hearers. From the age of five until he was seventeen he was to be carried about in this way on a succession of journeys, with never more than a few months' pause at home. Through his childhood and boyhood, then, he led a life of constantly changing surroundings, a life of coaches and inns, of waiting around indefinitely to be given an audience. The only sense of security for the boy, the only anchorage usually considered essential for healthy growth, lay in the mutual affection, the unfailingly agreeable relations of his family at home and abroad. Through his travels he remained a wholesome, natural child, with a child's love of play. Animated, eager, outgoing, instinctively responsive, he met people easily and made friends with them. Constantly confronted with strangers, he soon overcame any shyness or embarrassment, nor had he any occasion to be a show-off, because he never had to make a bid for attention. Making music was simply the day's work. The ladies who petted and fondled him, or echoed each piece with their "Ohs" and "Ahs," must soon have ceased to make any particular impression on Wolfgang. He was quite aware of what their musical judgment was worth.

The success of the first venture was evidently great enough to set Leopold thinking of a still larger one. When winter had turned into spring and summer, the family was ready for a longer and a more extensive pilgrimage. They left on June 9, 1763, for Paris via the southern German states and the Rhine Valley. Even on the first day a wheel of the carriage broke, was patched precariously by a local smith and wobbled to Wasserburg while Leopold and his servant walked behind. It was no life of ease. The lodgings often consisted of one small room for all four. At a court the elector would receive them at his convenience. They had to wait for an evening free of other entertainment or for his return from the hunt, or else seek him out in his summer quarters. Some sessions lasted as much as five hours, some kept them up late into the night. This protracted itinerary of traveling, playing and waiting around, together with what theatre or concert performances Wolfgang may have attended, might have been expected both to excite and overexhaust a boy of seven. A remark by Leopold from Frankfort, where he had had a particularly strenuous schedule, is reassuring: "Wolfgang is extraordinarily jolly, but a bit of a scamp as well."

They visited Aachen and played before the Princess Amalie, the sister of Frederick the Great. She was all zeal and advised Leopold to give up Paris and to go to Berlin. Leopold was less interested in her raptures and her advice than in her reward. He wrote (October 17, 1763): "If the kisses which she gave to my children, and to Wolfgang especially, had been all new louis d'or, we should be quite happy; but neither the innkeeper nor the postmaster are paid in kisses."

Often they had to sit idly for days until the paymaster called with the expected present, which might be a single gold coin in a jeweled snuffbox, a gold toothpick, a watch. Leopold wrote, "With snuff boxes and *étuis* and such stuff, we shall soon be able to fit out a shop." He examined all the trinkets coldly for their monetary value and weighed them against living expenses.

Visiting again the Bavarian Elector, now in his summer residence at Nymphenburg, Wolfgang displayed a fresh accomplishment, now ready for exhibition. He performed a concerto on the violin, adding his own cadenzas. From Munich they went to Augsburg, and lingered for two weeks while Leopold renewed acquaintances in his native town. Leopold managed three concerts by the children and bought a clavier for practice while traveling. They went to Ludwigsburg and thence to Schwetzingen, the summer residence of the Elector Palatine Carl Theodor, near Mannheim. It was an interesting visit, for the Elector had brought with him from Mannheim an orchestra, which Leopold put down (July 19) as "undeniably the best in Germany." They passed through Heidelberg, where Wolfgang played the church organ and where Leopold was reminded of Salzburg, gave two concerts in Mayence, although the Elector was ill, and four in Frankfort, where they arrived on August 9. At the first of them a boy of fourteen, destined for fame, was in the audience. It was Goethe, who was later to become Mozart's admirer. Goethe told Eckermann, who fully reported the recollection of Mozart in his *Gespräche*: " 'I saw him as a boy, seven years old, when he gave a concert on one of his tours. I myself was fourteen, and I remember the little fellow distinctly with his powdered wig and his sword.' "

In Coblenz and Brussels there were more concerts. Concerts could be more profitable than private performances before electors, for they amounted to a joint contribution by the social entourage, organized and, with luck, collected in advance. After a belated audience with Prince Carl von Lothringen, they headed for Paris behind four post horses. They reached the capital in four days, stopping at Mons, Péronne and Gournay. Leopold entered Paris November 18, 1763, laden with letters of introduction, few of which were to bear fruit.

IV

Paris, 1763, 1764

P ARIS WAS good territory for a new sensation, but first the attention of Paris had to be caught. Leopold found the French a strange people as to looks, language and ways. News of an *"enfant prodige"* traveling about Europe had been slow in crossing the Rhine. Leopold got his first foothold through people who spoke his own language. The Bavarian Ambassador, Count von Eyck received them on November 18, and housed them at the Hôtel Beauvais on the Rue Saint-Antoine, formerly the residence of Madame de Beauvais, lady-in-waiting to Anne of Austria. Driving through neighboring streets they had a glimpse of the filthy and ragged element in contrast to the gorgeousness of the *noblesse* they were soon to encounter. At first nothing developed, and Leopold was momentarily at a loss for his next step. Another fellow countryman came gallantly to his rescue. He was Friedrich Melchior Grimm, the distinguished writer and encyclopedist, a native of Ratisbon, who had been in Paris for fifteen years and knew his way about. It was he who arranged for their reception at Versailles, and who later organized and carried through the details of a profitable concert, who aided their first publishing venture and saw to having their portrait painted by M. de Carmontelle, and reproduced in engraving. "A man," wrote Leopold, "of good sense and a kind heart."

They established themselves at Versailles on Christmas Eve. They had been invited to stay two weeks, but had to find their own lodgings and to use sedan chairs, an expensive means of transportation. They had to live *"noblement"* says

Leopold, which included attiring themselves in the costume of the country. Since the court was in mourning for the Princess Isabella of Parma, granddaughter of Louis XV, Wolfgang was fitted out in a "black suit and French hat."

At the *grand couvert* on New Year's Eve, "my Wolfgang was affably privileged to stand beside the Queen the whole time, to talk constantly to her, entertain her and kiss her hands repeatedly, besides partaking of the dishes which she handed him from the table. The Queen [Maria Leszczynska, the Polish consort of Louis XV] speaks as good German as we do and, as the King knows none, she interpreted to him everything our gallant Wolfgang said. I stood beside him, and on the other side of the King, where M. le Dauphin and Madame Adelaïde were seated, stood my wife and daughter."

The presence of royalty as profitable objects for a dedication decided Leopold on taking the first step of circulating Wolfgang's music in print. The decision was prompted by Wolfgang's sudden and surprising development as a composer under the stimulus of music at court. "Every day," writes Leopold on February 3, "God performs fresh miracles through this child. By the time we reach home, God willing, he will be able to contribute to the Court music." Wolfgang accordingly wrote four sonatas "For Clavier with Violin Accompaniment" which became his first engraved works (K. 6, 7, 8, 9). The first two were dedicated to Madame Victoire, the second daughter of Louis XV, who played the violin; the other two were dedicated to Madame la Comtesse de Tessé, Lady-in-waiting to Madame la Dauphine. "Picture to yourself the furor which they will make in the world when people read on the title page that they have been composed by a seven year old child; and when the sceptics are challenged to test him, as has already been done, imagine the sensation when he asks someone to write down a minuet or some other tune and then immediately and without touching the clavier writes in the bass and, if it is wanted, the second violin part. In due course you will find how fine these sonatas are; one of them has an Andante [K. 7, Adagio?] in a quite unusual style." He writes at last: "We have built well, and now hope for a good harvest."

Leopold has much to say about the French, their customs, their gossip. The women are "painted up as unnaturally as dolls at Berchtesgaden," a sight "unbearable to an honest German." Madame la Marquise de Pompadour, *maîtresse en titre* to Louis XV, received the Mozarts in the magnificence of her separate apartments. Leopold found them "like paradise" and admitted to having been impressed by the lady who, whatever her morals, had "charmed a King." He finds that "she must have been very beautiful, for she is still good-looking. In figure she is tall and stately, stout, or rather well-covered, but very well proportioned." Marianne recalled, years later, that la Marquise lifted small Wolfgang to the table beside her, "but pushed him aside when he bent forward to kiss her, on which he indignantly asked 'who is this that does not want to kiss me? The Empress kissed me.' "

It was suggested that Leopold have his children inoculated for smallpox (but not with vaccine, which was still to be discovered). This he indignantly refused as an "impertinence." "For my part," concludes the fatalist, "I leave the matter to the grace of God. It depends on His grace whether he wishes to keep this marvel of nature in the world in which he has placed it, or to take it to Himself."

After Versailles, notice began to be taken of the Mozarts in certain houses of Paris. By a special dispensation, a private theatre in the house of M. Félix on the Rue Saint-Honoré was opened to them for two concerts in the Lenten season. The two children were set to show their paces. Wolfgang played on the clavier, organ, and violin in turn, accompanied a lady in an Italian aria without seeing the music, supplying the harmony extempore. He then improvised on this. Marianne played at sight difficult pieces by two resident composers, Johann Schobert, clavecinist to the Prince of Conti, and Johann Gottfried Eckardt, once a pupil of Emanuel Bach, thus silencing Schobert, who would have liked to minimize, if Leopold was correct, the musicianship of the little intruders. Other German composers, too, were influential in the French court, yet Schobert's scores, delicately phrased, showed French taste. Wolfgang's compositions were colored by Schobert's style. As for Leopold, he had no use for the French music he encountered. "The whole of it," he wrote, "is not worth a damn (*keinen Teufel wert*)." Eckardt and Schobert were different, being German. Schobert he praised grudgingly, for he suspected him of selfish motives.

The financial results of these concerts were also gratifying. Leopold had a system. "Not a sou is paid at the door. And no one without a ticket is admitted, whoever he may be. My friends sell the tickets a week beforehand each for a laubthaler or a federthaler, the equivalent of one-fourth of a louis d'or, and they collect the money. But most of the tickets, in blocks of twelve and twenty-four, are given to the ladies, who sell them the more easily, as out of politeness one cannot refuse to buy them. *Est modus in rebus,* or, in our language, *Franzosen wollen gefoppet seyn.*" ("Frenchmen like to be fooled.") At the first concert he took in 112 louis d'or, more than doubling the 50 he had belatedly received from the treasurer of the *Menus plaisirs* at Versailles.

V

London, The Hague, Salzburg,

1764-1767

ENGLAND, their next objective, lay beyond a terrifying body of salt water, approached with prayers on the part of Leopold. He wrote from London on April 25, 1764: "Thank God we have safely crossed the Maxglanerbach," comparing the English Channel in humorous relief to a small suburban stream of Salzburg.

Leopold surveyed the new situation—a people quite different from anything they had run into on the continent—and considered a course of procedure. First of all English hats were purchased for the mother and daughter, and dress clothes for "our big Wolfgang." The outfits may be imagined from contemporary paintings by Gainsborough or Romney. London, although a "godless" spot, was really a good prospect, for the Mozarts were fortunate in having monarchs of German blood to deal with. George III was a Handel enthusiast. Queen Charlotte of Mecklenburg-Strelitz both played and sang. The summons came on April 27, only two days after their arrival. Leopold's report was elated: "Their easy manner and friendly ways made us forget that they were the King and Queen of England. At all courts up to the present we have been received with extraordinary courtesy. But the welcome which we have been given here exceeds all others. A week later we were walking in St. James's Park. The King came along driving with the Queen and, although we all had on different clothes, they recognized us nevertheless and not only greeted us, but the King opened the window, leaned out and saluted us and especially our Master Wolfgang, nodding to us and waving his hand."

A second session, on May 19, was confined to the royal family, and became a real *Musikabend,* lasting from six until ten. The King placed piece after piece before the "invincible" boy to be read at sight: music of Wagenseil, his friend in Vienna; Karl Friedrich Abel, chamber musician to the Queen, once pupil of Sebastian Bach and a famous viola da gamba player; and George Frideric Handel. Sebastian Bach's youngest son, Johann Christian, was twenty-nine, and had been in London only two years. Handel was then five years dead. Mozart may well have heard oratorios of Handel in the winter months to follow, and operas by the popular "London Bach," which were also being performed. He was undoubtedly influenced by both composers, but by this Bach far more than by Handel.

Handel was out of fashion, except in England. The music of Handel and Sebastian Bach would be significantly revealed to him some years later. Now he was alert only to current taste, and the prevailing taste was for graceful melody set to a transparent harmonic accompaniment, aimed at uncomplicated, sensuous pleasure. Sebastian Bach, with his more sober and sturdy, closely worked contrapuntal style, had become quite outmoded. Even while he still lived, he began to be superseded by his sonata-writing sons.

Johann Christian Bach was for years passed by in Germany as a sort of artistic renegade. At nineteen he deserted Berlin and the house of his elder half brother Emanuel for Milan, where he became organist of the great Cathedral and adopted the Roman faith as a necessary concomitant to the job. He studied in Bologna under Padre Martini, who commended his counterpoint. Nevertheless he was lured to Naples, where the favorable climate for opera, more or less frowned upon in north Germany, inspired him to compose three successful *opere serie*. This led to his appointment as Composer to the King's Theatre in London. The youngest Bach had thus become "Giovanni" Bach, and then "Mr. John Bach." In the first transplanting he had become impregnated with Italian melodiousness, the ingratiating ways of *opera buffa*. He had renounced the severities of his father and the modified severities of his half brothers. He was pleased to cultivate the favor of London's gentleman patrons, and their society. The two portraits by Gainsborough show him in faultless brocades and ruffles, the right hand conspicuously jeweled. To his former colleagues he was *"der welsche Bach,"* who had embraced frivolous foreign ways; to Reichardt he was *"ein leichtgesinnter jovialischer Mensch,"* almost equivalent in Berlin to damnation. But London, Italy and France loved him. Mozart loved him both for his engaging music and his amiable self. It can be said that Mozart was led into a lifelong Italian style by way of "Giovanni" Bach.

Leopold decided at once to make Wolfgang's talents known to the gentry at large. Since the season was over and they were rapidly leaving town, he quickly assembled the musicians necessary for an orchestra, chose June 5 because many would have stayed for the King's birthday on June 4, delegated blocks of tickets as he had in Paris, and gave the concert on "two or three days' notice." He proudly reported that two hundred of the "leading people of London" were present, the net receipts almost 100 guineas. Probably on the strength of the profitable off-season concert, Leopold decided to linger "at least through the winter." Performances did not continue to prove justified by any particular demand. A charity concert arranged by Leopold for good will's sake (June 29) accomplished nothing in particular. The King's subjects were less interested than the King and Queen in the "wonder of nature."

In August, 1764, Leopold contracted from exposure "a kind of native complaint which is called a 'cold.'" He had himself "purged and bled," and removed in a sedan chair to Chelsea, then a separate village rather than a suburb, "with one of the most beautiful views in the world." The Mozarts were thus confined to Chelsea for seven weeks. The release from being shown about was fortunate for Wolfgang, for he had time to reorder his fresh musical experiences and try them out in music of his own. Not wishing to disturb his father by playing, he was soon at work on a symphony (K. 17). His sister tells that he turned to her and said: "Remind me to give something really good to the horns," instruments which Handel had made popular in England. His industry continued there and after their return to London in October. There were three sonatas of Christian Bach which he arranged as concertos (K. 107). Two more symphonies were forthcoming (K. 18 and 19). A set of six trios (K. 10-15) were dedicated to Her Majesty on January 18, 1765. The bright, fluent style of Johann Christian Bach is often reflected in these scores, the symphonies in particular. This young man quickly made friends with Wolfgang. "He liked to play with the boy," writes Jahn. "He took him on his knee and went through a sonata with him, each in turn playing a bar with so much precision that no one would have suspected two performers. Bach began a fugue, which Wolfgang took up and completed where he broke off."

"What he knew when we left Salzburg," wrote Leopold on May 28, "is a mere shadow compared with what he knows now. It exceeds all that one can imagine. He greets you from the clavier where at the moment he is seated, playing through *Kapellmeister* Bach's trio. My boy knows at the age of eight what one would expect only from a man of forty. Indeed, only he who sees and hears him can believe it. You yourself and all our Salzburg friends have no idea of Wolfgang's progress; for he is quite different now."

Wolfgang must have been taken to opera performances in London, for Leopold was encouraging his interest in that direction. The boy took singing lessons from Giovanni Manzuoli, a celebrated castrato and star of the Italian Opera season which opened in November. (Castrati were much prized, their voices ecstatically praised. Leopold speaks enviously of the 20,000 German gulden Manzuoli would probably earn that season.) There could have been no thought of developing Wolfgang's then treble voice, but the father had a good deal of awareness of what might be learned about the uses and possibilities of dramatic singing, about declamation, about acting; incidentally about the peculiar vanities of operatic singers, pampered castrati in particular. The tenor aria "*Va, dal furor portata*" (K. 21), then written for an occasion, shows that Wolfgang from the very first was proficient in operatic ways.

Further evidence of his operatic inclinations was shown in a quasi-scientific test of the boy's powers and a report published in *Philosophical Transactions* (1770) by the Honorable Daines Barrington. Mozart was given the manuscript orchestral score of an operatic air to read at sight, transposing the parts. He was also asked to improvise an operatic love song and a song simulating rage, which he promptly did, on nonsense syllables. These were among many tests, circumstantially reported as successful. The English scientist's last lingering suspicion about the boy's age disappeared when, "whilst he was playing to me a favorite cat came in, upon which he immediately left his harpsichord, nor could we bring him back for a considerable time. He would also sometimes run about the room with a stick between his legs by way of a horse."

As the spring and summer of 1765 came on, the novelty of beholding the "prodigies of nature," as the *Public Advertiser* described them, began to pall. Leopold, in quest of guineas, stooped to exhibiting Wolfgang and Nannerl as freaks. He invited the skeptical to their lodgings for proof of the children's abilities before they bought their tickets. July found them still in London, playing every day, according to the same periodical, "from 12 to 3 at the Swan and Hoop Tavern in Cornhill, on one clavier, the keyboard covered." The price was two shillings sixpence.

Leopold decided, after more than a year on a remote island, among strange people, that the time had come to move along. What guineas could be gathered had been gathered. Nor were the surroundings suitable for a properly reared German family. He had written as early as March 19: "I have made the decision, after careful consideration and several sleepless nights, that I will not bring up my children in such a dangerous place, where most of the people have no religion and where one beholds only evil examples. You would be astonished at the way children are brought up here; not to mention other religious matters." Leopold had little use for Protestantism. In Germany he tried to convert some Lutherans he had met to the only faith.

Having lingered through the summer for various reasons, he at length lent a willing ear to the protestations of the Dutch Ambassador that the Princess Caroline of Nassau-Weilburg would be more than eager to receive them. Accordingly, although Leopold had far more than overstayed his leave from Salzburg, they made their way to Holland in early September, 1765.

They had no sooner arrived at The Hague than Marianne contracted a fever and became delirious. A priest was called in. Leopold talked to the mother and persuaded the daughter, too weak to speak, that "what God sends must be endured." "We convinced her of the vanity of the world, and the happy death of children, when released from it." Later, he wrote his landlord: "My daughter was scarcely out of bed a week and had just begun to walk across the bedroom floor by herself, when on November 15th little Wolfgang contracted an illness which in four weeks has made him so weak that he is not only absolutely unrecognizable but has nothing left but his tender skin and his little bones, and for the last five days has been carried daily from his bed to a chair." Having ordered five masses to be read in four of Salzburg's churches, he now ordered nine for Wolfgang. Their recovery was certainly not due to any remote knowledge of the nature of their illness.

Wolfgang had performed at court in September, shortly after their arrival, for the Prince of Orange, William V, and for the Princess of Weilburg. For the Princess he composed a song (K. 23), and at Amsterdam his Symphony in B flat (K. 22) was performed. He played again at the March festival and turned out, together with arias for the Princess, six sonatas and sets of variations "for clavier with violin accompaniment," which were promptly engraved (K. 26-31). There was also a set of variations on the old Dutch National Anthem (K. 25).

A progress through towns of Holland and Belgium brought them again to Paris on May 10, 1766, where they spent two months, revisiting Versailles for four days. They then went to Switzerland, via Dijon and Lyons, stopping at Geneva, Lausanne, Berne and Zürich. In Geneva, Leopold remembered that Voltaire, living there in voluntary isolation, had been approached circuitously, in their behalf. The Baron Grimm's mistress, Madame d'Epinay, had been persuaded to write him about the two prodigies then traveling in his direction. He could not receive them when they visited, and he wrote to the lady: "Your little Mazar [sic] had chosen, I think, a poor enough time to bring harmony into the temple of discord. You know that I live two leagues from Geneva. I never go out. I was very ill when this phenomenon burst upon the black horizon of Geneva. Now he has gone, greatly to my regret without my having seen him." Leopold could have had no personal regret at missing what he considered a dangerous and despicable "atheist," but regret at missing a publishable statement from a celebrity.

On November 30, 1766, they were again in Salzburg. The child who had last seen his native home at the age of seven was now a boy of ten, emaciated by his recent illnesses, but now a master. His stay in Paris had been long, in London still longer. He had absorbed more than a little of the musical ways of those capitals. He had openly entered the lists of musical composers and proved by his works an alertness to every current combined with a talent quite his own. Three years of dwelling in foreign parts, interspersed by traveling, must have meant for Mozart a succession of impressions which would have completely bewildered another of his age. He must have heard a good deal unless we can assume that he wrote his first oratorios, operas, vocal music shortly to follow, from the knowledge of scores rather than actual experience. One thing is certain: at the time of his return to Salzburg, he was ready to compose, with ease and tolerable correctness, music in any form and to any text.

Anyone today would say that Mozart, as a normal boy (for he was a normal boy), after this vagrant, knockabout life among strange people in strange lands speaking strange languages, must have reached the point of an urgent need to stay quietly in one place, and that place his home. The time had come for less display of his performing abilities, less improvising, and more systematic study at regular hours. An exercise book now in the Mozarteum at Salzburg is attributed

by Jahn to this year. It goes through the paces of thorough
bass and counterpoint, drawing upon Fux's *Gradus ad Par-
nassum* for subjects, with corrections and notes in the father's
hand. To Mozart, apparently, even such practice work was
not dry. He labels his parts blithely in one place: *"Il sign.
d'Alto, il Marchese Tenore, il Duca Basso."*

Mozart's childhood symphonies are an echo of the adult
ways of others, but still astonishing by their entirely competent
handling of the current *"style galant."* As manifestations of
precocity they well served their purpose. Leopold perceived
in them something more than correctness. There were moments when the exuberance of invention, the turn of a phrase
in a slow movement were the composer's own. At this point
the teacher recognized a quality which he himself did not
possess. He became an amazed bystander. He could only
continue as technical guide, watching as the flower of his son's
talents opened, and making it his charge to protect and to
publicize that flowering without interference. This noninter-
ference is greatly to his credit. The genius of Mozart lay not
in facility, which was a common and expected trait in his day,
but in the unfailing source upon which that facility drew.

Leopold's respect for his son's qualities overweighs all his
mistakes in the personal relations of the two. The late Edward
J. Dent failed to make a point when he called Leopold "a
musical workman rather than an artist," who expected eventually from his son nothing more than "enough technical
skill to write successful and effective drawing room music."
To be sure, Leopold did not realize his son's true stature—
neither did anyone else (except perhaps Haydn) while he
lived. He was the better teacher for having enough intelligent
perception to leave the boy alone, and for having no originality of his own to impose upon his pupil. Leopold's compositions show a good technical competence. What if they were,
as Wyzewa bluntly put it after close study, "absolutely lacking
in invention, extraordinarily powerless to draw anything from
himself"? What Mozart needed was exactly what Leopold was
qualified to give him: systematic drilling in basic technique.
"Invention" his father could not give him, it had to come
"from himself." If the contrapuntal exercises were rigid and

dry, they did the pupil no harm. He fulfilled them obediently, nor is there any hint that he found his tasks onerous. At first complacent with the arbitary rules of Fux, he later let his imagination override them. He wrote in the strict style when and only when he saw fit. When he encountered the fugues of Sebastian Bach in his later years he enriched his own fugal writing accordingly. Meanwhile he continued to turn counterpoint to his own symphonic uses and eventually became a master of it absolutely supreme in ease and grace of handling.

The short year at home was not spent entirely with exercises. Leopold was careful to make sure that Salzburg in general, and the Archbishop in particular, should recognize the boy's greatly enhanced abilities. Wolfgang as composer was put to more ambitious tests than piano pieces or chamber sonatas. For the Archbishop Sigismund he wrote the first part of a three-part oratorio, *Die Schuldigkeit des ersten Gebotes* (K. 35), on "The Obligation of the First Commandment," Michael Haydn as concertmaster and Anton Adlgasser as court organist writing the other parts. It is a work of operatic proportions, requiring voices and orchestra, descriptive treatment. In the score, the helping hand of Leopold is evident in the recitatives. It is modeled on the Italian style. He wrote a Passion for Holy Week (*Grabmusik,* K. 42). In May he composed a "comedy" to a Latin text, for presentation by the students of the University of Salzburg: *Apollo et Hyacinthus* (K. 38). It is a full-length work, with solos and ensembles. In the spring and summer, Wolfgang evidently needed piano concertos for ready performance. Whether or not he had time to write original ones, the fact remains that four played in this season were transposed from sonatas by others, notably Abel and Christian Bach, the result of the scores carried back from London and Paris. These various and not unexacting pieces of Wolfgang's twelfth year are as competent in meeting their purpose as the work of the usual mature *Kapellmeister.*

VI

Vienna, 1767-1768

THE PLANS of Leopold for his boy would not allow home lessons and home composing to go on indefinitely. He was ready to start off on a new venture when a good opportunity offered, and that opportunity came before they had been at home for quite a year. When the announcement came of the wedding festivities of the Archduchess Maria Josepha and King Ferdinand of Naples, to be celebrated in Vienna, the family were told to pack their traveling clothes once more. They were off on September 11, 1767, for Vienna by way of Lambach and Mölk, with its monastery. Leopold saw his way to increasing his boy's fame considerably by a second visit to Vienna. By now he had made Wolfgang a subject of conversation in many western courts. Now, too, he was ready to put him to any composing test. The letters do not mention an intention of Leopold on facing Vienna again to have him compose an opera, but it was probably in his thoughts. A successful opera in Vienna by a boy of twelve was an exciting thought for an ambitious father, as he admitted later. *"Aut Caesar aut nihil"* was his favorite phrase.

This time misfortunes beset the Mozarts from the beginning. The Princess Josepha died of smallpox on the eve of the royal wedding festivities, October 17. "The Princess bride has become the bride of the heavenly Bridegroom," wrote Leopold. This meant the suspension of all concert activities. It also meant a serious epidemic, with an appalling death rate among the children who contracted the disease.

Leopold bundled his family off to Olmütz, where, in a miserable, cold inn, Wolfgang showed the dreaded symptoms.
"His cheeks were hot and very red, while his hands were
cold as ice." He was soon delirious. Leopold administered
the usual "black powder," found a doctor, and went in
despair to a Count Podstatzky, Dean of Olmütz and Canon
of Salzburg. "When I told him that my small boy had fallen
ill and that I feared that he might have smallpox, he told me
that he would take us in." Accordingly, Wolfgang was
wrapped in blankets and carried to the Dean's rectory. This
was extraordinary magnanimity on the part of the Count
in a moment when panic was general. He may indeed have
saved the composer for posterity. The red pox appeared,
but the danger passed. When Wolfgang looked in a mirror
and beheld his swollen nose, he said, "Now I am like little
Mayr," referring to a player in the Salzburg orchestra who
had a large nose.

Back in Vienna in January, they were received with kindness by the Emperor Joseph II and his mother, the co-
regent, Maria Theresa, and by those nobles who were not
at once terrified at a pock-marked face.

It was at this point that Leopold decided to take his boldest
step. "I must show what we can do. We must either succeed
or fail. And where is my boy more likely to succeed than in
the theatre?" He easily obtained the Emperor's assent. It
would have to be an *opera buffa,* and it could not be performed until after Lent. The delay was further extended, for
the Emperor visited Hungary and the Turkish borders and
would not return until June. Meanwhile no money was
coming in. Leopold, who since his appointment as *Vize-
kapellmeister* four years before had been at home only a few
months, was jeopardizing his position. The argument that he
hoped to build prestige for the Salzburg *Kapelle* by the
fame of one of its talented sons was less impressive to the
Archbishop than the indefinite absence of the father from
active service. Leopold was ready to admit that he had no
right to expect a continuing salary, and was satisfied when
word came that His Most Benevolent Highness would allow
him to stay away without pay after the month of March.

At length a libretto was handed to Mozart: *La finta semplice*. It was about an outwardly naïve lady, a "pretended innocent," who schemes to marry money and position. It was a play of Goldoni, slightly (and anonymously) doctored by the librettist Marco Coltellini, while this gentleman kept Wolfgang waiting, or gave him altered verses to recompose. Wolfgang was to learn by experience the many exactions involved in the production of an opera, in which the singers were the first consideration and must be individually satisfied with their arias. He readily met all demands and was never at a loss. The manuscript shows the emending hand of the father, but principally in such matters as stage directions. It is a finished piece of work which could have stood up to any that Vienna was hearing at the time. As a youthful feat, as a first attempt at a full-length *opera buffa,* the score is astonishing. There are twenty-six vocal numbers, connected by dialogue in recitative form. The voice parts are handled with understanding, the *recitativo secco* molded to the language and the expressive intent of the dialogue. The orchestra is resourceful and well matched to the voices. The score is gay and spirited throughout. The twelve-year-old composer treats the cynical discussion of matrimony as if he knew all about it. He is equal to every situation. When an aria calls for anger, for timidity, for sorrow, for ardor, Wolfgang, who has been using his ears, is quite ready to meet *buffo* custom and to add touches of his own. In character depiction, in melody as such, in the texture of ensemble, the intimations of the later Mozart are already discernible, only waiting to be lifted high and clear of contemporary routine. The two hundred pages of score bespeak the enormous industry of the boy at his desk, busily keeping up the pace while intrigue played around him and contrived obstacles.

By the end of June, Leopold was suspecting "deeply laid plots and malicious persecutions." Too much success for an outsider, and a small boy at that, might not have been agreeable to certain musicians at court. It was one thing to show off a *Wunderkind* at Schönbrunn, quite another to return with him as a composer of twelve and set him up in direct competition with the composers established there in the dignity of their adulthood. There was soon an undercurrent of opposition. Gluck, according to Leopold, was hostile, but there is no evidence of ill will on the part of that composer, then or later. The impresario Affligio, who had the principal financial stake in the production, showed caution and then open reluctance.

Everything lagged except the young composer's pen. Leopold was freshly alarmed when the report was spread that not the child but the father was actually writing the opera. To counter this he gathered some skeptics, asked them to open any text of Metastasio, the famous librettist then in Vienna, and put it before Wolfgang. "Wolfgang took up his pen and with the most amazing rapidity wrote, without hesitation and in the presence of several eminent persons, music for this aria with several instruments." Apparently Metastasio and a few others were on his side. But they were a helpless minority. Even the Emperor could not control Affligio's operatic ventures, for it was Affligio's and not crown money that was risked. Leopold wrote frantically that "envy pursues any person of talent according to the extent of his abilities. . . . Our adversaries are wicked liars, slanderers and envious creatures who would laugh in their sleeves if we were to become discouraged and depart, giving them the victory." And later: "The whole hell of musicians has arisen to prevent the display of a child's ability." The frenzies of Leopold had at least a core of truth—but they were in vain. When a plea sent to the Emperor brought no result, he extracted a declaration, so he tells us, from the composer Hasse and from Metastasio in favor of Wolfgang as a superior opera composer. Both were long-established authorities. Hasse, we know, was deeply impressed, for Leopold obtained from him, and carried later to Bologna, a strong letter of recommendation. By this time, Affligio was looking for no such proofs. He threatened, again according to the word of Leopold, that if he was pushed he would go ahead but ruin the production and consequently the composer's reputation. This is even harder to believe, for it would certainly have meant a flat loss for himself. Leopold believed it, and so was left helpless and beaten. It would have to be said that Wolfgang had failed as any small boy must fail who presumes to compose an opera. Leopold withdrew the score and took it back with him to Salzburg, where it was at length performed—after a fashion. In any case, Vienna was left to judge the young composer incompetent by implication.

The inexhaustible Wolfgang could have proved his competence by the little *Singspiel—Bastien und Bastienne—* which he composed during this visit. It was no public vindication, for it was written for a friendly performance and heard by a few in a little garden theatre. The host was Dr. Franz Anton Mesmer, the inventor of healing by magnetism, who was to be a lifelong friend of the Mozarts and who was to be lampooned later, more pointedly but still good-naturedly, in *Così fan tutte,* for by then the composer could instruct his librettist. The little operetta has been unduly condescended to. Its simplicity, freedom from *fioriture* or complexity of part-writing, would have been conditioned by the nature of the occasion and the limitations of the performers. This very simplicity suits the character of the naïve subject and the composer's young spirit—a happy combination. Here, as later, Mozart at his simplest is sometimes Mozart at his best.

There was at least a partial vindication in the dedication of a chapel on the Rennweg, near the Belvidere, for which ceremony Wolfgang composed an Offertory (K. 47), a Missa solemnis (K. 139), and a trumpet concerto (which has not survived). The ceremony was decorated by the presence of the whole royal family, backed by trumpets and drums. "The Court and the public," wrote Leopold, "was at last convinced of the wickedness of our adversaries." Having thus proved his point to an extent, Leopold put his family in a coach for home, and entered Salzburg on January 5, 1769, after an absence this time of fifteen months.

The Archbishop at last seems to have awakened to the fact that the small son of his Vice *Kapellmeister,* who had been the talk of every court in Europe, was worthy of interested attention, even official recognition. It would have been like Leopold to obtain an audience and remind him that the ability of his son and therefore the honor of Salzburg had been slighted in Vienna. In any case, the Archbishop ordered a production of *La finta semplice*. This was a concession in that neither his singers, his musicians, nor his palatial quarters were equipped for an *opera buffa*. A stage was erected in the *Residenz*. The title part was taken by Michael Haydn's wife, née Maria Magdalena Lipp, who, if Leopold may be believed, had points in common with Goldoni's unscrupulous character. After the performance, according to custom, a *"Licenza"* was performed, a separate piece exalting the patron. This may have been *"Sol nascente"* (K. 70). The Archbishop thereupon announced the appointment of Wolfgang as Concertmaster.

Since Wolfgang was to be called upon for church music in that year and for opera presently, he may have studied both forms in the quiet of his home. He composed a Mass, in D minor (K. 65) for performance a week after his arrival (January 14), and another on a larger scale, more proficient in development (K. 66), for the first missal celebration by his landlord's son Cajetan Hagenauer, who had taken orders at St. Peter's in his absence. Instrumental music included three sets of minuets (K. 103-105), a serenade (K. 100), and the two cassations (K. 63 and 99).

VII

Italy, 1770-1771

Nᴏᴛ ᴀ ʏᴇᴀʀ had passed since the return of the Mozarts to Salzburg when, on December 12, 1769, Leopold was off again, and this time southward. Italy was the climax of his ambition. Italy was music's heart and source. Music there was more general, more popular in more communities. All music of the Roman Catholic Church stemmed from there. Instrumental music was rivaled only in Germany. Opera everywhere had Italian roots, Italian librettists, Italian singers. *Opera buffa* persisted in Paris in a war of styles. In London the Mozarts had heard Italian opera; in Vienna, Wolfgang had been given an Italian libretto and confronted with an Italian cast. Leopold had very likely planned for *La finta semplice* as a step in the Italian direction. If Wolfgang could succeed with an Italian opera in Italy the Viennese skeptics would be well silenced. This was important, and Leopold, confident that his son could meet the test, was never more purposeful. Marianne no longer fitted in his schemes. She was now a young lady of seventeen, an excellent, a faithfully industrious pianist, but by no means a remarkable one. Her place henceforth would be at home; her function, a teacher with a regular stream of pupils. Now she could stay in her mother's care. Father and son alone could subsist more cheaply, and without subjecting the feminine element to travel hazards. The two could fend for themselves. Often they were received in monasteries, saving the cost of inns. Wolfgang at thirteen could be expected to meet social as well as musical requirements.

The letters describing the journey, the people encountered, the exploits of Wolfgang, were addressed on each post day to the mother. Leopold plainly had posterity in mind. Every experience was carefully described. The mother was repeatedly warned that every letter must be kept. Since every letter to Salzburg passed a censor, he had worked out a code for private information, consisting of the substitution of certain letters of the alphabet for the right ones. It permitted the free expression of uncomplimentary remarks about certain patrons. Wolfgang's letters begin at this time. They are at first postscripts to his father's—gay and affectionate messages to his mother and sister. With them he brings a personal, vivid picture of himself into the story of his life. He seems to write as naturally as he would speak, putting down whatever exuberant nonsense comes into his head. The postscripts begin at Wörgl, the first stop on their journey. He writes to his mother: "Dearest Mamma! My heart is completely enchanted with all these pleasures, because it is so jolly on this journey, because it is so warm in the carriage and because our coachman is a fine fellow. He drives at top speed when the road gives him any chance at all." He writes to his sister in good Italian, as if testing his language and hers. *"Carissima sorella mia"* gets joking messages to various friends, beginning with one to a Herr von Schiedenhofen: "Tell him that I am always singing 'Tralaliera, tralaliera' and that I need not put sugar in my soup now that I am no longer in Salzburg."

The two Mozarts approached Italy by way of Wörgl, Innsbruck and Bozen. They entered the province of Venetia through Steinach and the Brenner Pass and headed southward to Rovereto, where they spent Christmas; thence to Verona and Mantua and westward to Milan by way of Cremona. In each town, Leopold at once sought out any *Eccellenza* it might hold, any art patron or prominent musician who might help their cause. Of these there were plenty. They found a warm welcome everywhere. It was all very gratifying, except that public concerts brought them no fee at all. The patron simply opened these events to the populace. "From this you will realize," Leopold tells his wife, "that we shall not become rich in Italy." Excitement was quickly generated. Crowds gathered, miracle-minded. A story is told by Jahn that later at Naples people began to whisper, as Wolfgang played, that a ring flashing on his left hand was the secret of his ability. He removed the ring and continued. Hearing that the principal church in Rovereto had a good organ, Leopold somehow let it be known that the boy would play on it at a certain hour, with the result that "all Rovereto" had assembled there and they could hardly make their way inside. A similar incident happened at the Church of San Tommaso in Verona, where their stay of a fortnight enabled a painter, believed to be Cignarolli, to make one of the most charming portraits of the boy Mozart which have survived.

From Verona, Wolfgang wrote to his sister in Italian: "Now we hear all the operas," and proceeded to give a specific and perceptive account of the operas he had heard, the music, the orchestra, the singers one by one. In Mantua and Milan there were more operas and troupes to be summed up. Wolfgang writes to his sister from the latter city, which they reached by the end of January:

> The opera at Mantua was delightful. They played *Demetrio* [by Hasse]. The *prima donna* sings well, but not loud; and when you don't see her acting, but only listen to her, you would think she isn't singing at all. For she can't open her mouth, but whines everything. That's not new to us. The *seconda donna* looks like a grenadier and has a powerful voice too, and I must say doesn't sing badly, seeing that she is acting for the first time. The *primo uomo, il musico,* sings beautifully, though his voice is uneven—he is called Caselli. The *secondo uomo* is already old and I don't like him. As for the tenors, one is called Otini. He doesn't sing badly, but rather heavily, like all Italian tenors, and he is a great friend of ours. I don't know the name of the other one. He is still young, but not particularly good. *Primo ballerino*—good. *Prima ballerina*— good, and they say she isn't ugly, but I haven't seen her close to. The rest are quite ordinary. A clown was there who jumps well, but can't write as I do, I mean as sows piss. The orchestra was not bad. . . .

Very plainly, Wolfgang was being primed in operatic ways, including the practical human factors, and missing very little. They heard Piccinni's *Cesare in Egitto* in Milan, also Hasse's *La clemenza di Tito,* which subject Wolfgang was later to set. Wolfgang gave numerous concerts, and composed a symphony, sonata, or aria when needed.

The winter was exceptionally cold for northern Italy; Wolfgang suffered from chapped hands and face, and when they reached an inn he would hug the fire. A great lady presented him with some cold cream. The father hastens to assure the mother that he is fulfilling the motherly duties: "We sleep on four good mattresses and every night the bed is warmed so that Wolfgang, when he goes to bed, is always quite happy." He adds: "He eats carefully, and does not overeat. He eats very little, and none the less he is fat and cheerful and gay and jolly all day long."

In Milan they had the good luck to be befriended by the Governor-General of Lombardy, Count Carl Joseph von Firmian, whose younger brother had once been Archbishop of Salzburg. This Count was as well disposed as he was influential—he proved to be even more helpful than Grimm had been in Paris. He procured for Wolfgang the promise of a commission for an opera in Milan for the following Christmas. The *scrittura* (contract) was to be sent to whatever part of Italy he might be in. It was to be an *opera seria,* which meant a "grand" opera on a mythological subject, with much pomp and no humor. The recitatives would be sent in October, and Wolfgang would be expected in Milan in November, to allow for completion and performance in the following month. This suited Leopold perfectly. "It will take all our time to reach Rome for Passion week. You know that Rome is a place one must visit. Then we shall go on to Naples, which is such an important center that even if the *scrittura* does not bring us back to Milan to write the opera, some opportunity may easily develop to keep us there through the winter."

So fortified against any failure of promise, he delayed no longer in Milan. They took a coach to Lodi on March 15, and by the time of their arrival that evening, Wolfgang had composed his first string quartet (K. 80). At Parma, their next stop, they heard the celebrated singer Lucrezia Agujari, who bore the unkind (but probably technically justified) name "La Bastardella." La Bastardella entertained the two Mozarts at a midday meal, after which she astonished them both with her top notes. "In Bologna," writes Leopold, "Wolfgang is admired even more than he has been in all the other towns of Italy; the reason is that this is the center and dwelling place of many masters, artists and scholars." A combination of all three was Padre Martini, the Franciscan father who had made a science as well as an art of music. Leopold would have sought the seal of the Padre's approval for its worth; Wolfgang would (and did) eagerly enter into contrapuntal trials with him. Wolfgang wrote fugues on his subjects, accepted his advice. He sought him out as a special friend when they returned to Bologna on their way north, and was to address him later for a letter of recommendation to Munich. The two Mozarts arrived in Bologna on March 24, and reached Florence by March 30, where advance word had opened many doors for them. They hurried on to Rome and reached there on April 11, as Leopold had planned.

They made their way through the crowds at St. Peter's to the altar where the Pope was holding a service, although they had no pass. In the Sistine Chapel a famous feat of memory took place, thus described by the father (April 14, 1770):

"You have often heard of the famous *Miserere** in Rome, which is so greatly prized that the *musici* in the chapel are forbidden on pain of excommunication to take out a single part of it, to copy it, or to give it to any one. *But we have it already*. Wolfgang has written it down, and we would have sent it to Salzburg with this letter if we did not need it for use here. . . . So we shall bring it home with us. Since it is one of the secrets of Rome, we do not want to let it fall into other hands, and so incur immediate ecclesiastical displeasure."

Here was a case of the father with a nose for notoriety

---

* By Gregorio Allegri.

hastening to make the most of the son's extraordinary but guileless musical doings. Wolfgang does not so much as mention the feat in the letters. As for Leopold, if he did not put the boy up to it, he seized the opportunity to make it known once it was done. He sought out Christofori, one of the Sistine choristers, to confirm its correctness, made sure that this deed would be officially condoned, and proceeded accordingly. He reassured his wife about this bit of holy theft: "There is not the slightest cause for anxiety. . . . All Rome knows, and even the Pope himself, that he wrote it down." Wolfgang writes a postscript to this letter:

> I am a fool as everyone knows, and I am in a tight spot— there is only one bed in our room, and mamma can well imagine that beside papa I get very little rest. I hope we find better quarters. I have just been drawing the holy Peter with his keys and the holy Paul with his sword and the holy Luke with my sister, etc., etc. I have had the honor of kissing St. Peter's holy foot, and I was unfortunately too small to reach, so I, that same old dunce,
>
> Wolfgang Mozart—
had to be lifted up.

Describing the many encounters of his son, Leopold is moved to write (April 21):

> The further we have penetrated into Italy the greater has been the general amazement. Moreover Wolfgang's knowledge does not stand still, but increases from day to day, so that the greatest connoisseurs and masters are at a loss for words to express their admiration. Two days ago we were at the house of a Neapolitan Prince, San Angelo. Yesterday we were at the house of Prince Chigi, where amongst others were present the so-called King of England or Pretender* and the Secretary of State Cardinal Pallavicini. Before long we are to be presented to His Holiness.

This sort of thing was quite usual. A week later he mentions among momentary conquests Prince Xaver of Saxony, courtiers (unnamed) from Paris, Malta, Vienna, Sweden, a Count von Wallenstein, Duchesses of Bracciano and of At-

---

* Charles Edward (1720-1788)

tems, also a visit to an Augustinian monastery. Meanwhile Wolfgang seems to have been composing at all odd moments. He writes to his sister (in Italian) on April 25. He tells her of a game he has learned, called *boccia* (bowls), which he will teach her as soon as he gets home. He ends:

> After this letter I shall finish a symphony which I have begun [K. 81?]. The aria is finished [K. 82]. A symphony [K. 95 or 97?] is being copied (my father is the copyist, for we do not wish to give it out to be copied, it would be stolen). ... My greetings to all my friends and please kiss my Mamma's hands for me, for I am (Tralaliera)
> Wolfgango in Germania
> Amadeo Mozart in Italia
> Behind as before, and doubled in the middle.

On May 8 the two Mozarts left Rome, apparently not without a retinue, for they had four "*sedie,* or two-seated carriages." Pausing at Marino, Sessa and Capua to visit Augustinian monasteries at each place, they reached Naples on the twelfth. When more visits began, they were equipped for them. "We have left our five cloth suits in Rome," writes Leopold on May 19, "and have put on our two beautifully braided summer costumes. Wolfgang's is of rose-colored moiré, but the color is so peculiar that in Italy it is called '*colore di fuoco*' or flame-colored; it is trimmed with silver lace and lined with sky-blue silk. My costume is of the color of cinnamon and is made of piqué Florentine cloth with silver lace and is lined with apple green silk."

They set out from Naples to return to Rome on June 25, this time by mail coach, with the result that the journey which before had taken four days and a half was accomplished in twenty-seven hours. Leopold writes from Rome on June 27:

> As we had slept for only two hours out of the twenty-seven, and had eaten only four cold roast chickens and a piece of bread in the carriage, you can imagine how hungry, thirsty and sleepy we were. Our good Frau Uslenghi gave us some well cooked rice and two soft boiled eggs each. No sooner did we get to our bedroom than Wolfgang fell into a chair and at once began to snore in such a sound sleep that when I completely undressed him he showed no sign of waking. Indeed

he went on snoring . . . and I had to drag him to bed still
sound asleep. When he awoke after nine o'clock in the morning, he did not know where he was or how he had got to bed.
Almost the whole night through he slept in the same spot. God
be praised, we are well.

Wolfgang was approached for operas in Naples, Rome and
Bologna, which his father had to refuse, being bound to
Milan. Cardinal Pallavicini in Rome bestowed upon Wolfgang, in the name of the Pope, the Order of the Golden
Spur, whereby he became a Chevalier equal to Gluck, wore
a "beautiful golden cross," and was addressed as *"Signor
Cavaliere."* He wrote to his sister: *"Mademoiselle, j'ai l'hon-
neur d'être votre très humble serviteur et frère—Chevalier de
Mozart. Addio."* Publicly, unlike the Chevalier Gluck who
held the same decoration, he never bothered to use the
title.

On July 21, from Bologna (where they were to stay until
October), Wolfgang writes to his mother, congratulating her
on her name day, and adds a note to his sister (in Italian):

> May God keep you in good health and let you live another
> hundred years, and not let you die till you are a thousand. I
> hope you learn to know me better in the future, and then you
> can judge how much you like me. I haven't time to write much.
> My pen isn't worth a fig nor is he who is using it. The title of
> the opera which I am to compose in Milan is not yet known.
> Our hostess in Rome has given me the *Thousand and One
> Nights*. It is fun to read.

On the twenty-seventh they received the libretto for Wolfgang's opera. It was *Mitridate, rè di Ponto,* an *opera seria*
by Vittorio Amadeo Cigna-Santi, a poet of Turin, where
it had been performed three years before with music by
Abbate Gasparini. Whether Wolfgang was pleased with the
rather turgid story of ancient Rome does not appear. He
was obviously never asked. He had met and heard Signora
Antonia Bernasconi, the prima donna, Signor Ettore, who
was assigned the title role, and two castrati who were to be in
the cast—Santorini and Cicognani. When the young composer arrived in Milan on October 18, he had prepared some
of the recitatives. The arias had to be written in consultation

with the singers, who of course had a great deal to say about what they wanted. There were signs of underground opposition. An unnamed saboteur tried to disaffect Signora Bernasconi by putting before her the music of the old setting as preferable. The attempt failed. She was entirely happy with what Wolfgang had composed. Wolfgang had to write under pressure, while the father took care that his strength should not be overtaxed. While delays were caused by the late arrival of some of the singers, Wolfgang cheerfully kept up his end. He wrote to his sister even at the start of his labors, on August 4, "It is impossible for me to write a better hand, for this is a note-pen and not a letter-pen. My fiddle has been re-strung and I play it every day—I'm writing this because Mamma wanted to know whether I still play it. . . . Meanwhile I have already composed four Italian symphonies [K. 81, 84, 95, 97?] to say nothing of five or six arias [K. 77, 78, 82, 88, 143] and a motet." In answer to his sister's suspicion that someone has been claiming a cassation as his own, he gives the *incipits* of three, and remarks: "Who would dare to pass off as his own a composition by the *Kapellmeister's* son, whose mother and sister are in Salzburg? *Addio!* Farewell. My only amusement at the moment consists in dancing English steps and caprioles and pirouettes. Italy is a sleepy country! I am always drowsy!" His drowsiness had not kept him from being busy in every musical direction.

As the rehearsals progressed, incredulity at the ability of a boy, and a *tedesco* at that, to compose a passable opera gave way to amazement and enthusiasm from the whole company. Produced the day after Christmas, 1770, it was received with great applause and cries of *"Evviva il maestro! evviva il maestrino!"* *Il maestrino* was bound by contract to lead three of the performances. There were twenty. Wolfgang was given a new title by the Academy of Verona: *"Cavaliere Filarmonico."*

It would be expecting the impossible if we were to look for a great opera from Mozart under such circumstances. The characters were walking symbols, given to uttering overblown sentiments. To Mozart at thirteen, music was gay and insouciant. The text had some semblance, obscured by much later handling, of Racine's original. The boy was suddenly required to produce quantities of arias, ensembles, accompanied recitatives—on texts which he received out of order, which must favor the vocal equipment of each singer; pontifical, sententious verses on such matters—hardly within his young experience—as love thwarted, patriotic loyalty, noble sacrifice. Having recently become acquainted with operas by Hasse, Jommelli, and lesser lights, he had a working knowledge, and met his assignment. When it is at all possible, the characters come to musical life.

Bringing the Italian journey to a close, Leopold did not have a grievance to carry home, or the tale of a single serious misadventure. Italy, wherever they went, had taken Wolfgang to its heart. On the strength of his operatic success, he had bids for another opera in Milan, and for an oratorio in Padua. Still more tangible were the manuscripts of three new symphonies in the portmanteau (K. 84, 95 and 97). He had made them all properly Italian. After the labors over the opera and the climax of its production, Leopold delayed the return home by a visit, mostly for pleasure's sake, to the Carnival in Venice. They left Venice on the twelfth of March, 1771, and were in Salzburg for Easter.

VIII

Salzburg, Milan, Vienna, Munich,

1771-1777

Mozart, now fifteen, needed no longer to be pushed by his father as a wonder child. He was an opera composer respected in Milan, which meant a good deal. People who knew and who were listened to were ready to act in his favor. One of them was Count Firmian, who had done so much for him in Milan. A letter came from the Count in Vienna speaking for another personal friend, the Empress Maria Theresa. Her son, Archduke Ferdinand and Princess Maria Ricciarda Beatrice of Modena were to be married in Milan in the coming October. Wolfgang was forthwith commissioned to compose a *serenata* for the event—the usual complimentary piece for such occasions, with airs, choruses and ballets, set to an appropriate classical text, with complimentary allusions to the bridal pair. It was called *Ascanio in Alba*.

Wolfgang and his father arrived in Milan on August 21, but Wolfgang did not receive the text, he did not even see it, until September 7. The performance was less than six weeks away, but Wolfgang went calmly and cheerfully to work and had his score ready within ten days. The task could have been done by another, with automatic and sterile results. The stream of Mozart's musical current had always life and grace. It was his training, too, to make music in spite of obstacles— a happy outcome of Leopold's contrivances to amaze. While Wolfgang was composing the Overture to his *serenata*, he wrote to his sister (August 24): "Over our heads we have a violinist, downstairs another one, in the next room a singing-master gives lessons, and in another room opposite ours an oboist. That is good fun when you are composing! It gives you plenty of ideas." Those who have tried to think musically against contending sounds will say that, even allowing for Wolfgang's usual nonsensical exaggeration in his postscripts, this was truly a feat.

The performance of *Ascanio in Alba* on October 17, 1771, was, to depend upon Leopold again, "an extraordinary success." It was repeated a number of times, more often than Hasse's *opera seria, Ruggiero,* which had opened the festivities on the sixteenth as the principal event. Hasse's friendly relations with the Mozarts continued, nor had he reason to alter his earlier opinion, expressed in a letter of introduction borne by Leopold to the Abbé Ortes in Bologna: "Herr Mozart is a highly cultivated and polished man, his children are well brought up. The boy is, in addition, beautiful, lively, charming, and behaves in such a way that one absolutely cannot help loving him. . . . I have seen his compositions; they are certainly good and I have noticed nothing in them to be expected of a twelve-year-old boy. . . . One thing is certain: if his development keeps pace with his age, something wonderful will come of him."

Leopold delayed the return to Salzburg until the end of Advent, since "no concerts are held at court." He need not have worried about keeping in good standing with his Archbishop. The day after their arrival, which was on December 15, his Excellency died. There was no heartfelt mourning among the inhabitants of Salzburg at his passing; if there was regret it was from apprehension about his successor—Hieronymus Joseph Franz von Paula, Count of Colloredo. He had been Bishop of Gurk, a small Carinthian community, which for a man of forty does not signify any ecclesiastical standing. He was the son of the Vice-Chancellor of Vienna under Francis I, and the word went around Salzburg that he was possessed with the Emperor's zeal for reform, perhaps also his zeal for economy. The Archbishop Sigismund, his predecessor, by no means loved, had had at least the virtue of being easy-going and indifferent. Certainly Mozart never formed any liking or respect for the man who was now to be his employer. Still, the beginning promised well. The new Arch-bishop confirmed the old one's promised appointment of Wolfgang as *Konzertmeister,* a post which carried with it the possibility of composing whatever scores for church or palace might be required. An opera, or rather a complimentary al-legorical piece was in order for the installation, and Wolfgang was set to work upon a *serenata, Il sogno di Scipione* (K. 126). It was an old text by Metastasio, a relic of 1735, a patriotic piece having no connection whatever with the new Archbishop. It was considered sufficient to change the name Carlo in the text of the *licenza,* the panegyric, to "Girolamo," signifying "Joseph." Wolfgang otherwise fulfilled his home obligations with seven symphonies (K. 124, 128-130. 132-134), four divertimenti (K. 131, 136-138), the litany *De Venerabili* (K. 125), a *Regina Coeli* (K. 127). Six string quartets (K. 155-160) were begun in Salzburg and completed abroad. Two commissions had come from Italy: one from Padua for an oratorio (*azione teatrale*), *La Betulia liberata,* the story of the biblical city liberated by Judith; and the other for Milan, through the intervention of Count Firmian: *Lucio Silla,* an *opera seria* for the carnival season of 1773.

The father and son were off for Milan on October 23, 1772, for what was to prove the last visit to Italy. *Lucio Silla* (K. 135) was another piece on a worn plot—about an emperor who covets the fiancée of one of his subordinates but finally in an overwhelming burst of magnanimity gives her up and blesses the pair. It is hard to imagine the boy as warming to this piece of empty solemnity. He took hold of it cheer-fully and turned out, when the subject allowed, some beautiful numbers. There was as usual the short allowance of time. The opening performance was scheduled for the day after Christmas. On their arrival in Milan on November 4, Wolf-gang had written some recitatives, but these had to be changed, for the librettist, Giovanni da Gamerra, submitted the whole text to Metastasio for revision. The solo numbers had to await the arrival of the principal singers. These had to be consulted, their best notes favored. Maria Anna de Amicis, the prima donna, came from Venice on December 4. She had an extraordinary range and vocal agility, and the composer delighted her with airs tailored accordingly with ornate passages few others could perform. On December 5, Wolfgang told his sister: "I still have fourteen numbers to compose, and then I shall have finished. It is impossible for me to write as I have no news, and also I don't know what I'm writing, for I can think of nothing but my opera, and I should find myself writing you not only words but a whole aria." The tenor engaged as principal became ill, and another (Bassano Morgnoni) was hastily imported. He had never acted on a large stage. He arrived on the seventeenth, just before the first full rehearsal. There were mishaps at the opening. At five o'clock, the expected curtain time, the large audience was seated and everything ready. All had to wait, including the nervous singers, while according to Leopold, "The Archduke rose from his midday meal to write in his own hand five letters of New Year's greetings to their Majesties the Emperor and Empress; I should mention that he writes very slowly." The performance began at eight and ended at two. The opera soon found its pace and was repeated twenty-five times.

During this last Italian sojourn Mozart managed to compose, before and after the opera, a considerable amount of chamber music. He wrote a quartet (probably K. 155) to pass the time in Bozen at the start of the journey, and completed five more (K. 156-160). Besides these he wrote a divertimento (K. 186) and a wind octet, using pairs of clarinets and English horns. For performance by the castrato of the opera, Venanzio Rauzzini, he composed the fresh and exuberant motet *"Exsultate"* (K. 165). It requires an accomplished coloratura soprano to sing it today.

Leopold made a diplomatic effort to reach home in time for the first anniversary of the new Archbishop's installation, March 14, 1773. Their coach pulled in to Salzburg on the eve of that day.

When in the following summer the Archbishop made a journey to Vienna, Leopold took the occasion to go as well, and went with Wolfgang, on July 14. He would admit no special object in the journey, but lost no time in obtaining an audience with Maria Theresa. The Empress had been most kind on their first Vienna visit; she had promptly chosen

Wolfgang to compose *Ascanio in Alba* for her son's wedding in Milan. Now she was equally gracious, but heeded no hints. The astute Leopold had met his match in this practical and level-headed mother. If he could have seen a letter she had written to her young third son, the Archduke Ferdinand, then Governor of Lombardy, he would have revised his optimism. She had written on December 12, 1771, two months after the first performance of *Ascanio in Alba,* to the bridegroom of that festive occasion:

"You ask me about taking into your services the young Salzburg musician. I do not know in what capacity, believing that you have no use for a composer, or for useless people. If however it would give you pleasure, I do not wish to prevent you. What I say is intended only to urge you not to burden yourself with useless people, and not to give such people permission to represent themselves as belonging in your service. It gives one's service a bad name when such people run about like beggars; he has, besides, a large family."

The two Mozarts otherwise enjoyed their stay in Vienna, renewed old friendships, played and listened to much music, earning, however, no money. Wolfgang composed a *serenata* (K. 185), and worked upon six quartets (K. 168-173). The quartets, in the opinion of Wyzewa and Saint-Foix, mark the beginning of an important German phase in the music of Mozart. He may or may not have met Joseph Haydn at the time, for Haydn is not mentioned in the letters. There can be no possible doubt that he knew Haydn's recently published quartets, Op. 20, for his own closely imitate their style. On his return to Salzburg he may have come into closer contact with Michael Haydn, Joseph's younger brother, whom he had known from boyhood. Leopold disapproved of Michael Haydn's drinking habits, his laziness and his "dissolute" wife. Later he acknowledged this Haydn's importance as a composer. Wolfgang was quicker to find in him a valuable colleague in composition. He copied many of his scores. Wyzewa and Saint-Foix have discerned a close affinity between the two composers in the particular sense of "pure beauty" which pervades their works. They write of Michael Haydn:

The melodic line shows, even in his most careless works, a grace and delicious sweetness which is found repeatedly, and lends, for example, his quartets and quintets the aspect of works of Mozart from which only the soul of Mozart is missing. Just as in Michael Haydn's elder brother exactness of expression was always superior to invention of melody, with rhythm and modulation of striking beauty, so in the younger brother it seems as if poetic beauty always flowed effortlessly, a beauty often a little monotonous, closed within narrow limits, but as adorably fresh, limpid and *"galant"* as could be imagined.

This association was especially evident through Mozart's longest Salzburg sojourn, a period which began with his return from Vienna on September 26, 1773, and lasted four years, until September, 1777, with one welcome interruption, a visit to Munich from December 6, 1774, to March 8, 1775, for the production of the *opera buffa, La finta giardiniera*. It was as well that he otherwise stayed at home to draw the more quietly upon his greatly accumulated inner resources, for these proved to be notable maturing years. It would have been surprising if he had not composed a large amount of music, for it had already been noticeable that when Wolfgang was not loaded with performing duties and the dreary inactivity of days on the road he began to take musical account of himself. He composed as usual to meet occasions, but the occasions were not few, and he met them with music of incredible beauty as his genius probed, subtilized, expanded in each department of his art—each department, that is, except the stage. Only once was he called upon for a quasi-operatic piece in Salzburg. The Archduke Maximilian, the youngest son of Maria Theresa, visited Salzburg in April, 1775, and for the reception Wolfgang wrote *Il rè pastore* (K. 208), a bucolic work lacking in dramatic contrast, a pastoral serenade rather than an opera, but music of Mozartean simplicity in the best sense. It was during the Archduke's visit that Mozart wrote (and perhaps played) his first violin concerto (K. 207) which he shortly followed with four more, his great contributions to this form (K. 211, 216, 218, 219).

The commission from Munich for a stage work was of

course received by Wolfgang with delight. He had had no chance to write an *opera buffa* since his one and only attempt —*La finta semplice*. Since the offer came from Maximilian III, the Bavarian Elector, Hieronymus was not in a position to stand in the way.

La finta giardiniera was a typical *opera buffa* of the more scrambled sort* The text is attributed to Calzabigi. It was already current and popular in a setting by Anfossi. The plot could hardly have been arrived at except as an attempt to satisfy all concerned: the singers and their best styles, sometimes serious; the appetite of the audience for much comedy and occasional sentiment; the composer's needs for a suitable framework. There are the expected *buffo* parts— the Podestà, the usual wealthy and amorous old man (here a tenor), his servant Serpetta, the soubrette. There are also parts borrowed from the serious category—Arminda, a haughty and inconstant lady, and Ramiro, the languishing poet who courts her in vain. His part is for a male soprano, and is entirely serious. The title part of Violanta (Sandrina)—the lady who is in pursuit of her lost husband, has disguised herself as a lady gardener and has been employed by the Podestà—would not have been out of place in *opera seria*. To put the tangle of situations into a sentence—each of the seven characters (except one—the castrato) is wooed while wooing someone else. The composer was not dismayed. He depicted distinct musical characters, whether comic, lovelorn or impassioned, developed a new degree of melodic invention, handled the orchestra with new resource. In short, he produced a vivacious score which hangs together, progresses smoothly, and shows an advance in every respect over the earlier *La finta semplice*.

Friends from Salzburg visited the carnival. Wolfgang was embarrassed for some of them. One, Herr von Mölk, attended an *opera seria* performance for the first time. "He crossed himself so often that we were ashamed of him, for any one could plainly see that he had never been anywhere but Salzburg and Innsbruck." Lodgings were found by Leopold for Marianne, and she was bundled off from Salzburg, arriving in

---

* Wolfgang once wrote to his sister: " '*Opera buffa*' means 'Crazy Opera.' "

time for the opening performance. Why the mother was left at home we are not told—Leopold seems to have ruled otherwise. The opera was received with delight on January 13, 1775. The Archbishop himself had occasion to visit the Elector, but his stay came between performances. To Leopold's amused satisfaction he was compelled to listen at length to its praises "by the whole family of the Elector and by all the nobles, and to receive their enthusiastic congratulations. He was so embarrassed that he could only reply with a bow of his head and a shrug of his shoulders."

With the Elector it was a different story. He was an enthusiastic musician, a more than passable player on the bass viol. He insisted upon hearing some of Wolfgang's church music, which was promptly sent for from Salzburg. The Salzburg visitors noted how the Mozarts were entertained by the Elector, and whispered that Wolfgang might be expected to have a court appointment. Leopold was angry and called them fools, just as he had done when his visit to Vienna had stirred up similar talk at home. Leopold well realized that delicate possibilities when under consideration might be ruined by gossip.

The situation at Salzburg is reviewed by Mozart in a letter which he wrote to his teacher and friend in Bologna, Padre Martini, September 4, 1776. He was submitting for the Padre's opinion, which turned out to be of the highest, the *offertorium, Misericordias Domini* (K. 222), which he had written for the Bavarian Elector at Munich. "For the theatre we are poorly situated through the lack of singers. We have no castrati and will not find them easily since these folk wish to be well paid and liberality is not one of our vices. For my part I write chamber and church music." "Chamber and church music" covered a great deal of ground. For the Archepiscopal services he composed four Masses in the last part of 1776 (K. 257, 258, 259, 262)—and another in 1777 (K. 275)—the Litany in E flat (K. 243), the offertory, *Venite, populi,* for two choirs (K. 260), and the graduale, *Sancta Maria* (K. 273). There were also organ sonatas, performed between the epistle and the gospel. Music was expected for concerts by the court orchestra, and may have included concertos, duo sonatas, and solo works (he played the clavier before the Archduke Maximilian). Since he wrote no symphonies at this time, we can only suppose that there was no call for them. Serenades (*Tafelmusik*) were needed for formal parties. But these and chamber music in every form were in demand for uses quite apart from the court. "Night Music" was written for the fête day of Countess Antonia Lodron (the Mozarts were now cultivated by such aristocracy as Salzburg possessed). The wedding of the daughter of the merchant Sigmund Haffner occasioned the "Haffner" Serenade (K. 249 and 250). There was at least one divertimento (K. 251) which celebrated Nannerl's name day. The occasion of the *Serenata notturna* for two string orchestras (K. 239) is not known. These various suites of several movements, less developed than symphonies, usually opening with a march, were often performed in the street and listened to from the windows of those complimented. The "entertainment music" was composed mostly for Salzburg. Piano concertos and violin or solo sonatas were sometimes written for himself, sometimes for a pupil, and adapted to the pupil's ability. Mozart used a piano at this time although he did not abandon the harpsichord. The Piano Concerto in C major (K. 246) was written for the Countess Lützow whose husband was Commandant of the *Festung* on its rocky perch above their heads; the magnificent Concerto in E flat major (K. 271), for Madame "Jenomé" (Jeunehomme), a visiting French pianist. The Concerto for Three Pianos (K. 242) was performed by the three countesses Lodron, mother and daughters; four-hand piano sonatas he probably played with his sister.

As usual he was simply providing music where it was needed. Those whom he obliged enjoyed the lovely measures, appropriate to the moment, and promptly forgot them. Not one of them realized that they were being presented with something more than jolly tunes—music of undying beauty, infinitely superior to what other composers round about were giving them. A concert in Salzburg given by a violinist, Herr Kolb, for visiting businessmen, a group from the court orchestra furnishing the accompaniment, is described by Leopold. The host played one of Mozart's violin concertos, and a

"*Nachtmusik*" which may have consisted of movements from the "Haffner" Serenade. He wrote to Wolfgang in Munich September 29, 1777:

> As the music was so much praised and won extraordinary acclamation and applause, he [Kolb] announced: "You have been hearing the compositions of a good friend who is no longer with us." Whereupon they all cried out: "What a pity that we have lost him!" The concert took place in Eizenberger's hall. When it was over, they all got drunk and shouldered one another in processions round the room, knocking against the lustres, or rather against the large chandelier which hangs in the middle of the ceiling, so that they smashed the center bowl and other pieces, which will now have to be sent to Venice to be replaced.

One wonders whether there were many such Salzburg evenings with music drowned in alcohol; also whether the music now so highly prized won from Mozart's colleagues something more than a moment of surprised attention.

Leopold felt his position at Court intolerable. He was fifty-eight, and two younger men were over him, Lolli and Fischietti, a situation which did not increase his love for pre-empting Italians. Brunetti, who was the principal violinist in Salzburg, and too close to the Archbishop to please Mozart, may nevertheless have been the first performer of the concertos and fine divertimento movements composed by him in Salzburg. Hieronymus cultivated the violin, for a gentleman was expected to play an instrument. He would take part in concert performances while Brunetti stood behind him to support him in difficult spots, or, in passages on the E string, to take over altogether. Wolfgang, now twenty-one, with abilities admitted by everyone except, apparently, the new Archbishop, held a "half time" position. In return for his music for church services, concerts, celebrations, he was rewarded with the token pay of 150 gulden. Wolfgang, who otherwise had hard feelings towards none, openly hated Hieronymus. He did so in sympathy with his father's ill-treatment, and was led by the hostility which pervaded all Salzburg. The inhabitants, being conservative Catholics, disliked his free-thinking attitudes and resented both his repressive measures and the efficiency

with which they were applied. They had hated him even at
the moment he took office. The story was told by Koch-Stern-
feld that when he entered the Cathedral for his installation
the people in the street stood in silence. A small boy called
"Huzza," and promptly had his ears boxed by the man beside
him. The new lord was well aware of this feeling and he returned it. "He seldom expressed satisfaction with his officials.
His disdainful mode of address to all but those of the highest
nobility and the irritable tone of his conversation kept all
about him in timid subordination. Even his appearance (although he was of puny stature and sickly complexion), the
sharp glance of his gray eyes, the left eye rarely wide open,
and the decided lines around his mouth, commanded respect
and fear." Wolfgang probably nursed his own grievance, born
of a succession of slights. The air became oppressive. When
he journeyed to Munich for his opera production, he wrote to
his sister "how much good it is doing me to be able to breathe
freely."

Some have defended Hieronymus on the grounds that the
two Mozarts were of no great practical use to his court. Leopold's hostility would have made him a germ of dissension
in the choir. Both Mozarts were usually absent when they
might have been useful. Wolfgang made his fame elsewhere
instead of at home, particularly in opera, which the court of
Hieronymus could not have produced, putting him in the embarrassing position of the ill-equipped potentate. The very
presence of these two subjects must often have galled him.
Leopold petitioned for leave to depart with Wolfgang on another tour and was summarily refused. His Lordship would
not countenance "begging expeditions" from his court. On
August 1, 1777, Wolfgang wrote the letter asking for his own
dismissal. The required formal phrases of abject servility can
be turned to ridicule by cynical insinuations. Here is the
closing paragraph of this petition (which of course may have
been worded by Leopold):

I most humbly beg your gracious Excellency [etc.] to grant
my dismissal, since I am compelled to make use of the coming
autumn month in order not to have to travel through the following cold months in bad weather. Your gracious Excellency

[etc.] will not take this humble petition ungraciously, since three years ago when I asked permission to go to Vienna, you graciously told me that I had nothing more to hope for, and that I had better seek my fortune elsewhere. I most humbly thank your gracious Excellency for all high favors received and with the flattering hope of being able to serve you with more success in my maturer years, I am

Your gracious Excellency's
My gracious Prince and Master's
Most humble and obedient servant
Wolfgang Amade Mozart

The trip now contemplated by Mozart and his father was to encompass the three principal music centers of the westward continent: Munich, Mannheim and Paris. It was a doubly bold step, for it might have caused Leopold's dismissal. A position elsewhere would have been more than doubtful for a man past his prime ousted from a subordinate position by an employer who would rather ruin than recommend him. Leopold had already strained his own security often enough in his efforts to find a berth for Wolfgang. Now the Archbishop flatly refused to allow Leopold to leave Salzburg again.

Even for Wolfgang another job-seeking journey would be a desperate venture, for costs were much more certain than earnings, and the Mozarts had been unable to save. It was against the nature of the scrupulously honest Leopold to borrow, and especially to borrow from trusting neighbors, on an uncertain outcome. There was no alternative; Hagenauer again came to the rescue, and other friends, including Joseph Bullinger, a Jesuit priest and close companion of the family. "Our faithful Bullinger," Wolfgang called him. It was an additional dilemma that Leopold could not accompany Wolfgang on this critical venture, which would require the wary eye and the tactful approach, accomplishments which the direct, ingenuous and overtrusting Wolfgang entirely lacked. He was also completely inexperienced in the arrangements of coaches, lodgings, appointments, concerts, endless practical details which had always been taken care of by his father. Leopold turned as the only resort to his wife, who, knowing little more about such matters, could at least look out for his physical needs and by her presence keep him from wasting time and money in frivolities. Anna Maria Mozart was dismayed at being sent laden with these responsibilities into a largely unknown world. Her husband persuaded her that they had no other alternative. When the coach rolled off with mother and son on September 23, 1777, Leopold and Nannerl watched with heavy hearts as they disappeared down the valley, in the direction of Wasserburg. The family had always suffered a pang at separation, and this one was especially lugubrious. The mother was apprehensive both at leaving the father and daughter to themselves, and at the prospect of having to control her exuberant and unpredictable son. Wolfgang was secretly elated. At twenty-one, independent and traveling for the first time without a kindly but strict and watchful father at his side, he could hardly have been otherwise. He was conscious of his ability to do anything in music. This was his magic power. There was not a position in Europe he could not fill with distinction. He had only to show what he could do and the rest would follow.

IX

Augsburg, 1777

THE FIRST interchange of letters is characteristic. Leopold, self-pitying and ready to unburden himself about his troubles, writes of "the sad day which I never thought I should have to face." He was remorseful because, in the excitement, he had forgotten to "give his son a father's blessing." Nannerl had wept, and they had tried to console each other with a game of piquet. Wolfgang's first letter, from Wasserburg, is anything but gloomy. He wanted to cheer them, to assure them of his proficiency in practical matters. In fact he was rather enjoying the experience of being in charge, and looking out for his bewildered mother. "We are living like princes," he writes in Italian. *("Viviamo come i principi.")*

> Only one person is wanting—and that is Papa. Ah well, it is God's will. It will all work out. I hope that Papa is well, and as happy as I am. I am most attentive to my duty. I am quite a second Papa, for I see to everything. I have begged Mamma to let me pay the postillions, for I can deal with these fellows better than she can. . . . We both of us beg Papa to take care of his health, not to go out too early and not to worry, but to laugh heartily and be merry and always remember, as we do, that our Mufti H. C. [Hieronymus von Colloredo] is an ass, but that God is compassionate, merciful and loving.* I kiss Papa's hands 1,000 times and embrace my

---

* Leopold answers this: "My dear Wolfgang, I beg you not to write any more jokes about our Mufti. Remember that I am in Salzburg and that one of your letters might get lost or find its way into other hands."

scoundrel sister as often as I have taken snuff today. I believe I have left my diplomas at home? Please send them to me as soon as you can.

The diplomas which he mentions so casually were those which had been awarded him by the academies of Bologna and Verona.

Leopold in answer gave his son careful instructions on whom he should visit in Munich, particularly those connected with the court, those who could have access to the Elector. "You must be excessively polite to the courtiers, for each one has a finger in that pie." He was not to expect too much from "all the compliments and shows of friendship." He must be wary of financial agreements and not let it be known what miserable pay he had had from his Salzburg prince.

Wolfgang reported faithfully on each step he had taken. He had called on every likely person. He and his mother had been asked to one house after another; they had attended plays and concerts. Herr Albert, who was his host, had arranged a concert in his house and invited a court violinist named Dupreille. Mozart made the most of a miserable clavier and the clumsiness of Dupreille, who played wrong notes and omitted rests. At last Wolfgang seized his violin and played "the last Cassation in B [K. 287] until they all stared. I played as if I were the greatest fiddler in Europe." Of course Wolfgang did not mean this. He merely wished to please his father, who had long been after him to give more of his time to the violin rather than to the clavier exclusively. These performances brought him applause but led to nothing. Unable to obtain an audience with the Elector, he approached Count Zeil, Bishop of Chiemsee, who had been friendly with the Mozarts in Salzburg. The Bishop reported that he had spoken to the Elector at Nymphenburg, and had this reply: "It is too soon yet, let him travel in Italy and make himself a name, I do not refuse anything, but it is too soon yet." He seemed to have forgotten *La finta giardiniera,* and the church music he had once praised. The Electress, who also should have remembered, shrugged her shoulders at the suggestion and looked doubtful. Wolfgang then tried a more direct, if scarcely diplomatic course. He found access to the Presence but did so by interrupting him as he was about to start on a hunting party. Wolfgang reports the interview word for word (September 30):

When the Elector came up to me, I said: "I trust your Highness will allow me to lay my services and myself at your feet." "So you have left Salzburg for good?" "Yes, your Highness, for good." "Did you have a real argument?" "Not at all, your Highness. I only asked permission to travel, which was refused. So I was compelled to take this step, though I had really long been planning to leave, for Salzburg is no place for me, that is certain." "Good heavens, what a young man we have here! But your father is still in Salzburg?" "Yes, your Highness, he lays himself humbly at your feet, etc. I have been to Italy three times, I have composed three operas, I have been elected to the Academy at Bologna. . . . All this proves that I am in a position to serve any court. My greatest wish is to serve your Highness—" "Yes, my dear fellow, but I have no vacancy." "I assure your Highness that I would do honor to Munich." "No doubt, no doubt, but there is no vacancy." As he said this, he was already leaving me.

Wolfgang next turned to the German Theatre, which, like many of its kind, attempted operas, mostly in adaptation and translation from want of presentable native scores. Wolfgang expressed a desire to compose an *opera seria* in German together with "three *opere buffe* a year," as he put it, "which one can write for practice, and for something to do." Operatic comedy had only passing attention, and a court would withhold its best forces for an opera in the grand style. This was the true road to fame for an ambitious composer. Mozart was drawn to both sorts. He heard a *Singspiel* and walked out of the theatre "simply itching to compose." Albert, his kindly host, scratched his head over the young man's predicament and came up with a plan. Since the electoral budget was not to be counted upon, ten friends might be assembled and pledged to contribute one ducat a month each. It was simply a case for arithmetic. This would pave the way to Count Seeau, the Intendant of the theatre. Wolfgang eagerly caught at the idea. He could count on some return from Seeau, and surely a benefit performance. He could make at least 800 gulden a year and this would be enough to bring his family to Munich. It was more than they got at home. Even if the sum did not come to that amount he could live on very little. He explained the scheme to his father, and concluded: "As for food, I should not have to worry, for I should always be invited out, and whenever I had no invitation, Albert would be only too delighted to have me at table. I eat very little, drink water, just at dessert I take a small glass of wine."—A diminuendo of logic! "What do you think of this idea," he wrote. "Is it not a true act of friendship, and should I not accept it?"

Leopold answered kindly but drily that this was indeed an act of friendship, but "it does not appear to have occurred to you that these ten philanthropists and lovers of music will be difficult to find." What would they expect in return? This was nothing to count on. Here was a case of what he called Wolfgang's "fires of straw which burn up quickly and end in smoke." When Count Seeau was told of this plan, it hardly excited him. He quietly inquired whether the young opera enthusiast was getting any pay at home, which might be lightly supplemented. Finding that he was not, he at once lost interest. To Leopold, the combination of official coolness and the lack of an opening was quite enough. He advised his son to waste no more time in Munich listening to "fine words and bravissimos. As soon as you find there is nothing to be got, you had better move on." A makeshift arrangement in Munich would do him no good. "How the Archbishop would sneer! You can do that anywhere else as easily as in Munich. You must not make little of your talents, and throw yourself away; there is certainly no need for that." Mozart and his mother left for Augsburg on October 11.

The plan for Augsburg brought special directions from Leopold, for, being no electoral seat, but municipally ruled, it required a different technique. No money was to be had except from concerts. Leopold's brother Franz Aloys (a bookbinder who would be able to do up the manuscript scores for proper presentation later) would show him around and introduce him. Advance notices must be put in the Augsburg papers. He must visit at once Von Langenmantel, the town councillor and principal citizen. He did so, accompanied by his uncle. This magistrate, whom he described to his father by putting the name in Italian as "Longotabarro," received him coldly and made him play interminably while his uncle was left sitting "on a stool in the anteroom." Mozart did not like his manner and was incensed that his uncle, "a most excellent and lovable man and an honorable townsman," should be so treated. When Mozart met condescension, he stiffened into hostility. He was made to play before Von Langenmantel's "dressed up son and the long-legged wife and the stupid old lady." He writes, obedient to his father's counsel: "I was very polite, for it is my custom to treat people as I find them; it pays best in the end." When he mentioned that he was about to visit Georg André Stein, the maker of pianofortes as well as harpsichords and organs, the young Langenmantel offered to accompany him to the workrooms. He had planned, in a spirit of fun, to conceal his identity. He introduced himself as Herr Trazom (his name spelled backwards). The councillor's stupid son nearly bungled the joke. As soon as Mozart sat down and began to play an instrument Stein tore open the letter of introduction and embraced him. Mozart was much taken with the pianos, and set them above those of Späth in Regensburg, which he had until then preferred. The tone was even, the hammer action superior, the dampers (worked by the knee) cleaner in their effect. The wood was carefully weathered. Only the price was high, 300 gulden. (On this last point Leopold heartily agreed.) He asked to play one of Stein's organs in the church of St. Ulrich and when Stein protested that his talents were for better uses, he called the organ "the king of instruments."

The young Von Langenmantel had at once proposed a concert to be given in the *Stube* of the *Rathaus* for his colleagues, the "patricians" of the town. First Mozart was made to go to his house for lunch, meet a group of them, and play before and after the meal. He was greeted with the news that a concert would be impossible. At a meeting the patricians found that their funds were low, and they were not willing to pay a gold sovereign for his type of virtuoso. Mozart took this politely, played before and after lunch, and would have given them a violin concerto except that the orchestral accompaniment "was so bad it gave me the colic." All went to the theatre and returned for supper. Mozart was wearing the Order of the Golden Spur, which had been conferred upon him by Pope Clement XIV in Rome in 1770. Leopold had instructed him to wear it, not in electoral cities, but in municipalities like Augsburg. It was appropriate enough in such company, for these particular "nobles," in a city of religious factions, were mostly Catholics. They probably felt that he was a nobody putting on airs by flaunting what they themselves had not attained. They began baiting him about it.

Mozart describes the incident on October 17:

They kept saying to me: "Hello, you fine gentleman, Knight of the Spur." I said nothing, but during the supper things got beyond a joke. They asked me: "How much did it cost? Three ducats? Must one have permission to wear it? Does permission cost something too? We really must send for some crosses." A certain officer, a Baron Bach, said, "You should be ashamed of yourselves. What would you do with a cross?" That young ass Kurzenmantel winked at him. I saw him, and he knew it. Then there was quiet for a while. He offered me snuff, and said, "There, take some." I still said nothing. At last he began to get nasty again, and said "Tomorrow I'll send someone to your inn, and perhaps you will lend me the cross for a little while. I'd like to show it to our goldsmith. He is quite a character. If I ask him the value, he'll probably say: 'About a Bavarian thaler.' And that is all it's worth, because it's not gold at all, but only copper. Ha! Ha!" "You are wrong there," I said. "It is tin. Ha! Ha!" I was burning with anger. "But do tell me," he said. "I suppose that if necessary I can leave out the spur?" "Oh yes," I answered. "You don't need one, for you already have one in your head. I have one in mine, too, but of a different kind, and I should not like to exchange it with yours. Here, take a pinch of snuff?" I offered him some. He turned rather pale, but went on: "The other day, your order looked fine on that grand waistcoat of yours. . . . Here, take a pinch of snuff." "It is really very strange," I began, as if I hadn't heard him, "but it would be easier for me to win all the orders there are than for you to become what I am, even if you were to die twice and be born again. Take a pinch of snuff on that." With that I stood up. They all got up too, and were very embarrassed. I took my hat and sword and said: "I shall have the pleasure of seeing you tomorrow." . . . "Surely you don't mean to—" "I mean nothing. You are a lot of miserable beggars (*Bettlerei*)."

This is the first recorded instance of outspoken anger on Mozart's part. It is the more understandable in that he had gone to these young men in the friendly spirit of his peaceable nature, innocent of any offense in wearing his decoration, and had suddenly met their ill will as a guest in their midst.

The next day, Mozart told Stein and his musical friends— Gignoux, the organ builder, and *Kapellmeister* Graf—far more sympathetic company, about the proposed concert and what had become of it. He wrote to his father: " 'I am heartily sorry that I ever came here,' I said. 'I should have never in my life have believed that in Augsburg, my father's native town, his son would be so insulted.' You can imagine, dear Papa, how sorry and angry the three of them were. 'Oh,' said they, 'you must really give a concert here. We can do without the patricians.' "

Stein agitated for a concert to make amends for the insult. Many of the "Evangelic" (Lutheran) contingent of the *patricii,* gathered to hear him. Mozart played for the sake of good feeling. "A crowd of the nobility were there," he wrote his father: "the Duchess Smackbottom, the Countess Firejoy, to say nothing of the Princess Dunghill and her two daughters, who are married to the Princes Bulgefront from Swinetail."*

Those at home laughed over this last, but Leopold was angry: "One thing is very certain: they would never have found me at their miserable affair"—a remark partly referring to the fee of two ducats which had been handed to Mozart. About the Langenmantel affair there came a bit of fatherly advice:

---

* "*Es war eine menge Noblesse da, die Duchess Arschbörnnel, die Grafin Brunzgern, und dann die Fürstin Reichzumtreck mit ihren 2 Töchter, die aber schon an die 2 Prinzen Mussbauch von Sauschwanz verheirathet sind.*"

I have just received your letter of the seventeenth and I am very curious to read the continuation of the Augsburg story. Everyone knows about the beggarliness of the patricians and every honest man here laughs about it. That is why they are in the pay of the rich merchants. . . . As for young Herr von Longotabarro, he did not have to go far to learn his baiting and sneering ways—his *cher père* was the same sort. That is his upbringing, and indeed that was what the young patricians claim as their sole and particular privilege: to jeer at others, whenever they have the opportunity. In that alone lies their great nobility. Anyone who lowers himself to their vulgar level will arouse their jeering habits, which they usually employ toward people of their own class. You made yourself too cheap with that fellow. You went to the theatre together! You were merry! Instead of being sufficiently reserved you were far too familiar! In short you were too free and easy with that *puppy*, and he thought at once that he could make fun of you. Let that serve as a lesson to you to associate freely and naturally with intelligent people rather than with such ill-bred, unfledged boys whose only boast is that their father is the magistrate of the town.

Mozart answered this little sermon with spirit, if not quite convincingly: "Papa says that I made myself cheap with that young Von Langenmantel. Not at all. I was just natural, that was all. I think Papa imagines that the fellow is still a boy. Why, he is twenty-one or twenty-two, and a married man. Is it possible to remain a boy when one is married? Since that episode I have not gone to them."

On the nineteenth he visited the Heiligkreuzkirche with his uncle for the not unusual session of lunch-music-supper and more music. Remembering perhaps a recent plea of his father: "Do yourself credit and play with energy, with your whole heart and mind, yes, just as though you were the first violinist in Europe," he now played two concertos with the monastery orchestra, which he found better than the Augsburg Orchestra. His "Strassburg" Violin Concerto (K. 218) went like oil *("Es gieng wie Öhl")*, a favorite expression of his, which is indeed the keynote of the Mozart style. Afterwards, a clavichord was brought forth. Then he was asked to play the organ. The monks gave him a theme. "I put it through its paces and in the middle I went into the major key and played something quite lively, though in the same tempo, and after that the theme over again, but this time arseways. Finally I thought, why not use my lively theme for a fugue? Without wasting time I went right into it, and it went as neatly as if it had been fitted by Daser." (Daser was a tailor in Salzburg.) He read a fugal sonata at sight: "I played until eleven o'clock for I was bombarded with subjects for fugues."

He was made to listen to Maria Anna (Nanette) Stein, Herr Stein's daughter, aged eight, who was a child prodigy and the pride of the town. His report was unfavorable, and he advised the father on what must be cleaned up if Nanette was to succeed as a virtuoso. Nanette was to develop more practical ideas. She inherited her father's business, married in 1793 Johann Andreas Streicher, a piano maker from Stuttgart, and went down in history as the kind lady who befriended Beethoven, mended his frayed linen, straightened up his house, and otherwise made him comfortable.

Wolfgang found much diversion in the house of his uncle in the person of his cousin two years younger than himself, Maria Anna Thekla Mozart, whom he called *"Das Bäsle"* (the diminutive of *Basel,* "cousin"). He thus described her to his father: "I must say that if I had not found such good, delightful cousins I should repent ever having set foot in Augsburg. . . . Our little cousin is pretty, sensible, charming, clever, and merry; she knows something of the world, having been in Munich some time. We two suit each other exactly, for she is just a little wicked; we laugh at everybody, and have great fun." Wolfgang seems to have been diverted by this spirited girl rather than infatuated; his letters to her that have survived are more ribald than romantic. His heart as an adolescent had first been touched by the daughter of Dr. Barisani, physician to the Archbishop in Salzburg. When he had to leave her behind on his last two Italian journeys, he sent her cryptic messages by way of his sister as go-between: "What you promised me (you know what, you dear one!) you will surely do, and I shall certainly be most grateful to you."

His letters to the Augsburg cousin, the *Bäsle,* are on a very different level. They deal in a species of joking which is nowadays not only considered extremely inappropriate for a young man addressing a young girl, but was found actually unprintable until the courageous edition of the family letters, as translated by Emily Anderson, appeared in 1938.* Those who are shocked by these and distressed at the contradiction between filthy language and an imagination capable of the loftiest beauty should ask themselves which is the true Mozart and which the echo and custom of his time. Custom controls what subjects may be mentioned, and especially to ladies. Plumbing was less private at the time. A type of humor which mentions bodily functions was not excluded by South German provincialism. A letter from Wolfgang's mother to her husband, in her almost illiterate script, (Munich, September 26, 1777) will show that such humor was not confined to Wolfgang in the Mozart family:

> *Adio ben mio leb gesund*
> *Rick den arsch zum mund*
> *Ich winsch ein guete nacht,*
> *Scheiss ins beth das Kracht.*

Nannerl uses language of this sort in messages added to her father's script. The correct Leopold indulges in similar remarks in a letter of June 29, 1778. Mozart, obviously led on by the *Bäsle,* may have amused himself by testing her impermeability to shock.

The two went around Augsburg together a good deal. They once visited the Church of St. Ulrich, where Leopold had been a choirboy. Afterwards they went to a wineshop and were joined by a priest who insisted upon singing a canon:

A certain Father Emilian, a conceited ass and a poor specimen of his profession, was too interested in my little cousin

---

* "Even in Germany," writes Miss Anderson in an Introduction, "an excessive prudishness or possibly a certain unwillingness to admit that the writer, formerly regarded as the Raphael or the Watteau of music, should have been capable of expressing himself with such grossness, has hitherto prevented their publication *in toto.*"

and wanted to joke with her, but she only made fun of him. Finally he became a little bit tipsy and began to talk about music. He sang a canon which he called the most beautiful he had ever heard. I said: "I'm afraid I can't join in, nature has never granted me the gift of intoning." "That doesn't matter," he said, and began. I took the third voice, but I invented quite a different text "Pater Emilian, you idiot, lick my arse, I beg you." All this *sotto voce,* to my cousin. Then we laughed together for another half hour.

Leopold did not quite like this developing interest in the *Bäsle* who, rumor said, was free in her flirtations. Wolfgang's earlier rapturous description of her beauties implied that he had somewhat lost his judgment, if the rather coarse-featured girl in a pencil portrait now in Salzburg is an accurate likeness. If he had not been about to leave Augsburg, Leopold might have used something stronger than light sarcasm: "I am altogether delighted to hear that my niece is beautiful, sensible, charming, clever and gay, and far from having any objection to make, I should like to have the privilege of meeting her. Only it seems to me that she has too many friends among the priests. If I am wrong, I shall be pleased to beg your pardon on bended knee. But I only say 'It seems to me—' . . . Now you can laugh as much as you like! I am quite pleased to hear that she is a bit of a rogue; but the ecclesiastical gentlemen are often far worse."

X

Mannheim, 1777, 1778

AFTER MUNICH, Leopold's greatest hopes for immediate returns and an eventual position for Wolfgang lay in Mannheim and Paris. Mannheim they had visited fifteen years before, when Wolfgang played as a child of seven for the Elector Carl Theodor and his court. Leopold then heard the court orchestra and pronounced it "undeniably the best in Germany." Carl Theodor was still the Elector of the Rhenish Palatinate. He had continued in his efforts, and at great expenditure, to maintain his court as the most cultured in the German principalities.

Arriving in Mannheim on October 30, 1777, Mozart lost no time in getting acquainted with the Elector's court musicians. He established cordial relationships with some of them before he had even obtained an audience with the Elector. He heard the orchestra in the *Kapelle* on All Saints' Day and wrote: "The orchestra is very good and strong. Ten or eleven violins on either side, four violas, two oboes, two flutes and two clarinets, two horns, four cellos, four bassoons, four basses, trumpets and drums." Later he wrote: "You cannot think what a splendid effect a symphony makes with flutes, oboes and clarinets—Oh, if we only had *clarinetti!*" The clarinet was not unknown, but it had been used crudely, in band music. It had never been used elsewhere as an important, expressive, individual instrument. Mozart here came to realize the solo possibilities of woodwinds, over and above their usefulness in doubling or group alternation. The Mannheim orchestra cultivated expressive refinements which no other had attempted. J. F. Reichardt, who had recently traveled around Europe for musical comparisons, wrote of "the masterly effect produced by the Mannheim Orchestra by the swelling and diminishing of a long note, or of several successive notes, which gives to the whole coloring a darker or lighter shade. This would be considered too great an innovation by Hasse [in Vienna] or Graun [in Berlin]."* Schubart in *Ästhetik,* puts it more romantically: "No orchestra in the world has ever surpassed that of Mannheim in execution. Their forte is a thunder, their crescendo a cataract, their diminuendo a crystal streamlet babbling away into the far distance, their piano a soft breath of early spring." In this description we can already visualize the "Paris" Symphony, soon to follow. The new opening up of orchestral possibilities was a stimulus of the first importance to Mozart. His music shows it at once and continues in increasing degree. Mozart found less to praise in the *Kapelle.* The two organists were inferior, and it soon became evident that he could play circles around them.

The orchestra had many players of the highest distinction. Trained into a new conception of ensemble by Johann Stamitz (then dead twenty years) they had given Mannheim its reputation as the German "musical paradise." Christian Cannabich, a native of Mannheim and a violin pupil of Stamitz, had studied in Italy under Jommelli. He became concertmaster of the Mannheim orchestra in 1759, and later *Kapellmeister* and co-conductor with Holzbauer. In 1777 the concertmaster was the aging Töschi. Friedrich Ramm was a fine oboist. Johann Baptist Wendling was the first flute, Georg Wenzel Ritter first bassoon. Franz Lang and his brother Martin were the horns. On the day after Wolfgang's arrival, Christian Danner, one of the violinists (who remembered the boyhood visit), took him to the *Kapelle* rehearsal and introduced him to the players. "Some of them," wrote Mozart, "who knew me *per renommée,* were polite and respectful; but the rest, who did not know anything of me, stared in the most ludicrous manner. They think because I

---

* *Briefe eines aufmerksamen Reisenden*

am little and young that there can be nothing important or mature in me. But they shall soon see."

Mozart was always sensitive about his small stature. He tried to laugh off this incident to his father, but he was obviously humiliated by his having the eternal status of an outsider, unemployed, belonging nowhere. Eager by nature to make friends, he quickly felt hostility or rebuff in those who considered him beneath their notice. He had learned from his father to be mistrustful of strangers. Those who praised his playing, protested friendship and even made promises were sometimes really interested in nothing else than their own security, which might be threatened by a formidable rival. However, most of the principal musicians now welcomed him freely as one of their circle. Cannabich at once invited him and his mother to his house. He came to be expected at meals and at evening parties where Wolfgang amused them with his readiness for fun and sometimes by his jokes of the known vulgar variety. There was of course much music. Cannabich and his wife soon treated him as a son. Their daughter Rosa, then thirteen, played the clavier. Wolfgang found her playing not all that it might be, but not beyond repair. He wrote a sonata for her "exactly like Mdlle. Rose herself" (K. 309). The Andante in particular was pronounced a true picture of the little girl whom Wolfgang described as having "a staid manner and a great deal of sense for her age; she speaks but little, and when she speaks it is with grace and amiability." The flutist Wendling and his family were also most friendly. They had a daughter, Augusta, who was said to have been once chosen by the Elector for one of his mistresses.

An obvious and pleasant way of repaying hospitality was by music as a return compliment. Wolfgang wrote French songs for "Mdlle. Gustl" Wendling (probably K. 307 and K. 308), and a fully worked out concert aria for the mother, Dorothea; he chose a text from Metastasio's *Dido* (K. 486a). Mozart had mentioned his lukewarm feelings about flutists, and when teased about this he said to Wendling's brother: "Yes, but it is quite another matter with your brother. He is not a piper, and one need not always be in terror lest the next note be too high or too low—*he* is always right, you see; his heart and his ear and the tip of his tongue are all in the right place, and he does not imagine that blowing and making faces is all that is needed; he knows too what 'adagio' means." Mozart's caution about woodwind solo parts until this time may well have been due to the poor intonation then prevalent —a malady which Mannheim was the first to rectify. He composed an oboe concerto (the original score is unfortunately lost) for Ramm, who greatly liked and often played it.

Mozart had nothing good to say about Abbé Vogler, the second *Kapellmeister*. His musical opinion was undoubtedly colored by personal dislike, which he shared with the other musicians who considered this man's haughty self-importance ridiculous. Vogler had built a reputation as a sight reader, which was tested at a large party when Mozart's concerto (K. 246) was brought in. "The first movement," writes Mozart (January 17, 1778), "went prestissimo, the andante, allegro, and the rondo really prestissimo. After all, it is much easier to play fast than slow; notes can be dropped out of passages without being noticed; but is that desirable? The rapidity allows the right and left hand to be used indiscriminately, but should that be so? In what does the art of playing at sight consist? In playing the piece correctly, in strict time, giving the proper expression to every passage and every note, giving the impression that the player had composed the piece himself. Vogler's fingering is atrocious; his left thumb is like Adlgasser's, and he makes all the runs for the right hand with his first finger and thumb."

The Elector's court possessed an Academy of Science, an art collection considered the best in the German states, a splendid theatre where dramas and operas were elaborately produced. In 1775 Carl Theodor had established a German nationalist society for the encouragement of plays and operas in his own language. The drama until then had been mostly French, and opera was imported whole from Italy. The Elector brought in the best German poets, and tried to retain them: Klopstock, Anton Klein, Lessing, and later Wieland. The attempts were not always successful, but they did implant something of *Sturm und Drang* fervor into the Mannheim circle. The poetic urge found its way, though fitfully, into the operas, which remained by the weight of tradition basically Italian. Mozart's acquisitive ear here first caught something of *Sturm und Drang* sentiment.

When the Mozarts arrived in Mannheim, *Günther von Schwartzburg* by the court composer, Ignaz Holzbauer, to a German text by Klein, was still being played. It was vaunted as German throughout—subject, book, music, performers. Mozart listened to it, not as propaganda, but as music in the theatre. He reported to his father: "Holzbauer's music is very fine; far too good for the poetry. I am amazed at the spirit of so old a man as Holzbauer, for you would not believe the amount of fire in his music." His praise was not without reservations. Mozart would have been able and willing to compose an opera in any language or any style—German, Italian, even French, if he were only given the chance. Italian was his preference, Italian *opera seria,* for then *opera seria* was a higher order of art. Wieland was then in Mannheim, and his *Alcestis,* set by Anton Schweitzer, was in production. In *Alcestis* Mozart found some good points—more weak ones. His description of Wieland is quotable as an instance of his many word portraits in the letters: unsparing, vivid, jocular (December 28, 1777):

> He is slightly affected in his speech. He has a somewhat childish voice: he keeps staring at you through his glasses. He indulges in a sort of pedantic rudeness, mingled sometimes with a stupid condescension. . . . People gawk at him as if he had dropped from Heaven. Everyone seems embarrassed in his presence, no one says a word or moves; all listen intently to every word he utters; and it's a pity they often have to wait so long, for he has a defect of speech that makes him speak very slowly and he can't say six words without stopping. Apart from that, he is what we all know him to be, a most gifted fellow. He has a frightfully ugly face, covered with pockmarks, and he has a rather long nose. In height he is, I should say, a little taller than Papa.

The Elector's singers were, to take Mozart's judgment, something less than extraordinary, but acceptable. They were almost all German. Dorothea Wendling, the wife of Johann Baptist Wendling, the first flute in the orchestra, was outstanding. Her sister-in-law Elisabeth was married to Franz Anton Wendling, one of the violinists. Francisca Danzi was shortly to marry the first oboist August Lebrun. The most illustrious of the singers was an imported one, the tenor Anton Raaff. He was sixty-three. He had by then only the remnants of a voice, compensated by a style and understanding which delighted Mozart. Raaff became a helpful friend, and was destined to sing in the title role of *Idomeneo*.

There was a close interchange of letters between Mannheim and Salzburg as Leopold watched every step, every new encounter and its consequences, if any. Wolfgang reported to his father as faithfully as his less methodical nature allowed. The lag in the mail (it took at least twelve days to send a message and receive the answer) caused considerable confusion as letters continually crossed. Leopold visualized his son as wasting his time indefinitely in Mannheim, enjoying his new friends, composing sonatas gratis, making no money to offset the 450 gulden of his own standing debt, and delaying his departure for Paris. The winter was almost upon them, and his wife should not be subjected to that long journey through snow and mud. Meanwhile Wolfgang filled his letters with his usual jokes to cheer his father, while his father was only annoyed; he wanted, instead of a string of light talk, specific information, some assurance that Wolfgang was not simply idling away expensive days. There resulted sermons which Wolfgang considered unjust and resented as much as any son of twenty-one, and on his own, would resent parental reproaches. Leopold wrote (November 24, 1777): "You should have more important things on your mind than practical jokes; you should be endeavoring to arrange a hundred things in advance, or you will find yourself suddenly in trouble, and without money—and where there is no money, friends are no longer to be found, even if you give a hundred lessons for nothing, compose sonatas and, instead of occupying yourself profitably, play the fool every evening from ten o'clock until midnight. Then ask for money credit!

Suddenly jokes will cease, and in a moment the most smiling countenance will become serious."

This was not altogether just. Wolfgang was "arranging things in advance," but not "a hundred things." That was the difference between them. Wolfgang was irrepressible, always ready to laugh and make others laugh. He was ever sanguine, kept his eye dutifully on the main chance, did not occupy himself with a hundred details, and tried to cheer his father, writing casually: "Come what may, all is well so long as a man enjoys good health. For happiness consists—simply in the imagination." This was a perfect description of Wolfgang, who sustained his spirits and composed out of a joyful imagination. A generally accepted dictum, agreed the father, but he posed a question: Is a traveler who sits stranded and moneyless in an inn or a post station to find happiness in the imagination?

Mozart was meanwhile faithfully maneuvering for a position. He described in his best narrative style, with quoted dialogue, how he waited for an opportunity to meet the Elector and contrive a series of passing encounters through Count Savioli, the intendant of the orchestra, who was close to the throne; how he penetrated to the residence of the actress-mistress and induced the governess of the four bastard children to work in his cause. Two of the children were studying music and their abilities were discussed. These were excuses which enabled Mozart to play before the Elector. When it was several times urged that Mozart would like nothing better than to stay in Mannheim for the winter, but that it would have to be made financially possible, his Highness intimated his consent but did not specifically give it. Finally, when pushed by Count Savioli, he gave a negative answer. This prolonged and degrading suit resulted in nothing but a gold watch, of which Mozart already had four. Carl Theodor has been praised as an enlightened patron of the arts. His personal life and his part in Mozart's biography hardly commend him.

A plan for a journey to Paris had already been discussed by Mozart's musical companions (so Mozart reports on December 11), and when Wendling was told of the Elector's defection he said, "red in the face with anger, 'We must find some way out. You must stay here at least for the next two months until we can go to Paris together.' " Wendling and Ramm, who knew and were known in Paris as a flutist and oboist of the first order, would make the journey with him in Lent, the favorable concert time. Etienne Lauchéry, the *maître de ballet* at court, would make a fourth. "Mamma would stay here, probably with the Wendlings," wrote Wolfgang to his father. "Wendling assures me that I shall never regret it," he adds with his usual ardor in a new and wonderful solution to all problems.

He has been twice to Paris; and has only just returned. He maintains that it is still the only place where one can make money and a great reputation. He said: "Why, you are a fellow who can turn your hand to anything. I will tell you the way to set about it. You must compose all sorts of music, *opera seria, opéra comique,* oratorio—everything in fact. Once a man has written a couple of operas in Paris, he is sure of a settled yearly income. Then there is the *Concert Spirituel* and the *Académie des Amateurs,* which pay five louis d'or for a symphony. If you take pupils, the fee is three louis d'or for twelve lessons. Further, you can have sonatas, trios and quartets engraved *par souscription.*"

Meanwhile, to meet immediate expenses in Mannheim, Wendling had induced a Dutch amateur flutist, De Jean, probably a pupil, to order "three short, simple concertos and a couple of quartets for flute" for a fee of 200 gulden. Wendling suggested that a set of duets for clavier and violin could be engraved, by subscription, that Wolfgang could have all his lunches and suppers with him. Mamma would have her meals at Herr Danner's house and Herr Danner would receive lessons in return. Wendling had an answer for everything. When he heard that Leopold was counting heavily on help from Baron Grimm in Paris, this helpful flutist said at once that Grimm was his "bosom friend." His first step on arriving in Paris would be to call on Grimm. The Queen of France might be addressed by a letter from such an influential friend as Herr Mesmer in Vienna. The whole thing was so completely worked out, so absolutely flawless, that Wolfgang expected his father's consent quite as a matter of course. "I am so certain of this, that if it were now the time to travel, I should go off to Paris without waiting for an answer."

Mamma, wrote Wolfgang, need not be subjected to the cruelly long journey. She could be sent home alone. Mamma always agreed to do what she was told. Overwhelmed by a flood of words about the Paris plan, she could not object and was made to add her assent to the letter: "Herr Wendling has assured me that he will be a father to Wolfgang, whom he loves as if he were his own son; and Wolfgang will be looked after as well as if he were with me. As you may imagine, I myself do not like to let him go, nor do I like to have to travel home alone, it is such an awful distance. I can't bear to think of it. But what can we do? I am too old to undertake that long journey to Paris, and besides it would cost too much. . . . It is bitterly cold here. I am so frozen that I can hardly hold my pen." Wolfgang had gone out to look for cheaper lodgings for her. The poor woman's principal duty in Mannheim had been to keep down the expenses to almost nothing. She would put 14 kreutzers' worth of wood in the stove each morning, the same amount in the evening, and freeze all day. In short, she was in all things compliant with the wishes of her men well knowing which of them made the decisions. About Wolfgang's journey to Paris she wrote, "You must think it over and let us know if you approve."

The father's answer was cautious. Of course these gentlemen, his traveling companions, were counting on Wolfgang. "They need a fourth, and where will they get such a fourth as you are? . . . All friendships have their motives." If the Dutch gentleman comes forth with his 200 gulden, well and good, but he must not be counted upon. "In general, I quite approve of the present plan. But for the time being Mamma must not be made to live alone—that I will not have." For different reasons, each of them must have an eye on the other. Some arrangement must be made for her return to Salzburg alone, but not until after the severe cold of the Christmas season. He was still hopeful that the Elector would grant some sort of temporary appointment; he felt that Wolfgang should have pressed his case even further. A certain amount of "cringing" for important results he considered as sometimes advisable, although not beyond the point of fundamental self-respect. Wolfgang might do well to compose a Mass and present it to the Elector. If Mannheim could be established as a base, journeys such as the proposed one could still be made. Details were accordingly discussed for the new move. The mother was to be sent to Augsburg, where her brother-in-law would see that she would be safely conveyed to Salzburg in one of the empty coaches which carried Salzburg merchánts in the other direction. The big trunk was to go to Paris with Wolfgang, carrying all of his music and his clothes, a wardrobe to be added to for a proper appearance in that city of elegant fashion.

The date for departure was set for about the middle of February. On January 17, Wolfgang wrote of a planned journey to the Princess of Orange at Kirchheim-Bolander, about ten hours' drive—"a short day's journey" from Mannheim. "I shall get eight louis d'or at least. Since she is passionately fond of singing, I have had four arias copied for her, and, as she has a nice little orchestra and gives a concert every day, I shall also present her with a symphony. Moreover the copying of the arias will not cost me much, for it has been done by a certain Herr Weber, who is accompanying me there. He has a daughter who sings admirably and has a lovely, pure voice; she is only fifteen." The "certain Herr Weber" was Fridolin Weber, a poorly paid underling at court, who sang bass and did minor duties. His daughter was Aloysia (the youngest daughter, Constanze, then a child of fourteen, and Sophie, a year younger, he seems not to have noticed; nor is the eldest, Josefa, then nineteen, mentioned). As Wolfgang admitted, Aloysia had not yet learned to act. Her range and vocal skill he highly praised. She could easily manage the difficult coloratura air he had written for De Amicis in *Lucio Silla*.

Leopold knew from experience that Wolfgang's keen and dependable musical judgment could become less objective where a beautiful female voice was concerned. He had written ecstatic pages about a young soprano in the opera in Munich named Käsur, ecstasies which others did not seem to share. To fall in love with a voice might lead in his case to falling in love with what was behind it. Leopold guardedly generalized about "women—who run after young people of talent in order to get their money, draw them into their net and even land them as husbands." He adds uneasily: "God and your own good sense will preserve you."

The next letter from Wolfgang (on February 4) had to report that the expedition to Kirchheim had not proved a triumphal affair. Arriving on Friday night, Wolfgang, the father and daughter were not admitted to the presence until the following evening. They were ushered to the *officier-tafel* after their reception, which is to say they ate with the servants. They gave concerts on Monday, Tuesday and Wednesday; Wolfgang played a dozen times, Fräulein Weber sang and played. Wolfgang received only 7 louis d'or, the Webers 5. Wolfgang paid half the expenses instead of his third share, ending with 42 gulden. "At least," wrote Wolfgang, "I had the inexpressible pleasure of making the acquaintance of a thoroughly honest, good Catholic Christian family."

The letter continued with a new scheme which was to throw his family into consternation. "Now I am coming to an important point," wrote Wolfgang, "about which I want you to reply at once." He then proceeded to throw his bombshell. He was suddenly turning his back on the Paris plan. "Wendling, though an excellent fellow, unfortunately has no religion whatever. His daughter has been 'somebody's' mistress. Ramm is a decent fellow, but a libertine." Wolfgang had all at once developed a distrust of them, for "friends who have no religion cannot be our friends for long." In short, he had made his excuses to Wendling and Ramm. He would like to pledge his fortunes with Herr Weber and his two older daughters Josefa, who also sang, and Aloysia. "Herr Weber will try to get engagements here and there for concerts with me, and then we shall travel together." He adds: "He is just like you." He would be helpful in the same way. "I have become so fond of this unfortunate family that my dearest wish is to make them happy; and perhaps I may be able to do so. My advice is that they should go to Italy." Leopold is asked to inquire about openings and terms for a prima donna in Verona or Venice. They would all stop, Wolfgang concluded, at Salzburg for a pleasant visit, presumably on their way to Italy. There would be a joyful family reunion, and an immediate friendship between Aloysia and Marianne. Wolfgang, developing his thesis with mounting enthusiasm, proposes to write an opera for Verona for Aloysia "for fear that she may be victimized. . . . Do not forget how much I long to write operas. I envy anyone who is composing one. I could really weep for vexation when I hear or see an aria. But Italian, not German, *seriosa,* not *buffa.*"

Adding her own letter to this one of February 4, the mother begins shrewdly: "You will have seen from this letter that when Wolfgang makes new acquaintances, he immediately wants to give his life and property to them." She has evidently been talked into disapproval of the infidel friends; as for the Paris project, she is obviously awaiting orders. Of romance, she says nothing, realizing that she stands between her two men, certain to disagree. She is careful not to be drawn into their dispute. "I am writing this quite secretly, while he is at dinner, and I shall close, for I do not want to get caught—*Addio.*"

Mother and son must have waited in fearful anticipation for Leopold's answer to this sudden undoing of all his laborious efforts and continuing expenditures. They had a long wait, at least twelve days, according to the postal facilities of the time. This moment of critical decision between a hot-headed young man and a long-suffering father could have been worked out with far less distress on both sides if it could have been more direct. Two letters from Leopold which crossed the letter of February 4 must have given Wolfgang many a pang of remorse at what he had written.

The first letter from Leopold, dated February 5, is full of last-minute advice about the expected departure for the distant, foreign, and dangerous city of Paris. It is sententious—Polonius speaks again—but it is full of the tender and affectionate care of the parent whose every thought, whose very life, is devoted to his son. The journey to Paris was to be the final, desperate effort. It was a gamble on which

Leopold had staked his all, even his future, for he had by this time borrowed to the extent of 700 gulden. In spite of giving lessons and paring pennies, he saw no prospect, short of Wolfgang's success, of repaying his trusting and loyal friends. Aware of Wolfgang's kind of judgment where an appealing girl is concerned, and this Wolfgang must have read with particular discomfort, he fears lest easy joking and fondness for fun will lead him into an entanglement with a female, and bog down his career in household drudgery. He ends: "From my heart I give you my paternal blessing and remain until death your faithful father and your surest friend."

The dreaded answer, arriving at last and dated February 11-12 began: "I have read your letter of the fourth with amazement and horror." There follow three thousand words of protest. Leopold is outraged, but less angry than offended that Wolfgang, who has always trusted his judgment and found it right, should suddenly cast it aside. "My dear son," he writes, "I implore you to read this letter carefully—and take time to reflect on it. . . . Listen to me, therefore in patience!" He thereupon proceeds to demonstrate, point by point, the monstrous absurdity of everything Wolfgang has said. "It now depends upon your good sense whether you become a famous *Kapellmeister,* or whether captured by some woman, you die on a bed of straw in an attic full of starving children." He notes that Wolfgang, having highly praised Wendling and become his intimate friend, suddenly dismisses him and takes up with a Herr Weber. "In the transport into which your kind and too open heart has thrown you, you think all your ill-considered fancies as reasonable and practical." Wolfgang expects to take a young thing who has a good voice, but who has never been on the stage, to critical, competitive Italy and at once make a prima donna of her. "As for your proposal to travel about with Herr Weber and, be it noted, his two daughters—it has very nearly made me lose my reason! My dearest son! How can you have allowed yourself to be bewitched even for an hour by such a horrible idea, which must have been suggested to you by someone or other! Your letter reads like a romance. For could you really make up your mind to go trailing about the world with strangers? Quite apart from your reputation—what of your old parents and your dear sister? To expose me to the mockery and ridicule of the Prince and of the whole town which loves you?" After going into the complete futility of traveling on such a basis, he concludes: "Off with you to Paris! And that soon! Find your place among great people! . . . From Paris the name and fame of a man of great talent resounds through the whole world."

This letter would have completely demolished Wolfgang's argument if Mozart had persisted. But even before he had received it, he was talking differently, considering Paris, the chance of an opera there. The "straw fire" was already vanishing into smoke. Answering the letter on February 19, he tried hard to save face. He was hurt that his father should accuse him of not respecting his judgment. Mentioning the proposed journey with the Webers, he writes: "I never had any such intention—I mean of course, in our present circumstances." Leopold may have reread the earlier explicit statement, sighed, and smiled.

In truth, Wolfgang's wild, and to Leopold ruinous, plan was not simply a momentary aberration, nor was it a case of losing his head over a girl. It was rather the cumulative result of circumstance. The imagination of the composer Mozart was ready to expand. Mannheim had been a great stimulation, it had opened up to him new orchestral possibilities, and likewise operatic possibilities to match his inquiring and maturing interest in voice and stage. Stirred in these directions, he had been confined, by lack of opportunity, to composing nothing more than small pieces for young pupils and, under pressure for money, a brace of works for the flute, an instrument then distasteful to him. Goaded to make money, he had to spend part of each day giving tiresome lessons—the last resort of any indigent musician, and an interruption of his composing hours. At court, after interminable waiting around, he had had to bow to the ruling prince like any servant begging for a job, only to be waved aside by a man of prodigious power and no particular musical judgment. He had no standing in Mannheim, and was thrown upon the charity of the friends he had made. His position

had become humiliating and at length unbearable. He had
no recourse but to nurture the "pride and self-love" which
his father mistakenly taunted him with.

At this point the very atmosphere in Mannheim became
unsettled and tense. The Elector Maximilian in Munich had
died of smallpox in December. Carl Theodor was immediately summoned to take his place. Mannheim came under the
silent pall of mourning, and the opera *Rosamunde* by
Schweitzer, which was about to be produced, was suddenly
withdrawn. There were rumors of armed invasion of Bavaria
by Austria and Prussia with their rival claims. There were
cautious whispers on what the succession might be. Eruption,
impending change, pervaded the air. These developments as
well as his more personal dilemma may have contributed in
bringing Mozart to the point of casting sensible fatherly
counsel to the winds and taking a headlong emotional course,
a course more alluring than a laborious assault upon another
citadel more forbidding than Mannheim. He was in the mood
for a sudden infatuation with a thrilling soprano voice and
the comely soprano as well. Aloysia Weber was not the
first cause of his revolt from the line of duty laid out for him.
Wolfgang, aged twenty-two, needed just this final, contributing excitation. The blissful vision of Aloysia as a triumphant
prima donna, subduing all Naples in an opera created for
her by himself, was so glittering a possibility that it swept
from all but an uneasy corner of his consciousness a thousand
obstacles, including, of course, an outraged parent. It was
what would be called in our time by those who believe themselves qualified to give a psychological opinion (which of
course means everybody) an "escape"—the casting aside of
an oppressive dilemma, the grasp at romance, the rejection
of the very thought of possible failure.

"Composing operas is now my one burning ambition," he
writes again to his father. And earlier in the same letter there
is this striking statement: "I am a composer . . . and I
neither can nor ought to bury the talent for composition
with which God in his goodness has so richly endowed me
(I may say so without conceit, for I feel it now more than
ever)." These are not only true words—they have the ring

of a sudden exciting sense of release from inaction and from a complex of obstructive cares. This realization came upon him as he was sitting in a Mannheim parlor, so he tells us, waiting for an uneager pupil who had neglected to appear. Mozart thought of the concerto he had had to leave uncompleted for this stupid appointment and suddenly his heart was filled with rebellion. Leopold answered his cry from the heart—"I neither can nor ought to bury the talent which God has given me"—by writing: "Who says you ought to bury your talent? But that is precisely what you would be doing if you were to roam about in gipsy fashion." These two conflicting protests bring to a focal point the whole anguished interchange of long letters between the two men at this time. Leopold saw no other course than to find a foothold, a kapell-meistership for his son, under which he could proceed to compose. Wolfgang did not question this, for he would not have faced the thought that no court in Europe could give him the freedom, the independence which his God-given talent would require. His outburst was an imperious impulse; it overrode practical planning, it was a deep, ultimate truth, which Leopold, not suspecting the depth of possibilities in his son, could not understand.

Peace was made within this loyal family, their devotion never shaken by dissension. Wolfgang finally wrote tenderly to his father in these words: "I have full confidence in three friends, all of them powerful and invincible—God, your head, and mine. Our heads, I admit, are very different, but each in its own way is good, serviceable and useful, and I hope that in time mine will by degrees equal yours in those branches in which it is now inferior. Well, good-bye! Be merry and cheerful. Remember that you have a son who has never knowingly forgotten his filial duty to you, who will endeavor to become more and more worthy of so good a father."

XI

Paris, 1778

So it was decided that the mother should accompany Wolfgang to Paris. The journey was long, but she should not be subjected to returning home by herself. Leopold took comfort in the thought that her presence in Paris might have a restraining influence upon his impulsive son. Wolfgang had had enough of Mannheim, and his habitual optimism rose at the thought of new territory. "I have set all my hopes on Paris," he wrote, "for the German princes are all skinflints (*Knicker*)." Unable to sell their chaise, they found a driver to take them over the rough spring-rutted roads and then to purchase what was left of the vehicle. The journey took nine and a half days. It was tiring and "boresome," but could have been worse, for the season of intense cold had passed.

Arriving in Paris in the afternoon of March 23, 1778, Mozart lost no time in paying the calls on his prepared list. The first was their old friend, Baron Grimm, with whom Leopold had communicated. There was also the Minister from the Palatinate, Herr von Sickingen. There was Joseph Legros, the director of the *Concert Spirituel*. There was Jean Georges Noverre, whom Wolfgang had known as the ballet-master in Vienna and who now held the corresponding position at the Grand Opera. Wendling, whom he found at once, had paved his way with every opening he knew. The friends continued as if nothing had happened in the nature of private unkind remarks by Wolfgang. It is to be hoped that no hint of these ever reached the ears of the "godless" Wendling. The tenor Raaff was also in Paris. "He is staying with

M. Legros," wrote Mozart, "so that we meet almost every day." Madame "Jenomé," for whom he had composed his great piano concerto in Salzburg, was also there.

The first lodgings that they found were completely cheerless. Frau Mozart sat all day alone in a small dark room looking on a court, "as if I were in jail!" The room was too small to hold Wolfgang's clavier or his desk, and he had to compose at the quarters of Legros, leaving his mother alone, with scarcely light enough to knit. Her landlord, Herr Mayer, and his wife at least spoke German. Mozart's first long account of the musicians of Paris was hopeful, even though he found their singing atrocious, their language unmusical and their musical taste unreliable. Legros professed great warmth, asked him to compose numbers to follow a *miserere* by Cannabich for the *Concert Spirituel,* and a sinfonia concertante to be performed by his old friends Wendling, Ramm, and Ritter—the Mannheim bassoonist—together with Giovanni Punto, the hornist, who played *"magnifique"* according to Mozart, and was later to inspire Beethoven's Horn Sonata. The choral music had to be written in too great haste, and the "best" of it was omitted at the last moment. Legros deliberately left the manuscript score for the Concertante (K. 297b) on his desk uncopied until it was too late to have it ready for the concert, and then lost it—this to the annoyance of the players, and of Mozart, who put it down as hostile intent, and called it *"Hickl-Hackl."* Noverre, not even as reliable as Legros so far as results were concerned, promised him the commission for an opera—"I think it is to be called *'Aléxandre et Roxelane',"* reported Mozart. A librettist drafted a first act, but nothing came of it. Only operas by established composers had a reasonable chance of performance and neither the theatre managers nor the composers present were interested in an unknown young German. Piccinni, who had once befriended him in Milan, went no further than a courteous bow. Joseph Gossec, whom he met after a *Concert Spirituel,* called his choral music *"charmant,"* but was not heard from again. Grétry, then a leading figure in the opera, he may never have met. Gluck had left Paris for Vienna on the first of March, but the opera war was still a topic. Piccinni had been set up against Gluck as a champion of French opera, with his *Roland* produced in January. Piccinni was Italian to the core, he knew little French, and in setting this, his first French text, he had to be coached line by line. Least of all did he wish to be pitted against the famous, the securely renowned, Gluck. Gluck's *Armide,* which had been first performed in the September previous, was superior in the treatment of the language, and in most other ways. It was no triumph from a "nationalist" point of view, for Gluck was more interested in his subject and the dramatic truth of its treatment than in catering to any operatic fashion. The opera was disturbing to factionalism because it confounded expectations —it was greater than its time. There was no such thing as a third, a neutral, position, nor would any *entrepreneur* have considered confusing the issue by coming forward with a young and unknown German composer. No one could have known that this obscure newcomer, who cared not a fig for theoretical talk and who would have leapt at the chance to compose in any style at all, was capable of turning out a *tragédie lyrique* which would have astonished and puzzled both factions, but also gripped their attention. *Idomeneo,* which he was to be asked to compose for Munich three years later, he could easily have composed in the original French language of the libretto, with its striking choruses, its ballet spectacle, its powerful declamation dear to the French heart. It is interesting to speculate on how an *Idomeneo* by Mozart would have been received in Paris. His *Idomeneo* would approach Gluck in theatrical force, and owe much to him. As a musical score it was far richer than either Gluck or Piccinni could produce.

These potentialities no one in Paris knew or suspected— not even Grimm. Some would have preferred to keep them unknown. With no fees, no commissions in sight, Mozart was compelled, as he had been in Mannheim, to seek pupils. Grimm recommended him to the Duc de Guines, who actually played the flute well and had a daughter who was a good harpist. Mozart wrote for them the Concerto for Flute and Harp (K. 299), although, as Jahn put it, "these were the two instruments he could not endure." The daughter he taught composition, trying at patient length to coax a single musical idea from her little head. His father urged him to hunt out pupils, but he answered (May 1, 1778): "You write that I should pay plenty of visits and make new acquaintances and renew old ones. It is really impossible. To go on foot takes too long and makes one dirty, for Paris is inconceivably filthy; to drive costs four or five livres a day; and comes to nothing. The people pay compliments and nothing more; they engage me for a certain day, and then I play, and they say: *'Oh! c'est un prodige, c'est inconcevable, c'est étonnant!'* and then adieu. I have already spent money enough in that way, and often uselessly, for the people have been out."

Grimm had given him a letter to the Duchesse de Chabot. The result of this visit is vividly described in the same letter:

I was left waiting half an hour in a large, icy cold room, with no stove. At last the Duchesse de Chabot came in, apologized politely for the clavier, which was not in good condition, and asked me to try it. I said I should be delighted to play but that my fingers were numb with cold, and I begged her to take me to a room where there was at least a lighted stove. *"Oh, oui, Monsieur, vous avez raison"* was her only answer. Then she sat down and began to draw for at least an hour with some gentlemen who all sat around a large table. Meanwhile I had the honor of standing and waiting. The doors and windows were open, and very soon not only my hands but my feet and my whole body were stiff with cold, and my head began to ache. No one spoke to me. If it had not been for M. Grimm I would have walked out. At last I played on the wretched, miserable pianoforte. The worst of it was that Madame and the gentlemen went on with their drawing, without paying the least attention, so that I was playing to the walls and table and chairs. All this was too much for my patience. I began the Fischer variations, stopped half way through, and rose. Then followed no end of *éloges*. I said what was quite true, that I could not do myself credit on such a clavier, and that I would be pleased to appoint another day, when I could have a better one. But she would not agree and insisted that I wait another half hour, till her husband should come in. He came, and sat down beside me, and listened attentively. Then I forgot cold, and headache, and annoyance, and played on the wretched clavier as you know I can play when I am in a good humor. Give me the best clavier in Europe but an audience who do not or will not understand and feel with me when I play, and I lose all pleasure in it. I told the whole affair to M. Grimm.

Noverre was one of those people who make unmeaning promises and use the talents of another to their own advantage. He asked Mozart to contribute dances for a ballet, *Les petits riens,* to be performed with Piccinni's *Le finte gemelle,* added them to six numbers of his own, let himself be known as the composer, and paid Mozart nothing. The only music by Mozart which was properly heard and noticed in Paris was the "Paris" Symphony (K. 297), played at a *Concert Spirituel* (June 18, 1778). The rehearsal went badly, and the composer, who attended the concert with Raaff, was in an angry mood and ready to "snatch the violin out of the hands of Lahoussaye [the leader] and conduct it myself!" To his surprise it went well, and had a marked success. The audience's enthusiasm was such that it broke into applause at an effective passage in the middle of the Allegro, and again in the finale—such was the custom in 1778.

Mozart described this to his father on July 3. In the same letter he spoke of his opera prospects as completely indefinite. A French translation of Metastasio's *Demofoonte* had been mentioned, but nothing more than mentioned. Leopold had been clinging to two prospects—one was that Mozart might write an opera, adapting himself to the French style with his usual imitative skill. The other prospect was the position of organist to the court at Versailles. Mozart answered that this was out of the question. He would have to be at Versailles six months of the year, away from music. Anyway, the salary was insufficient. This was the beginning of the end of his hopes for Paris.

In the first days of June his mother's health had begun to fail. She did not want to have a doctor, especially a French-speaking one, and resisted when neighbors urged that she should be bled. Mozart was worried and helpless. At last a surgeon was called in who took her blood and diagnosed her trouble with the usual all-covering phrase—"internal inflammation." Mozart sat by her side for days, and did not dare to leave her even long enough to fetch a doctor. Suddenly, she lost her hearing. A doctor, an old German of seventy, came and gave her "a rhubarb powder in wine." He forbade water, which the fevered patient longed for and which Mozart, in agony, had to refuse. On the twenty-sixth the doctor visited her again. "Imagine my feelings when he said to me quite unexpectedly: 'I fear she will not last out the night . . . you had better see that she makes her confession.' " Mozart ran out and obtained a German priest. She seemed to improve slightly but then became delirious and her son remained at her bedside day and night. In the late afternooon of July 3 the death agony began, and in the evening the end came. Mozart wrote about it to Bullinger, the family friend in Salzburg, for he wanted him to break the news gradually to his father: "She lost all sensation and consciousness. I pressed her hand and spoke to her—but she did not see me, she did not hear me, or seem to feel anything. She lay thus until she died five hours later at twenty-one minutes past ten. No one was present but myself, Herr Haina (a kind friend whom my father knows) and the nurse."

Sitting up through most of that night, he wrote two long letters, the first to his father, preparing him for the shock, but pretending that his mother was still alive. To Bullinger he related everything and asked his friend to tell his father and sister. To his father he wrote: "I have very sad and distressing news to give you. My dear mother is seriously ill. . . . She is very weak, and is feverish and delirious. They give me hope—but I have not much. For a long time now I have been hovering day and night between hope and fear—but I have resigned myself wholly to the will of God—and trust that you and my dear sister will do the same."

To Bullinger he wrote: "I beg you, most beloved friend, watch over my father for me and try to give him courage so that, when he hears the worst, he may not take it too hardly. I commend my sister to you also with all my heart. Go to both of them at once, I implore you."

Again he wrote his father on July 9:

When I wrote you she was already enjoying the blessings of heaven—for all was then over. I wrote to you during that night and I hope that you and my dear sister will forgive me for this slight but necessary deception; for as I judged from my own grief and sorrow what yours would be, I could not indeed bring myself suddenly to shock you with the dreadful news! . . . I have indeed suffered and wept enough—but what did it avail? So I have tried to console myself; and please be resigned, my dear father, my dear sister! . . . You do not yet know your brother's good heart—for I have not yet been able to prove it. My two loved ones! Take care of your health. Remember that you have a son, a brother, who is doing his utmost to make you happy. . . . At length we shall live together as peacefully, honorably and contentedly as is possible in this world.

Mozart was now acutely conscious of the loneliness of his position in Paris. He missed any stimulation in the musical life around him, nor was he yet befriended by any of the musicians. He was never at ease except with his German companions from Mannheim. His unfailing good nature, his habitual cheerfulness, which still brightened his letters from Mannheim, gave way in Paris to a new note of despondency. He had written on May 29: "I often wonder whether life is worth living—I am neither hot nor cold—and don't find much pleasure in anything." This was completely unlike Wolfgang, and the remark alarmed his father. His mother's death, coming shortly after this, was certainly a moment of trial for him. Having subsisted on the warmth of family, friends and music-making, he was now quite alone, for his Mannheim friends had left Paris. He was ignored and without money.

The hours of depression passed. He hardly knew which way to turn, but his fundamental high spirits were not defeated, and soon the old resiliency returned. The letters after his mother's death were those of a self-sufficient young man who was feeling his twenty-two years, beginning to acquire judgment, facing his problems in his own way, no longer the obedient and compliant son except by affection and obligation.

He had the pride of independence but no money in his

pocket to sustain it, and it pained him to accept Grimm's bounty and at the same time to be treated by him as an incompetent. Grimm's advice, repeated in a letter to Leopold, was the more unpalatable in that there was some truth in it. Grimm wrote that the young man was "too good-natured, unenterprising, too easy to dupe, too little occupied with the means which can lead to fortune. If one is to penetrate here, one must be tough, audacious." He said that what Mozart needed was half his amount of talent and twice his cleverness at insinuating himself. Talent was unappreciated. The public paid attention only to the well known, and at the moment was ridiculously excited over the two opposed names of Piccinni and Gluck. "It would be difficult for your son to succeed, standing between the two factions." It was only the "mediocre and detestable musicians who make immense fortunes."

Mozart felt that he needed no patronizing advice from Grimm, for he saw at least as clearly how things stood. He knew that Leopold's suggestion, that he enter the lists with an independent opera and make the controversy three-cornered, was the impossible view of an outsider. Mozart was able and ready to write an opera, to a French text if need be —even though "the devil himself must certainly have invented the language of these people." Piccinni, who knew far less French than he, in fact almost none at all, was doing it. Johann Christian Bach had been commissioned to compose an opera (*Adamis de Gaule*), for Bach was a name. "The French are and always will be asses, and as they can do nothing themselves, they are obliged to have recourse to foreigners. I spoke to Piccinni at the *Concert Spirituel*. He is most polite to me and I to him when—by chance—we do meet. Otherwise I do not seek acquaintanceship, either with him or any one else. I understand my job—and so do they— and that is enough." Knowing in his heart of hearts that no commission would be forthcoming, he lapsed, as he had been forced to do in Mannheim, into giving lessons. He asked for no other privilege than to compose unhampered. He wrote in a long letter on July 31: "My nature is so full of music that I am immersed in it all day long. I love to plan works, study and meditate. Well, I am prevented from all this by my way of life here." He was continuing only until he could find some opening elsewhere. He had an eye on Mannheim, to which the Elector was expected to return from Munich. He and his father discussed the possibility, a humiliating one to Wolfgang, of his return to Salzburg, provided that a reasonable and dignified status could be obtained.

Mozart wrote to the Abbé Bullinger (August 7) about the situation at Salzburg and a new note of cynicism appeared in his remarks. He could hardly face, after Mannheim, the thought of the Salzburg orchestra. "For the last five or six years the musicians at Salzburg have always been rich in what is useless and superfluous, but very poor in what is necessary, and absolutely destitute in what is indispensable; and that is just the case now." There had been unsuccessful attempts to obtain an intelligent *Kapellmeister* there. "Half a dozen *Kapellmeisters* should be always in readiness so that if one drops out another can be immediately put in his place. But where at present can they get hold of one? Even this would be dangerous. It will not do to allow order, peace and intelligence to gain the upper hand over the orchestra, for the harm would only spread until nothing more could be done about it. Are there really no antiquated periwigs with asses' ears to be found, no lousy heads who could restore the outfit to its former lame and halting status?" He wrote to his father: "Ah, if only the orchestra were organized as they are at Mannheim! Indeed I would like you to see the discipline which prevails there and the authority which Cannabich wields."

In writing this, Mozart was holding out against the inevitable—the last resort. Leopold proceeded to make the best of the situation. On August 31 he wrote that he had found what looked like an opening. Leopold had sounded out the situation without a direct application. He wanted the offer to come from the Archbishop. Adlgasser had died on the organist's bench in the middle of a service; Lolli, the *Kapellmeister,* had died too, leaving those posts open. Leopold talked with the canon, Count Starhemberg, with the ever helpful Bullinger, and finally with Marie Franziska, the Archbishop's sister, and found that Wolfgang was wanted. At last he could expect a proposition. Wolfgang would be organist and concertmaster. He would receive 500 gulden a year and Leopold would receive the same amount. Wolfgang would be privileged to compose operas for other parts and travel when he wished to produce them. Leopold knew that Wolfgang would be reluctant, and he added inducements. Munich was a future possibility, for Carl Theodor was establishing his court and his illustrious forces there. A commission from Munich would be desirable, for that city lay conveniently at eighteen hours' traveling distance. Finally he mentioned, not without guile, that "the Prince and the whole court" were interested in Mlle. Weber and might be persuaded to acquire her.

Wolfgang received the idea with polite "joy"—joy, that is, at the prospect of being reunited with his family. Otherwise he accepted the proposition as one bites into a sour apple. He did not relish the thought of sitting in as violin in the Salzburg orchestra, dwelling once more in a town where music was bread and butter, not an art. He could not forget the Mannheim orchestra. "Oh, if we only had clarinets too! You can't imagine the glorious effect of a symphony with flutes, oboes and clarinets!" He asks whether Herr Feiner, the oboe, "can play the *Cor Anglais*?" He could not readily accept the idea of being shut off from association with the trends of music in each European center, the foremost composers and their works. "A man of mediocre talent remains mediocre whether he travels or not; but a man of superior talent (which I cannot without hypocrisy deny that I have) will deteriorate if he always remains in the same place."

Mozart's pride would not admit failure in Paris, even to his father. His claim that he could find a place there if he persisted is not convincing. He had had enough. He had developed an acute, barely concealed grievance against Grimm. The Baron and Mme. d'Épinay, his mistress, had harbored him in their house after the death of his mother. Grimm's patronage became intolerable when it failed to be backed by confidence in his prospects. An implication of lack of faith

in his talents was the unpardonable offence. Grimm wrote
to Leopold advising that the boy go elsewhere. He lent Wolfgang 15 louis d'or, which Wolfgang, on his dignity, could not
repay. When Grimm arranged for his departure by a slower
coach in order, so Wolfgang believed, to have him out of the
way a few days sooner, Wolfgang stiffened and barely held on
to his temper. Indeed, he had no reason to stay longer than
would be necessary to collect his dues for lessons and find a
publisher, if possible, for his piano concertos and piano
sonatas. In other words, to settle his affairs and provide himself with traveling money.

With all his profession of eagerness to return and embrace
his father and sister once more, his journey homeward was
marked by much lingering. He went out of his way to revisit
Mannheim, which Leopold considered a senseless waste of
time. He knew that Wolfgang would be tempted to stay even
longer in Munich. Most of his friends of the Mannheim
orchestra were there, and more important still, Aloysia Weber
was there. Leopold no longer disapproved of Aloysia, since
she and her father together would now have a salary even
better than what he and Wolfgang would receive in Salzburg.
Herr Weber he still looked upon with suspicion as having
cultivated Wolfgang solely for what he could get from the
boy's kindness and ready talents.

Wolfgang's disinclination for Salzburg grew as its distance
away lessened. He arrived in Munich on Christmas day and
only on his father's insistence made the final stretch of his
journey by mid-January. There was much that could have
detained him in Munich. First there was Aloysia herself. She
was to sing in the pending production of Schweitzer's *Alceste,*
which Wolfgang waited to hear. She had been given only a
small part, and Wolfgang provided her with his own setting
of Alceste's first aria, in full bravura, which he had sketched
in Paris, and shaped it to her then already considerable
abilities (K. 316). In it there were oboe and bassoon obbligati for his friends Ramm and Ritter. The girl herself was
pleased with the striking and effective music, but she was not
carried away by the compliment. She had cooled off considerably. The protestations of love seem to have come mostly

from Wolfgang all along. His was the broken heart (though, as it proved, not past mending) and his the injured pride. His cousin, the *Bäsle,* came from Augsburg, presumably to see him, for he had skipped her city on his return journey. Perhaps she diverted him with her fooleries and brought some in return. She went on to Salzburg and stayed in her uncle's house. The letters give no hint of any serious interest between the two cousins. Immediately after the first performance of *Alceste,* Wolfgang left for home. He was received with open arms in mid-January, 1779, by family and friends. His room was in order, with the cupboard and the practice clavichord he had asked for. Therese, the cook, had prepared capons in large quantities.

The tension between father and son was not lessened through Mozart's re-establishment at Salzburg, which was to last until November of the following year. What could sometimes be resolved by tact and ameliorating delay in letters could not be handled so easily when they were face to face. The bond of affection between the two and their singleness of purpose would not have permitted any open cleavage. Nevertheless, Mozart's right to his own adulthood was long overdue. He was about to take to himself the privilege of leading his own life, making his own judgments, his own mistakes.

XII

Salzburg, Munich, 1779-1781

Mozart's reinstatement in Salzburg could not have been a happy period, but it was a busy one, for a large amount of music came from his pen. The orchestral music written in Salzburg in the months after his return includes the two symphonies, in G major and B flat (K. 318 and 319), the *Sinfonia concertante* for Violin and Viola (K. 364), the Concerto for Two Pianos (K. 365), and the "Post Horn" Serenade in D major (K. 320). In the year 1780 there followed the Symphony in C major (K. 338). All of this music shows a refinement of part-writing, an independent treatment of the woodwind parts and the horns, a delicacy of detail, a use of crescendo and diminuendo, contrast of forte and piano, which unmistakably reflect his experience in Mannheim. He refused to sit and play with the violins, and avoided playing violin solo, but drilled the orchestra as best he might, standing, trying to instill subtleties strange to their experience. His cousin, then visiting Salzburg, teased him for his extravagant antics as a leader, important to himself and his purpose but only ridiculous to her. As organist, he was expected to perform; and for his performance he wrote new sonatas (K. 328, 329, 336). Choral music for all services he furnished in abundance. There were the Masses (K. 317 and 337) and the Vespers (K. 321 and 339). Brevity was still exacted. He could not develop the text in expression of its devotional meaning, or in fulfillment of its contrapuntal form, or its bravura possibilities. The music is usually engaging, melodious, apt to its purpose. It often goes deeper in the ardor of the subject than its surface brightness and color would indicate; deeper than the musical perception of the church-goers or their conformist mood.

Mozart's hunger to compose an opera had been perpetually stimulated by those he had heard in Mannheim, Paris, Munich, while he waited in vain to be asked to write one himself. He made the most of two rather unpromising openings in Salzburg. A visit there by the theatrical troupe of Schikaneder resulted in a revision and expansion of the incidental music he had provided for the play *Thamos, King of Egypt* by Baron von Gebler. Mozart furnished five entr'actes and three choruses (K. 345). A second project was a *Singspiel* in German, to be posthumously titled "*Zaïde*" by André. The text (incomplete) was provided by Andreas Schachtner, the court trumpeter. The piece is simply written and tailored to the capacities of Böhm's troupe, for which it was intended. It shows signs of haste. It foreshadows in subject and treatment *Die Entführung aus dem Serail.*

These attempts were soon forgotten when the long-awaited opening came in the form of a commission from Munich. The Elector Carl Theodor wanted an opera for the Carnival of January, 1781. He had evidently been influenced by Mozart's warm advocates in Munich, transplanted from Mannheim— at least those of them who had verbal access to the Prince. The opera was to be *Idomeneo, King of Crete.* Now at last he had some control in the preparation—acquaintance with the performers, from whom he knew what to expect, assurance of a proper spectacle by the most sumptuous forces in the German states. The libretto was adapted from the French by the Abbé Giambattista Varesco, court chaplain at Salzburg, under the composer's eye. It was derived from a rather antiquated opera, *Idoménée,* by Campra, to the text of Danchet, which had been performed in Paris in 1712. The libretto retained a certain French poetic flavor, and choruses in the French tradition. Leopold made the point that the result was wholly a Salzburg product, for the Abbate Varesco and Mozart worked together upon the text and music at Salzburg. Leopold too had a supervising hand in the completion of the Italian libretto, sending on to Munich from

Salzburg the final installments as they were written by Varesco according to the last-minute needs of the composer and the singers.

Idomeneo was welcomed by both Wolfgang and Leopold as a belated but exciting opportunity for fame and success. What Wolfgang had written for the theatre in Salzburg was merely local and did not count in this sense. What he had composed for Milan and Vienna were regarded as remarkable manifestations of precocity—operas written and led by a mere boy. *La finta giardiniera* in Munich had been enjoyed, applauded, and forgotten, like most pieces of its type. An *opera buffa* was then taken as a lower form of art, frank entertainment, and a new one was looked for at each carnival season. An opera seldom had what we would now call a repertorial life, since the interest then was always in a new work rather than the repetition of a familiar one, or at least a new setting of a familiar libretto. The interest in a new *opera seria* was high, the attention keen, the production elaborate. The vogue for this form would soon pass, but in 1781 it was still a composer's goal: the dream of a young man making his bid for world recognition. The time would come when *Idomeneo* and all of its fellows would fall into disregard, for public interest would soon weary of this artificial and convention-ridden form, where heroes and heroines of Greek mythology sang in polished periods of their loves and woes, their destinies subject to the anger or favor of the gods of Olympus. One's first reaction is surprise that Mozart could have put his heart and utmost effort into the dilemma of a Cretan king who is commanded to sacrifice his son to Neptune, a story which seems to defeat warm-blooded, human characterization.

Mozart entered upon *Idomeneo* gladly and without expressed reservations. The singers were his loyal friends and would not make difficulties. Cannabich and Count Seeau, close to the Elector, could of course be counted upon to favor his cause. A success in Munich would at least strengthen his standing at home; it might lead to an appointment in the Bavarian court. It is not surprising then that he put willing and intense effort into the final preparations and rehearsals.

Anton Raaff, assigned the title part, gave him some anxiety. In spite of his intelligence as an artist, his vocal quality was no more than could be expected of a tenor at the age of sixty-seven. More disturbing still, he quite lacked ease or grace of carriage as an actor. The two female parts of Ilia and Elettra were given to Dorothea and Elisabeth Wendling, the wives of the brothers Johann Baptist and Franz Anton Wendling of the orchestra. He knew their abilities; they knew his and were of course delighted with their beautiful arias. The castrato part of Idamante was important because it was the lover's part, and because it involved the tragic dilemma between him and his father (Idomeneo). The part had been given to Dal Prato, and with him Mozart had his greatest difficulty, for he found his voice production poor ("he has no method, no intonation, no feeling"), his ability to understand a dramatic situation almost negligible. Mozart drilled him endlessly in his part, referred to him in gay alliteration as *"mio molto amato castrato Dal Prato."* Mozart "created" the performances as well as the music. He coached the singers separately and together. He was on the stage, in the orchestra, everywhere, instilling into all involved the concept of his opera, unifying the style. This spectacle of Mozart in full charge is heartening, for it shows him for the first time allowed to be more than a hired scribbler of music for the stage, allowed at last to carry it through and dictate to the singers and players. It also shows him as that *sine qua non* of a true composer of operas—a practicing worker in the theatre. His father was uneasy about his zeal, remembering how he had used more energy than tact in drumming new musical ideas into the Salzburg orchestra. Leopold in his letters became the worried parent. He stood over Varesco and warned him not to sacrifice clarity to brevity in the recitatives. His suggestions to Wolfgang amounted to interference; he even advised him how to treat the subterranean voice of the god in the last act. Wolfgang answered equably, but quietly used his own judgment. He knew exactly how he wished to handle the trombones in this scene. He was well aware of the problem of the amount of expository recitative the audience would take without becoming distrait, and soon found that he must reduce it considerably. He needed no advice, and when he cut an important dialogue between Idomeneo and Idamante it was because in rehearsal Raaff and Dal Prato stood on the stage like a couple of sticks instead of like father and son in a terrible predicament.

Mozart reported to his father that the rehearsal of the first act aroused the enthusiasm of the troupe. Friedrich Ramm and Franz Lang of the orchestra went to the house of Cannabich, "beside themselves with joy," to tell Frau Cannabich about it, and could not wait to embrace the composer. The second act caused still greater enthusiasm, and the third, they agreed, would surely carry by its climax of action. The Elector was present at a full rehearsal just after Christmas. "After the first act the Elector called out to me quite loudly: 'Bravo.' When I went up to kiss his hand, he said, 'This opera will be charming and will not fail to do you honor.' " When he prepared to leave, two special parts were gone over out of place for his benefit: Ilia's aria *"Se il padre perdei"* with its wind obbligato parts, and the exciting storm scene with its choral outcries. "He again expressed his approval in the kindest manner, and said with a laugh: 'Who would believe that such great things could be hidden in so small a head?' " Mozart counted on making a terrifying impression upon the audience with the storm music, and an even greater one with the voice of the god in the last act. "The accompaniment consists of five instruments only, that is, three trombones and two French horns, which are placed in the same quarter as that from which the voice proceeds. At this point the whole orchestra is silent." These were innovations, derived from Gluck, but truly striking at the time, before the nineteenth century had invented new excesses in the way of terrifying or supernatural music.

The sense of anticipation grew as the date of performance approached. Leopold and Marianne arrived in Munich at the last moment, and so did many of the Salzburg friends, a larger number than had made the journey for *La finta giardiniera.* We may assume that *Idomeneo,* produced January 29, 1781, was a success, and that the word traveled to other parts of Europe. There is no verbatim report. If Leopold had not been present, posterity would have had the benefit of a detailed description by Mozart in a letter to Salzburg.

After the production, *Idomeneo* was not to be performed again publicly in Mozart's lifetime. It has gone into history as his supreme achievement in nobility of declamation. He could certainly have achieved still greater heights in tragic opera if he had had the opportunity later in Vienna, and a more sympathetic text. He made the most of this one. Among the grand mythological stage spectacles nurtured by the courts but doomed by the Revolution, *Idomeneo* stands unique. It should not be weighed against Gluck's great "reform" operas, for, lacking their driving dramatic power, it far surpasses them in the fullness and variety of the score. While Gluck lived only in the theatre and focused his strong theatrical instincts upon the sung texts, using a sparse orchestra to support the singers, Mozart used the theatre as an opportunity for his far superior symphonic abilities. Beside the musical wealth of *Idomeneo,* Gluck's orchestral scores seem almost barren with their thin instrumentation, their dependence upon tremolo and other facile effects, their monodic part-writing and choruses in block harmonies. Gluck was indeed wise in stressing "simplicity" as the direct means of concentrating upon intensity of mood in the vocal line. Mozart undoubtedly profited from the true and impressive declamatory style of that great artist of the stage, his orchestral theatricality, his pictorial effects, his depiction of the supernatural. Gluck made valid in practice the continuing faith in accompanied recitative as the way to preserve and enhance the noble elevation of ancient Greek tragedy. The meaning and beauty of poetry was conveyed by its syllabic stress, its accent, and music was the art to heighten the accentuation, intensify the dramatic situation. There was a sincere effort in the eighteenth century to underline the spirit and the letter of Greek tragedy with music. Metastasio was a practical intermediary in a noble aim, and Gluck and Mozart brought it to a short of ultimate peak. The listener who can become accustomed to the conventions of repetition, embellishment, literary hyperbole, finds in the highly charged or pathetic lines of Idamante or Ilia, the intensive outpourings in some of the concert arias, a truth of dramatic expressiveness never since touched by later composers, in which the lines are invariably sacrificed to the musical purpose. The art was mannered and could not survive. Its demise was nevertheless a loss to the musical stage.

Mozart at twenty-four, making his first real effort in *opera seria,* was not in the least conscious of the controversial side of the subject. He was embracing what to him was the highest mission of the stage, the medium upon which he had been sharpening his skill in various theatrical productions, in concert arias in the grand manner, from the age of nine. As always, he entered upon the composition of *Idomeneo* without preamble and finished it with dispatch. At work he was to a degree an assimilator, a co-ordinator, but never a deliberate reformer. He would never have become one, for his was not a fighting nature. If he had lived to Gluck's ripe age and attained a similar position of might in the operatic world he would certainly have held out for better librettos and treated them to greater ends in his own way, quite without theoretical expostulation. Mozart was well aware of Gluck's efforts to drive artificiality out of opera in favor of the "natural," to combat the domination of leading singers anxious only to show their voices. Mozart did not oppose the singers. He kept them contented with difficult passages shaped to their abilities, but those passages, even though ornate, turned out to be beautifully expressive. So too with his audiences and his sometimes arbitrary patrons. Leopold need not have admonished him as he did in the midst of the labors over *Idomeneo* (December 11): "I advise you when composing to consider not only the musical but the *unmusical* public. You must remember that to every ten real connoisseurs there are a hundred dull listeners. So do not neglect the so-called popular style which tickles long ears." The advice was quite superfluous. Mozart's way, even from his childhood symphonies, had been to favor popular expectations and so coax "long ears" into the more rewarding paths of beauty. Hardly a page of his music is otherwise. Nor is there the slightest sign that disinclination went with necessity.

In *Idomeneo,* Mozart faced the problem—which Gluck and every opera composer had faced—of satisfying the audience by making the story intelligible, not submerging the text in the music, and yet not bringing the music to a dead standstill in the attempt to make the lines understood. Gluck had stressed the orchestrally accompanied recitative as preferable to the dry sort with its clavier chords.* Mozart used *recitativo secco* where he was overloaded with expository dialogue. He kept what he considered essential for an audience to follow the plot, and he made sure that it could be clearly heard. He used *recitativo accompagnato* where the text became emotionally intense, and here he alternated each phrase with a telling orchestral commentary. In the arias the principal interest is often in the orchestra. The orchestral writing alone sets *Idomeneo* above any opera composed until that time. The arias, though sometimes too long, are developed, constantly renewed, and do not fall into the undramatic fault of literal reiteration. *Idomeneo* has its particular musical flavor, its own distinctive style. The characters Idamante, Elettra, Ilia, draw our sympathy and are integral to a score which grows with long acquaintance. *Idomeneo* is as *sui generis* as each of the comedy operas to follow.

Idomeneo was defeated in the next century as a performable work on account of its subject and text, a less than average product of a defunct courtly form. The score is prized by musicians for its great beauty, its splendid scenes, and particularly its choruses foretelling the temple scenes of *The Magic Flute* but affording far greater variety. Unable to hold a place in any standard company of today, which must reconcile its repertory with its box office, it has proved a prime subject for those independent operatic projects dedicated to the resurrection of the greater unknown past.

Leopold had worried about Wolfgang's overstay of his six weeks' leave from Salzburg, which lengthened with the post-

---

* And yet he used *recitativo secco* even in his "test" opera, *Alceste,* and likewise the "exit aria."

ponement of the production of *Idomeneo* until January 29. Wolfgang did not worry. He wrote on December 16: *"A propos!* how about the Archbishop? Next Monday I shall have been absent from Salzburg for six weeks. You know, my dear father, that it is only for love of you that I remain in Salzburg, for, by heaven! if it rested with me I would have torn up the agreement and resigned my appointment before I left home this time. It is not Salzburg, but the Prince and the proud nobility who become more insupportable to me every day. I would welcome with delight a letter saying that he no longer requires my services."

The matter resolved itself when the Archbishop went to Vienna, probably on account of the death of Maria Theresa on November 28, 1780 (that event had caused the Mozarts to fear a declaration of mourning in Munich and a cancelation of *Idomeneo*). The Archbishop took with him a part of his performing forces and summoned Wolfgang to Vienna. He accordingly left Munich on March 12. Except for once, briefly as a visitor, he was destined never to return to Salzburg.

XIII

Vienna, 1781

MOZART ARRIVED in Vienna on March 16, 1781, in his most optimistic mood. He had the score of *Idomeneo* with him and intended to play it to the Emperor Joseph II, with some fugues which His Majesty was said to be fond of. He had influential friends in Vienna. Pupils could be found. Concerts were reported to be profitable. A position at court was a future possibility, for Giuseppe Bonno, the *Kapellmeister,* was old and infirm. Gluck was the most honored opera composer in Vienna—but he was sixty-seven. Antonio Salieri was chamber composer to the throne. A movement was afoot for the establishment of German opera, and for this neither the Italian Salieri nor the venerable Gluck, a wholly Franco-Italian composer despite his origin, were in the least suited.

Mozart soon found out that this broad path was not unobstructed. The Archbishop as his employer kept him under close surveillance and saw to it that this youngest member of his retinue did not simply walk into the kind of fame and income he had been denied at home. The Archbishop by the privilege and custom of his position gave concert entertainments at one house or another, taking his musicians with him. Having the employer's claim on the time of his performers, he refused Mozart permission to give a concert or to play except at his own orders. When Mozart had to forgo an appearance at a fashionable concert for the benefit of the widows and orphans of Vienna musicians, he was especially disappointed. He would have played the "beautiful fortepiano" made by Stein and owned by the Countess Thun, and the Emperor would have heard him from a proscenium box. The Archbishop's refusal to allow his pianist to play for this particular cause, without pay, was considered as discourteous. "All the nobility of Vienna have made a grievance of it," wrote Mozart, and indeed the Archbishop had no choice but to yield for the next occasion. Obviously, the already explosive relationship between Mozart and his lord and master was deteriorating rapidly. To be highly regarded and befriended by a considerable part of the Viennese nobility and at the same time to be openly treated with haughty contempt as a servant in such a way that even these friends were aware of it, soon brought Mozart to the breaking point. The eruption had to come soon.

Mozart's account in the letters is excitable and biased, but the tenor of the situation is plain enough. The Archbishop was annoyed at the attention the young member of his court was getting elsewhere, and still more annoyed by his insolent attitude. He countered by suppressing him and keeping him strictly in his place. Mozart, humiliated and balked, was seething with offended dignity. Dismissal was no longer a threat to him. He was past caring. The trouble began on the very day of his arrival. He wrote to his father on the day following that he had been quartered in the Archbishop's establishment, while Brunetti as violin soloist, and Ceccarelli as castrato, the luxury item in the performing forces, were separately housed. Mozart was given his lunch at the servants' table. "Our party consists of the two valets, the body and soul attendants of His Worship, the *Contrôleur,* Herr Zetti, the Confectioner, the two cooks, Ceccarelli, Brunetti, and—my insignificant self. By the way, the two valets sit at the top of the table, but at least I have the honor of being placed above the cooks." The more exalted officers, the private secretary and the chamberlain, were placed at a separate table. This sort of thing was customary in the households of archbishops and princes; it was particularly galling to Mozart just then.

When the Archbishop was to visit Prince Galitzin, the Russian Ambassador, Mozart was instructed to be taken to the Palace by Brunetti, placed in the anteroom, and escorted by a valet, when wanted, into the salon where the guests were assembled. Mozart ignored the procedure and arrived on his own accord at the appointed hour. He wrote (March 28): "When I got upstairs, I found Angerbauer standing there to direct the lackey to show me in. But I took no notice, either of the valet or the lackey, but walked straight on through the rooms into the music room, for all the doors were open—and went straight up to the Prince, paid my respects and stood there talking to him." This bit of defiance of class etiquette could not have passed unnoticed.

The inevitable final confrontation with the Archbishop soon came. Hieronymus, after repeatedly delaying his departure and keeping everyone in a state of uncertainty, gave the order that Mozart was to return to Salzburg by public conveyance on Wednesday, May 9. Mozart sent back word that he could not collect fees due to him until Saturday and would leave then. There had been two audiences. A third, on May 9, he describes:

When I entered the room his first words were "Well, fellow, when are you going?" [This in the contemptuous second person.] I—"I intended to go tonight but the seats were all engaged." [This was probably a concocted excuse.] Then he burst forth that I was the most dissolute fellow he knew, that no one had ever served him so badly, that if I didn't leave this very day he would have my salary stopped. I couldn't get in a word, for he kept firing away. I listened to it all calmly [!]. . . . He called me a scoundrel, a rascal, a vagabond. I cannot really remember all he said. At last my blood began to boil, and I said "So your Grace is not satisfied with me?" "What, do you dare to threaten me, you scoundrel? There is the door! Be careful, for I will have nothing to do with such a miserable wretch." At last I said: "Nor I with you!" "Well, get out!" As I left, I said "This is final. You shall have it in writing tomorrow." All the remarks which this fine servant of God made to me had such an excellent effect on my health that in the evening I was obliged to leave the opera in the middle of the first act and go home and lie down. For I was very feverish, I was trembling in every limb, and I was staggering along the street like a drunkard. I also stayed at home the following day, yesterday, and spent the morning in bed.

Leopold was inexcusably blind in not realizing that his son had burned his bridges, that the time for caution and the swallowing of pride for self-interest had passed. He should have known Wolfgang well enough to accept so final a step. Mozart had once and for all taken his destiny into his own hands. Leopold's answer is lost, but Mozart's letter of May 19 shows how he could meet his father's blunt counsel of expediency with the strength of self-reliance:

> I must confess that there is not a single trace in your letter of the father I know—You say that the only way to save my honor is to change my decision. How can you make such a contradiction! When you wrote this you surely did not bear in mind that such a recantation would prove me to be the basest fellow in the world. All Vienna knows that I have left the Archbishop, and all Vienna knows why! They all know that it was because my honor was insulted—and, what is more, insulted three times. Am I publicly to prove the contrary? Am I to make myself out to be a cowardly groveler, and the Archbishop a worthy prince? No one would like to do the former, I least of all. As for the latter, God only can accomplish that.

He closes:

> Dearest, most beloved father, ask of me anything you will except that. The very thought of it makes me tremble with rage. Adieu. I kiss your hands a thousand times and embrace my sister with all my heart, and am ever your obedient son.

The story of this flare-up between Mozart and Hieronymus naturally arouses our sympathy for the one and indignation against the other. Some have defended Hieronymus as acting in his own interest, for he could not have had the glimmer of a notion that this particular musician in his hire would go down in history as a great figure in music, and that he himself would survive in the memory of man only as the hated opponent. To him, Mozart was a young hothead, whose talents were extremely useful, but whose insurrectionary qualities had become increasingly difficult to keep within bounds. He would still have liked to patch things up and retain Mozart. He avoided the final break, and may have hoped that Leopold in Salzburg would use persuasion. Leopold had indeed written a letter to Count Karl Arco of the archiepiscopal household. The letter was ill-timed and ill-advised. This very count, acting as buffer in the Archbishop's antechamber, where Mozart sought admission to the Presence to demand his formal dismissal, became abusive (goaded no doubt by Mozart) and ejected him with "a kick in the behind."* Mozart made a furious vow that if he ever met Arco in the public street, he would return the kick in kind. "The heart shows the true nobleman," he wrote, in recounting this, "and, although I am no count, I am more honorable perhaps than many a count; and whether it be a footman or a count, whoever insults me is a scoundrel."

Leopold was far too slow to realize that what Mozart called his "honor" had a special meaning. It was the defense of the dignity and inviolability of his inmost nature, his faculty to compose. He called it "God-given," and instinctively protected it. He had no thought of immortal fame. He was aware, although he never spoke of it in so many words, that he could write music at any time, at a moment's notice, in any form, which would at least equal the best. The opportunity to use this function freely was his first right. When his readiness to compose encountered open indifference or latent hostility, he withdrew into his sense of pride, as one will do when what one stands for as sacred is belittled.

Looking back at the boyhood letters, we find a different Mozart. There were no fits of anger then. His affectionate nature was completely trusting and would have had no defense against rebuff. In his family he was surrounded with protective love. Traveling about Europe as a child he was still protected by his father from the ugly side of humanity, and would observe people and things with his irrepressible humor. He was incapable of meanness. His descriptions of stupidity in musicians are sometimes brutally candid as well as pointed and witty, but it should be remembered that they were confidential, even a letting off of steam after polite

---

* "*Giebt mir einen Tritt im Hintern.*" Pauline D. Townsend, the Victorian translator of Jahn, delicately renders this: "He pushed him towards the door with his foot!"

restraint.* They relieved the sense of impatience and annoyance which he may well have spared the people themselves. His opinions of other musicians were sometimes unsparing, but never colored with envy. He was quick to recognize true musical value. Duplicity, insincere protestations, he learned to expect in Vienna. The unpardonable attitude, which always sent the blood rushing to his head, was contempt of his ability.

Installed once more in Salzburg, the Archbishop had difficulty in finding an organist, a composer, a clavier player and teacher in one, to replace the man he had lost. He made an offer to Leopold Kozeluch, regarded as the foremost clavier player in Vienna. Mozart wrote to his father on July 4: "The Archbishop secretly offered a thousand gulden to Kozeluch, who however, has declined, saying that he was better off in Vienna and that unless he could improve his position, he would never leave. But to his friends he added: 'What deters me most of all is that affair with Mozart. If the Archbishop lets such a man go, what on earth would he do to me?' "

Mozart, salaryless, faced the cold necessity of finding an income. He could no longer be dependent on his father, and felt the obligation to send some money in repayment of his long-accumulated debt. He mentioned bringing his father and sister to Vienna and supporting them. But not just yet. The midsummer of 1781 now hung over the city, and had driven many of its most likely people into their country houses. He had been able to keep only one pupil, the Countess Rumbeck. Countess Thun, already his most loyal friend in her class, worked up a subscription for six clavier sonatas. As the winter set in, he found a few pupils, and picked up an occasional concert engagement. A letter to his sister bespeaks loneli-

---

* An example of this is his description of Josephine Aurnhammer. Mozart lodged for a while with the Aurnhammer family, until the daughter, who was his pupil, showed a personal interest in him, and started gossip. Mozart hastened to set his father straight on this point by describing her as "loathsome, dirty and horrible." He wrote: "She is as fat as a peasant, perspires revoltingly, and goes about so scantily dressed that it is as if she plainly said: 'Just look at me.' "

ness, even a bit of homesickness. He craves news and misses the Sunday evening "bolt-shooting parties." He describes a typical day as his excuse for writing too seldom (February 13, 1782): "My hair is done by six o'clock in the morning, I am dressed by seven, and write until nine. From nine to one I give lessons. Then I dine except when I am invited out at two or even three o'clock, as for example today with Countess Zichy and tomorrow with Countess Thun. I can never work until five or six in the evening, and even then I am often prevented by a concert, but compose when possible until nine. . . . When I come home early I usually compose something before I go to bed. I often write until one, and am up again at six!"

His attention as early as June, 1781, had been drawn to the theatre, for the reason that a German-speaking company of high quality was a path in the direction of true German opera. He wrote to his sister, who was fond of the theatre, that his principal entertainment consisted in plays. "I wish you could see a tragedy performed here! I know no other theatre where every kind of play is given to perfection. Every part, even the smallest and worst, is well filled." Joseph II had lifted the theatre to this excellence by giving it full state support, and popularizing it as well. He had also attempted to follow through this national impulse as long before as 1777 by building a German opera company at the *Burgtheater* as the *"Nazionalsingspiel."*

It was an ambitious undertaking, for German operas worthy of the name had seldom been performed in Vienna. Most of the singers were Italian. It was elsewhere, mostly in northern Germany, that efforts had been made to develop the *Singspiel* into a respectable musical form. The *Singspiel* was a product of the spoken theatre, where songs would be inserted in a play and sung by the actors, who were not trained singers. At first the songs were simply interpolations to please the crowd. The next step was to build the musical part, to integrate the music with a text in the vernacular, to attain a genuine native opera, as it had been attained in Italy, and to a degree in France. In those countries a national opera developed, as apparently it always must, by going hand in hand with the spoken theatre, by reaching some sort of fusion between the "grand" style and the popular stage. Popular opera had grown from light stage entertainment by imitating successes in the higher form in the vein of parody. Parody meant competing with the imported, which was necessarily the Italian variety, by using the native language and introducing tunes with which everyone could feel thoroughly at home. The Germans had the instinct for music but awaited its formal development. The *Volkslied* had yet to be lifted into full artistic expression by Mozart, Weber, Beethoven, Schubert and the continuing German line. In 1781 a true national idiom for the musical stage was the project of certain high-minded poets and princes but not yet an achievement. Goethe, Wieland, Lessing, hoped to make the *Singspiel* a work of art and failed, partly because the theatres were ill-equipped musically, mostly because there were no adequate composers available. There were plenty of dull ones and some earnest ones, like Johann Adam Hiller, the Cantor at Leipzig. Not one of their stage pieces has survived to take its place beside such triumphant pioneers of popular endeavor elsewhere as *The Beggar's Opera* in England and *La serva padrone* in Italy.*

Joseph II felt impelled to pursue this high patriotic aim. He did so more from a sense of duty than from any motive of personal enthusiasm, for his taste ran to the Italian style and language. He had grown up upon the operas of Hasse or Piccinni. Salieri had been his favorite composer for years—"the idol of the Emperor," he was called. It was therefore by a lucky chance that a lukewarm emperor attached his best singers to the *Burgtheater* and opened the way for a great composer at last to take advantage of the situation. The new project had opened in 1778 with *Die Bergknappen* by the resident composer Ignaz Umlauf. The piece was praised but made no great stir (Mozart, for one, thought little of Umlauf's ability). The repertory lapsed into translations from French *opéras comiques* by Gossec, Grétry or Monsigny, with an oc-

---

* The *"guerre des bouffons"* in Paris had produced no enduring masterpiece, but at least a large amount of zealous encyclopedic *brouhaha*.

casional adaptation from the Italian. In April of 1781, Gluck and Salieri each had a try, but Gluck's *Die Pilgrimme von Mecca* was a concocted translation from his *La Rencontre imprévue,* and Salieri's *Der Rauchfangkehrer* could not begin to provide music at one with the language. The situation was ripe for a *Singspiel* of high musical quality, music with (necessarily) an Italian formal basis but a true German flavor, not only to match but to belong to its comic German text.

There are signs that Mozart sensed his opportunity. Mozart was not only the best candidate, he was the only one worth considering at all. By the process of elimination, if for no more perceptive reason, those in control of the opera looked to him. Mozart had multiple hopes. He had brought *Idomeneo* with him, and arranged to have parts of it sung at the house of Countess Thun. He had had the text translated into German by Schachtner in Salzburg. He even had the score of his Salzburg *Singspiel,* later named *Zaïde,* ready to show, and brought it forth for the inspection of Gottlieb Stephanie, the younger of two actor brothers, who was both a poet and the Inspector of the *Nationalsingspiel.* Stephanie obviously had his instructions from Director Rosenberg, who in turn was subject to his Emperor. Stephanie read and liked the opera, particularly on account of its oriental subject, which was traditionally popular. He was skeptical probably because it had too little comedy and too much moral sentiment to please Vienna, and because it was written for the modest forces of a traveling company, not for the illustrious forces of Vienna. It was fortunate in any case that this piece was not chosen, for the opera decided upon was to prove a far more advanced score, of more sustained beauty. The result of a conference at the end of July was the final choice by Stephanie and the immediate acceptance by Mozart of a *Singspiel* in the Turkish style, to be adapted from a text by Christoph Friedrich Bretzner, and worked over by Stephanie. The libretto, here taken without any by your leave, had previously been set by Johann André and recently produced in Berlin as *Belmont und Constanze,* or *Die Entführung aus dem Serail.* There had been further antecedents on the favorite subject of European ladies captured and held in a harem and with true Western spirit keeping the sultan or pasha at a respectful distance.

Mozart plunged with great eagerness into the music. As he worked upon his score through the remaining months of 1781 and into the following year, a fresh romance blossomed in his life. It so happened that while he was composing this opera about two engaged couples in a dilemma, he too became a fiancé with problems of his own.

XIV
Vienna, 1781, 1782

O<small>N LEAVING</small> the Archbishop, Mozart had established himself as a boarder with the Weber family. There had been changes. Aloysia, after giving Mozart his dismissal in Munich, had obtained in 1779 a permanent position in Vienna with the new German opera troupe. Established in the capital with her parents and sisters, she was immediately successful, confirming Mozart's earlier high opinion of her voice as more than personal bias, and also confirming his confidence that she could learn to act. Her father died a month after their arrival, and in 1780 Aloysia married Josef Lange, a prominent actor in the *Burgtheater*. Mozart wrote his father, on May 16: "I was a fool about Lange's wife, that is true, but who is not when one is in love? I was indeed in love with her, and I feel that I am not yet indifferent to her, and it is as well for me that her husband is a jealous fool who never lets her out of his sight, so that I seldom see her." He wrote of the marriage that she "flung herself at a comedian." Lange could act serious parts as well. He was a tolerable painter and would later oblige his sister-in-law and her illustrious husband by making their portraits. Mozart's slight opinion of the girl who had summarily dropped him was based on pride, but not altogether unjust. Aloysia was the kind who would choose a husband to the advantage of her career, and would hardly hesitate between an unemployed pianist and a successful actor.

Mozart found the living quarters of the Weber family to consist of a house *"Zum Auge Gottes"* on the Petersplatz.

Frau Weber rented rooms and furnished meals and other domestic conveniences on a rather crowded basis. There was a special attraction for Mozart. When he had attached himself to the Webers in Mannheim he had not so much as mentioned the third daughter, Constanze, then fourteen. Now she had turned eighteen. The fact that Mozart was living in a household considered none too reputable, and that he had been seen a few times in the Prater with her, was enough to start gossip about them. The talk even reached Leopold, who wrote at once telling Wolfgang that he must live elsewhere. Mozart was indignant at gossipers who leapt at conclusions. "I have never thought less of getting married than right now —God has not given me my talent to attach to a wife and so waste my youth in idleness." Here he was echoing his father's favorite precept. He admitted: "I fool about and have fun with her when I have time, which is only in the evenings when I have supper at home; for I work in my room in the mornings and am seldom in the house in the afternoons. If I had to marry all those with whom I have joked, I should have two hundred wives at least." This offhand remark has been quoted out of context to make of Mozart a sort of Don Giovanni. His explicit statement "I am not in love with her" did not convince his father. If it was not yet love it was very close to it. He promptly left the "Eye of God" and moved into a miserable little "closet behind the kitchen" in the house, well nicknamed the "rat hole," of Herr Aurnhammer.

Mozart not only minimized his feelings about Constanze— he held back the news of his engagement to her, well knowing how it would be received. Leopold had too often pictured what married poverty could do to an artist in pursuit of a career. Constanze was a moneyless member of this miserable family who had never had any interest in Wolfgang beyond getting what they could out of him. Leopold soon received from his son, who had so emphatically denied any intention of marriage, an avowal which was overdue, preceded by news which had already reached him in the line of gossip, both from Vienna and from Mannheim. Nasty things had been said about Constanze's character. This filled Mozart with rage and lessened his persuasive point to his father that a wife, and especially Constanze, would prove after all a convenience and an economy. Mozart wrote (December 15):

> My effort now is to find a small but assured income, to add it to what chance may bring in—and then—to get married! You are shocked at the idea? But I entreat you, dearest, most beloved father, to listen to me. Since I have had to reveal my intentions to you, you must also listen to my reasons, which indeed are very well founded. Nature speaks in me as urgently as in others, more so, perhaps than in many a hulking peasant. I simply cannot live as most young men do now-a-days. In the first place, I have too much religion; in the second place I have too great a love for my neighbor and too high a feeling of honor to seduce an innocent girl; and in the third place I have too much horror and disgust, too much dread of disease to play around with whores. So I can swear that I have never had anything to do with women of that sort.

His next task was to prove to Leopold that a member of the Weber family could actually be desirable as a wife:

> But whom is it that I love? Do not be shocked again, I entreat you. Surely not one of the Webers? Yes, one of the Webers, but not Josefa, nor Sophie, but Constanze, the middle one. I have never found such differences of character in a single family. The eldest [the mother] is a lazy, gross, false woman, and as cunning as a fox. Mme. Lange is a false, evil-minded person, and a coquette. The youngest is still too young to be anything in particular—she is just a good-natured, frivolous creature! May God protect her from seduction! But the middle one, my good, dear Constanze, is the martyr of the family, and, probably for that very reason, is the kindest-hearted, the cleverest, and therefore the best of them all. She makes herself responsible for the whole household and yet is never credited with doing anything right. Oh, my dearest father I could fill whole pages with descriptions of the scenes I have witnessed in that house. If you want to read them I shall do so in my next letter. But before I leave off bothering you with my talk, I must make you better acquainted with the character of my dear Constanze. She is not ugly, but at the same time not really beautiful. Her whole beauty consists in two little black eyes and a pretty figure. She has no wit, but she has enough common sense to enable her to fulfill her duties as a wife and mother. She is not at all extravagant—that is

an absolute falsehood. On the contrary, she is used to being poorly dressed, for the little that her mother has been able to do for her children she has done for the two others, but never for Constanze. It is true that she would like to be neatly and cleanly dressed, but not fashionably, and she is able to supply most of a woman's needs by making her own clothes. She dresses her own hair every day. Moreover she understands housekeeping and has the best heart in the world. I love her and she loves me with all her heart. Could I wish for myself a better wife?

If this description of his betrothed and his prospect of wedded life was lacking in certain elevated ardors of young love, and shaped to appease a more than reluctant parent, it had a good deal of truth in it. Constanze was trained in music, like all the Webers, and would respect it. Mozart did not look for a lofty mating of kindred spirits, but an affectionate domesticity on a comfortable bourgeois level. It would be enough that the affection of the pair would carry them through decidedly skimpy living conditions without serious strain or thought of break.

Mozart pleaded for his father's consent, but it was plain in his letters that he would marry with or without it. He had to admit that the mother was a trouble-maker and a shrew, that she "liked wine, and more so, I admit, than a woman should." Her daughters, he hastened to add, drank only water. After the death of her husband, a Johann von Thorwarth, auditor of the theatre and inspector of the wardrobe, had undertaken the guardianship of the family. He made Mozart draw up a marriage contract, promising to marry Constanze within three years, or if he should change his mind, to pay her an annuity of 300 gulden. Mozart agreed readily, knowing that he would "never forsake her." He wrote to his father: "What did the angelic girl do when the guardian was gone? She asked her mother for the document and said to me: 'Dear Mozart! I need no written pledge from you. I believe what you say,' and tore up the paper." Mozart felt the need of "rescuing" the eighteen-year-old girl, often in tears under the mother's baleful eye and sharp tongue, from the degradation of that household. The Baroness von Waldstädten, who was a matchmaker at heart, received her in her home in the suburb of Leopold-stadt, and when Mozart heard that police intervention by the Webers was imminent, he asked the Baroness to put an end to an impossible situation by arranging for an immediate wedding in her house.

On July 31 Wolfgang made a last plea for his father's blessing. It came, with his sister's, but after the wedding, which took place August 4, 1782. Wolfgang answered August 7: "There was no one present at the ceremony but the mother and the youngest sister, Herr von Thorwarth as guardian and sponsor for us both, Herr Landrath von Cetto, who was witness for the bride, and Gilowsky for me. When we were actually united my wife and I both began to weep. Everyone, including the officiating priest was moved to tears by the sight of our happiness. Our wedding festivities consisted solely in a supper given us by the Baroness von Waldstädten."

Leopold had not hesitated to remind the prospective bride-groom that he had once involved himself in considerable debt to send his son across Europe. He expected no immediate repayment, but Mozart as a husband felt obliged to give an account of his expectations. There were occasional sums to be collected when he published a set of chamber works by subscription. In Lent he could give concerts and count on a good attendance, but this was seasonal. The only steady returns would be from pupils, which he disliked because he was deprived of his best composing hours. On January 23, he wrote that he had three of them at 6 ducats a month from each. "With one more, a man and his wife can manage in Vienna if they live quietly and in the retired way which we desire; but, of course, if I were to fall ill we should not make a groschen." The optimist continues: "My affairs cannot get worse; on the contrary, they must continue to improve." They did not improve except sporadically; Mozart was burdened with lesson-giving for the rest of his life.

There was, of course, the new opera, which had busily taken shape through the period of his engagement, and had been performed on July 16, 1782, nineteen days before his wedding. An opera could not be expected to support a family.

Die Entführung aus dem Serail brought him a single fee and presumably the return from one benefit performance.

It was not through any fault of the composer that *Die Entführung* waited through a year of delays before it was produced. When Mozart received his commission on July 31, 1781, he expected it to be performed within six weeks, and the score progressed by rapid strides. He acquainted his father with the news of the commission on the day following: "The libretto is quite good. . . . I intend to write the overture, the chorus in Act I and the closing chorus as Turkish music. Mlle. Cavalieri, Mlle. Teyber, M. Fischer, M. Adamberger, M. Daner and M. Walter are to sing in it. I am so delighted at having it to compose that the first songs for Cavalieri and Adamberger and the trio at the close of first act are already done. The time is short, for it is to be performed in the middle of September, but the circumstances of the production will all be favorable. And indeed everything combines to raise my spirits, so that I hasten to my writing table with the greatest eagerness, and can't leave it." The "circumstances" was the expected visit of the Grand Duke Paul Petrovitch from Russia.

The Abduction from the Seraglio grew in the making. It could hardly have been rounded out into the magnificent score we know if its composer had been held to a six weeks' schedule. As it happened, there were further postponements. The visitors did not arrive until October, and for their visit three operas by Gluck were decided upon.* Mozart's letters of September 26 and October 13 are full of the progress of the opera. His enthusiasm was such that "what would at other times require fourteen days to write I now do in four." The delays were most fortunate, for they enabled him to recast and amplify the libretto. Mozart took hold of his task as full master and sole creator. The principal singers, who were superb, inspired him to do the utmost for their voices and particular abilities. We owe the wide compass and the *fioriture* in the part of Constanze, the captured heroine, to the

---

* *Iphigenie auf Tauris* in German (October 23), *Alceste,* and *Orfeo ed Euridice* in Italian (December 3 and 31).

accomplishments of Katharina Cavalieri, a prima donna of deserved fame, and actually a German singer. The part of her lover, Belmonte, was shaped for Adamberger, a first tenor in whom Mozart delighted. The librettist had given the part of Osmin, the pasha's villainous overseer, almost nothing. Mozart favored Fischer, a magnificent *buffo* actor and singer, and built his part into the principal one, with songs of "comic rage," giving "full scope" to Fischer's beautiful, deep notes. Some of the verses supplied by Stephanie had no poetic value. They were explosive and nonsensical, often none too singable,* but they served the composer to drive home the character formed by his own lively imagination. Mozart stood over Stephanie and gave him no peace. He made him recast any pages unsuitable to music, reorder the third act and the finale of the second. In a letter to Salzburg he exulted in his new power to change the text into the utmost musical effectiveness, to exclude any literary prerogative for the poet, such as too much concern with rhymes and verbal elegance.

Bretzner, the original librettist, was disturbed about the final result and published a complaint about "a certain person named Mozart" who had pre-empted his book, but librettists were quite unprotected in those days. He could no more than disclaim the additions. The story of a Christian girl rescued from a Turkish harem was nothing new, nor was Bretzner's version of it particularly distinguished. Mozart did not succeed in drawing the elements together into a wholly smooth and satisfactory play. Sometimes the music freezes the action, as Constanze's long coloratura aria *"Martern aller Arten,"* really a concert number, and other arias which he later shortened. The opportunities for alternate fun and sentiment were enough to fire his enthusiasm. The beautiful score was certain to delight the hearers of his first full-rounded *Singspiel* and the expostulations of Osmin were enough to assure it as a comic stage piece. The songs of the first pair of lovers, splendidly sung by Cavalieri and Adamberger, became a milestone in German Romantic musical treatment. Mozart's

---

* For example, this in rapid patter: *"Wenn Sie euch zum Richtplatz führen, und die Hälse schnüren zu, schnüren zu, schnüren zu."*

effervescent spring of comedy *alla Turca,* his sheer exuberance, would perpetuate the new *Singspiel* while all previous
Turkish confections (Gluck's *Pilgrims of Mecca* included)
were destined to pass into oblivion.

There was an organized cabal. The first two performances
were described by Mozart: "Can you believe that the opposition was even stronger on the second evening than on the
first? The whole of the first act was drowned out, but they
could not prevent the bravos after every song." The piece was
an immediate hit. Mozart reported to his father a succession
of full audiences as it went through seventeen performances,
ceasing only with Lent and the departure of Fischer for Paris.
It went the rounds of German theatres and by 1788 had been
performed in twenty-five of them.

Mozart was established as a composer of German opera to
be reckoned with. Gluck, in his exalted position as *Kammermusicus,* and Salieri, the King's darling, had reason to look
askance at the newcomer who had at once vindicated the
Emperor's nationalistic project and raised the claptrap *Singspiel* to full artistic respectability. Both composers were
smoothly polite. Salieri, Mozart continued to suspect of concealed hostility. There is no evidence that the Chevalier
Gluck, a world figure, had any small-minded tendencies, although Mozart's father was always ready to believe the worst
of him. He was warmly courteous and enthusiastic, sat in a
box at Mozart's Lenten concert in 1783, praised the music,
and invited the couple to Sunday dinner.

These two composers need not have worried about the
new boost to the German theatre. The *Nationalsingspiel* soon
disintegrated, for the good reason that an opera company
cannot subsist on one opera. Again a succession of translated
pieces and new ones ordered from local mediocrities fell flat.
The singers were drawn back into the Italian company. Mozart watched this happen with bitter disappointment. He
continued to look for a German libretto as well as an Italian
one, and when in 1785 there was a plan afoot for reopening
German opera in the *Kärntnerthortheater,* he wrote to Anton
Klein in Mannheim, who had sent him a script for consideration, and spoke of the "slackness and stupidity" which the

effort usually encountered. "If there were a single good patriot in charge, things would be different. But then, perhaps, the German national theatre which is sprouting so vigorously would actually begin to flower; and of course it would be an everlasting blot on Germany if we Germans were seriously to begin to think as Germans, to speak German, and, heaven help us, to sing in German! Do not blame me, my dear sir if I go too far in my zeal. It is because you are a fellow *German* that I speak quite freely. This is so seldom possible that after unburdening my heart I feel quite privileged to go out and get drunk."

Thus speaks the man who had just composed the first great German opera, and who would have to bide his time and make his own opportunity to compose a second and greater one.

XV
Vienna, 1782-1785

D*ie Entführung* has been called a "fiancée's opera." There is certainly a curious analogy, for Mozart was striving to "rescue" his Constanze from the degrading clutches of the shrewish mother at the very time when he was dealing with the rescue of his stage Constanze from the harem of the pasha.* His own Constanze was even "abducted" by the Baroness Waldstädten, who harbored her in her house until Mozart carried her off as his bride. He jokingly called the event *"Die Entführung aus dem Auge Gottes,"* for the house on the Petersplatz, where the Webers lived, was called "The Eye of God."

If the *Singspiel* blessed the event, it did not solve the money problems of the happy couple. Although, by Mozart's estimate, it took in 1200 gulden (about 270 ducats) in the first two nights, the composer apparently received a flat fee of 50 ducats from the Vienna Opera coffers, lost any claim on performances elsewhere, and beheld a pirated piano reduction in the shops. Money was not plentiful in the Mozarts' second-floor flat on the Hohe Brucke (now 25 Wipplingerstrasse), where the two set up housekeeping. (The mother-in-law, as Mozart made clear to his father, did not and never would live with them.) It was not long before many musicians visited their apartment, and warm friendships were formed. Much music was tried out, often supplied by Mozart himself.

---

* It was of course only an accident that Bretzner's Constanze bore the same name as Mozart's fiancée.

The concerts among friends met no grocers' bills; where the friends were patrons, the principal reward was still often in the enjoyment of music. Musical experience rather than ducats would have been derived from the meetings each Sunday from noon until two at the house of the Baron van Swieten, Commissioner of Education. (They began in 1782.) These were reading sessions, rather than performances for company, the vocal parts taken by the Baron, Mozart, and anyone else available. The purpose was to become acquainted with unknown music, and this music was mostly by Sebastian Bach and Handel. In Berlin, where the Baron had been Ambassador from Vienna to the Court of Frederick the Great from 1770 to 1778, he had acquired a taste for these composers, favored there by a conservative royal faction, but disregarded elsewhere as boresome and hopelessly outmoded contrapuntists. Van Swieten was a pompous and overbearing gentleman (he wrote symphonies which Haydn remarked were "as stiff as himself"). The composers whom he championed nevertheless proved him to be a musician of extraordinary perception: he readily singled out Bach and Handel from the past, Mozart and Haydn from the then present, and later befriended Beethoven. He became a loyal friend of Mozart, and Mozart became the willing object of his propaganda in favor of the baroque composers. There is no mention of the "old Bach" in Mozart's correspondence until this point. Of Handel, Mozart remembered that there were six fugues on a shelf at home, probably brought back from London, and he wrote immediately asking his father to send them. Remembering his own contrapuntal scores, he wrote again asking for any Masses or shorter services of his own that might be on hand, and Michael Haydn's as well. "We should also like, dearest father, some of your own church music," he tactfully added. Mozart had until then confined his fugal writing to religious scores; he had often improvised fugues on the keyboard but never wrote them down. Constanze, a listener at these Sunday gatherings, reproached him for this—a sign that her musicianship extended beyond the ability to vocalize (that common achievement among the Weber sisters) and to furnish a clavier accompaniment when needed.

This unexpected appetite for counterpoint on Constanze's part may have had something to do with Wolfgang's decision to compose the Mass in C minor. He made a vow to write a Mass in the ardor of his pledge of betrothal. He never finished the score of his Mass in C minor (K. 427), but arranged a later performance at Salzburg. The solo soprano part was then sung by Constanze—it has considerable coloratura and a wide range. Van Swieten rather than Constanze is to be credited with the impulse that brought forth this music (with its unmistakable Handelisms) in Vienna, where nothing of the sort was asked for. Later works prove how Van Swieten led Mozart (or pushed him, a willing victim) deeply into the choral part-writing of Handel and the fugal marvels of the forgotten Bach.

The irregular income in Vienna was hardly enough to support a wife who was used to living on momentary means but who never quite learned to make the most of what they had. In spite of their shabby living quarters (frequently changed but seldom for the better), the debt problems and her illnesses later (mostly connected with child-bearing), they were essentially an affectionate and a united couple. Constanze had no adequate idea until after his death that her husband was something more than a skillful musician who nevertheless had to struggle for attention and means of support. She was less literate than he, but he did not require high intellectual companionship. He was a devoted husband. His affectionate nature went out to her as it had to his parents and sister; he was considerate of her comforts, eager to cheer her when the situation was gloomy. Nissen, who married the widow Constanze in 1809 and wrote of Mozart under her eye, has made the cryptic remark that she "cared perhaps more for his talent than himself." If the affection was more on his side, he had an irresistible coaxing way, and she could not have failed to respond. Niemetschek, who knew them both, wrote: "Mozart was happy in his union with Constanze Weber. She made him a good, loving wife, who accommodated herself admirably to his ways. . . . He loved her sincerely, confided in her always, not concealing his faults, and she rewarded him with tenderness and faithful care. All Vienna knew of their mutual affection, and the widow cannot think without emotion of her days of wedded life."

Nissen tells that Mozart used to go riding at five o'clock in the morning, and would never fail to leave a note for his wife when she should wake up; for example: "Good morning, my darling wife, I hope that you have slept well, and that nothing has disturbed you; I don't want you to get up too early, not to take cold, not to stoop, not to stretch, not to scold the servants, not to fall over the doorstep. Do not be vexed over anything before my return. May nothing happen to you! I shall be back at —— o'clock."

Constanze was like Wolfgang in being fond of a good time, and had no choice but to put up with his expensive tastes. He was addicted to fine clothes. Seeing a beautiful red coat he wrote, "I must have a coat like that, for it is one that will really do justice to certain buttons that I have long been hankering after. . . . They are mother-of-pearl with white stones around the edge, and a fine yellow stone in the middle." This communication, we regret to say, was a hint addressed to the Countess von Waldstädten.

Mozart reports (January 22, 1783) an all-night dance at the apartment they had recently taken, on 17 Wipplingerstrasse, third floor. They had a large room, "1,000 feet long and 1 foot wide" Mozart jokingly called it, and had the use of two adjacent vacant rooms for their party. Their landlord was the Baron Wetzlar, a man of wealth who became a helpful friend. Mozart also attended public *Redouten,* and went to one dressed as Harlequin. He performed in a pantomime in the carnival season with a group which included his sister-in-law Aloysia as Columbine. Of course he provided the music (only fragments of a first violin part survive). He liked to cut a well-dressed figure in the noble establishments he frequented. This particular vanity must largely explain the melting away of the handsome concert returns that sometimes came to him.

It was as a clavier virtuoso and as an improviser of variations rather than as a composer that Mozart continued to be principally known in Vienna, even after *Die Entführung* had succeeded and made its way elsewhere. The Emperor, having heard him play the clavier, and being informed of a visit by Muzio Clementi, the celebrated virtuoso from London, had commanded a joint performance of the two in January, 1782. It was more than a joint recital—it was, according to a custom which would carry over into the next century, a contest, even a combat. Joseph laid a wager on Mozart, and won, by whose decision we are not told. Any evidence of hostility between the rivals would have lent zest to the occasion. This time there was none, or at least none on the surface. Mozart wrote to his father: "After we had paid each other all manner of compliments, the Emperor gave the signal that Clementi should begin—He preluded, and played a sonata. The Emperor then said to me *'Allons, d'rauf los!'* I preluded and played some variations. Then the Grand Duchess produced some sonatas by Paisiello (in his own miserable manuscript), I had to play the allegro, and Clementi the andante and rondo. Then we each took a subject and carried it out on two pianofortes. By the way, I had borrowed the Countess Thun's piano for myself, but only played upon it when I played alone. The Emperor wished it to be so. The other instrument was out of tune, and had three keys that stuck: 'Never mind,' said the Emperor.'" By stacking the cards (apparently an emperor's prerogative), he had signified his aproval of his favorite. Dittersdorf reported in his memoirs the following conversation: "Emperor—'Have you heard Mozart?' Myself—'Three times already.' Emperor—'How do you like him?' Myself—'As every connoisseur *must* like him.' Emperor—'Have you heard Clementi also?' Myself—'I have heard him also.' Emperor—'Some people prefer him to Mozart. What is your opinion? Speak out.' Myself—'In Clementi's playing there is merely art, but in Mozart's there is both art and taste.' Emperor—'That is just what I said to myself.'"

Afterward, each player gave his private opinion of the other. Clementi wrote: "I had never heard so delicate and graceful an execution." And Mozart, confidentially, to his father: "Clementi is a good player, and that is all one can say. He plays well as far as the execution of his right hand is concerned. His best point lies in passages in thirds. But he has not an atom of taste or feeling, in fact he is a mere *mechanicus*."

For this concert, Mozart received 50 ducats. On the strength of it he organized a concert for the third Sunday in Lent. He brought out selections from *Idomeneo,* his Piano Concerto in D major (K. 175), substituting a new rondo (K. 382), and at last improvising. In May, Philipp Martin, a young enthusiast from Regensburg, organized a series of concerts on Sundays in the Augarten, together with open-air serenades. The players were mostly amateurs. The concerts were sanctioned by the Emperor and were sold by subscription. Mozart presumably collected his share of the profits. At the first of them he played his two-piano Concerto in E flat with his pupil Fräulein Aurnhammer, and a symphony (probably the one in C, K. 338). These concerts were not continued, but there was an increasing demand for Mozart's own concerts in Lent, and at these, new piano concertos and occasional symphonies were expected. He asked his father on January 4, 1783, to send what scores might be on hand; the Serenade (K. 204), the symphonies (K. 182, 183, 201) and the "Haffner" Symphony (K. 385). This last he had composed for Salzburg the year before as a serenade, at his father's request, hastily, between other duties.

A concert given by Aloysia on March 11, 1783, became his, for he supplied most of the music as well as his fingers. A concert of his own on March 23 included the "Haffner" Symphony, the piano concertos, in C (K. 415) and D (K. 175), with the new finale, the Finale from the "Post Horn" Serenade (K. 320), and piano solos. Aloysia Lange sang *"Se il padre perdei"* from *Idomeneo,* and the concert rondo *"Mia speranza adorata"* (K. 416); the tenor Adamberger and the soprano Therese Teiber, who had sung in the opera, sang arias. The Emperor was in his box, and led the applause. "His delight was beyond all bounds," wrote Mozart. At a concert given by Mme. Teiber a few days later, the Emperor was again present and pointedly applauded Mozart.

Mozart planned to take his bride to Salzburg to meet his father and sister. It would be a sort of reconciliation, for the father's written approval, after the event, had an air of grudge.

There had been an interchange of polite notes, an exchange of small gifts between the sisters-in-law, which seemed insufficient to establish good relations. Constanze was painfully aware that her faulty spelling and grammar would not make a good impression. Mozart felt, as other husbands have, that a parent or sister need only to know his wife to love her as he did. The visit was necessarily postponed, first because of his spring concerts and lesson duties, then because of her first confinement, which was expected in early June, 1783, then because certain overimaginative friends had warned him that the Archbishop would have him arrested for deserting without formal dismissal.

The baby was born on June 17. "Congratulations," he wrote on the eighteenth. "You are a grandpapa! Yesterday at half past six in the morning, my dear wife was safely delivered of a fine sturdy boy, as round as a ball. Her pains began at half past one in the morning, which gave us no rest or sleep that night. At four o'clock I sent for my mother-in-law—and then for the midwife. At six o'clock the child began to appear and at half past six the trouble was over. My mother-in-law by her great kindness to her daughter has made full amends for all the harm she did her before her marriage. She spends the whole day with her."

Mozart, advised on all sides out of the bungling ignorance of the eighteenth century on child care, was afraid of milk fever, opposed alike to feeding by the mother or by a wet nurse. "I was determined that my child was not to take milk from a stranger! I wanted the child to be brought up on water like my sister and myself." He was talked out of this last theory. What nourishment was decided upon does not appear. Wolfgang and Constanze departed at last for Salzburg at the end of July, presumably leaving their baby (christened Raimund Leopold) behind, in whose care we are not told, for the letters naturally cease during the visit, which was to last three months. The child died on August 21. To survive babyhood was indeed a problem in those days.

Constanze's reception at Salzburg was polite but strained. The father's bitterness was too apparent. Marianne's attempt to be agreeable was stilted and unconvincing. The visit lasted through the summer, and the crowded condition of the household, which included three pupils of Leopold, did not make the situation easier. Throughout the visit, Mozart continued to be musically active. There were conferences with the Abbé Varesco, for Mozart was in search of an Italian libretto for an *opera buffa* that Vienna might accept, and he turned to his friend, the Italian adapter of *Idomeneo*. Varesco worked industriously on what was to be called *"L'oca del Cairo."* The subject was not too promising nor was the "poet" a master of wit. Mozart nevertheless was soon deep in the music for the first act. The Mass in C minor (K. 427), which he had composed with Constanze in mind, was performed in St. Peter's Church on August 25, Constanze taking the soprano part. The Mass was incomplete, and movements were presumably borrowed from earlier scores. Michael Haydn had been ordered by the Archbishop to provide duets for violin and viola. When Mozart heard that he was ill and could not compose, he went to his friend's bedside and wrote for him the beautiful unaccompanied duets (K. 423, 424). They were performed as Haydn's, nor did the Archbishop detect in them Mozart's obvious workmanship.

Mozart returned to Vienna on October 30, 1783, laden with sketches for his intended opera, but stopped at Linz long enough to give a concert on November 4. Since he had no symphony with him, he composed one on the spot (almost certainly K. 425). A more immediate and practical reason pushed *L'oca del Cairo* aside. He wrote his father on February 10, 1784: "I have works which at the moment are bringing in money." These money-making "works" which caused him so readily to put away his opera sketches were nothing less than the six piano concertos of 1784—six superb masterpieces which reached a new peak in his music and set a pattern for the matching of piano and orchestra in a way that had never been and never would be approached by another. These six (K. 449, 450, 451, 453, 456, 459), of extraordinary diversity and elevation, showing no lapse in a single bar into routine, are the more astonishing as the unquestioning fulfillment of the demands of the moment, in the scant hours at his disposal. "The whole morning is taken up with pupils," he wrote, "and almost every evening I have to play." The would-be opera composer could not think of opera in Lent, for he became in the spring of 1784 the most popular clavier player in Vienna, and he was wanted on every side. A list of twenty-two engagements between February 26 and April 3, noted down for his father, tells the story. Most of them were given in the salons of Prince Galitzin and Count Jean Esterhazy, two of the numerous nobles who ardently cultivated music and gave private concerts and even private opera performances for their guests. Four concerts were given by Mozart on a subscription basis in this period. The Concerto in E flat (K. 449)* was completed on February 9, the Concerto in B flat (K. 450) on March 15, the Concerto in D major (K. 451) on March 22, the Concerto in G major (K. 453) on April 12. The Quintet for Piano and Winds (K. 452) he wrote for these concerts on March 30. Composing a concerto involved also writing out parts, rehearsing and performing. Mozart sometimes did not have time to write the score, but only the various parts, which he would give to a copyist to duplicate. The piano part existed mostly in his head. The manuscript would have little more than blank staves with cues or an occasional modulation indicated.

This feat, one of the most incredible miracles of the creative Mozart, was apparently not regarded by him or his father as a miracle but simply as in the day's work. Mozart until this moment had never in his letters spoken of the quality of a new work, but only of its acceptability and its success, duly reported for his father's satisfaction. Now for the first time he shows pride in what he had done. Sending home the copies of the first four concertos, he asks curiously for the family's preference. This elation is natural, for the composer had, almost to his own surprise, felt his powers deepen, become more resourceful, more subtle, and at the same time more abundant than ever before. The same burgeoning transformed and lifted another medium, the string

---

* Written for his pupil, Barbara Ployer. The Concerto in B flat (K. 456) and the one in F (K. 459) are dated September 30 and December 11.

quartet. The six which he dedicated to Joseph Haydn were composed between 1782 and 1785.

To musical Vienna, which meant mostly the nobility, Mozart was a wonderful pianist rather than a composer. He could write his own concertos as any piano virtuoso was expected to do. His sonatas, particularly the easier ones, were cultivated, his opera was praised, but little remembered after its one season. His string quartets were found puzzling and too involved. This opinion was shared by the royal dilettante Joseph of Austria, who cultivated string quartets, but rejected Haydn's and Mozart's in favor of simpler ones by their more obliging contemporaries.

For his piano playing and for his agreeable ways, Mozart was invited to many a noble house, and treated to many a meal. The extent of his popularity is proved by a list which he put down for his father of 182 subscribers to his concerts in 1784, most of them princes, counts, barons, or their wives. Those were occasions when any titled person who wished to be considered a musical connoisseur could hardly have afforded to be absent. In Lent of the following year, Leopold made his first visit to Vienna since Mozart had settled there. A letter to his daughter reports what he has seen and heard. The old man's pride in his son's success was dampened by the fact that Wolfgang had accomplished the long-sought goal quite by himself. From the moment of Leopold's arrival, at one o'clock on Friday, February 11, 1785, life became a continual round of visits, rehearsals and concerts. After a concert at the Mehlgrube on the very first evening, he wrote to his daughter: "We had a new and very fine concerto by Wolfgang [in D minor, K. 466], which the copyist was still working on when we arrived, and its rondo which your brother did not even have time to play through since he had to supervise the copying.* You can well imagine that I met many acquaintances there who all came up to speak to me."

Leopold was taken to a quartet session with Haydn, and on the next evening to another concert. "Your brother played a glorious concerto which he composed for Mlle. Paradis

---

* Supervision of copyists was necessary to prevent not only errors but theft.

in Paris [in B flat, K. 456]. I was sitting only two boxes away from the very beautiful Princess of Württemberg and had the great pleasure of hearing so clearly all the interplay of the instruments that for sheer delight tears came into my eyes. When your brother left the platform the Emperor waved his hat and called out 'Bravo, Mozart!' " This was Sunday, February 15. On Tuesday Mozart played the D minor Concerto again, "most magnificently." On Wednesday there was another concert at the house of Herr von Ployer from Salzburg. Leopold notes that Mozart had "fine quarters" on the Schulerstrasse, that his rent of 460 gulden was more than covered by his receipts from a single concert. He figured that Wolfgang, if free of debt, should be able to put 2,000 in the bank. In the course of the week there were more concerts. He was entertained at lunch in various houses, including that of Frau Weber, who turned out to have one point in her favor—she was a good cook. It was lavish fare for Lent, but not as lavish as the pheasants, oysters, glacé fruits and champagne later served by the junior Stephanie. Two days later the actor Müller entertained him with twenty others. "We never get to bed before one o'clock and I never get up before nine. We lunch at two or half past. . . . Every day there are concerts, and the whole time is given up to teaching, music, composing and so forth. I feel rather out of it all. If only the concerts were over! It is impossible for me to describe the rush and bustle. Since my arrival your brother's fortepiano has been taken at least a dozen times to the theatre or to someone's house." Leopold, returning to Salzburg, bewildered by the furious pace of musical and social life in Vienna, was destined never to see his son again. He had seen at its peak the acclaim that surrounded Mozart as pianist and the accompanying gold. The vogue was not to last.

Whether or not Leopold was more impressed by what his son was composing than by the glitter of gold and social success, he certainly should have been. When he went on February 12 to a reading session of Mozart's newest quartets, the last three of the six to be dedicated to Haydn, Haydn, whom he may have met for the first time, spoke to him earnestly. "Haydn said to me," Leopold reported to his daughter (February 16): " 'Before God and as an honest man I tell you that your son is the greatest composer known to me either in person or by name. He has taste* and, what is more, the most profound knowledge of composition.' "

Impressed as he must have been, Leopold could not have realized the full import of this remark. That he was puzzled by certain passages in his son's works is indicated by his expressed doubts over the sharps and flats on receiving the copyist's parts for the Piano Concerto in C (K. 467). The introduction to the last of the "Haydn" quartets (K. 465) was not recognized by those who first encountered it, as a poignant and newly significant dissonance in Mozart's writing.

Mozart wrote (in Italian) this touching dedication of the six quartets to Haydn:

To my dear friend Haydn!

A father who had decided to send his children into the world at large, thought best to entrust them to the protection and guidance of a famous man who fortunately happened to be his best friend as well. Behold here, famous man and best friend, my six children. They are, to be sure, the fruit of long and arduous work, yet some friends have encouraged me to assume that these children will not go quite unregarded, and this flatters me into believing that they may one day bring me some comfort. You yourself, dearest friend, have shown me your approval of them during our last stay in this capital. Your praise above all encourages me to recommend them to you, and leads me to hope that they will not be entirely unworthy of your good will. May it please you therefore to receive them kindly and to be their father, their guide and their friend. From this moment I surrender to you all my rights in them, but beg you to regard with leniency the faults which may have remained hidden to the partial eye of their father, and, notwithstanding their shortcomings, to persist in your noble friendship for him who loves them so dearly. Meanwhile I am from all my heart, etc.,

W. A. Mozart

Vienna, September 1, 1785

---

* "*Geschmack*," used by connoisseurs at the time, would have meant a distinguished sensitiveness to beauty.

The music tells us even more eloquently than these words how Mozart had become engrossed in the possibilities opened up by Haydn. In his turn he wrote quartets of greater subtlety and depth of feeling. Haydn was then in turn influenced by the workmanship of the younger man. The esteem, the indebtedness of each to the other was freely admitted by them both. Mozart remarked to a friend who expressed surprise at his dedication of the quartets: "It was due from me, for it was from Haydn that I learned how quartets should be written." Niemetschek wrote: "It was quite affecting to hear him speak of the two Haydns or any other of the great masters; one would have imagined him to be one of their enthusiastic pupils rather than the all-powerful Mozart." Haydn missed no opportunity to point out Mozart's extraordinary genius. His admiration was not confined to the quartets. Carpani has quoted him as saying that he had never heard one of Mozart's compositions without learning something from it. After Mozart's death he once declared that if his friend had written nothing but the quartets and the *Requiem* he would have sufficient claim to immortality. When Haydn was asked by the intendant at Prague in 1787 to provide an opera for production with *Figaro* and *Don Giovanni,* he wrote that he refused to put himself "in competition with the great Mozart." He added: "If I could only inspire every lover of music, especially among the great, with feelings as deep, and comprehension as clear as my own in listening to the inimitable works of Mozart, then surely the nations would contend for the possession of such a jewel within their borders. Prague must strive to retain the treasure within her grasp—but not without fitting reward. The want of this saddens the life of a great genius, and offers small encouragement for further efforts to follow. I feel indignant that Mozart has not been engaged at any imperial or royal court. Pardon my wandering from the subject—Mozart is a man very dear to me."

The friendship between the two men has been attested to by a number of those who saw them together. They used the familiar *"du,"* then unusual between an older and younger man (Haydn was fifty-three at the time of the dedication of the quartets; Mozart was twenty-nine). Mozart always called Haydn "Papa." Haydn was then little regarded in Vienna. He was an outsider, for he had a Hungarian patron. His operas were not even considered. His quartets were disregarded in favor of simpler, more conventionally agreeable ones. His liberties in modulation, his whimsical humor, were adversely criticized.

This very neglect of the two foremost living composers in their time drew them together, for each understood the importance of the other as did no one else. There has never been such a close, such a mutually helpful association of two composers before or since. Together, they developed the string quartet from a rudimentary chamber sonata into the most intimately expressive of all instrumental forms, the most subtle of all chamber forms, and provided a basis without which Beethoven could never have written what he did.

XVI

Vienna, 1784-1786

THE RE-ESTABLISHMENT, by Imperial wish, of an Italian opera company in Vienna in 1783 (specifically by the performance of Salieri's *opera buffa, La scuola dei gelosi* on April 22) was an important development for Mozart. Not that he was asked to partake in it, for the Emperor still looked upon him as a pianist and did not even consider him as a prospect for Italian opera. Mozart felt differently, as will soon appear. An immediate effect of the operatic development was to bring a number of musicians into his life. Two Italians of the older generation, Giovanni Paisiello and Giuseppe Sarti, visited Vienna in 1784. Paisiello had befriended Mozart in Naples years before, and Mozart had long known his music well and was influenced by his graceful style. Both newcomers were cordial, and to both he responded by using a popular theme from one opera by each for a set of variations.*

Mozart acquired as pupils in 1785 two young Englishmen drawn to Vienna by the operatic magnet, who not only became close companions as well, but led to the formation of a jovial British group often to be found at his house. Thomas Attwood, aged twenty, and Stephen Storace, twenty-two,

---

* Paisiello's *Salve tu, Domine* (K. 398); and *Come un agnello* (K. 460) from Sarti's *Fra due litiganti*. This air he would later introduce into the supper scene of *Don Giovanni*. Sarti's later criticism of the string quartets as the work of a clavier player chained to enharmonic relationships argues honest professional obtuseness rather than ill will.

both studied composition with him. Stephen was soon to succeed as an opera composer in Vienna and London. He was also a good singer, and his sister Nancy (Ann Selina), nineteen, was a still better one. She had achieved the status in Italy of prima donna, and had been engaged in Vienna for the newly formed Italian opera. She was destined to be the first Susanna in *Figaro*. Michael Kelly, an Irish tenor, born in Dublin in 1762, came from Italy, where he had adapted himself to the operatic surroundings in Naples and Rome, Florence and Venice, and had won a special reputation for his acting in comedy. He was to be engaged for the same opera in the two parts of the wily Don Basilio, and Curzio, the stuttering advocate.

Mozart's lesson-giving hours were not all tedious. Johann Nepomuk Hummel was the youngest of his pupils, and came to him at the age of nine. Mozart kept "Hans" in his house, grew fond of him, and put him to use when a piano part was to be played. Mozart would sometimes correct the exercises of a pupil with more than half an eye on a game of bowling, or he would put him to a test of billiards instead of harmony. The pupils never resented this—no one expected laborious method from Mozart. Those who were at all capable found inspiration in him. Michael Kelly, who could write a melody as well as sing one, asked to be taught how to make a full harmonic setting. Mozart tactfully advised him not to plunge into the intricacies of composition at that advanced point of his career as singing actor. " 'You may take my word for it,' " Kelly quotes him as saying, " 'Nature has made you a melodist, and you would only disturb and perplex yourself. . . . Melody is the essence of music. *I* compare a good melodist to a fine racer, and contrapuntists to hack post-horses, therefore be advised, let *well alone,* and remember the old Italian proverb—*"chi sa più, meno sa"*—Who knows most knows least.' The opinion of this great man made on me a lasting impression."

Kelly describes Mozart in his entertaining memoirs with an esteem amounting to adoration. Allowing for the fact that he wrote them in 1826, when Mozart had become generally deified and when to have known him was something to boast about, there is no mistaking the genuine affection and comradeship between the two. Kelly describes quartet evenings at which Haydn and Dittersdorf took the first and second violin parts, Mozart the viola and Vanhall the cello. Mozart usually

> favored the company by performing fantasias and capriccios on the piano-forte. His feeling, the great execution and strength of his left hand, particularly, and the apparent inspiration of his modulations, astounded me. After this splendid performance we sat down to supper and I had the pleasure to be placed at table between him and his wife, Madame Constance Weber, a German lady of whom he was passionately fond, and by whom he had three children.* . . .
>
> After supper the young branches of our host had a dance and Mozart joined them. Madame Mozart told me that great as his genius was, he was an enthusiast in dancing, and often said that his taste lay in that art, rather than in music.
>
> He was a remarkably small man, very thin and pale, with a profusion of fine, fair hair, of which he was rather vain. He gave me a cordial invitation to his house, of which I availed myself, and passed a great part of my time there. He always received me with kindness and hospitality. He was remarkably fond of punch, of which beverage I have seen him take copious draughts. He was also fond of billiards, and had an excellent billiard table in his house. Many and many a game have I played with him, but always came off second best. He gave Sunday concerts, at which I never was missing. He was kindhearted and always ready to oblige, but so very particular when he played that, if the slightest noise were made, he instantly left off.

We can be sure that Mozart would not do this in such a way as to cast a chill of reproach upon his guests, as his friend Baron van Swieten did at his own house with his terrifying frown of disapproval. When we read of the listening habits of those days, we can understand that something had to be done if the music was to be heard at all. The lengths of divertimentos, often played at banquets, and their numerous repeats were adjusted to the tendency of the guests to

---

* The Mozarts actually had six children, of whom four died in infancy.

converse freely and listen when and where they pleased. An effective movement in a symphony or a concerto was punctuated with bravos and often encored. Box holders at the opera would occupy themselves by visiting back and forth, playing cards, or eating ices. Chatter would cease only when the prima donna or primo uomo stepped to the footlights to deliver an important aria, and this would often be accompanied by shouts of acclaim, or abuse.

When the Italian opera company was in process of reorganization in Vienna, the German project having fallen into disuse, Mozart was at once aware that he might be able at last to be heard there in an *opera buffa*. Since no offer came to him, he began to make a personal search for a libretto. He was now determined that the book must conform to his musical scheme and not the reverse. "I have not found a single satisfactory one," he wrote his father. "So many changes would have to be made that, even if the poet would undertake them, he could more easily write an entirely new text." He was becoming libretto-conscious and taking the matter into his own hands. The hunt was discouraging, for librettos in those days were mostly dull and tradition-ridden, built altogether on type characters in stock comic situations.

A new poet had lately arrived in Vienna, Lorenzo da Ponte. He was quite inexperienced as a librettist, but had almost at once insinuated himself into a position of favor at court. Mozart met him, but hesitated. There was no way to sample his abilities or adaptabilities. On top of this, Da Ponte was an Italian and therefore suspect; he might be in secret league with Salieri. He promised to write a new libretto for Mozart, but this might be nothing more than voluble talk. Mozart reported the conversation to his father, and added: "Who knows whether he will be able—or willing —to keep his word?" Obedient to fatherly advice, he was counting on no one, and watching for every chance. He urged his father to approach Varesco, to propitiate him for past liberties taken with the *Idomeneo* text, and sound him out for a good *opera buffa*. "It must be really comic." It must "introduce two equally good female parts, one of those to be *seria,* the other *mezzo-carattere. . . .* The third female character, however, may be entirely *buffa,* and so may all the male ones, if necessary." Here we have the prescription for *Figaro* to come. The specifications are significant in showing that he had already sized up the troupe for which he was to compose; they are still more significant in that they reveal his intention of drawing upon serious opera custom for developed characters to be turned into high comedy, and set side by side with *buffo* farce. Mozart did not yet mention *Figaro.* He may have received the text of the play *Le Mariage de Figaro* from Beaumarchais whom he had met in the year previous. Its more farcical predecessor, *Le Barbier de Séville,* would have suited him far less well. Paisiello's setting of this he would have missed, for its production on August 13, 1783, took place during his visit to Salzburg.

His effort to extract a libretto from Varesco in Salzburg was bound to have been unfruitful, for Varesco was quite lacking in the kind of wit he needed. Varesco had prepared a text called *L'oca del Cairo,* about a lover who conceals himself in a sort of mechanical goose and so makes his way into a stronghold to rescue his lady. The script was labored and inept. Mozart gave it up after composing the first act, and worked upon another of its kind, *Lo sposo deluso,* which he also abandoned.* After laying aside his operatic sketches for his series of concerts in Lent, he was reluctant to take up again tasks which had reached no proper degree of ardor, and while he searched elsewhere his association with Da Ponte was renewed and more warmly developed. When they found a subject and began to work upon it, one of the rarest of all collaborations for stage music was at once happily established.

Da Ponte was a Venetian Jew (Emmanuele Conegliano) who had taken Christian orders at fourteen, and had adopted the name of his bishop patron. He was an adventurer, still looking for a foothold, and so far without operatic experience. Banished from Venice for immoral conduct, he had not dared show his face in Vienna while the moral reformer Maria Theresa was alive. He arrived there in 1782 with a

---

* Alfred Einstein believed that Lorenzo da Ponte was the author of *"The Deceived Husband."*

letter of introduction to Salieri, and on the death of Metastasio in that year he had made use of his genius for ingratiating himself in high places, hoping to be appointed by the Emperor as *"poeta cesareo,"* or poet to the throne, over Giambattista Casti, also a newcomer but undoubtedly his literary superior. Da Ponte's first assignment was an opera for Salieri, *Il ricco d'un giorno*. *Riches for a Day* (December, 1784) fell flat because of an impossible subject, not of his own choosing, so Da Ponte is careful to explain in his memoirs. Salieri, disgusted, turned to Casti, now a direct rival. The result, *La grotta di Trofonio* (October, 1785) was well received, and Da Ponte was put into the position of having to prove himself worthy of his high trust. He at once turned to two composers, both of whom were yet to have their Viennese baptism in *opera buffa*—to Martín y Soler, the Spanish composer who had recently come to Vienna, and to Mozart, whom he had met at Wetzlar's house in 1783. He had obtained the Emperor's support for a collaboration with Martín.

Mozart did not share Martín's royal favor—in fact the Emperor showed no particular interest in him. This left Da Ponte hesitant about tying himself with a composer entirely unsupported. Mozart had hit upon Beaumarchais' play, *La Folle journée,* or *Le Mariage de Figaro,* quite by himself, for Da Ponte admits as much. Mozart must also have been full of its possibilities and communicated his enthusiasm to Wetzlar, his friend and benefactor as well as his landlord, for Wetzlar sang its praises before Da Ponte, and even offered to back the project of *Figaro* in London if it should not be taken in Vienna. Da Ponte agreed to translate the play into an Italian libretto. Mozart was hard at work on the music in November, 1785. Meanwhile, Martín quickly set Da Ponte's adaptation of Goldoni's play *Il burbero di buon' cuore,* which was produced on January 4, 1786. Obviously Da Ponte was not going to risk his fortune with a single composer, especially an unaccepted one. It is hard to believe that he approached the yet unproven Mozart with any true perception of his abilities. To be sure he wrote in his memoirs, with the eloquent hindsight of 1823, how he had lifted from neglect and obscurity "the priceless jewel buried in the bowels of the earth and hiding the refulgent excellence of its splendors." It is doubtful whether at the time the poet had much idea of the pricelessness of the jewel, for his understanding of music was confined to its verbal needs, and his judgment of it throughout his memoirs is determined invariably by the degree of glory each collaboration brought to himself.

It is particularly significant that *The Marriage of Figaro* was Mozart's initial choice. It was a bold choice for many reasons. It was, in the exclusively French sophisticated theatrical manner, too long, with too many characters to accommodate the usual *buffo* custom of six. Mozart's father thought the choice unwise, considered the play "tedious," and foresaw headaches as between composer and librettist. He was wrong on both counts—the two seem to have embraced it as anything but tedious, and worked it out readily enough. Da Ponte found a point in the fact that Louis XVI had at first banned the play in France as "immoral" and thereby created an enormous curiosity and interest in it. It had been finally produced in Paris on April 27, 1784. In Vienna it was prohibited. Whether Joseph would acquiesce to the opera remained to be seen. The two decided that instead of bringing a summary refusal on their project they would risk their labors, quietly complete the score, and present it to the monarch as an accomplished fact. This in itself indicates Da Ponte's faith in Mozart as well as in *Figaro*.

Da Ponte relates that they went at it together and finished *Le nozze di Figaro* in six weeks. It probably took more, for Mozart was at work upon it at the beginning of November, and put down in his own record that the overture was completed April 29, 1786, which was two days before the first performance. He wrote the overture last of all to allow the fullest time for the stage rehearsals.

Da Ponte proved to be not only Mozart's principal librettist—he was the only adequate one he ever found. His sense of the theatre was keen. His usefulness to Mozart in making singable syllables, witty turns of phrase, good versification for arias, and effective theatrical continuity are constantly evident in *Figaro* and *Don Giovanni*. When he was thrown upon his own resources for a story, as in *Così fan tutte,* the result was far from a masterpiece until Mozart made it one. *Figaro* was conspicuously his best libretto because it was a fairly close translation, speech by speech, a condensation and an adaptation to musical purposes of a first-rate piece of stage literature. To realize Da Ponte's brilliant part in the deed, one need only compare it to the frank *buffo* convenience of *Le Barbier de Séville* as translated by Petrosellini for Paisiello in 1782, and Sterbini's similar job for Rossini in the next century.* Da Ponte preserved in *Figaro* the distinction of the satire, its elegance and colloquial charm, while eliminating its wordier by-play. Beyond any doubt he served Mozart well. Without his contribution the play could not have been immortalized in music.

In another sense, Mozart found in Da Ponte a fortunate co-worker. Never good at pushing his own advantage, he needed an adroit courtier who could counter intrigue with his own brand of tact. Da Ponte tells us of how he went to Joseph with the score under his arm, and told him what the two had been doing.

"What?" he said, "Don't you know that Mozart, although a wonder at instrumental music, has written only one opera, and nothing remarkable at that?"

"Yes Sire," I replied quietly, "but with your Majesty's clemency I would have written but one drama in Vienna."

"That may be true," he answered, "but this *Mariage de Figaro*—I have just forbidden the German theatre to use it!"

"Yes Sire," I answered, "but I was writing an opera, and not a comedy. I had to omit many scenes and to cut others quite considerably. I have omitted or cut anything that might offend good taste or public decency. It will be a production which your Sovereign Majesty may well patronize. The music, I may add, as far as I may judge it, seems to me marvelously beautiful."

"Good! If that is the case, I will rely on your taste as to the

---

* *The Barber of Seville* would in any case have been inferior material for Mozart. It was little more than broad farce. It had been originally designed by Beaumarchais as a play with musical numbers.

music and on your wisdom as to the morality. Send the score to the copyist."

Da Ponte's claim to have cut out the offensive passages in the play was partly true. Figaro's inflammatory speech against the sorry lot of the soldier-pawn is deprived of its bitterness in *"Non più andrai"*;* his long and ferocious attack in the last act on the injustice of noble privilege becomes in *"Aprite un po' quegl'occhi"* nothing more than Figaro's disillusion about women in general and Susanna in particular. The dialogue is elsewhere toned down, legitimately so, since both composer and librettist were aiming at a gay social satire rather than a subversive one, quite aside from the risk of censorship. In any case, the text had to be condensed to plot essentials, reduced from five acts to four, which was still at least one more than operatic custom. The two collaborators had to eliminate all leisurely dialogue to make way for the expansions and repetitions of musical form. Mozart naturally lingered upon the emotional experience of his characters, but gained time in concerted plot development by rapid and closely integrated ensembles. In an introduction to the first printed libretto, Da Ponte apologizes for the unavoidable length of his book, which he hopes will be compensated by "our special purpose, which is to offer a new type of spectacle to a public of refined taste and assured understanding." He seems to have been more concerned that his public might miss the subtleties of *Figaro* than that they might be disturbed by its morals, for this aspect he does not even mention. Nevertheless, the "immorality" which Louis had objected to remained the ineradicable thesis: a noble count presented in the worst possible light as at once lecherous and jealously suspicious of his loyal and innocent wife, lusting after his wife's personal maid, who is also his servant's fiancée, outwitted and insolently exposed by the servant himself. Napoleon's remark about the play, quoted by St. Beuve: *"C'était la révolution déja en action"* does not

---

* Beaumarchais ends the speech: "A good soldier, *morbleu!* Weather-beaten, ill clad, carrying a heavy gun, right, left, forward, march to glory, and never swerve from your course—unless of course a cannon shot . . ."

make it deliberately inflammatory. On the surface, it is a straightforward depiction of a social condition. Beaumarchais stated in his long apologia, with a sly air of innocence, that he was no more than presenting types as he saw them, and as all others were at liberty to see them and draw their own conclusions.

Vienna was not disturbed by implications or "immoralities." Nor was Mozart concerned with anything except to clothe the very human characters and their intrigues with captivating music. He creates in Cherubino a charming picture of young adolescent fervor, a Susanna who is loyal, lovable, and sufficiently pert, a gentle and forbearing countess, a contriving Figaro who wins our sympathy by his wit in saving for himself a virtuous bride. These persons created by music dwell in our hearts through the generations, infinitely more alive, more close to us than the excellently drawn but sometimes bookish figures of Beaumarchais. Beaumarchais indeed designed the characters. Da Ponte faithfully transferred them. Mozart through the more direct, more emotionally probing art of music, responding to the task with his own human understanding, gave them actual, pulsing life. The axiom that opera is an "artificial form" is momentarily defeated when a great composer is so engrossed in his characters and so engrosses the hearer as in this case. It has happened rarely, perhaps in Wagner's Sachs, Debussy's Mélisande, Strauss's Marschallin. Nowhere else has Mozart given us the true inner being, the intimate moods of his characters as in *Figaro*. There is no more vivid demonstration than this one of the intimate delineative power of music as compared to fiction or the spoken stage.

Mozart readily laid aside his score when other music was called for. The Emperor ordered a one-act opera *"Der Schauspieldirektor"* for the entertainment of the Governor-General of the Netherlands on February 7, 1786, and this was performed in the small theatre at Schönbrunn. The text by Stephanie is overburdened with talk, but the subject lent itself to humorous contrast between a sentimental and a bravura singer. It was an old and much used subject. Mozart missed not a point in lampooning both while giving each an effective number. Also in this period, concerts, lessons and the fulfillment of composing obligations continued. The thematic catalogue which he then kept shows the three magnificent piano concertos, in E flat (K. 482), A (K. 488), and C minor (K. 491), and the Violin Sonata in E flat (K. 481).

Meanwhile other composers were pushing for precedence in the mounting of their own operas—this according to Michael Kelly. "There were three operas now on the tapis," he wrote in his *Reminiscences*.

> One by Regini [Righini's *Il demogorgone*], another by Salieri (*The Grotto of Trophonius**), and one by Mozart, by special command of the Emperor. . . . Each composer claimed the right of producing his opera for the first. The contest raised much discord, and parties were formed. The characters of the three men were all very different. Mozart was as touchy as gunpowder, and swore he would put the score of his opera into the fire if it was not produced first. His claim was backed by a strong party: on the contrary, Regini was working like a mole in the dark to get precedence.
>
> The third candidate was *Maestro di Cappella* to the court [Salieri], a clever shrewd man, possessed of what Bacon called crooked wisdom, and his claims were backed by three of the principal performers, who formed a cabal not easily put down. Every one in the opera took part in the contest. I alone was a stickler for Mozart, and naturally enough, for he had a claim on my warmest wishes, from my adoration of his powerful genius, and the debt of gratitude I owed him, for many personal favours.
>
> The mighty contest was put an end to by his Majesty issuing a mandate for Mozart's *"Nozze di Figaro,"* to be instantly put into rehearsal; and none more than Michael O'Kelly, enjoyed the little great man's triumph over his rivals.†

---

* Kelly's memory was at fault about Salieri's opera, which was produced on October 12, 1785, a month before Mozart began to compose *Figaro*.

† Michael Kelly had appeared on the bills in Italy as "Ochelli," and the name stuck. He sang both Don Basilio and Don Curzio—a double chance for his special clowning ability. He insisted upon making Don Curzio stutter, according to the text of Beaumarchais, and so established an operatic tradition. Nancy Storace sang Susanna.

Kelly, like the other members in the original cast, had the advantage of the

instruction of the composer, who transfused into their minds his inspired meaning. I shall never forget his little animated countenance when lighted up with the glowing rays of genius; —it is as impossible to describe it as it would be to paint sunbeams—I remember at the first rehearsal of the full band, Mozart was on the stage with his crimson pelisse and gold-laced cocked hat, giving the time of the music to the orchestra. Figaro's song, *"Non più andrai, farfallone amoroso,"* Bennuci gave with the greatest animation and power of voice.

I was standing close to Mozart, who, *sotto voce,* was repeating Bravo! Bravo! Bennuci; and when Bennuci came to the fine passage, *"Cherubino, alla vittoria, alla gloria militar,"* which he gave out with stentorian lungs, the effect was electricity itself, for the whole of the performers on the stage, and those in the orchestra, as if actuated by one feeling of delight, vociferated *"Bravo! Bravo Maestro, Viva, viva, grande Mozart."*

Even during the late stages of the rehearsals there was underground activity, and Da Ponte found that there was something brewing between Casti, the rival poet, and Count Rosenberg, the theatrical director. Da Ponte tells how the Count, finding that there was to be a ballet in *Figaro,* and that this could be objected to as against regulations, had a sharp interview with him and tore out the pages from the libretto at this point. Da Ponte knew how to counter this kind of sniping. The Emperor attended the dress rehearsal, and was mystified when, in the wedding celebration of Act III,* the music continued without dancing or singing, while the Count and Susanna made silent gestures. Da Ponte showed him the score and he ordered the ballet dancers summoned at once.

Da Ponte wrote of the opening (May 1, 1776): "In spite of the Count, of Casti, and a hundred devils, it was a success with the public." Of course he must add: "The libretto too was reputed beautiful." Kelly wrote: "Never was anything more

---

* Da Ponte could not have remembered his librettos very well—he mentions the ballet as occurring "at the end of the first act."

complete, than the triumph of Mozart, and his *Nozze di Figaro,* to which numerous overflowing audiences bore witness." Unfortunately, the record does not bear this out. *Le nozze di Figaro* was warmly applauded, but not more so than most of the pieces then put on; far less so than Martín's *Il burbero di buon' cuore,* which preceded it, or the same composer's *Una cosa rara,* which shortly followed. *Figaro* was not heard again in Vienna until 1789. There can be only one reason for this. The countless subtleties of the orchestral score, its descriptive detail supporting the characterization in the vocal parts, the shaping of melodic development to the moment, the complexity of the ensembles, their swift dramatic progress—all these points, grasped in part by trained musicians working with the score, were missed by a casual audience accustomed to a broader *buffo* treatment.

The descent of Mozart's material fortunes through the last four years of his life can be accounted for in no other way than by just this tendency toward subtilization in his music. Although admired, befriended by many, he had developed to a point beyond the ready comprehension of the majority in Vienna, and this included many of the professional musicians as well. It was in vain for Haydn to praise his quartets. The set of six dedicated to him were published with some hesitancy by Artaria and had no sale. Those six had reached a new degree of balanced subtlety in detail which was to be even further refined in the last quartets and quintets. The piano concertos of 1785 were more quickly applauded. Here too there was refinement of detail in orchestral treatment, modulatory boldness, fantasy which seemed wayward. The composer at the piano, marvelously adept, easily overrode resistance to the unusual. The transparent combination of the light pianos and light orchestras of the time, the whole deliberately contrived to entertain, could not fail to please even a dull audience. Mozart had written to his father (December 28, 1782) of the piano concertos (K. 413, 414, 415), that they were at "a happy halfway point between what is too easy and what is too difficult; they are very brilliant, pleasing to the ear and natural, without being empty." They had in them something for the "connoisseurs" and something for the uninitiated, whereby everybody was pleased. This was one of the rare cases where Mozart spoke of his aim as artist. The attitude applies to all the music he wrote. Making music was to him giving pleasure—the impulse was natural and instinctive. To let his personal fantasy take hold, but so adroitly as not to upset the "less learned," was quite to his purpose. The obligation to please was inherent in his training from childhood. It was taken for granted by father and son as a requisite for survival. If Mozart had lived long enough to win general acceptance as among the "great," as a figure of authority, he might have been bolder in his music, less complacent in the patterns of custom. As it was, he showed no sign of being restive or impatient with the path of convention. He never felt moved to defy custom, to pursue personal fantasy with disregard of his audience. He was neither the challenging artist at odds with his time, nor the despicable caterer to fashion. He was before all others an artist of instinctive inner equilibrium. He never bothered himself with aesthetic problems, but with complete assurance and infinite resource simply met the moment in a persuasive way that solved problems by not ever bringing them up. This applies to every form, but most spectacularly to the debated form of opera.

We of a later century find it difficult to understand how any music of Mozart could have been found disturbing by contemporary audiences, or even unappealing. The wealthy population of Vienna, supposedly avid for music, were quite able to forget him. His spring concerts, once so profitable, fell off for lack of subscribers, and ceased. He wrote only two piano concertos after 1786, (K. 537 and 595), and they were for private uses. He apparently never wrote a symphony expressly for performance in Vienna. Through the Vienna decade he wrote one for Linz (K. 425), and one for Prague (K. 504). There is no good indication that the three great symphonies of 1788 were performed at all in his lifetime. Thus the creative course of a great artist could be controlled by momentary circumstances. Because Viennese taste was principally interested in piano concertos, piano solos and vocal numbers, and an occasional symphony to piece out, not necessarily a new one, Mozart composed only five during the ten years of his full maturity. The final three he may have composed as a spontaneous outlet after an accumulation, stimulated by Haydn's example, of unexpressed power in the greatest of instrumental forms. Viennese taste on the other hand may be thanked for the masterly and incomparable piano concertos of these same years.

The two Masses of the Vienna period, the first of them unbidden, also give the impression of pent-up energy, the release of zeal for a favorite form which has been long in abeyance. *Eine kleine Nachtmusik,* an idealized serenade, may also have been the fulfillment for his own pleasure of a type of music no longer called for. Mozart's most intensive efforts in Vienna were concentrated upon opera. His heart was in the opera house, over and above the fact that in opera lay fame and success. Recognition came too slowly in Vienna, more slowly than in Prague, or in a mounting succession of German theatres.

Figaro ran through nine performances until December, at which point Martín's *Una cosa rara* superseded it and engaged Vienna's delighted attention. As usual *Figaro* brought its composer nothing beyond the initial flat fee of 100 ducats and presumably the customary proceeds from a single benefit performance. His family cares increased. His second child, Karl Thomas, born on September 21, 1784, fifteen months after his first, was destined to survive him. He became a pianist of a sort, but had a non-musical official career and died in 1858. A third child, christened Karl Johann Thomas Leopold (again his father was remembered), was born on October 18, 1786, and died a month later (November 15).

Mozart, realizing by hard necessity that he had no immediate prospect of regular income from the court, and musical rather than financial satisfaction from his activities in other circles, was persuaded by his English friends, especially Stephen Storace, into contemplating London as a more profitable city. Obviously not willing to leave poor Constanze with a small child and a failing infant, he asked his father to take the two children while he and Constanze went to England. Leopold answered tartly that he would do no such thing, even if paid, failing to mention that he was at the time taking care of Marianne's son. One cannot say with any assurance that posterity would have been better off for such a venture. Haydn would presently make a fortune in England and compose his best symphonies. But Haydn had a wider fame to commend him to the British public. London was musically remote and musically provincial. Its opera had the air of an imported product, nor did Da Ponte make out well there. That Mozart then and later when he was in more need of money gave nothing more than thoughts to an English visit would indicate that the atmosphere of Vienna, and Vienna only, generated music deeply in his heart. The Storaces, Attwood and Kelly returned home in February, 1787, to Mozart's sorrow at losing four of his best friends.

The list of Mozart's works from June until the end of 1786 show numerous arias, songs, piano pieces which musical evenings in private houses would have brought about, together with a continuing succession of works which may have been similarly prompted, and which show consummate mastery:

June 3 — Piano Quartet in E flat (K. 493)
June 10 — Rondo for Piano (K. 494)
June 26 — Concerto for French Horn, in E flat (K. 495)
July 8 — Piano Trio in G (K. 496)
August 1 — Sonata for Piano, 4 Hands, in F (K. 497)
August 5 — Clarinet Trio (K. 498)
August 19 — String Quartet in D (K. 499)
September 12 — Variations for Piano, in B flat (K. 500)
November 4 — Variations for Piano, 4 Hands (K. 501)
November 18 — Piano Trio in B flat (K. 502)
December 4 — Piano Concerto in C (K. 503)
December 6 — Symphony in D ("Prague") (K. 504)

XVII
Vienna, Prague, 1786, 1787

Aʙᴏᴏsᴛ ᴛᴏ Mozart's spirits, if not to his purse, came from Prague in the new year of 1787. Prague was a more thoroughly musical center than Vienna, even without Vienna's wealth and equipment, in the way of performing forces. In Prague, music was systematically taught in the schools and systematically practiced. In Vienna, music was a diversion; in Prague, it was a passion, as Mozart soon learned. Prague had heard and enthusiastically received *Die Entführung* in 1783. *Figaro,* introduced there in December, 1786, had been greeted with wild enthusiasm. Mozart made the journey with Constanze at the hospitable invitation of Count Johann Joseph Thun, and the pair were also entertained by Franz Duscek, whom Mozart had met in Salzburg. He wrote to Gottfried von Jacquin, his pupil in Vienna, on January 14:

As soon as we arrived (on Thursday noon, the 11th) we had to scramble to get ready for lunch at one o'clock. After the meal old Count Thun entertained us with some music performed by his own people, which lasted for about an hour and a half. This kind of *true entertainment* I could enjoy every day. At six o'clock I drove with Count Conac [Canal] to the so-called Bretfeld ball, where the cream of the beauties of Prague always gather. That, my friend, was a spectacle! I can imagine you running after all those pretty girls and dowagers—or rather stumbling after them! I neither danced nor flirted with any of them, in the first case because I was too tired, in the second because I am naturally bashful. But I looked on with the greatest pleasure while all these people wheeled about in sheer delight to the music of my *Figaro* arranged as quadrilles and waltzes. For here they talk only about *"Figaro."* Nothing is played, sung, or whistled but *"Figaro."* No opera draws like *"Figaro."* Always *"Figaro,"* indeed a great honor for me.

"Songs from *Figaro*," wrote Niemetschek, "were heard in the streets, in gardens, even the wandering harp player before a tavern was obliged to strum out *Non più andrai* if he expected to attract an audience."

When it became known at a performance of *Figaro* in the Opera House on January 17 that the composer was in the audience, there was great excitement and straining of necks, demands for repeats. Two days later Prague heard the new symphony which the great Mozart brought with him (K. 504).

Seventeen Eighty-seven was to be the year of *Don Giovanni,* otherwise of works few but important—notably the string quintets, in C (K. 515) and G minor (K. 516), composed in April and May. *Eine kleine Nachtmusik* (K. 525) was dated August 10—what particular event brought it about we do not know; there seems to have been no call for serenades from Mozart in Vienna. It was in May that he was asked to listen to a pianist of sixteen lately arrived in Vienna —Ludwig van Beethoven. Mozart (so Jahn writes), sensing arrogance in his reserve (he was really awed before the master) refrained from praise, but when Beethoven had improvised in a way as astonishing as Mozart's exhibitions of the sort at the same age, he remarked afterwards that the young man was worth watching—"the world will hear from him."*

The news came of the death of his father in Salzburg on May 28. Leopold had missed the satisfaction of hearing *Figaro*. Mozart, learning of his illness, had written a long and affectionate letter on April 4, and to Jacquin on May 29: "On returning home today I received the sad news of my most beloved father's death. You can imagine the state I am in." His affection had become a memory. The correspondence had

---

* The story is unconfirmed. Ries, in his *Notizen,* writes merely that Beethoven "received some lessons from Mozart."

long since dwindled to the barest exchange of news. The letters from the father in the Vienna years, whether from the general carelessness in the Mozart household or the resentment of Constanze, were not preserved. Comments from Leopold on Wolfgang's career, which may have included valuable information about the planning of *Die Entführung* and *Figaro*, have survived only in brief messages written to his daughter.

Mozart's last letter to his father, the letter of April 4, nevertheless indicates one strong bond of understanding between them, the bond of their faith revivified by their adoption of Freemasonry. Mozart had joined the order late in 1784, and his father had joined it during his visit to Vienna in the following spring, whether or not by his persuasion. Wolfgang had reached a contemplation of death, not as a "miserable sinner" in terror of the "Day of Wrath," depicted by the Masses he so well knew, but quite peacefully. "As death, when we come to consider it closely, is the true goal of our existence, I have formed during the last few years such close relations with this best and truest friend of mankind, that its image is not only no longer terrifying to me, but is indeed very soothing and consoling! . . . I never lie down at night without reflecting that—young as I am—I may not live to see another day. Yet no one of all my acquaintances could say that in company I am dispirited. For this blessing I daily thank my Creator and wish with all my heart that each one of my fellow creatures could enjoy it."

This cheerful and rational state of mind (which does not mention repentance) would have been congenial to Leopold. He had always regarded death, a frequent and sometimes unannounced visitor in those days, as an eventuality "in God's hands," to be accepted with calm fortitude and resignation. A practical man, he had resorted to ritual observance as he did to purging and bleeding—these were precautionary measures which might help but could not be relied upon. Leopold's faith in God was fundamental, direct, unquestioning. He communicated this faith constantly to the growing Wolfgang, who accepted it both obediently and readily, nor did either of them have cause to be much impressed by certain church mummery in Salzburg and elsewhere. Both men, as intelligent artists, were liberal-minded and so too was Haydn, who became a Mason at about this time. Of the three, Mozart was the most zealous member. He was more strongly impelled by humanitarian impulses than his father, less docile under the rigidity of the crown, which frowned officially upon the order. He was undoubtedly influenced by many warm friends who became his fellow Masons. The music he wrote for them, and more especially his masonic opera, *The Magic Flute*, are eloquent testimony of how deeply he received the creed into his heart. The composer of the Mass in C minor and the *Requiem* remained a good Catholic, but an enlightened rather than a dogmatic one.

It was in Prague, in January, 1787, that the bid came for *Don Giovanni*, while *Figaro* was filling the opera house there with applauding audiences and corresponding cash for the impresario Pasquale Bondini. This gentleman was quick to seek out the visiting composer and obtain his promise for a new opera in the following autumn. Mozart, immediately after his return to Vienna, had laid this before Da Ponte, who came up at once with the subject of the Spanish libertine who had his just due in the end. Mozart took to the idea at once, and was soon deep in the music. There was nothing new about the idea of *Don Giovanni* for an opera. The legend was as old as time and had been treated since the early seventeenth century in the Spanish, French, Italian, German, even the English-speaking theatres. Through the eighteenth century it had appeared often in opera. Vienna had Gluck's Ballet, *Don Juan*, in 1761, Righini's *Il convitato di pietra* in 1777.

Don Giovanni, cluttered with farcical stage associations, would have given pause to a purist with serious intentions. To Mozart, interested in any musical possibilities, it was an unalloyed opportunity. It was a story one could always count upon to entertain an audience. One beheld the Don involving himself in one affair after another and what was still more interesting, extricating himself in spite of a considerable amount of overlapping. The sense of public morality was reestablished and a titillating spectacle assured at the final curtain as the villain was drawn down to hell amidst dancing devils and flickering cloth flames. Mozart probably first visualized the piece for what it had always been—a straight comedy with plentiful intrigue, and chances for humor in the characters. Only when he began to compose did the tragic aspects grow upon him—the pathos of the wronged ladies: Donna Anna, whose father is murdered almost before her eyes; Donna Elvira, a noble and dignified señora who is the slave of her passion. The ruthless Don with the quickness of wit and tongue necessary for seduction and for escape from its consequences, and his servant Leporello with his peasant humor, caught in his master's scrapes, a coward and something of a rogue, afforded the only consistently comic situations. Leporello was the clown of the piece, and in Italy had been known as "Arlecchino," in Germany as "Hans Wurst." Each of these characters acquired a new, lifelike vividness in Mozart's imagination as he worked upon his score. The scene where the statue of the murdered Commendatore first speaks and the final scene of the libertine's consignment to perdition became truly awesome and terrifying. The closing sextet before the curtain brought the required happy ending as those who had at last escaped the Don declared their intention of enjoying a virtuous and undisturbed life thenceforth. If *Don Giovanni* had opened with the murder and ended with the horrors of hell, the over-all impression would have been rather grim for a comedy. The prologue by Leporello and the final, cheery "vaudeville" made a difference. The result was farcical routine lifted into a vital and substantial drama, whereas *Figaro* was farce lifted into high drawing-room comedy. *Don Giovanni* remains overt comedy, for in every scene except the first and last, a grisly outcome is barely avoided. At moments the two sides of the dramatic mask are in conflict, as when Donna Elvira, a lady in pitiful distress, is made a fool of. The total result is the most powerful of Mozart's works, universal in that it embraces the comic and the tragic to the enhancement of both. Modern dispute about its category is quite beside the point. Neither Mozart nor his eighteenth-century fellows bothered about stylistic rectitude. Their first concern was to make the most of the available singers and their talents and to catch the audiences. Mozart differed from the rest in following through from these premises and producing a stage work unique and unclassifiable. Careless about nomenclature, he labeled it a *"Dramma giocoso"* (not his own term), but listed it in his personal record as *"Opera buffa."* He was equally casual about changes in the course of production. He readily doctored the score to bolster lagging attendance in Vienna, and it may have been for the same reason that he there dropped the final sextet.

Da Ponte's creative resource was called upon for this libretto as it had not been in *Figaro*, where he had a single, smoothly integrated play with dialogue of superb wit to draw upon. Here there was no end of source texts, many variants, most of them poor and unsuitable. The subject was considered low comedy, anything but elegant, and when Gazzaniga's *Don Giovanni Tenorio* was produced in Venice on February 5, 1787, nine months before Mozart's opera, the librettist, Giovanni Bertati* saw fit to provide a prologue, in which the opera troupe humorously apologizes for stooping so low as to present this vulgar subject. They must resort to it, continues the spokesman, to avoid bankruptcy. Da Ponte and Mozart too must have known *Don Giovanni Tenorio*, for they both drew upon it. Da Ponte in particular incorporated the First Act into his own, improving the dialogue. In the Second Act he tightened the plot, dropped two characters and developed those he kept, or rather opened the way for Mozart to develop them. The peasants Zerlina and Masetto became very much alive. Donna Anna, Donna Elvira and Don Ottavio were rather wooden figures until Mozart breathed musical life into them. On the other hand, the sinister gaiety of Don Giovanni and the protests of his servant are managed by the poet with true wit and point. Leporello's aria warning Donna Elvira by cataloguing his master's past conquests is a gem of *buffo* patter which the composer met in kind.

Mozart, together with Constanze, returned to Prague in September, 1787. Bondini according to contract had lodgings for him at the inn, *"Bei drei Löwen."* His old friends the Dus-

---

* Bertati is still known by Cimarosa's *Il matrimonio segreto,* for which he provided the libretto in 1792.

ceks, however, encouraged his free use of their garden with a stone table, on which he wrote the pages necessary to complete the score, cheered rather than hindered by the conversation and games of bowling going on around him. There were of course last-minute changes to oblige the singers. Da Ponte did not arrive until October 8, and had to leave before the performance on October 29—his short stay coming between two of his productions in Vienna. Casanova was in Prague at the time, and posthumous sketches in his hand strongly indicate that this flesh-and-blood Don Giovanni, then a reminiscent libertine of sixty-two, was called upon for alterations in the dialogue.

There are many tales about the preparation of *Don Giovanni* in Prague. Most of them are as undependable as usually happens when a positive record of an important event is wanting and stories are handed down. Rumors about Mozart's affairs with the female performers can be reduced to what may have been a mild flirtation with one of them—Caterina Micelli, the Donna Elvira. Other stories may be discounted: Teresa Saporiti, the Donna Anna, had annoyed him by referring to his small stature, and Caterina Bondini, the Zerlina, was the director's wife. It is related that when Zerlina, embraced off stage by Don Giovanni in Act II, was supposed to utter a cry of terror, Mozart gave her a pinch to make it genuine and convincing. This would have been a purely professional liberty. It is said that Luigi Bassi, the Don Giovanni, complained of having no grand bravura air, and made Mozart recast his duet of seduction with Zerlina (*"La ci darem la mano"*) five times before he would accept it. Before condemning him for this bit of effrontery we should admit that the last must have been the best since it is impossible to imagine any previous version as having been quite equal to it. The story was vouched for by Constanze that on the night before the first performance Mozart composed the overture while she kept him awake with punch and fairy stories, that it was completed and hurried to the copyist at seven in the morning, performed from parts still wet at the premiere, that Mozart whispered to the musicians near him before the curtain rose: "Some of the notes fell under the desks, but on the whole it went splendidly." Some have taken the edge from this story by trying to place it on the night before the last rehearsal. In any case, Mozart, who certainly need not have waited until the danger point, enjoyed putting himself to the test of speed.

The audience was excited to behold their beloved Mozart presiding at the piano. Mozart (and probably Bondini) had qualms about the success of *Don Giovanni* because it was entirely different from *Figaro*. All the parts were a strain upon the modest abilities of the singers, and since there were only six available, Bussani had to double as Masetto and the Commendatore. Mozart's doubts vanished as the performance progressed. Singers as well as players were on their mettle. The composer of *Figaro* was applauded before the first note had sounded, and newly acclaimed at the end as the composer of another masterpiece. After the fourth (benefit) performance, Mozart wrote to Jacquin in Vienna: "I only wish my good friends (particularly Bridi and yourself) could be here for a single evening to share my triumph. Perhaps it will be performed in Vienna. I hope so. Everyone here is urging me to stay two months longer and write another opera; but, flattering as the proposal is, I cannot accept it."

Perhaps *Figaro* and *Don Giovanni,* in spite of their indifferent success in Vienna, brought a certain realization to the Emperor that Mozart was something more than a pianist. Perhaps he listened to favorable comments, more convincing than the denigrations of not disinterested opponents. At any rate he granted him official recognition.

Gluck died on November 15, 1787, in his seventy-fourth year, and Joseph, on December 7, gave Mozart the vacant post of *Kammermusicus*. It was no occasion for rejoicing, for neither the former honor nor the former salary went with the position. Mozart received 800 florins although Gluck's salary had been 2,000. His duties were to be nothing more than to provide dances for the masked balls in the Redoutensaal during the carnival seasons. Pieces came quickly from his pen for the short remainder of his life—minuets for the noble masks, country dances and German dances for the general crowd. Officially, therefore, he was without fame, and actually without a living income. The post was no disgrace in itself; Haydn had from time to time furnished the royal dance music and Beethoven would later do so. These chores left his true skill untouched, and brought the bitter remark (quoted by Niemetschek): "Too much for what I do, too little for what I could do."

XVIII
Vienna, Berlin, 1788, 1789

NEWS OF *Don Giovanni* does not seem to have stirred any particular interest in Vienna. *Figaro* was for the time being forgotten. It had won momentary attention and some discussion, but other operas created an equal or greater excitement each season and most of them passed into oblivion as a new one came along. Mozart's surface style—smooth, gay and entertaining—was regular musical currency. A dozen composers in Vienna during the seventeen-eighties could turn out deft, professionally competent and appealingly tuneful operas. Gluck had seniority and fame—his great penetration in tragic or pathetic musical description was not unperceived in his time. Dittersdorf's *Doktor und Apotheker* had had an enormous success in the year previous, and was repeated twenty times in five months. In contrast to Mozart's experience with *Die Entführung,* Dittersdorf was commissioned to write two more German operas in the same season. Nevertheless the Italians were in the ascendancy. Salieri had an official advantage over Mozart. Piccinni and Paisiello, Italians who had spread their fame over Europe, would have been ranked by many as more important than Mozart. Cimarosa was immensely popular. Sarti and Righini were slightly less so, but the Spaniard Martín y Soler became for a while the rage. The predominant native Italian operas were preferred because the orchestral score provided nothing more perplexing than an obvious melodic line over a light accompaniment of conventional chords in bouncing rhythm, ensembles quite uncomplicated, duets in a routine mating of voices, melodies which were no more than good tunes to catch the ear, repeated rather than developed, the bravura passages nothing more than frank exhibitions, vocal acrobatics. Mozart's orchestra was far richer in texture, often thematically developed, his musical depiction was easily missed because it was subtle and fleeting. His intricate ensembles, too, dazed and bewildered, or simply annoyed the sluggish listener. It is hard for us to understand how the incredible profusion of great melodies in *Figaro,* as compared to two or three catch tunes in an average opera, could have failed to impress its first audiences as far above its run-of-the-mill fellows. If *"Non più andrai"* became popular at once, why not the arias of Cherubino, Susanna, the Contessa? The truth probably is that each has a special, delicate treatment which makes it an integral revelation of the character and the emotional moment. Only an opening phrase or two provided the obvious kind of "tune" a layman could carry in his head. Each is developed as an intimate communication. Cherubino's *"Non so più cosa son"* is a special depiction of adolescent ardor and would be unmeaning apart from the context. Figaro's *"Se vuol ballare"* has its undercurrent of defiance, of vengeful malice. The initial simplicity of Mozart's vocal melody is therefore a deception. His melody has its characteristic purity as compared to the frankly sensual vocal style of Italian opera. Viennese taste preferred the Italianate melody of Salieri or Cimarosa. Italy itself for the same reason remained for many years indifferent to Mozart's operas. Even Rossini in the next century, while making a sincere obeisance to the image of Mozart, could not do otherwise than turn out a superficial nineteenth-century version of the *opera buffa* as if that composer had not existed.

Da Ponte, with a shrewd eye upon the collaborations which would best pay off, had been careful not to put all his eggs into one basket, however much he later protested in his memoirs his friendship for Mozart as his favorite. While writing *Don Giovanni* for Prague he had had an eye on Vienna too. He had simultaneously worked on *Axur* for Salieri (a translation of the rather pompous *Tarare* by Beaumarchais) and *L'arbore di Diana* for Martín, giving his mornings, afternoons and evenings to the three in turn (or so he tells us). The pieces by Salieri and Martín were performed shortly before and after *Don Giovanni.*

Don Giovanni was performed in Vienna on May 7, 1788, with an excellent cast including Albertarelli as Don Giovanni, Aloysia Lange as Donna Anna, Cavalieri as Donna Elvira. Although this talent was far above anything Prague could furnish, the applause was listless. The Viennese audiences were puzzled by the new setting of a familiar story deprived of some of its broader humors, with music which had a way of turning suddenly from gaiety and taking on a dark, disturbingly tragic caste. A judgment by a Berlin critic (of a German version, in 1790) is typical of the noncomprehension which first met *Don Giovanni*: "Variety, eccentricity, fancy, have created *Don Juan,* not the heart." Attempts were made to save the production by various additions, such as the aria *"Mi trada quall' alma ingrata"* to give further display to the talents of Cavalieri, and *"Dalla sua pace"* for Morella, the Don Ottavio, who demanded a number less taxing to his abilities than *"Il mio tesoro."** *Don Giovanni* lasted through fifteen performances and only at the later ones did the magnificence of Mozart's opera begin to dawn upon the Viennese public. Nevertheless, it was shelved until after its composer's death.

Except for the Piano Concerto in D (the "Coronation"), Mozart wrote no original works in the larger forms in the year 1788, until the summer, when he composed his last three symphonies, the summit of his orchestral writing. According to entries in the notebook the three were completed within a space of about six weeks: the Symphony in E flat (K. 543), on June 26, the Symphony in G minor (K. 550), on July 25, and the great "Jupiter" Symphony, in C (K. 551) on August 10. The variance of character and rapidity of writing in the three masterworks has been used to strengthen the supposition that Mozart must have composed his more important music in his head, retained it accurately in his memory, and

---

* Purists have advocated the omission of these added numbers as interpolations which delay the action. They are usually retained for the more cogent reason that they are too beautiful to be missed.

put it down on paper as nothing more than a labor of record-ing. That he was not bothered by company about him while writing would indicate that actual notation was not an act of the imagination which would have required quiet and con-centration. How Mozart managed to compose at his speed and level will never be accounted for. Equally astonishing in this prodigious act by Mozart in a few summer weeks is that for the first and last time in his life he was apparently com-posing without prospect of performance or return, and solely for his own satisfaction. There is no mention of the symphon-ies before his death, no record of a performance. His sym-phonies were no longer called for in Vienna. It is unlikely that they were intended for the journey to Berlin in the fol-lowing spring, for that journey happened by a later and ap-parently unexpected invitation from Prince Lichnowsky.*

The joy which speaks in these symphonies is belied by the miserable circumstances of his life in that summer. *Don Gio-vanni* was still running at the *Burgtheater,* while its composer, who had no more returns from it, was writing pot-boilers and trying to borrow to meet present expenses, pushed by his landlord and other creditors, living on the hopes of a planned concert which never took place. He wrote to Michael Puch-berg, a fellow Mason: "If you my worthy brother do not help me in this predicament, I shall lose my honor and my credit, which of all things I wish to preserve." And in the same letter he wrote about "black thoughts which often come to me, thoughts which I push away with a tremendous effort." This was written the day after he had completed the E flat Sym-phony, and two days before the death of his only daughter, Theresia, his fourth child, at the age of six months. The note of despair had not appeared in his letters except in 1778, when his efforts to establish himself in Paris had reached a dead end. From the summer of 1788 until the end of his life he was burdened by mounting debts and forced to borrow on his prospects. He had no regular income other than the quarterly 200 florins from the court—the equivalent of about

* Mozart did not give a public concert in Berlin. He did give a con-cert of his own works in Leipzig, in April, 1789, and presented a symphony (unspecified).

70 dollars. The vogue of his concerts had all but disappeared, whatever the reason might be. He could not enlist subscribers for them. His pupils had dropped off too, in these last years, owing perhaps to his innate reluctance to give hours of his time to struggling beginners. The return from an opera was far from commensurate with the time and effort put into it. The list of his compositions from the last three symphonies until the final months of his life consist of one opera, *Così fan tutte,* two string quartets for the King of Prussia, three piano trios (in E, K. 542; in C, K. 548; in G, K. 564), two superb string quintets (in D and in E flat, K. 593 and 614), and the Piano Concerto (in B flat, K. 595). The chamber music would have been provided for private gatherings. There are otherwise various short works, piano pieces and arias, the first sort to oblige pianistic friends, the second to oblige a singer, or to be inserted in the opera of another. Few of his works were published in his lifetime, and those brought him little return. On the other hand, the household expenses of the Mozarts seem to have been modest enough. Only the care of an invalid wife depleted by unsuccessful child-bearing involved additional costs for doctors and cures at Baden. There is only one way to account for the increasing weight of debt, the continual pinch which kept Mozart in a desperate state of misery and embarrassment. He was careless of money, and his high spirits seemed to require dressing elegantly and entertaining handsomely.

It would be a mistake to suppose that Mozart subsided into a state of gloom, or showed a long face to his friends. In good company he put his troubles behind him. In summer these friends were reduced by the absence of titled ones, which eliminated subscription concerts. He wrote to Michael Puchberg, to whom he was repeatedly to turn in need, that he had planned to give some at home "in order to be able to meet at least my present and frequent expenses. . . . A fortnight ago I sent around a list for subscribers and so far the only name on it is that of the Baron van Swieten!" The Baron may not have brought much money Mozart's way; he had a reputation of being close with it. There can be no doubt that he was immensely profitable to him musically. The indefatigable "classicist" had kept him busy in the previous autumn. He would gather subscriptions from other gentry, engage the opera orchestra and the best singers he could, rehearse oratorios in his house and present them in whatever auditorium, public or private, he could obtain, as invitation matinées. Mozart arranged Handel's *Acis and Galatea* in November, 1788, *The Messiah* in the following March, and subsequently *The Ode for Saint Cecilia's Day* and *The Feast of Alexander*. In those times a revived score of an old master was simply brought up to date, and not presented inviolate as a "period piece." Van Swieten summed up the point of view when he wrote to Mozart of his purpose to "satisfy the modern taste while preserving the integrity of the subject." Mozart freely filled in the harmonies of Handel with added string parts, gave color variety to the woodwinds, adding clarinet parts, and even put in thematic touches.

A concert-giving tour on the pattern of the earlier years was a natural recourse, and when in the spring of 1789 Prince Carl Lichnowsky, the nephew of the Countess Thun, invited him to share his carriage in a journey to Berlin, he was quick to accept. Mozart had not been further from Vienna than Salzburg or Prague since 1781, and he had never been in Saxony or Prussia. He was known in Berlin by performances of *Die Entführung,* and Frederick William II, accounted a musician of broader taste than Frederick the Great, had expressed a desire to see and hear him. The pair set out on April 8, making stops at Prague, Dresden and Leipzig. Mozart was entertained by chance friends in each city, and of course was asked repeatedly to perform. He played at court in Dresden, and in Leipzig played for an hour on the organ of the Thomaskirche, in such a way that Cantor Doles declared that his master and predecessor, Sebastian Bach, had "risen again." In Berlin he was received with respect as the composer of *Die Entführung,* which was much admired. Lichnowsky took him at once to the King, who was delighted with his playing. Frederick was fond of string quartets and took the cello part in performances of them at Potsdam.

Mozart was persuaded by Prince Lichnowsky to travel back to Leipzig to give a concert before leaving Berlin. Since the attendance was poor and consisted largely of free tickets, and since the traveling expenses came out of his own pocket, Mozart gained nothing from it but the pleasure of a cordial reception in a program entirely of his own music. The players told the tale that in rehearsing the first movement of a symphony the orchestra were thrown out by his fast tempo and that in trying to enforce it he stamped his foot so vigorously that a piece of his shoe buckle flew off. He explained afterwards to friends that he was trying to goad the older players into alertness. It was not simply incompetence on their part, for he also played one of his concertos without rehearsal and without mishap.

He returned to Berlin, but did not give a public concert, reserving his talents for the King and Queen. Before he left, the King gave him a present of 100 friedrichsd'or with a request for some quartets. Mozart planned to compose six, and completed one of them (K. 575) immediately on his return to Vienna. Two more were written in May and June of the following year (K. 589, 590). These three were the last string quartets he wrote. Out of deference to his Prussian Majesty he worked prominent cello parts into each of them. The present from Friedrich, together with one of 100 ducats from the Saxon Elector, were his only profits from his journey.

The legend that Friedrich at Potsdam offered Mozart the post of *Kapellmeister* at a sum handsomer than he had ever hoped for in Vienna is unlikely. Mozart would surely have told Constanze of such an offer, but he wrote to her on May 23, five days before his departure: "You and I must be satisfied with the fact that I am fortunate enough to stand in the King's favor—this is between ourselves." The amount he carried home would have been larger if Lichnowsky had paid his expenses at Potsdam and taken him home, instead of which he borrowed 100 gulden from him.

The Berlin journey brings up again the doubt whether Mozart's lifelong quest for a secure and remunerative court position could ever have succeeded. In Vienna only, with proper recognition, could he have found the intelligent musicianship, the degree of congenial musical activity he seemed to require. Even in Vienna, composers at best were court servants and sycophants. Gluck's honorable position had been exceptional, and had been based on veneration built on his long and illustrious career. Gluck had had his knockabout years. At Mozart's age he had been an itinerant player upon musical glasses, more than ready to play for favor as a composer. Most of the courts were poorly equipped, and even Esterház, which was tolerably well equipped, would have made Mozart restive with its confinement and isolation more quickly than it wearied Haydn. Karl von Dittersdorf (whose name was an ennobled form of Ditters) served in a succession of courts inferior even to Salzburg, and had never been able to entrench himself in a secure position. His memoirs show that he had to make the most of miserable musical forces, derived from cooks or liverymen whom he had to train into the semblance of an orchestra. Dittersdorf was the most compliant of young men, always ready to ingratiate himself where advantage was in sight. He learned to delight all hearers with music which was tailored to their taste but which seems colorless to us now. He returned from a visit to Berlin, unlike Mozart, laden with gold, having praised Friedrich Wilhelm's musicians, befriended the royal mistress, and made himself popular right and left. Mozart could not face mediocrity with a benign smile. He was more truthful than tactful in mentioning to the sovereign where there was room for improvement, and had he lingered as long as Dittersdorf did, Reichardt and Duport, the musical rulers there, would have become his open enemies. Dittersdorf penetrated the confidence and friendliness of the Emperor Joseph in Vienna far more readily than the forthright and touchy Mozart. His social technique was the quick and witty answer, just bold enough to stimulate good humor without overstepping. The method was to play up to the monarch's vanity about his musical judgment. Dittersdorf quotes in his memoirs the following conversation, which shows his way of shaping Joseph's judgment by his own insinuation:

Emperor: What do you think of Mozart's compositions?

I: He is unquestionably one of the greatest original geniuses, and I have never yet met with any composer who had such an amazing wealth of ideas; I could almost wish he were not so lavish in using them. The hearer is left out of breath; for hardly has he grasped one beautiful thought, when another of greater fascination dispels the first, and this goes on throughout, so that in the end it is impossible to retain any one of these beautiful melodies.

Emperor: He has one single fault in his pieces for the stage, and his singers have very often complained of it—he deafens them with his full accompaniments.

I: That surprises me! One can introduce and blend harmony and the play of accompaniment without spoiling the cantilena.

Emperor: You have this gift to perfection. I have observed it in your two oratorios, *Esther* and *Hiob*. What do you think of Haydn's compositions?

I: I have not heard any of his dramatic pieces.

Emperor: You lose nothing in that, for he writes exactly as Mozart does. But what do you think of his chamber music?

I: Why, it is making a world-wide sensation, and justly too.

Emperor: Is he not often too playful?

I: He has the gift of sportiveness, but he never loses the dignity of art.

Emperor: You are right there. (*After a pause*) Sometime ago, I drew a parallel between Mozart and Haydn; I wish you would do the same, that I may see whether you agree with me.

I (*After a pause*): Before I do so, will Your Majesty allow me to ask you a question?

Emperor: Certainly

I: What do you think of a parallel between Klopstock and Gellert?

Emperor: Hm! They are both great poets. To understand all of Klopstock's beauty one must read his works over and over again, whereas Gellert's merits are patent at the first glance.

I: Here Your Majesty has my answer.

Emperor: Mozart, then, may be compared with Klopstock, and Haydn with Gellert?

I: That is my opinion, anyhow.

It is not hard to understand why the Emperor would have passed by Mozart in favor of a composer who would entertain him in conversation, and with his operas flatter his self-conceit as a connoisseur instead of confusing him with his "deafening accompaniments." It must be added, however, that Dittersdorf, with all his clever diplomacy, never grew rich by Joseph's favors. He died in poverty.

The money Mozart brought home from Prussia must have been swallowed by standing debts, for in July, 1789, a few weeks after his return, he wrote three letters of piteous appeal to Puchberg, whom he had already drawn upon. "Great God!" he began, "I would not wish my worst enemy to be in my present position. And if you, most beloved friend and brother, forsake me, we are altogether lost, both my unfortunate and blameless self and my poor sick wife and child. Only the other day when I was with you I was longing to open my heart to you, but I had not the courage." He wrote that he had been ill and unable to work. His wife, pregnant again, was alarmingly ill, and he would have to send her to Baden for a cure. There were doctors' bills. Three days later, having no answer, he wrote again. He concluded this letter: "If you can and if you will entirely relieve me, I shall return thanks to you as my saviour, even beyond the grave, for you will be enabling me to enjoy further happiness on earth. But if you cannot do this, then I beg and implore you, in God's name for whatever temporary assistance you can give me." He had asked for 500 gulden. Puchberg noted on the letter that he had sent him 150 "on the same day." These humiliating letters were to be resumed and continued almost monthly through the following year. Mozart kept living on expectations and never meeting the moment. Puchberg sent smaller amounts as his faith in the continuing expectations diminished. Sometimes he did not answer at all.

XIX

Vienna, Frankfort, Prague, 1789-1791

FIGARO was again put on the stage on August 29, 1789. Audiences began to find that there was more in it than they had realized, for it prospered, attained eleven performances by the end of the year, and had fifteen more in the year following. Joseph too may have begun to suspect that there was more to *Figaro* and its composer than he had noticed before. At any rate there came a sudden commission in September, 1789, for an *opera buffa*. Mozart was not consulted about the subject. "It was not in his power," wrote Niemetschek, "to decline the commission and the libretto was provided without consultation of his wishes." Whatever part Da Ponte had in the choice, he was not proud of the result, for he barely mentions *Così fan tutte* in his memoirs. He was handicapped by having no libretto of a predecessor to lean on. The consequence is a routine *opera buffa* plot, based on absurd situations, and only occasionally witty in the dialogue. We know nothing of what Mozart felt about the assignment, or whether he had a hand in the planning of the book. This was not the first instance where he cheerfully accepted indifferent stuff and proceeded to turn it into gold. The composer who was always ready to shape into music of beauty any theme that was given to him to vary, who had composed several works with flute in Mannheim when the flute was particularly distasteful to him, who would compose pieces for such an insipid contrivance as musical glasses in the last year of his life for the same reason (a fee was a fee) was complacent about an opera subject when he had no alternative. *Figaro* was the only operatic comedy entirely of his own choosing, and the only book which had true unity of style. Mozart's choice of *Figaro* may have been more fortunate than astute. He had to grasp at his chance always. If Mozart was less than eager about the assignment, a royal commission which he would not have refused, there is no sign of reluctance in the result. The libretto has too often been put down as an impossible piece of artificial trumpery. Artificial it is, and absurd. It could not have elicited from Mozart what Beaumarchais did. It is a neat bit of artificiality, nevertheless, put together by a librettist who could have been as plausible as he wished, and by doing so would have quite dulled the point of the piece. He contrived a completely rational plot on an irrational premise, and, plainly aware of Mozart's various musical propensities, provided him with plentiful ensembles, love scenes, scenes of trenchant drama, scenes of slapstick comedy, all ordered with a canny sense of effect by contrast.

As Mozart composed *Così fan tutte* we can imagine him tackling each of the successive numbers head on, shaping the characters in his music as he dealt with them, fulfilling the moment from the invention that never lapsed. He readily injected human warmth into situations even where the lines were unhelpful, where instead of having one character to portray, he had virtual twins. When the two sisters in the story bid farewell to their fiancés it matters not that the whole thing is supposed to be a hoax—we are treated to the tenderness, the heartbreak of separation in the fullest degree. The scenes where the maid Despina tricks the ladies by disguising herself as a doctor and later as a notary are the broadest farce, and bring out to the utmost Mozart's delectable sense of musical fun. The scene where the sister Fiordiligi is overwhelmed with self-reproach at her inconstancy, and the scene where the two men in turn are in despair on discovering that their sweethearts have failed them, these moments become in the music full emotional drama, and would not have been out of place in *opera seria*. Indeed, the opera comes close to a parody of the grand heroic manner.

Da Ponte's plain purpose was not to prove the trite generality that all women are fickle, nor does he really convince us on that point, but to set up the romantic types of grand heroic opera, with their impossibly exalted sentiments, their declamatory recitatives, their *fioriture,* to be punctured by a cynical bachelor, and a down-to-earth serving maid who looks upon such subjects as love and matrimony as a simple matter of the right opportunity. Mozart fell in with this purpose, but he proved inadequate as a parodist. Underlining Guglielmo's disillusion and Fiordiligi's remorse with intended exaggeration, he only made their predicament more vivid for us. The style he was attempting to lampoon was too deep a part of his nature. The sisters' accents of gentle longing for their "absent" lovers, expressed with undulating woodwinds and muted violins, work such complete enchantment that the ridicule later heaped upon them stirs our resentment. No one can wish that Mozart had curbed his affections and his flowing pen, depicted Fiordiligi and Dorabella with less of his heart. If there is a certain irreconcilability in the score, an occasional jolt as our sympathies are pulled two ways, we need only to turn to the all-pervading delight of the music itself.

Così fan tutte has suffered a full century of neglect by those who, bothered by the "bad taste" of the book, have overlooked one of Mozart's gayest and most delightful scores. The Vienna which first heard it was not shocked by the depiction of women's frailty, for Vienna was quite accustomed to obliging women—the story is said to have been based on an actual incident of two young blades and their fiancées (or mistresses). The first audiences were no worse than slightly bored by a plot which developed on a strained thesis. They made the mistake of dismissing the opera on account of its text without half examining the music that went with it. The subtle action that was built into the music, particularly in the marvelous quintets and sextets, passed them altogether. The romantic nineteenth century simply rejected the plot as preposterous and unfair to the sex, with the result that the music was seldom heard at all. The book was translated, adapted, rewritten in attempts to make the opera acceptable, but in vain because the tale was irremediable anyway, and because the perfectly fashioned score was marred wherever it was touched. It has required the present generation, less solemn about operatic morals or plausibilities, to become intrigued instead of alienated by the neatly paired equilibrium of the characters, the sophisticated wit of the comedy of manners. Only in the last few years has this *opera buffa** taken its secure and rightful place with its two illustrious predecessors in the same genre.

The thesis of the title—"So do they all"—that fidelity among women is, like the mythical phoenix, found only in literature, was nothing new; the key verse was specifically quoted from Metastasio's *Demetrio*. It was no stuffy pronouncement but a subject for light banter over a bottle of wine between a cynical bachelor and two romantic young men, each newly engaged. There is no reason to be disturbed when Dorabella and Fiordiligi succumb too quickly to their suitors in disguise and in reverse. To justify the title they could hardly do otherwise. If the girls are too readily taken in by the false mustaches, and too promptly won, there is a good reason for this too; the plot must move at its brisk pace. And so it does, with music which is the life of the piece in all its moments—gay, serious, farcical, tender.

Così fan tutte, first performed January 26, 1790, might have had a longer run than it did.† On February 20, Joseph II died and the national mourning closed the theatres. If Mozart expected more from the new monarch, Leopold II, who took the throne on March 13, he was to be disappointed. Joseph had wished to be considered as a musician of taste, had embellished his court with some care and considerable expense, upholding it as the best in Europe. Mozart had at least passing attention from him; from the new Emperor he had none. The Emperor Leopold not only did not care

---

* Over the first printed libretto it was called a *dramma giocoso,* also Mozart's designation for *Don Giovanni,* as if he were conscious of having lifted the *opera buffa* for once and all into a new category.

† After ten more performances in the summer following, it was shelved and not performed in Vienna until 1804 (in German translation by Treitschke). It was performed in Prague, in Italian, in 1791, before Mozart's death.

for music, he became impatient with his opera company as an incubus of intrigue, and wearied of listening to their personal grievances. Salieri and Da Ponte, its official composer and principal librettist, had each made the fatal tactical error of taking as mistress one of the foremost singers: the Signore Cavalieri and Ferrarese respectively. (Cavalieri had been the first Donna Elvira, Ferrarese the first Fiordiligi). Personal rancor begot a general feud. Salieri resigned, knowing he would be better off elsewhere. Da Ponte took refuge in Trieste, and when his pleas to be reinstated were unanswered, departed to London. Joseph Weigl took Salieri's place and Ugart replaced Rosenberg. Mozart, who was never the sort to push his cause, wrote a modest petition, asking to be made assistant *Kapellmeister,* mentioning that before coming to Vienna (but not since) he had been required to compose a large amount of church music, and had met his requirements. He also asked to be taken as teacher to the two princes. His petition was not granted.

Mozart so continued miserably in debt. He wrote to Puchberg in April, May and June, and again in August, 1790. He could not find subscribers for a concert. He had only two pupils. "Do your best to make it known that I am willing to give lessons." Puchberg, whether he had come to the end of his prudence, his resources or his friendship, sent sums as small as 25 gulden.

Mozart's hopes for royal recognition were further discouraged when Leopold entertained the visiting King of Naples in September with operas by Salieri and by Weigl, and did not even invite Mozart to court. When for his coronation in Frankfort on October 9, 1790, he took with him a large musical retinue, Mozart not included, Mozart figured that the gathering of titles and wealth for that event would afford the opportunity for profitable concerts. He accordingly went to Frankfort as a personal venture, taking with him his brother-in-law Franz Hofer. He gave a concert, playing two of his concertos (K. 459, and K. 537, the so-called "Coronation" Concerto, actually composed in 1788). He also visited Mayence; Mannheim, where *Figaro* was being performed; and Munich, where he was invited by the Elector to play at a concert for the King of Naples, an event which satisfied his hurt pride. It is doubtful whether he was able to take any earnings home with him.

In December, 1790, John Salomon, the impresario from London, appeared in Vienna and persuaded Joseph Haydn to accompany him back to England and to compose twelve symphonies for the Philharmonic Society of London. Haydn accepted, to the good fortune of posterity—the distance was great, but the inducement strong when measured in pounds sterling. Mozart was invited by Salomon to fulfill a similar mission, but he had already refused an offer made in October by the director of the Italian Opera in London to travel there and compose two operas for a fee of 300 pounds. This was three times the amount he would have received in Vienna, where he could not count on a commission for one opera, let alone two. Since Haydn reaped a fortune in England, Mozart with operas as well as symphonies might have done still better. Whether because he did not wish to set himself in rivalry with his dearest friend, whether he could not either take or leave the ailing Constanze who was once more pregnant, or whether his unprofitable journey to Frankfort had sapped his pioneering courage, he refused. He bade an affectionate farewell to Haydn, depressed by the feeling that he would never see him again. And so it proved.

Mozart's load of debt increased in the year 1791, for there was no public demand for his services, no possibility of subscription concerts. When a commission came his way, he fulfilled it handsomely. The two marvelous string quintets (K. 593 in D major, and K. 614, in E flat) were composed in December, 1790, and April, 1791, probably for Johann Tost, a wealthy Hungarian amateur violinist who had ordered two sets of quartets from Haydn. These were destined to be his farewell to chamber music. A piano concerto composed for a concert given by the clarinetist Joseph Bähr in March (K. 595 in B flat) was to be his twenty-seventh and last in this form—and there again he ended on the very highest plane of his accomplishment.

These works made a small portion of his composing activity. Early in the year, he and Emanuel Schikaneder hatched an operatic plan. Schikaneder had long since been the actor-manager of a traveling theatrical troupe and had become friendly with the Mozarts when the company had a five months' run in Salzburg in the season 1780-1781. Schikaneder in his younger days had acted leading hero parts—even Hamlet—but now, at the age of forty, and having acquired considerable girth, he made himself popular as the first comedian in extravaganzas, where his gags together with magic, spectacular effects and stage monsters were relied upon to fill the house. He had rented the Theater Auf-der-Wieden, a barnlike wooden structure, and had occupied it for two seasons. He put on a succession of *Singspiele* relying mostly on the fairy tales of Wieland, and it was this poet's *Der Stein der Weisen* and *Lulu, oder die Zauberflöte* which furnished the basis for the newly proposed opera.

It was probably early in May that Schikaneder broached to Mozart *The Magic Flute* as the subject for a musical piece for his theatre. Mozart was interested at once. *Così fan tutte* was already no more than a memory, there was no imperial command in sight, his load of debts was unrelieved. On top of this, such a project appealed to him because he would have more freedom and more control. From Schikaneder's point of view Mozart was a natural choice. He was a proven theatrical composer, unengaged, a fellow Mason, and the kind who would not stand too much on his rights, but allow Schikaneder's own comic part full scope and trim the music to his limited singing abilities. Schikaneder's theatre was in debt. As he was soon to learn, he could not possibly have found a better road to recovery. (It is said that Mozart got little of the profits, and that Schikaneder quietly appropriated the score.) Schikaneder planned his production for the autumn of 1791. He kept an eye on Mozart and installed him for working purposes in a little summerhouse in the garden of his theatre, a way of being sure that the score was progressing.* The legends which have clustered about *The Magic Flute* and its two collaborators have it that Schikaneder

---

* The summerhouse has been moved to the garden of the Mozarteum at Salzburg.

exhausted Mozart by holding him to his task, and also that, in the absence of Constanze, he led him into wild dissipation that hastened his illness. Both tales may have a small grain of truth. In any case, Mozart, who never had to be pushed to meet a deadline, had drafted all but a few pages of his score by late July.

While he worked upon it, a gloom settled on his spirit, belying the gay lilting measures and the tender optimism of the music. It is likely that his final illness was oppressing him. There were other contributing causes. The Emperor had definitely passed him by, his wealthier friends were at their summer resorts, Constanze he had sent to Baden, with their son Karl and her sister Sophie, early in June, for she was ill and expecting her sixth child. The apartment on the Rauhensteingasse was deserted, for he had dismissed his servant. It was silent, except when he stirred empty echoes by trying a passage on the piano. Mozart had always clung to family life, and his family now included Constanze's two sisters, their husbands and even the mother-in-law. He was forlorn in a silent house. How he clung to Constanze is evident in the letters which he wrote during every separation—his journeys to Berlin and to Frankfort, and during the summers when she was in Baden. He was always affectionate and solicitous and craved the letters from her which were less frequent than his own. There can be no doubt that the two were fundamentally faithful. She attested after his death that his friendships with fair pupils or fair singers sometimes led to infidelities which he at once confessed to her and which she freely forgave. She would have been less confiding than he about her own frivolities at parties common in Vienna at the time, for he was far from complacent on such matters. The current of gossip always ran high. On account of it he could not continue to live in her mother's house when the two were engaged. When she stayed with the Baroness von Waldstäten, and at one of that lady's overgay parties had allowed her calf to be measured by a young man in a game of forfeits, he had remonstrated in a long letter. Even in the summer of 1791, when he had sent her to Baden, he was disturbed about the proprieties at the Casino, and asked her to refrain from dancing until his arrival. In Baden from the beginning of June until mid-July she received letters from him daily. They are full of concern about her health, about the baths, medicaments, exercise. He tried, but unsuccessfully, to avoid mentioning expense problems. The letters show that in the absence of titled friends he at least had found bourgeois ones. It appears that he was usually up at five in the morning. He would work on *Die Zauberflöte,* lunch with Schikaneder, or Leutgeb, the hornist and cheesemonger who had set up his shop "in a shell," or Puchberg, or Joseph Deiner, whom he called "Primus," or his composer pupil Franz Xaver Süssmayr ("Snai"), then twenty-five, who was helping him with the opera as copyist. Wealthier friends were out of town in June. His efforts to appear cheerful when writing to Constanze are unconvincing. He ended a letter on July 6:

> The greatest possible pleasure you can give me is to be happy and jolly. If I know for certain that you have everything you want, then all my trouble is a joy and a delight. . . . Love me forever as I do you and be always my Stanzi Marini, as I shall always be your
>
> Stu! Knaller Praller
Schnip - Schnap - Schnur
Schnepeperl-
Snai!
>
> Give _____ a box on the ear and tell him that you simply must kill a fly which I have noticed on his face! Adieu—Look there! Catch them—bi—bi—bi—three kisses sweet as sugar, are flying over to you!

But the next day "Stanzi" must have been disturbed by a note of gloom—totally unlike him—which crept into his letter:

> My one wish now is that my affairs should be settled, so that I can be with you again. You can't imagine how I have been aching for you all this long time. I can't describe what I have been feeling—a kind of emptiness which is very painful, a kind of longing which is never satisfied; which never stops; persisting and increasing every day. When I think how merry we were together at Baden—like children [He had just visited her]—and what sad, weary hours I am spending here! Even my

work gives me no pleasure, because I miss stopping now and then to talk with you. Alas! this pleasure is no longer possible. If I go to the piano and sing something out of my opera, I have to stop at once, for it disturbs my emotions too deeply.

He writes " *Basta!"* and brushes the mood away.

Constanze's confinement almost coincided with the completion of *Die Zauberflöte*—her son was born on July 26.*

Probably within the next two weeks (the exact dates are not ascertainable) two unexpected commissions came to Mozart and delayed the last pages of the opera manuscript. The first of these was a visit from a stranger who handed him an unsigned letter asking for a Requiem. Mozart was in no position to refuse an offer with an advance of the fee (probably 50 or 100 ducats) in hand. He welcomed it in any case, for he had never been asked to compose a church work for Vienna, and still hoped to be appointed to the royal *Kapelle,* which Leopold had re-established. Aside from such advantages, he must have had a deeper urge, if we can judge by the result. There was nothing "mysterious" about the transaction. A gentleman of means wished to acquire a Requiem and pass it off in a private performance as by himself. Later subject to sick hallucination, Mozart came to believe that the Requiem was to be his own. Popular opinion, even more inclined than he to mystification and to look for premonitions of death, built the picture of the unnamed emissary, appearing without announcement, a tall stranger dressed in gray, his finger to his lips. The man was no doubt in proper servant's uniform. His master turned out to be a Count Walsegg, an amateur musician who wished to have performed a Requiem Mass in memory of his wife, and to

---

* Franz Xaver Wolfgang Mozart may have had his first two given names from Süssmayr, who presumably stood as godfather. Of the six children only he and Karl Thomas (September 21, 1784–October 31, 1858) survived infancy. Franz became a pianist and composer and so earned a living, but the weight of his father's name was too oppressive. He died July 29, 1844. The other children were: Raimund Leopold (June 17–August 21, 1783); Karl Johann Thomas Leopold (October 18–November 15, 1786); Theresia (December 27, 1787–June 20, 1788); Anna (born and died November 16, 1789).

impress his friends with his ability by this not entirely unusual bit of deception.

Almost on top of this came an order from Prague. Leopold was to be crowned King of Bohemia on September 6. Prague officialdom rather than Vienna officialdom had decided upon Mozart as the composer of the proper opera for the coronation ceremonials. It was to be *La Clemenza di Tito*, a libretto Metastasio had written in 1734, about the glorious benevolence of an emperor of ancient Rome, with implications which would be supposed to fit the present case. It was a typical *opera seria* in the old, outmoded style and was improved but not saved by being remodeled by Mazzolà. It was an anachronism in 1791, two years after the French Revolution, and perhaps for that reason an attempt to vindicate the virtues of monarchy. This text with its sterile pomposity was a strange choice to be thrust upon the composer who had just been pouring his heart into the gaiety, the gentleness, the earnestness of *The Magic Flute*.

Mozart may have hesitated for a moment, but he could not have refused. The fee and the opportunity for royal recognition were imperious, as well as imperial, reasons. He could not have hesitated long, for the event itself was about four weeks off. He took a coach to Prague with Constanze and Süssmayr, the latter for the purpose of writing the dry recitatives to connect the twenty-six numbers. Mozart composed all twenty-six, and began his notations in the carriage. The composer who never failed in an assignment, and always gave better than was expected of him, came through handsomely with a fully rounded, brilliant, skillful score. The performance (September 6), on the evening of the coronation, made no great impression. The Empress Maria Luisa, daughter of the King of Naples, called it "a piece of German stupidity" (*"una porcheria tedesca"*), a phrase that was passed around. Nevertheless it was remounted and liked in Prague and made its way to London. As an attempt at a successful stage piece, *La Clemenza di Tito* could not have been otherwise than stillborn. It could not hold the stage in another century, but is highly admired for purely musical reasons.

Exhausted by his labors over *La Clemenza di Tito* and

dispirited by its cold reception, Mozart returned at once to Vienna, where the final work upon *The Magic Flute* was urgently awaiting him. He completed the opera by September 28, two days before the performance. These numbers were the last in the score: the final chorus of the priests, Papageno's *"Ein Mädchen oder Weibchen,"* and the Finale, as well as the two purely instrumental numbers, the Overture and the March. He led the opening performance from the piano.

The first audience was unresponsive; they were probably too astonished to applaud. The alternation of the delicate Mozartean orchestra, the spectacle of Schikaneder galloping about plumed like a bird and singing songs of nursery-like simplicity, and the solemn priestly ritual may well have left them somewhat bewildered. Mozart after the first act was in a state of despair, and may have wondered how he could have let himself be drawn into this variegated concoction, played in a haunt of low comedy where music of lofty appeal was hideously out of place. On subsequent nights he was reassured. *Die Zauberflöte* soon caught its public and became more popular with every performance. It had a solid run through October. Here was proof at last that he could count on living by his music.

The first popularity of *The Magic Flute* has been attributed to its Masonic element. It was never censored, but it might have been. The literature of Freemasonry was incorporated; the printed libretto reproduced Masonic symbols. It was whispered that the Queen of Night stood for the late Queen Maria Theresa who had remained, until her death in 1780, the outspoken enemy of the brotherhood. Although the Masons were numerous and the more zealous of them would have taken delight in this kind of defiance of authority, it is doubtful whether the Masonic scenes rather than the sparkling tunes and the comedy continued to fill Schikaneder's theatre and others elsewhere.

When Mozart labeled *Die Zauberflöte* a *Grosse Oper,* he implied a work of depth and grandeur. He had called his other German opera, *Die Entführung,* a *Komisches Singspiel,* and basically this was also one—a spoken comedy with songs interspersed. It was also of course a great deal more than that. In *Die Entführung* he had lifted a pattern of routine stage entertainment to true musical importance. In *The Magic Flute* he carried his quest further and reopened the path toward a German national opera which his Emperor had defeated by dissolving the whole endeavor. Mozart had continued eager to set another German text. When the opportunity came, he had seized upon it at once. The book as it emerged was anything but promising. It was a gratuitous putting together of any fantastic character, comedy bit, or turn of magic that had pleased Schikaneder's audiences in the past. They were familiar with *Oberon* by Wranitzky, produced by Schikaneder earlier in the same season, and also *Kaspar, the Birdcatcher* by Wenzel Müller produced at the rival Leopoldstadter theatre on May 3. In each text a prince hero was sent by a fairy queen to release her daughter from the control of an evil magician. The hero was provided by the fairy with a magical musical instrument. In the latter case his clown companion, Kaspar, was also equipped with a protective instrument, specifically a bassoon. The captor was confounded, the lady rescued, and the lovers united, according to the invariable rule of fairy tales.

Strange reversals and contradictions appear in the libretto of *The Magic Flute,* as if there had been a change of plan toward the end of the first act. The good fairy queen turns out to be evil, the evil magician turns out to be the benevolent Sarastro. It is not known just what hands went into the drafting of the book. Schikaneder took full credit for it, but years later (in 1818, after Schikaneder's death), C. L. Giesecke* claimed that he had written the libretto. He probably had a great deal to do with the versification, for although *The Magic Flute* is far from a good piece of literature, Schikaneder was not to be relied upon as a poet, and was still less trustworthy on matters of credit, in fact quite capable of taking the glory

---

* Carl Ludwig Giesecke (his real name was Johann Georg Metzler) was a mineralogist who temporarily deserted science to become a comedian and librettist in Schikaneder's troupe. He prepared the libretto for *Oberon, King of the Elfs* (from Wieland), music by Paul Wranitzky. He sang the part of the first "boy" in *The Magic Flute.*

of authorship to himself. We can be sure that the dialogue for his own part, plentifully provided with humor, was his own. The probabilities are that Mozart, if he did not have a hand in the text itself, was responsible for the apparent switch in the plot. In this case, Schikaneder would have had to listen to him—his theatre is said to have been on the verge of bankruptcy and there was no other composer available who could be counted on to pull it up again. Mozart seems to have had his way not only about the libretto but about the performing forces. The vocal parts were exceedingly difficult and exacting. They would take arduous drilling. The orchestra required was far larger and more expert than the resources of the *Auf-der-Wieden*—it included clarinets and basset horns, then scarce, three difficult trombone parts, and a glockenspiel. Mozart and no one else would have wanted to interpolate scenes of Masonic ritual in order to express in music the faith that was then possessing him. Schikaneder was also a Mason, and would have sensed the advantage of a veiled declaration for the brotherhood when it was under official suppression by the throne. He was not the sort to be carried away by religious zeal, being far closer in character to Papageno than to Sarastro. Nor would his keen sense of the theatre have advocated solemn and static scenes of moral exhortation before his usual patrons assembled for farcical entertainment.

At any rate, the decision to turn *The Magic Flute* into a Masonic piece made necessary a drastic change in the plot. The Masonic scenes could not have been tied up with the Queen of Night as a good fairy, for queens (even good queens from Maria Theresa down) had no place in the Masonic philosophy, which made a point of subordinating women. To eliminate the Queen of Night would have meant dropping the principal coloratura part and also Josefa Hofer, Mozart's sister-in-law, for whom it was written. To open the opera with a temple scene would have alienated the audience at once, and would have required the rewriting of the whole first act. The test of virtue by the ordeal of fire and water could not be reconciled with the rescue of the heroine by magic means.

Mozart may have received the numbers piecemeal (as usually happened) to compose in haste, without knowledge of what would follow. The Queen of Night as she first appears is a grieving mother whose affection for her captured daughter is as believable to the audience as to the hero, Tamino. Her aspect at first is awesome, supernatural, but not necessarily evil. The "three ladies," servants of the queen, are amiable, and engagingly human in having an eye for Tamino's good looks. They give virtuous advice, including a gentle caution to Papageno about truthfulness and a practical lesson to drive it home, and provide Tamino and Papageno each with a delightful instrument whose beneficent notes will keep them from being lost and shield them from danger. The trio even guide them to the three genii (*Knaben*) who are admittedly good spirits. Not until Tamino tries to penetrate the three portals of the temple does he learn from the Priest that Sarastro (not yet encountered) is no wicked magician but a man of God. The story at first has no geographical bearings except that the subject was traditionally oriental, and that in the first libretto Tamino is referred to as a "Japanese prince." The Temple, when adapted to Masonic tradition, becomes Egyptian. Pamina, until then a faithful daughter, is told that she must reject her mother as a "haughty woman"—*"ein stolze Weib."*

From this point the altered plot is consistent. Sarastro, in one of the finest scenes in the opera, lifts it to its highest point. In the second aria for the Queen of Night, Mozart makes her evil indeed. It is music of frenzied frustration (recalling Elettra's final aria of defeat in *Idomeneo*) and ends with wild coloratura passages. Tamino and Pamina are blessed within the sacred precincts and Papageno, who does not belong in this righteous territory at all, finds his mate outside of its borders. The priestly scenes do not belong to comedy —their need, solemn and earnest, was applicable to free-thinking citizens of Vienna in 1791, and ludicrous in fairy-land, where the moralities, being either black or white, need no discussion, and where any speculation on problems of conduct is conveniently circumvented by magic spells. Tamino as a Masonic novitiate would not have been expected to encounter a dragon, and Pamina, whose emotions and instincts are warmly human, is hardly believable as the daughter of an evil enchantress. Papageno fits into the story only because it was built around him in the first place—his ingenuous, down-to-earth realism puts Sarastroan contemplation at a disadvantage and makes him no proper husband for the supernatural Papagena.

Mozart proved once more that he was equal to any assignment by accomplishing forthwith the most incredible of the many miracles of his career. He took the subject into his heart and transformed it into music of one piece. The true magic of *The Magic Flute* is its stylistic integration.

The overture (composed last) is the key to its style—elementary melodic simplicity, set with intricate counterpoint and a wealth of delicate detail. The characteristic Mozartean purity of the music pervades alike the running gaiety of the allegro and the solemnity of the priestly chords. There is not a commonplace bar in the whole opera. This purity of style elevates the temple scenes into a special atmosphere of their own. It affects each character. It ennobles Tamino's courageous quest, Pamina's distress. It makes Papageno, with his frank appetites, an innocent and almost lovable child of nature. The Queen of Night becomes weird rather than malignant. Her subject Monostato is grotesque rather than gruesome. The three "ladies," with the beauty of their part-singing and their delicate and feminine orchestral background, make us forget that they are on the wrong side of the moral line.

With such wiles does Mozart endear his characters to all his hearers. The magic power of superlative music can subdue the human reason and make the preposterous acceptable. The magician Wagner has bewitched his admirers into accepting a sudden and complete plot reversal by introducing an absurdity called a "love potion." Mozart was an even greater magician. Accepting casually, and because it came his way, a patchwork text of many sources, he transformed it into music which charms the layman and the discerning listener, each in his own province, compromising neither. He has even bewitched learned critics in another century into accepting the tale as a sound allegory.

Die Zauberflöte is the complete Mozart. It contains his

most deep-felt expression of faith in humanism; in the parts of Tamino and Pamina he opens the way to full romantic expression. In Papageno's part he transfigures the style of the street song into the purest beauty. The choral writing shows an advance over anything he had done by its refinement and "mystic" penetration. The use of instrumental color is also a fresh development, with entrancing results. His utimate stage masterpiece is the most mature of all in workmanship. It lays the cornerstone for German opera in two centuries to follow. As in his last symphony, the gaiety which had pervaded all that he wrote is somehow lifted to a different plane. It has been said that the last three symphonies, written in a single summer, complement each other to express all of Mozart. In a sense his three greatest operas follow a similar succession, *Figaro* having the carefree gaiety of the E flat Symphony, *Don Giovanni* also showing his darker nature, as in the G minor, the rarefied *Die Zauberflöte* becoming a sort of operatic "Jupiter."

What proved to be Mozart's fatal illness was already upon him in the last stages of *The Magic Flute*. Perhaps Schikaneder pushed him too hard in compelling its completion for performance on September 30. In the two remaining months of his destined life, he composed the Clarinet Concerto (K. 622) for Anton Stadler in early October, and the Masonic Cantata (K. 623) in November. Otherwise, he struggled to complete the *Requiem*.

XX

Vienna, 1791

As *The Magic Flute* continued to draw crowds at Schikaneder's theatre, Mozart took pleasure in attending performances. He keenly sensed that he had found the public pulse while giving his best. He once played the glockenspiel off-stage as Schikaneder went through the motions of playing as usual, and, as a joke, threw him off with a sudden cadenza. He took his small son Karl to a performance and watched the effect upon him. He was pleased when Salieri heard the opera and praised it. Sitting in a box at another time he noticed that his neighbor continued laughing in the temple scene, and called him a "Papageno." All this was quite unlike Mozart. He had always been careless about each of his completed works when they were once established in performance. It was the carelessness of the artist aware that at any moment he could sit down and match what he had done with another as good. Now he was convinced that this was to be his last opera. His imaginative life was in the theatre, and to relinquish the merry course of this one would have left his thoughts in a misery of blank finality. When he became too weak to go to the theatre he imagined each scene, watch in hand.

He worked feverishly on the *Requiem,* with the aid of Süssmayr, and here again was heartbreak, for he knew that he was racing with death. He was being defeated at last in meeting an assignment. He worked in his bed until the excitement exhausted him, and the manuscript had to be taken away. It was on November 15, when he had somewhat recovered his strength, that he wrote his last completed work, the short Masonic cantata for male voices, to a text of Schikaneder. Then he tried to resume his sketches for the *Requiem* but soon had to give them up, and was unable to leave his bed. The composer whose ease and rapidity have never been matched on such a plane was deprived of his function at the very top of his powers. He was obsessed by thoughts of death and believed, when his body was swollen by dropsy, that he had taken poison. Mozart had faced the thought of death with equanimity and expressed his thoughts in letters to his father. It was the natural end, the inevitable course, the way of God. He then believed that he could meet it cheerfully. Now at thirty-five, in all the abundance and resource of his musical instincts, it was another matter. Death is for one who has lived his full years and, quiescent, has found resignation. Mozart's spirit was younger than thirty-five, and his music was youth itself. There was nothing withdrawn, retrospective, in his last opera. It was visionary but also eager, forward-looking, expanding into richer ways. The *Requiem* is proof in an entirely different way that Mozart could no longer face the end with complete calm. This fearful and awe-inspiring article of faith was embraced by the dying man with a terrible earnestness. He was more than meeting an order with a proper setting of the text. Mozart never wrote music of more persistent gloom, more solemnity. In a way this was his most remarkable accomplishment. It opens up what might have become a new Mozart—an artist of serious stature, who could turn away completely from the style of graceful entertainment when the subject drew him. The most astonishing part of the *Requiem* is the clarity of purpose, the undiminished skill in every bar of the sketches, which the sick composer barely managed to put on paper. With physical dissolution, the creative brain was never dimmed.

The last days have been described by Constanze, and by Nissen from her account. While he was still conscious, his music was always in his thoughts. The day before his death he began to sing the first song of Papageno, but his voice was barely audible. *Kapellmeister* Roser, who was sitting beside him, went to the piano and finished it, to his delight. On the same day he asked for the manuscript of the *Requiem*. He began to sing the alto part while Hofer took the tenor and Gerl (the first Sarastro) the bass. Schack, the Tamino, who tells this story, took the soprano. When they began the Lachrimosa, which Mozart had not finished, he wept convulsively, and laid the score aside.

On the evening of his death, he was possessed by thoughts of his *Requiem;* when he could no longer speak, he blew out his cheeks as if imitating the trumpets. After midnight on December 5, 1791, he turned with his face to the wall as if to sleep, and within an hour he was gone.

The fatal illness had lasted about six months and had progressively taken his strength. Medical knowledge at the time was unequal to a diagnosis. Post-mortems in our century generally incline to the theory of nephritis, inflammation of the kidneys, as the final cause of death.

The funeral took place on the day after his death. The service was held at St. Stephen's Church. A large group of friends were present, but a storm was raging, and according to an account in the Vienna *Morgenpost,* no one accompanied the bier to the burial at the churchyard of St. Mark's. Van Swieten, who took charge of the funeral arrangements, had ordered a "third class" funeral at 11 florins, 36 kreutzer, whereby the coffin was put in a common grave and its identity lost. The Baron has been much blamed for this final economy. It would be kinder to remember him as the companion in the investigation of Handel and Sebastian Bach, a more loyal friend than most in his station of life, who may have put numerous fees in his hand when he could enjoy them.

The personal possessions of Mozart were scanty, his debts were large. Constanze, left with two children and in a difficult position, went to the Emperor and put her dilemma before him. Her husband's debts amounted to 3,000 florins. The Emperor advised her to give a benefit concert which he would sponsor. In this way the debts were paid.

There is a widely expressed opinion that Mozart had spent the strength of his frail body by constant work and the misery of poverty. This is contradicted by Mozart's unfailing joy in composing, and by the spirit which created *The Magic Flute,* the very affirmation of life and youth, the spirit, too, which was for the first time savoring the sweet taste of popular success without compromise. This would have meant public respect and consequent independence. Mozart had everything to live for.

The spirit of youth is also the spirit of growth. His composing energy at the end was not that of a man who was through with life. The composer who created The Overture to *The Magic Flute* with his last illness heavily upon him, who struggled to complete the *Requiem* until paralysis actually stopped his hand, had the will to live, to continue functioning. The spring of his invention was never quite so abundant as at the point when death took him. He would have continued in that particular combination of elementary simplicity expanding into delicate beauty, that matching of facility and quality which is the rarest the world has known.

The Music of Mozart

Introduction

THE ACTUAL bulk of Mozart's music, prodigious by modern standards, is not as large as that of some of his contemporaries, who were ready to provide new works as a matter of course for any and every concert. The bulk is impressive for a man who died at thirty-five, and was possible only because he began at eight. This also means that he composed almost half of his works (numerically speaking, for his earlier works are shorter) before he came of age. The early works are not to be despised or overlooked. In a way they are the foremost miracle of the composing Mozart. The small boy, learning his profession by imitating the gallant style of his elders, the composers about him, constantly comes forth with fresh invention, melodies which are the effervescence of youth itself. The supreme melodist seems never to have had to learn how to write a melody. Not one of the earlier symphonies, sonatas, or Masses, is without surprises of this sort. For a long while he is constrained to write polite music for polite gatherings. Gradually, in his teens, the personal Mozart takes control and the starch of elegance disappears. Borrowed fervor in a slow movement becomes his own personal impulse, the acquired formula for brilliance in a rondo becomes his own personal exuberance. He who passes by the special treasures which capture in tone this first romantic bloom of adolescence can never say that he truly knows Mozart. Here and there the music is transformed as the composer's enlivening imagination breaks up the old rigidities of phrasing, accompaniment, artificial graces. The growth of the artist will never cease through his life, but at about the time of his coming of age there are astonishing spurts. The five violin concertos of 1775, the "Jeunehomme" Piano Concerto of 1777, the "Paris" Symphony of 1778, *Idomeneo* of 1780, the *Kyrie* in D minor of 1781—each of these reveals the sudden awakening of what in its amplitude and independence amounts to a new grasp of each form, leaving precedent far behind.

The remaining ten years in Vienna are of course the great years, while here, too, the growth continues. The operas expand consistently in scope, where their subjects allow. The symphonies rise to their peak in 1788. The chamber works, the string quartets and quintets in particular, reach at last the highest point of all in craftsmanship. In the final three years, Mozart shows an increasing tendency to turn away from the *style galant* altogether. He is less under compulsion of entertaining frivolous audiences. Considered rebellion is not in his nature—the old habits of phrase repetition, formal cadence, da capo, ornamentation, linger, and will indeed linger in others into another century, for this was ingrained musical thinking. Nevertheless, Mozart's imagination, taking fire, leads him into new ways which modify formality. He probes the highly charged dramatic, the tragic and somber aspects of his art. The composer of the G minor Symphony and the Quintet in the same key, the Piano Fantasia in C minor, the *Requiem,* was turning away from a polite century and finding a romantic one. But not with rejection. As if to prove that his lifelong musical gaiety was not to be forfeited, he left a final opera to top all his works in sheer high humor.

The Operas

THE RECORD of Mozart's life and many remarks in his letters make it plain that opera was his first ambition. It was more than the highroad to fame; it was his dearest delight. When he had a reasonably congenial text he composed with joy, threw himself into the preparations, and carried through the rehearsals with such zeal that the performers caught his fire. It was his operas that elicited every aspect of his genius—his vocal melody and his choral writing at their highest; his orchestral writing, too, for the focal point is often in the pit, where there is not only symphonic brilliance, but, when the occasion calls for it, concertante quality. He shaped concert and chamber elements to his theatrical ends entirely in his own way. No other composer has been so at home both in and out of the theatre (except perhaps Strauss) and no other has even approached his greatness in this combined respect.

He is the only eighteenth-century composer whose operas still hold the stage in any standard repertory. Operas being more subject to fashion than other music, his have had to contend in another century with the sensational paraphernalia of Wagner, Verdi and Puccini, with the elimination of speech or recitative, the fusion into continuous musical narrative. These innovations have put Mozart's contemporaries into the class of those only occasionally performed. Mozart's operas once suffered a partial eclipse, and barely held their own at the Romantic peak. The renascence has come in our own century. Mozart in the theatre may well survive certain more demonstrative composers by the sheer élan and inner wealth of his scores and their theatrical truth. With many repetitions of standard operas it becomes apparent that Bellini, Verdi and Bizet had no exclusive ownership of human emotion. Norma and Violetta tore passion to shreds largely because the composer behind them had a formula. Donna Anna and the Queen of Night had another formula behind their making —a formula which had a lower voltage of automatic devices to quicken the pulse of the listener and could not so easily counterfeit genuine fervor or musical worth. Mozart was at least as dramatic, at least as romantic, in the terms of his earlier esthetic. Mozart's lovable characters, Cherubino and the Countess Almaviva, even such mild rogues as Leporello and Papageno, such saucy servants as Despina and Susanna, have a more enduring place in our hearts than their operatic fellows in another century, because the composer drew more deeply from his own human and musical nature to create them.

We accept the eighteenth-century formalities—the da capo arias, the phrase repetitions, the extended cadences, because, though they are long since obsolete, Mozart has made them musically delightful, even natural according to the musical logic of his time. In this matter of dwelling in the past, Mozart has one appeal to us which is accidental—the charm of the period piece. The costumes and sets which now make *Figaro* and *Così fan tutte* an opportunity for the designer and a spectacle for the eye were to Mozart entirely contemporary and normal. His gentle friend the Countess Thun may have dressed and graced a *fauteuil* very much as the Countess Almaviva did, and in a similar salon. Equally natural to his time was the graceful charm which then pervaded all music, and which to us can be refreshingly piquant—a pleasant contrast to modern onslaughts of sound. Thackeray in *The Virginians* had one of his characters speak impatiently of *"Cosi fan tutti"* (he spelled it so) as hopelessly "old-fashioned." *Così fan tutte* has long since passed the stage of being out of date like a piece of worn, hand-me-down furniture. It has entered the timeless category of a precious "antique" from a historical past.

Mozart's childhood operas, dating from *La finta semplice,* composed when he was twelve, are quite accomplished and performable—extraordinary manifestations of precocity. Needless to say, an opera of lasting importance needed more maturity, even in Mozart, than he could put into his early stage pieces for Italy and for Salzburg. *La finta giardiniera,* which he wrote for Munich at eighteen, was a more mature and finished work, but was defeated by its text. From this point Mozart was constantly eager to compose an opera, but was frustrated on every hand. Visiting Mannheim and Paris, where opera flourished, he hoped in vain for a commission. When at last he received the order for *Idomeneo* in Munich, at the age of twenty-five, his eagerness was great, as the letters show. Settling immediately afterwards in Vienna, he built up great hopes, went through "hundreds" of librettos (so he wrote), and made several beginnings, which were defeated by the miserable, tradition-bound hackwork that passed for librettos. *The Abduction from the Seraglio,* ordered for the National Theatre in 1781, had an indifferent text, but enabled him to compose the first important opera in German, which took a quick hold in German towns. Not until late 1785 did he succeed in getting another commission from the Emperor. It was *Figaro,* in Italian, the only text he ever found that was entirely of his own choosing and the only one entirely worthy of his abilities. The success of *Figaro* in Prague led to the commission for *Don Giovanni* there in 1787. *Così fan tutte,* his second *opera buffa* for Vienna, was produced in 1790. Nothing more was asked of him by imperial Vienna. He composed *The Magic Flute* in 1791, the last year of his life, and interrupted it for *La clemenza di Tito,* hastily written in a few weeks' time for Prague. *The Magic Flute,* a private venture with Schikaneder for a popular theatre, had a resounding success at once, and became the cornerstone for German opera—but only after its composer had died.

The story of the great operatic Mozart spending most of his years waiting for a chance to compose, writing only three operas for Vienna by order of the crown, and writing his last too late to taste the fame which should long since have come to him, touches us the more deeply when we realize that Mozart, who allowed himself six weeks to compose an opera (though he usually took more) could, if asked, have turned out one each season and doubled the number through his glorious Vienna decade.

Early Operas and Other Stage Works

Die Schuldigkeit des ersten Gebotes, Religious *Singspiel, K.* 35 (Composed in Salzburg, 1766–1767).

Mozart, aged ten, composed the first part of this musical morality play on *The Obligation of the First Commandment* ("Thou shalt love thy God"); Michael Haydn, as concertmaster, the second; and Adlgasser, as court composer and organist, the third. Mozart's part consists of a sinfonia, eight arias and a final trio. The music is completely adequate, rising dutifully to the rigidly righteous text.

Apollo et Hyacinthus, Latin Comedy in one act, K. 38 (Composed in Salzburg, May, 1767)

This was a spring production by the students of the University of Salzburg. Mozart provided nine numbers, including choruses and duets.

Bastien und Bastienne, Operetta in one act, K. 50 (Composed in Vienna, summer, 1768)

The French subject, *Bastien et Bastienne,* had been much knocked about, being the simple romance of a shepherd and shepherdess who have a falling out and at length patch up their differences, thanks to the advice of an older man who pretends to be a magician and is really no more than a man of kindly tact. *Bastien et Bastienne* had a history. It was at first *Le Devin du village,* an *intermède* composed by Jean Jacques Rousseau, a "back to nature" piece which had delighted Paris sixteen years before, as part of the vogue at Versailles for "simplicity" and the cultivation of an imagined Arcadia of silks and ribboned crooks. The piece was parodied by Madame Favart who annihilated the artificial never-land by appearing in sabots and singing in *patois* like a true rustic. It was translated into German by F. W. Weiskern and had been performed in Vienna four years before it was handed to Mozart. Wolfgang had no concern with the French background. What was put before him was a succession of solo airs with duets and a trio, connected by dialogue, in his own language, wherein the two lovers are alternately jealous, prettily angry, and joyfully united after the air of their advisor which brings in some amusing hocus-pocus.

Originally using spoken dialogue, *Singspiel* fashion, Mozart apparently later added dry recitative (as far as the Duet, No. 7). There are also short accompanied recitatives.

La finta semplice, *Opera buffa* in three acts, K. 51 (Composed in Vienna, 1768)

Mozart's first *opera buffa*, composed at the age of twelve, in and for Vienna, but not performed until his return to Salzburg, exists in the complete autograph score of twenty-six numbers. The text, by Marco Coltellini, is based on the machinations of Rosina, the "pretended innocent," to induce proposals of marriage from two hesitant bachelor brothers. A Hungarian officer, Fracasso, and his servant, Simone, are quartered in the house of the two wealthy bachelors, Cassandro and Polidoro, and their beautiful and desirable sister, Giacinta. The officer falls in love with Giacinta, and his servant falls in love with her maid, Ninetta. The two brothers oppose this double engagement. Polidoro, the younger bachelor, who is shy with women, is dominated by his cynical and domineering brother, Cassandro, who categorically denounces love and women on principle. Fracasso, the officer, in order to break down this barrier to the course of true love, brings in his clever sister, Rosina, to practice her wiles on each brother in turn, overcome their reserve and compromise their stand on the subject of matrimony. She succeeds in winning a proposal of marriage from each of them. The denouement is the engagement of "*La finta semplice*" and Cassandro, and his sanction of the marriage of the other two engaged couples.

Mitridate, rè di Ponto, *Opera seria* in three acts, K. 87 (Completed in Milan, December, 1770)

The text was by Vittorio Amadeo Cigna-Santi, and was derived from Racine's tragedy. The opera consists of twenty-three numbers, seven of which Mozart rewrote.

While Pontus is at war with Rome, and King Mithridates is with his army, his betrothed, Aspasia, is secretly courted by both of his sons, Farnace and Sifare. The brothers quarrel, but it is evident that Aspasia is in love with Sifare. The King returns and learns of his fiancée's infidelity. When he finds that both sons are ready to betray their country to the Romans he orders their execution, and the execution of Aspasia as well. Both brothers, however, show their valor in attacking the enemy; Mithridates is killed in battle; and Sifare and Aspasia are united.

Ascanio in Alba, *Serenata teatrale* in two acts, K. 111 (Composed in Milan, September, 1771)

This piece for a wedding festivity, to a text by Abbate Giuseppe Parini, contains twenty-seven numbers, choruses, airs and ballets, scenically set. It depicts a mythological union in which Venus is shown as the matchmaker, depicted with complimentary allusions to Queen Maria Theresa, who was the mother of Archduke Ferdinand, the bridegroom of Beatrice d'Este. Venus, numerously attended, descends from Olympus to arrange the marriage of her grandson Ascanio with Silvia, a shepherdess descended from Hercules. Cupid causes Silvia to behold Ascanio in a vision, to her delight. In a sacrificial ceremony celebrated by the shepherds of the land the couple is to rule, the constancy of Silvia is tested and proved. The piece ends with a joyful chorus.

Il sogno di Scipione, *Serenata drammatica,* K. 126 (Composed in Salzburg, March 1772)

This complimentary allegory to a text by Metastasio was performed in honor of the consecration of Hieronymus as Archbishop of Salzburg. It consists of twelve numbers. It is derived from Cicero's *Somnium Scipionis.* Scipio in a dream is visited by Costanza, the deity representing steadfastness and valor, and Fortuna, representing the softer, voluptuous delights. He must choose between them. The ghosts of his ancestors counsel him, but cannot control his choice. As he makes the inevitable virtuous choice, there is a thunderous outburst by the rejected Fortuna. The *licenza* in praise of the Archbishop follows.

Lucio Silla, *Dramma per musica* in three acts, K. 135 (Composed in Salzburg and Milan, October-December, 1772)

The text is by Giovanni da Gamerra. The antagonists are Lucio Silla, dictator in Rome, and Cecilio, a senator who has been banished. The potentate Silla wishes to marry Junia, but

Junia is in love with Cecilio. Silla tries to force the situation by publicly announcing Junia as his intended bride. Cecilio, having secretly returned to his country, rushes in with drawn sword, but is arrested and condemned to death. At the last moment the ruler is seized with remorse, pardons his would-be murderer, and blesses the pair.

La finta giardiniera, *Opera buffa* in three Acts, K. 196 (Composed between September, 1774, and January, 1775, in Salzburg and Munich)

La finta giardiniera, "the lady disguised as a gardener," taking the name Sandrina, is in search of her husband, who in the past had stabbed her in a fit of jealousy and left her, thinking her dead. She encounters him (the Count Belfiore) in the garden of the Podestà (a minor official) and, concealing her identity, beholds him interested in Arminda, the Podestà's niece. The Podestà, who possesses title, wealth, years and amorous intentions (being the first buffo) looks upon the "gardeneress" with an acquisitive eye. A young poet, Ramiro (a castrato part) is in love with Arminda, who is far more interested in Belfiore (the husband on trial). There is also Nardo, engaged as gardener, but actually the cousin of Sandrina, sharing her anonymity. Nardo is in love with Serpetta, the Podestà's servant, but Serpetta, money-minded, has her eye on her master. To put it briefly, everybody in the cast is suffering from unrequited love. In the last act, Sandrina and her husband, who has recognized her, go mad in a dark spot in the woods and believe they are a shepherd and shepherdess, thus throwing the other characters and the story itself into a state of complete confusion. They recover their sanity in time for an all-around matching of proper couples before the final curtain.

Il rè pastore, Dramatic festival opera in two acts, K. 208 (Composed in Salzburg, April, 1775)

The text of this pastoral piece by Metastasio had been set before, and would be set again by others. The occasion was the reception of the Archduke Maximilian in Salzburg. The production aimed at brilliance. The orchestra was large. The principal singing parts had elaborate bravura. The male soprano, Tomaso Consoli, who took the principal lover's part (Amintas) and the flutist Becke were both brought from Munich. The excellent

overture promises gaiety but formality rules the pastoral story
and its treatment. The love of the shepherd and shepherdess
Amintas and Elisa is the idyllic subject of the first act. There
develops a complication, for Amintas is not a shepherd at all
but the rightful heir to the throne of Sidon. Alexander, the Mace-
donian conqueror, the personification in eighteenth-century minds
of heroic virtue, summons Amintas to his duty as ruler of his
people and ordains that Tamiris become his queen. Tamiris, however, is in love with Agenor, a Sidonian noble. After a struggle
between love and duty, the desired pairing is brought about with
the blessing of the great monarch. The whole ends with a rather
routine choral finale in praise of the guest: *"Viva l'invito duce!"*
Mozart managed to make a score of much beauty out of his
unpromising assignment. The orchestra sometimes fulfills a traditional accompaniment pattern, but in several of the numbers,
and in the long introductions to arias, attains new life and distinction. The part of Alexander is brilliantly, even regally treated,
with trumpets in his first and last arias, with solo flute in *"Se
vincendo vi rendo felici."* The two lovers, Amintas and Elisa,
close the first act with an affecting duet, and Amintas' aria avow-
ing constancy (*"L'amerò, sarò costante"*), with a violin obbligato,
has elements of a concerto slow movement worthy of the year
of the great violin concertos.

Thamos, King of Egypt, Incidental music to the Heroic Drama
   by Tobias Philip, Freiherr von Gebler, K. 345 (Composed in
   Vienna, 1773, and in Salzburg, 1779)

Mozart wrote the opening chorus (without an overture) and
the chorus which opens the last act at the instance of the play-
wright for the early Vienna production. When the play was
brought to Salzburg in 1779 by Böhm's troupe, he rewrote these,
added entr'actes between each of the five acts (the third is music
under a speaking voice) and added a choral close, to a text provided by Andreas Schachtner. At that time the play had gone
the rounds of the German theatres.

The music is for the most part solemn and ceremonial, mas-
sively treated, and dramatic, aiming at stage effect. It is also
curiously interesting. The revision predates *Idomeneo* by a year
and *The Magic Flute* by eleven, and yet it has an affinity with
both.

The dilemma of the play is the succession to the throne of
Egypt. Thamos rules, not knowing that the rightful heir, Menes,
supposed to be dead, is still living, and is in hiding in the guise

of a priest. Nor does he know that his advisor, Pheron, is traitorously plotting to seize the throne. Menes will not make himself known, for he loves Thamos, and would like his daughter, Saïs, to become Thamos' Queen. This, after tragic misadventure, is the happy outcome.

Since Mozart had not yet encountered Freemasonry, and did not choose the subject, he would not necessarily have been enamored over a tale of priestly rites in ancient Egypt, the worship of the sun, and the triumph of virtue as a solemnly declared principle. Yet the three great C minor chords that open the first entr'acte, the trombone choirs, the exhortative choruses, have the very atmosphere of the Temple of Isis and Sarastro. Other pages are still closer to *Idomeneo,* such as the storm scene after the last act, where, as in that opera, Mozart summons every tonal means his century can offer, trombones included, to terrify his audience with music of doom. The fearsome lines of the Priest and the awe-stricken pianissimo of the crowd also point directly toward *Idomeneo.* This (added) final scene turns to brilliant jubilation, with joyous figures in the strings as the composer reaches what one might dare to name as the most uplifting of his stage finales.

Zaïde (Title by André), *Singspiel,* K. 344 (Composed in Salzburg, 1779)

The text is by Johann Andreas Schachtner, of Salzburg. The posthumous score, lacking an overture and finale and connecting texts, came to the attention of Constanze in 1798. It was published in 1838 by André under the title *"Zaïde."* It was Mozart's first attempt at a full-length German *Singspiel.* There is here more sentiment than humor. Three virtuous characters are under the control of the Sultan Soliman: Gomatz, who is his prisoner; Zaïde, who is his favorite; and Allazim, a prince in disguise who is in his employ. Gomatz and Zaïde, who are in love, try to make their escape with the help of Allazim. They are caught and condemned to death. The intended solution to this predicament is not known, but it might have borrowed from the predecessor of the piece—"The Seraglio, or the Unexpected Encounter in Slavery by Father, Son and Daughter," by Joseph von Friebert. It there appears that Allazim is the Prince Ruggiero, who saved the Sultan's life years before, and Gomatz and Zaïde turn out to be his children. The general happiness at their pardon would have been dampened by the embarrassing discovery that they are already closely related.

Later Operas

Idomeneo, rè di Creta, Opera seria in three acts, K. 366. Text by Abbate Giambattista Varesco, after Antoine Danchet (Composed in Salzburg and Munich, October, 1780-January, 1781)

Idomeneo was not only Mozart's first great operatic opportunity. It was his only opportunity to put the ardent application of his powers into the noble and dignified sentiments of classical tragedy in a full scaled production. *La clemenza di Tito,* composed in the last months of his life, when he was ill, pushed for time, and forced to interrupt the progress of *Die Zauberflöte,* could not and did not capture his heart and draw his best energies.

At twenty-four, having waited long and in vain for a commission, aware of his accumulated powers, he suddenly found a superb company, including the best orchestra in Europe, at his disposal. *Idomeneo* became his one heroic opera in the fullest sense. It elicited some of the most nobly moving stage music he ever wrote. Succeeding generations have come to know the operatic Mozart almost exclusively for his gay and sparkling music, with its moments of tenderness. His more solemn and tragic powers have been largely shut off from the general consciousness because the *opera seria* is of the past. Even at the time of *Idomeneo* it was an expiring form, still maintained only in certain courts. Opera audiences of a later day are no longer held by mythological subjects set forth at great length in a somber, declamatory style, with little relief. The story of *Idomeneo* is one of protracted anguish, imposed by a Greek god whom we find it difficult to take seriously, a dilemma resolved by the noble integrity of the Cretan Prince Idamante, and Ilia, whom he loves. The composer draws us into sympathy with the terrible ordeal of King Idomeneo and the pair of lovers. He does so with a score in an antique style which in other hands would be entirely monotonous but which in his hands becomes as varied and resourceful as any he ever composed. This variety is not in the solo voices, which are finely adapted to the text but stylized. It is in the orchestra, the choruses and the ensembles. In the solo arias and the many pages of accompanied recitative the orchestra never merely supports with string tremolo or emphatic chords. It dramatizes, alternates, enriches, even embellishes in a way no other composer of *opera seria* has approached (not excepting Gluck, who had nothing like Mozart's command of orchestral writing). Mozart was aware of the splendid wind players at his command. (He composed Ilia's aria "*Se il padre perdei*" at the beginning of Act II for wind obbligati with his colleagues in mind.) The Trio in the Second Act and the Quartet in the Third are his first great examples of ensemble writing. The choruses expressing the Trojan captives' joy of liberation, the people's terror of the storm, the ritual in the last act, are Mozart's fullest and most varied in any stage work, for the simple reason that this one gave him his fullest choral opportunity.

The opera is placed in Crete, after the Trojan wars. We first behold Ilia, the daughter of Priam of Troy, a captive princess in an enemy country, who is torn between loyalty to her people and her as yet unspoken love for Idamante, the son of the ruling King, Idomeneo. Idomeneo has been away for years with his fleet. On his return he is threatened with shipwreck and vows to Poseidon that if he is granted a safe landing he will sacrifice to the god the first living creature whom he encounters on the shore. The one whom he meets is none other than Idamante, his own son. At first he pushes Idamante away, and will not admit the vow he has made. He plans, at the counsel of Arbace, his advisor, to send his son secretly out of harm's way by having him escort Elettra, the visiting queen, back to her home. Poseidon is angry at this ruse. He sends a monster to destroy the inhabitants and a storm to drive the ship back. Now Idomeneo is forced to confess what he has done. The sacrifice must be made. Idamante offers himself to the knife, but Ilia demands that she be taken in his place—the prince must be saved for his people. At this point impressive trombone chords are heard amidst dead silence, and a subterranean voice commands that the couple are to be spared and made the rulers of Crete. Idomeneo must abdicate. Elettra who has loved Idamante from the beginning of the opera, and aspired to the throne, and who is furiously jealous of Ilia, now realizes that her hopes are defeated. She sings the last of her three great arias—music vivid, highly charged, now hysterical. This is as superb a musical characterization as the gentle and wholly feminine characterization of Ilia. Ilia's soprano part is matched effectively with that of her lover, Idamante, a castrato. The full effect of their duets is somewhat lost in modern performance, where a mezzo-soprano is necessarily resorted to. The important part of Idomeneo, a tenor, was also effectively matched with the castrato in the dramatic first-act scenes between father and son.

The score of *Idomeneo* is great music because Mozart believed in his task and put his utmost into it. The opera is not for the seeker after stage entertainment. For the seeker after rich musical reward it is full of treasure, as occasional zealous extra-repertorial productions have proved.

Die Entführung aus dem Serail, *Komisches Singspiel* in three acts, K. 384 (Composed in Vienna, between July 29, 1781, and May 29, 1782)

The Abduction from the Seraglio, Mozart's first full opera in the German language, takes place in the Orient, has two Turkish characters—the pasha and his overseer, Osmin—and of the four remaining, two are English girls. Their origins are incidental to an opera that could not have been more German, both in music and characterization. The name of the soubrette, Blondchen, belies her statement that she is an *"Engländerin"* who takes no nonsense from importunate barbarians. She is an unmistakable German *Fräulein,* and her part merely echoes the tradition which looked upon English women as the most high-spirited of their sex. It all went back to the *Roxelane* of Marmontel, a play about an English girl who reduced a proud sultan to fatuous submission.

The opera tells how Belmonte, the first tenor, manages, not without difficulty, to rescue from thralldom under a Turkish potentate his beloved Constanze, her maid Blondchen, and his servant Pedrillo, all three having been captured before the story begins.

The scene is at the portals of the Pasha Selim's palace. Belmonte arrives on his quest, his first song a lover's prayer that he may succeed. The refrain has already served as a quiet middle section (there in the minor) to the bright and gay overture with its Turkish trappings of bass drum, cymbals, triangle and piccolo. Osmin, the pasha's overseer, enters with a ladder and basket, and proceeds to gather espaliered figs while he sings a song of his own. He has the longest part in the play, with a wide range and some difficult buffo patter. His is a bluff and grudging part. "Poison and daggers" is his stock farce line. He would like to have the head of any Christian, but particularly that of Pedrillo, Belmonte's captured servant, who has become the pasha's gardener, for Pedrillo is loved by Blondchen, supposed to be his own prize by capture.

As Osmin sings while gathering figs, he is interrupted by the newly arrived stranger, Belmonte, who wishes to know whether this is the Pasha Selim's Palace. When Osmin finds that the newcomer is a friend of Pedrillo he rages against them both. Belmonte soon encounters Pedrillo, who assures him that the two ladies are well and safe. Belmonte, alone, sings his aria of passion and hope, "*O wie ängstlich, o wie feurig klopft mein liebevolles Herz.*"* He hides when a chorus of Janissaries, to "Turkish" music, usher in the pasha (a speaking part). This potentate wants Constanze's love and asks her consent, but, being a benevolent despot, will not force it, even when, in an anguished aria, she admits that she loves another. Pedrillo approaches the pasha with Belmonte and introduces him as an architect. This appeals to the pasha, who, like every prince of the period, is a perpetual improver of his estate, and the pasha engages him. Osmin enters and tries to drive Belmonte and Pedrillo away, but they, confident on account of Belmonte's new position, defy him and insist upon entering. This is the subject of an amusing trio which ends the first act.

Act II opens with a scene between Osmin and Blondchen. He claims full rights over her but she defies him as an independent English girl who will not tolerate a bullying male. Only with tenderness and flattery can a woman's heart be won. Osmin, being quite incapable of either, is put in his place. Constanze, in a scene with Blondchen (neither of them know yet of Belmonte's arrival) sings a sorrowful andante of great beauty. The pasha presses Constanze again, and this time with the threat of "all kinds of torture" unless she yields. One suspects that this unkind remark was put into his mouth to give her a subject for her aria of defiance: "*Martern aller Arten.*" Selim is thereupon constrained to listen for six minutes to this concert number with a concertante group of flute, oboe, violin and cello, with much vocal display. Pedrillo tells Blondchen about Belmonte, and plans an escape. Pedrillo will dispose of Osmin, the main obstruction, by inducing him to take wine, against his Mussulman principles. Blondchen sees freedom ahead and sings the most joyful aria Mozart ever wrote, and one of the most *völkisch*: "*Welche Wonne, welche Lust!*" Pedrillo, who by stage tradition must be something of a coward, fortifies himself for his truly dangerous attempt, with the aria "*Frisch zum Kampfe!*" There follows the drinking scene, the funniest in the opera. Pedrillo persuades

---

* Mozart wrote to his father (September 26, 1781): "This is the favorite song of all who have heard it—myself included, and it is exactly right for Adamberger's voice. You can imagine how it expresses the beating of the heart—the violins in octaves. One can see the trembling, the hesitation, the very swelling of the breast expressed by a crescendo; one can hear the sighs, the whispers, rendered by the muted violins with one flute in unison." Mozart's description is apt in every detail.

Osmin just to taste the forbidden drink, and when he hesitates, says, "Do you suspect that I have poisoned your bottle?" and takes a drink from it. (He neglects to mention that he has instructed Blondchen to put a sleeping draught in Osmin's cup.) They sing the duet *alla Turca,* "*Vivat Bacchus,*" after which Osmin embraces his "enemy" as his devoted friend, collapses into the gardener's wheelbarrow, and is rolled off. The act ends with a remarkable quartet. Constanze and Belmonte meet for the first time. Both couples see escape ahead. But the two men have some doubt as to whether the two ladies have been completely successful in holding off their Turkish suitors. The ladies act according to character—Constanze is hurt by the question; Blondchen is furious and slaps Pedrillo's face. When these matters are straightened out the quartet ends with an Andantino of complete harmony and felicity.

The Third Act opens with an aria by Belmonte (often omitted in performance), and a serenade by Pedrillo, which is supposed to be a signal. It is in the quasi-Moorish style, with a delightful modality really Mozart's own, sung, of course, to a pizzicato accompaniment. At this point the plan goes askew. Osmin, though still groggy, discovers them and they are seized. He sings his great aria of triumph, "*Ha! wie will ich triumphieren.*" Constanze and Belmonte, in a touching duet, express their love and their willingness to die together. The pasha finds out that Belmonte is the son of his unforgivable enemy, but decides at the last moment to shame them and overwhelm them with his kindness by pardoning them both.* In the final "vaudeville" the characters sing in turn a verse in rejection of revenge as a motive; each followed by a refrain from all. Only Osmin cannot accept this sentiment, and he puts in his angry final protest.

L'oca del Cairo, *Dramma giocoso,* K. 422 (Composed in Salzburg, October, 1783)

Setting this comedy during his visit from Vienna to Salzburg, with Vienna in mind, of course, Mozart abandoned it after composing in sketch eight numbers of the first act. The plot is built upon an offer by Don Pippo (a buffo part) that Biondello (tenor) may have his daughter Celidora for his wife if he can

---

* This was in the tradition of praising the monarch in stage pieces as always magnanimous. In the libretto of Bretzner from which this one was lifted, Belmonte was discovered to be the pasha's abandoned son and was pardoned accordingly. The choice seems to have been between unlikely character and unlikely circumstance.

penetrate the tower where she is confined. It so happens that Biondello has an ingenious companion, and that Celidora has a companion in captivity by the name of Lavina. The two young men contrive an oversized artificial goose which is exhibited at the local fair, and which Don Pippo's wife purchases for the girls. The goose of course contains the two men. It is unfortunate that Mozart allowed himself to believe in so slim a story, so clumsily written, and to waste good effort on it.

Lo sposo deluso, ossia La rivalità di tre donne per un solo amante, *Opera buffa* in two acts, K. 430 (Composed in Salzburg, autumn, 1783)

The text (author unknown) of *The Deceived Husband,* or *The Rivalry of Three Women for a Single Lover,* came to Mozart while he was at work on *L'oca del Cairo,* and probably caused its abandonment. This project too was abandoned after he had composed the Overture and four numbers. Mozart had apparently reached the point where he could not go through with a hackwork text which fell short of his musical ambition. This one is about a pair of lovers, Emilia and Annibale, who are separated. Emilia, believing Annibale dead, is induced to marry Sempronio, the *primo buffo caricato,* who through various complications becomes the "deceived husband."

Der Schauspieldirektor, Comedy with music in one act, K. 486 (Composed in Vienna, February, 1786)

While Mozart was completing *Figaro,* shortly after composing the piano concertos K. 482 and 467 and the oratorio *Davidde penitente,* shortly before composing the piano concertos 488 and 491, he was called upon for music to a play by the younger Stephanie, to be performed at the little theatre in Schönbrunn for royal guests.

The Overture is rapid, spirited, and in Mozart's best *Singspiel* vein. According to the story, the theatre director is visited by two applicants for the part of prima donna in an opera. Mme. Herz arrives first and sings a heartfelt arietta of unrequited love, ending with rather ridiculous coloratura. Mme. Silberklang enters and sings in her "silvery" voice a rondo of coquetry, equally ornate. There follows a trio in which each lady, furiously jealous, claims the privilege of *"erste Sängerin,"* while M. Vogelgesang tries to pacify them. Mme. Herz has a pathetic solo within this number, with the word "adagio" for her text, whereupon Mme.

Silberklang sings "allegro, allegrissimo" with great brilliance, and M. Vogelgesang sings beneath them, "piano pianissimo." In the final ensemble they make up their differences, and since every piece must end with a moral, they decide that the artistic project comes before personal ambition. Mozart admirably meets the occasion.

Le nozze di Figaro, *Opera buffa* in four acts, K. 492. Text by Lorenzo da Ponte (after Beaumarchais) (Completed in Vienna, April 29, 1786)

The opera, like the play which it closely follows, takes place on the estate of the Count and Countess Almaviva, near Seville. They are still a young couple for, according to Beaumarchais, only three years have passed since his earlier play, *The Barber of Seville*, where Almaviva, a dashing lover, has carried off the fair Rosina as his wife. In *The Marriage of Figaro* (which Beaumarchais called "*La Folle journée*" since the action happens in a single "mad day") it soon appears that the young husband has developed extramarital inclinations.

In the opening scene, a nearly bare room between the chambers of the count and countess, we first find two of their servants, Figaro, the valet of the one, and Susanna, the personal maid of the other. The two are to be married that very day, and Figaro looks upon this room as just right for them; he can answer the master's bell and she the mistress's with the utmost convenience. Not so, says Susanna, the charming and innocent fiancée who nevertheless has wide open eyes—the count, although he has magnanimously abolished the feudal privilege of the lord of the manor, a first claim upon the virtue of one of his servants when she marries, would like to make a private exception in this case. Figaro, furious, makes use of Harlequin's traditional custom of confiding in the audience when he sings "*Se vuol' ballare, Signor Contino,*" and reveals his intention of outwitting his master and keeping his bride for himself. This time the servant will call the tune. An older couple enters—Dr. Bartolo and his housekeeper, Marcellina. Both would like to prevent the wedding of Figaro and Susanna—Bartolo has a grudge against the valet from the previous play; Marcellina would herself like to marry Figaro and holds his written promise, given in exchange for a loan. They will try to manipulate the count's desires and his short temper to their purpose. A duet between Marcellina and Susanna, each aware that the other is her enemy, is a masterpiece of spiteful, mock-polite interchange in music. Cherubino, a young protégé in the household (the part of an adolescent boy, taken by a mezzo-soprano) approaches Susanna. Cherubino is an innocent in love with love. In the words of Beaumarchais, the basis of his character is "a restless and a vague desire." All women fill him with rapture. He loves the countess at a respectful distance; he flirts with Susanna; he has been found in the room of Barbarina, the gardener's daughter, aged eleven but little younger than himself. The count unexpectedly enters, and Cherubino, in order not to be caught alone with Susanna, hides behind an armchair (the only piece of furniture in the room). The count tries to persuade her to meet him in the garden that night. He will "pay for the favor." Don Basilio is heard approaching. He is the music teacher who has been working for the count to procure Susanna's compliance. The count quickly conceals himself behind the chair, but not before Cherubino, unseen by him, has slipped into the chair itself, this by the adroitness of Susanna, who throws a dress over his huddled figure. Basilio tries persuasion on Susanna once more, but also proceeds to hint that Cherubino is far too interested in the countess. The count at this point angrily makes himself known. (counts may indulge in a little philandering, but countesses may not.) Susanna, thoroughly alarmed at this developing situation of double concealment, shows signs of fainting, but when the two men start to place her in the chair on top of the hidden Cherubino, she makes a sudden recovery. Cherubino is nevertheless discovered, and a trio follows combining the alarm of Susanna, the amused skepticism of Don Basilio, the anger of the count. Cherubino, whose every innocent move seems to invite trouble, has committed the additional crime of overhearing the whole of the count's proposition to Susanna, even though he has "tried not to listen." At this point Figaro brings in the retinue of peasant vassals, who sing a chorus of grateful homage to their lord for having abolished the *"Droit du Seigneur,"* the "first-night privilege," and offer the white crown and bridal veil to be placed by him on Susanna's head in token of the event. Thus Figaro has nearly forced his hand, but he postpones the formal gesture until the wedding party. The count is asked to forgive Cherubino on account of his youth, and reluctantly agrees, but his forgiveness consists in sending him off (and out of the way) at once as an officer in his regiment. Figaro then sings the air of cynical godspeed, *"Non più andrai,"* commending the boy to the glories (and incidentally the hardships) of a military life—a life quite without the agreeable pleasures of a ladies' darling.

The Second Act shows the boudoir of the neglected countess,

who sings her aria of heartbreak—"*Porgi amor*." Susanna can give her no reassurance about the count's infidelities, but Figaro, who comes in singing a gay and confident phrase of *Se vuol' ballare*, has a plan. Susanna is to agree to the garden meeting with the master, but Cherubino, dressed in Susanna's clothes, is to go in her place. The count will then be publicly discovered and disgraced. The countess, at first hesitating because of her fear of her husband's jealousy, aroused, she sadly admits, by vanity rather than love, soon agrees. Cherubino is brought in, and after he has sung his love canzonetta "*Voi che sapete*" to Susanna's guitar but addressed to the countess, he is dressed up in girl's cap and bodice, to a delightfully "busy" aria by Susanna while she bids him "turn around," "hold still," etc. The count's knock is heard at the door, to the consternation of all three. Cherubino hides in the inner room, and the count, finding his wife alone, is filled with suspicion by her obvious confusion, a suspicion increased when she refuses to unlock the door of the inner room. The count goes to get the key, but takes her with him to prevent further deception. While they are gone, Susanna is in a panic about what to do with Cherubino, who solves the problem, amid apt music of fluttering alarm, by leaping out of the window and fleeing. The count and countess return, and the countess, alarmed for Cherubino, and knowing nothing of his escape, confesses that it is he who is inside. She tries to explain that it has been a harmless bit of fooling. She feels it wise to warn her husband that Cherubino, as part of the game, is not fully dressed. The count unlocks the door and, sword in hand, orders Cherubino to come forth. To the astonishment of both, and to music of breathless suspense, it is Susanna who appears triumphantly before them. The count is properly humbled, and begs forgiveness. There is one point however to clear up. He has received an anonymous letter revealing that his wife is unfaithful. Susanna tells him, and this is true, that Figaro has written the letter as a hoax; Figaro is to blame, otherwise it has no meaning. Figaro comes in to announce that the wedding party is ready to begin. "One moment," says the count, "do you recognize this letter?" Figaro hesitates, not knowing what has happened, while Susanna is unable to warn him. He says "I know nothing of it." On top of this, Antonio, the gardener, enters ("rather drunk"), carrying a broken potted carnation. He has seen a man leap from the window to his flower bed, and run off. The conspirators look mutely to Figaro to help them out, and Figaro, playing for time, points out that the man is too drunk to know what he is talking about. He then announces that it was he, Figaro, who jumped out of the window. When Antonio protests that it looked like "the boy," Figaro reminds them that Cherubino had long since departed on horseback according to orders. The gardener then produces a paper which he has picked up in the flower bed. The count snatches it and demands that Figaro tell him what it is. Again Figaro is caught, but Susanna conveys to him that it is the page's military commission, and Figaro, thinking fast, explains that he was holding the paper for a proper signature. There now comes a final dilemma. Marcellina enters with Bartolo and Basilio, flourishing her marriage contract with Figaro. To this problem, for the moment, Figaro has no answer. For this long and rapidly developing action, from the point of Figaro's entrance, Mozart has provided one of his most masterly ensembles, a complex which is also a clear unfoldment, delineative and dramatic in the highest degree.

The Third Act is laid in the assembly hall of the palace. Susanna encourages the count, according to plan, in a duet of smooth coquetry. The count is exultant but, having overheard a remark by her to Figaro, becomes suspicious of a new plot and gives expression to his anger in his principal aria, "*Vedrò, mentr'io sospiro.*" Figaro's legal case and Marcellina's claim for his hand is tested before the stuttering (and completely stupid) lawyer Curzio, with the count as judge. The investigation suddenly reveals that Figaro is the lost child of Marcellina and Bartolo; he was stolen shortly after his birth. Thus Figaro's worst obstacle to his marriage is removed without need of his own wit. Susanna enters to behold Marcellina and Figaro embracing, and not yet knowing that they are mother and son, boxes his ears. This particular climax is reached by a superb sextet, compact with action. The countess, alone on the stage, sings her famous aria of the abandoned wife, "*Dove sono.*" She dictates to Susanna a letter to the count in which Susanna proposes a meeting. The duet takes its form as each phrase is sung by the mistress, repeated by the maid. The wedding festivities close the act with singing and dancing. Figaro observes his fiancée slipping a letter into the count's hand, and believes her unfaithful after all.

The final act, in the garden, opens with a sorrowful cavatina by Barbarina, who has lost the pin which the count has removed from Susanna's letter and given her to return as the pledge of the meeting. Figaro extracts the story of the pin, and now believes the worst of Susanna's intentions. He sings the aria "*Aprite un po' quegl'occhi,*" on the inconstancy of women, leaving the orchestra to make the final point of cuckoldry by horn calls. Hiding, he beholds the countess and Susanna, each dressed in the clothes of the other. The countess, whom he believes to be Susanna, retires into the appointed meeting place, "under the pines." Susanna sings her lovely soliloquy of the tender and expectant bride: *"Deh, vieni, non tardar."* The count makes love to the woman he supposes to be Susanna. She is of course his wife, and leads him on, for she is now in a position to humble him completely, which she does when the mistaken identities are duly straightened out. The final denouement is swiftly worked, another masterly piece of ensemble writing.

Don Giovanni (Il dissoluto punito), *Dramma giocoso* in two acts, K. 527. Text by Lorenzo da Ponte (Completed in Prague, October 28, 1787)

The scene is in Seville, before the house of Dónna Anna and her father, the Commendatore. Don Giovanni, to whom all women are fair game, has entered the house with obvious intent, and his servant Leporello, the character who provides the most comedy in the story, is outside, awaiting eventualities. He sings a sort of prologue, describing his thankless position—he must share the dangers and take only the knocks from his master's exploits. Don Giovanni emerges from the house, masked by his cloak, and after him Donna Anna, whom he has attempted to seduce under cover of darkness. Her father, the Commandant, rushes out, sword in hand and, after sending his daughter into the house, compels the intruder to fight. The Don slays the old man (murder is not among his pastimes, but he has no choice) and takes flight. Donna Anna calls Don Ottavio, her betrothed, and makes him swear to find the unknown villain (for she has not recognized him) and avenge her father. In a second street scene Don Giovanni beholds a veiled lady and approaches her, only to discover that she is Donna Elvira, whom he has betrayed and abandoned. She reproaches him, but it is plain that she is still in love with him. He makes Leporello engage her in conversation, and escapes. Leporello tries to persuade her in his "catalogue" aria to forget the most inconstant of all lovers. She is only one of thousands of all sorts in many countries, whom he has used for his pleasure and dropped for others. The next scene shows a peasant wedding party in progress. The Don, all politeness, makes himself known to the couple: Zerlina, who is not unsusceptible to the charms of the grand gentleman, and Masetto, a country lout, who is sullen but awed and helpless before him as he touches the handle of his sword. His *buffo* aria, *"Ho capito, Signor, sì,"* shows his grudging submission. Leporello having led Masetto away, the Don asks Zerlina to be his wife. He will take her into his palace, near by, for a life of bliss and ease. In the duet *"Là ci darem la mano"* he takes her hand and wins her hesitating consent. Donna Elvira suddenly appears and denounces her lover in the violent aria *"Ah, fuggi il traditor!"* Donna Anna and Don Ottavio come upon Don Giovanni and, not realizing that he is the man they are looking for, ask for his assistance. He assures them that he will do everything in his power to uncover the villain. Elvira intervenes and denounces him again, but he assures them (in a dramatic quartet) that the lady is crazed and not to be listened to. They are thrown into doubt, and Donna Anna suddenly perceives and later confides to her fiancé that this is indeed the murderer of her father. Their course is now clear, and Donna Anna vents her feelings in the highly charged emotional aria *"Or sai chi l'onore."* Don Ottavio's principal aria, *"Dalla sua pace"* is his assurance of sympathy and devotion. Don Giovanni, intent upon Zerlina, instructs Leporello to prepare a party for all the peasants at his palace. There must be plenty of wine. There is a "lover's quarrel" scene between Zerlina and Massetto. He is jealous and angry, but she tells him that she is faithful, and unharmed. In her aria *"Batti, batti, o bel Masetto,"* she wins his forgiveness. In the final ensemble, the party scene, a great deal happens. As the dancing begins, Donna Elvira, Donna Anna and Don Ottavio enter, an avenging trio, but concealed by masquerade costumes. Three orchestras play simultaneously a minuet, a country dance and a German dance, signifying that the nobility and the common people are both being served. In the course of it, Don Giovanni forces Zerlina into the house. Suddenly her screams are heard by all. Don Giovanni tries to make it appear that it was Leporello who seized Zerlina but he is generally denounced. In the confusion he suddenly makes his escape.

As the Second Act opens, Leporello tells his master that after the latest escapade, which might have resulted in his death, he has had enough. Don Giovanni offers him four gold pieces which he accepts, suggesting that the Don stop his endless quest of women. The Don only laughs at this preposterous idea, and says that he has taken a fancy to Donna Elvira's maid. He forces him to exchange their clothing. Leporello, as the Don, will under the cover of night detain the mistress while he, appearing as Leporello, will go after the maid. Donna Elvira is taken in by Leporello's words of love as Don Giovanni, and Don Giovanni serenades the maid with his canzonetta. *"Deh, vieni alla finestra,"* to a guitar accompaniment. Masetto, now determined to kill Don Giovanni, encounters him, but mistakes him for Leporello. The Don acting the servant's part, tells Masetto he too has had enough of that villain. He will join Masetto in the deed and asks what weapons he will use. Masetto hands him a musket and pistol. He takes them, beats Masetto unmercifully and leaves him lying in the street. Zerlina finds him, comforts him, and sings her love song of complete reconciliation: *"Vedrai, carino."* Donna Anna and Don Ottavio discover Leporello with Donna Elvira and, joined by Masetto and Zerlina, seize him, thinking they have found the Don at last. They are about to kill him when he reveals himself. This episode is accomplished in a magificent sextet, followed by Leporello's aria begging for mercy.

The cemetery scene follows. As Don Giovanni is relating the outcome of still another affair, a sepulchral voice is heard: "Your laughing will end before dawn!" The voice comes from the statue of the Commendatore. Leporello is terrified. The Don is incredulous and forces his servant to read the inscription: "I here wait to take vengeance on the villain who killed me." The Don further compels Leporello at the point of his sword to invite the statue to supper. The statue nods its head. In a brief scene in Donna Anna's house, Don Ottavio urges her to marry him at once but Donna Anna in her aria *"Non mi dir"* tells him that she loves him but that her father's death is still too heavy upon her. The final scene is in the banquet hall of Don Giovanni's house. The table is set for two. "Table music" is played: airs from two contemporary operas and *"Non più andrai"* from *Figaro*. Donna Elvira comes in, kneels at his feet and entreats him to repent before it is too late. He only laughs. As she runs out, her scream is heard, for she has been confronted with a dreadful apparition. There is a knock on the door, and Don Giovanni commands his servant to open it, but this time has to do so himself, for Leporello is crouched under a table. The statue in solemn and weird tones refuses his invitation to supper and invites him in turn, holding out his hand. Courageous to the last, the libertine refuses to repent. The marble grip is the grip of doom. "Flames shoot up and Don Giovanni, shouting, sinks and disappears." The others enter, and told by Leporello of his master's fate, sing a moral sextet about the retribution which surely befalls those who lead an evil life.

Così fan tutte, *Opera buffa* in two acts, K. 588. Text by Lorenzo da Ponte (Composed in Vienna, 1789–1790)

In the Overture there is an amusing contrast between the ponderous pronouncement of the motto theme: "So do they all," and the general buffo gaiety which surrounds and submerges it. The scene is laid in Naples. We first behold two very romantic and very love-stricken young men, Guglielmo and Ferrando, in conversation with Don Alfonso, a bachelor, who infuriates them by claiming that no women are to be trusted. A wager is laid. The two lovers will pretend to go to war, return disguised and each woo the fiancée of the other. The two sisters, Fiordiligi and Dorabella, whose response to this test will decide the bet, are at least as romantic about love as the men. Their first duet shows that their emotions on the subject are on a more exalted plane than any *opera buffa* point of view. It also shows them as in an identical situation. Each exactly echoes the other musically—even the other's coloratura sighs. The supposed farewell of the two couples is music of heartbreak even though the men are pretending, and though Don Alfonso is injecting an aside: "I shall soon burst out laughing." The next scene is the ladies' boudoir. Despina, their maid, is on duty and complains of her tasks. Enter Dorabella and Fiordiligi, overcome with noble grief, and furious when the practical Despina reminds them that even if their men should be lost in battle there will be plenty of men in the world left to choose from. Don Alfonso bribes Despina to further his cause. He tells her that he is about to bring two new suitors to meet their mistresses. Ferrando and Guglielmo enter disguised as Albanian nobles, with false mustaches. Despina does not recognize them, nor is she impressed. The ladies are outraged at their intrusion and their pointed compliments. When they have gone, Fiordiligi proclaims in a highly emotional aria, *"Come scoglio,"* that her faithfulness is "like a rock." The sopranos who seize upon this as a concert piece because of its magnificent vocal display may not all realize that this very magnificence is meant as a travesty of the grand heroic manner, and also a huge piece of irony, for the "rock" is about to succumb to temptation. Guglielmo next sings his air *"Non siate ritrosi,"* exultant that the ladies have so far proved faithful. Ferrando is moved to tender reflection in his *"Un' aura amorosa,"* one of the most beautiful tenor arias of Mozart, and completely serious. Don Alfonso will not admit defeat; he insists that the two men push their trial further. They stagger into the ladies' presence as if on the point of death. Don Alfonso explains that they have taken poison in despair at the haughty rejection. They call for Despina and send her for a doctor. She re-enters disguised as a doctor and, singing "through the nose," revives them by the newly discovered mesmerism,* waving a giant magnet. The hearts of the ladies, after their alarm and relief, show signs of melting.

The Second Act opens in the sisters' house. Despina reminds the ladies that life is meant to be enjoyed; also that flirtation is the weapon by which men are ruled. The sisters are intrigued. They decide that it would be fun to give the suitors a little encouragement. The next scene is on the shore of the Bay of Naples. From a boat and to the strains of a wind octet ("serenade" fashion) Ferrando and Guglielmo sing a romantic duet. Guglielmo succeeds in coaxing from Dorabella a locket with Ferrando's picture. Fiordiligi does not yield at first, but she is obviously weakening and sings her aria of remorse: *"Per pietà, ben mio."* Both men are bitterly disillusioned, and the Don, who has now won his bet, advises them to marry the two anyway, to take them as they are and not expect too much from fickle women. A double wedding is arranged by Despina for the men in their disguise. She appears in the gown of a notary and holds a mock ceremony. At this moment military music seems to announce the return of the true lovers and throws the girls into dismay. The "Albanians" disappear and return as themselves. The deceit is explained, the suitors are properly switched about and two real weddings bring the final curtain.

La clemenza di Tito, *Opera seria* in two acts, K. 621. Text by Pietro Metastasio, revised by Caterino Mazzolà (First performed in Prague, September 6, 1791)

Mozart composed his last opera in eighteen days, on a sudden order from Prague, where Leopold II was to be crowned King of Bohemia. He put aside the urgent completion of *The Magic Flute* to do it, and the likewise urgent commission for the

---

* Dr. Mesmer and his family were close friends of Mozart, and lived in Vienna. This hilarious allusion could well have been Mozart's idea.

Requiem, which had just been handed to him. The opera was coldly received in Prague but had a certain success elsewhere, shortly after his death. To have composed a score as dramatically and warmly appealing as *Idomeneo* under such conditions would have been manifestly impossible. Mozart lived up to the letter of his assignment with his unfailing skill and resource. A certain amount of beautiful music permeated the barrier of artificial, arid rhetoric.

The plot is based on the generous spirit of the Roman Emperor (Titus Vespasian), who proves his "clemency" twice: first by giving up the hand of Servilia when he learns that she is engaged to Annio; at last by pardoning Sesto, who has plotted his death and fired the palace, and Vitellia who has instigated the deed. This display of imperial virtue, while gratifying to a courtly audience, is hardly good dramatic or musical material. The only truly dramatic character is Vitellia, who secretly loves Tito. When she learns that he intends to marry Servilia a double dilemma arises, for Servilia is Sesto's sister, and is already engaged to his friend Annio. Vitellia is filled with jealous rage, and wants to destroy Tito. She turns to Sesto, who loves her (in vain), and induces him to become her dupe and to commit treasonable arson and murder. Just before this event Publius, the Captain of the Emperor's bodyguard, brings to Vitellia the message that Tito will have her for his wife. It is now too late, she is unable to stop the carrying out of the plot. The First Act ends with the burning of the palace (an opportunity for stage spectacle). To the ensemble are added the cries of the horrified citizens who believe that their Emperor is lost.

In the Second Act, Sesto is caught, brought before the Senate, and condemned to death. Tito suddenly appears before the people, having escaped the conflagration in disguise. He is moved by his former esteem for Sesto, and is ready to pardon him if he will make a full confession of the plot (a reasonable precaution). Sesto is silent. He refuses to incriminate Vitellia, whom he loves. The sentence therefore stands, but Vitellia comes forward and confesses that hers was the first guilt. The Emperor pardons them both. The opera ends with a chorus of popular acclamation.

Royal audiences and their entourage actually welcomed this sort of spectacle. Metastasio's libretto, composed for Caldara in 1734, had been set by many composers (Abert names twelve) for various courts in Italy and the German states. Caterino Mazzolà, revising the text, had enlivened it with ensembles, hitherto not used, and had considerably reduced the vast amount of secco recitativo, a style of narrative which, even as late as 1791, audiences actually seemed to enjoy.

Of the six parts only two, Tito (tenor) and his officer Publius (bass) are sung by men. The rest, including Sesto and Annio, are sopranos. Since these parts were not given to castratos in the Prague production it can only be supposed that blind tradition persisted when castratos were either not desired or not available. The resulting duets between two sopranos would have been more effective with a duality of tone color. (Mozart's first sketches for the part of Sesto score him as a tenor.)

Although Tito has the principal male part, he has only one solo air. (The part was taken by Baglione, the first Don Ottavio.) The burden of action and singing falls to the two sopranos, Vitellia and Sesto. Sesto's final aria (No. 19) is on a heroic scale, and Vitellia's final rondo (No. 23) is the better Mozart, its beauty increased by an obbligato basset horn, obviously intended for Stadler. Stadler was also given a more conspicuous but a more obviously imposed clarinet obbligato for Sesto's aria in the First Act (No. 9). Most of the solo numbers are short, in two parts, without ritornello. Sometimes, where intensity would have been expected, the composer gives light grace, as if he had an eye upon his audience. The trios and larger ensembles have been admired—Mozart could not have written a really dull one at this point in his life. The choruses, the overture, the march music have a certain ceremonial vacuity, as if the composer of *The Magic Flute* were drawing upon his skill without having been given advance time for contemplation, for even a hurried warming up of his musical imagination. The same may be said of the score as a whole, which must have been composed in not much more than the time required for the physical act of putting it upon paper.

Die Zauberflöte, *Grosse Oper* in two acts, K. 620 (Composed in Vienna, between July and September, 1791)

The focal point of the plot of *The Magic Flute* is the Temple and the Sacred Grove of Isis and Osiris, where Tamino, the young hero of the story (and of course the first tenor), undergoes the test of virtue and is admitted. These precincts however do not appear until the end of the First Act. Tamino is first seen in an encounter with a dragon. His arrows are gone, he faints from exhaustion. Three veiled ladies with silver spears appear momentarily and slay the dragon. Papageno comes in and describes himself in a song as a bird-catcher who snares birds by the notes of his pipe. The two men are strangers; Tamino is of royal blood, Papageno is a simple witless fellow, a coward at heart, in fact the clown and principal comedian of the piece. Papageno, seeing the body of the dragon, first assures himself that it is safely dead and then boasts that it was he that killed it. The three ladies, who are subjects of the Queen of Night, return and punish him for fibbing by putting a padlock on his lips. This results in a song which he can only hum. The ladies give Tamino a portrait of Pamina, and explain that she is the daughter of the Queen; she has been carried off by an evil magician. Tamino is enraptured by the portrait and sings his principal air in her praise. There is a clap of thunder, the stage darkens and the Queen appears, surrounded by stars. The music is awesome, but the Queen's words are gentle. She tells Tamino that her daughter is beyond her power of rescue. If he will accomplish the deed, he shall have her for his bride. The ladies return and give Tamino a golden flute of magic powers to protect him on his quest. Papageno, they say, must accompany him. Three boys, beneficent spirits, will guide them to the castle. Papageno is anything but eager for danger. They give him a set of chimes (a glockenspiel) with similar protective properties.

The next scene is the room of Pamina in the palace of Sarastro. Monostatos, a wicked Moorish slave, is about to force his will upon the terrified Pamina. Papageno makes his way by accident into the room, and the two men retreat, each terrified by the other. Papageno tells her of Tamino and their mission of rescue. A sacred grove is seen, with three temples. The three spirits lead Tamino in and leave him. Tamino tries to enter the portals—the one at the right is inscribed "Reason" and the one at the left is inscribed "Nature"—but is stopped by the command from within—"Stand back." The middle door, over which is inscribed "Wisdom," opens and a white-haired priest appears. He asks Tamino what sanctuary he seeks and Tamino tells him the home of love and virtue. When he further vows vengeance on Sarastro as the wicked captor of Pamina, the priest tells him that he has been falsely advised by a chattering woman. Sarastro has indeed taken Pamina from her mother; more he cannot say. He withdraws and Tamino is assured by an unseen chorus that Pamina still lives. Tamino plays his flute and birds and beasts appear charmed by its tones. He is seeking Pamina but the music draws Papageno to his side instead. Papageno and Pamina next meet each other. Monostatos finds them and is about to put both in chains, but Papageno plays upon his magic chimes and the slave is compelled to dance helplessly to its measures. A march with trumpets and drums announces the approach of Sarastro and his attendants, to the terror of both Papageno and Pamina. Pamina asks Sarastro to return her to her mother but Sarastro gently tells her that this "haughty woman" would only do her harm. Her destiny is different: "A man must guide your heart." Tamino is brought in and the two behold each other for the first time and embrace before the assembled company. Monostatos is condemned to the bastinado.

In the Second Act, Sarastro tells his priests that the young couple wish to enter the Temple, and that they are worthy of the ordeal. Tamino is to be initiated into the mysteries and united with Pamina. They are conducted to the threshold of the Temple and Sarastro sings a solemn invocation to the Egyptian gods, Isis and Osiris. Tamino and Papageno are questioned on their intentions and rectitude. A vow of silence is imposed on them both. In the next scene the three ladies return, sent by the Queen to turn them against Sarastro and the holy rites. They are driven away. Pamina is next seen in a garden, asleep on a bench. Monostatos creeps in, and before awaking her, sings an exotic song of lust. (It is reminiscent of Osmin in *Die Entführung.*) The Queen of Night suddenly appears, and sings her aria of vengeful fury. She gives her daughter a dagger, commands her to kill Sarastro, and vanishes in a clap of thunder. Monostatos seizes the dagger and turns upon Pamina, but Sarastro intervenes. In the moving song *"In diesen heiligen Hallen,"* he gently explains to her that this is a community of good will where love rules and vengeance does not exist. She must forget her mother, who will not be harmed but confined to her own evil domains. Tamino and Papageno are put to the test. Papageno beholds his destined bride, who appears to be an ugly old woman. The three Spirits caution Tamino about his imposed silence. Pamina rushes in and greets Tamino, but (like Orpheus) he cannot answer. Believing that he does not love her, she sings her moving air of sorrow, *"Ah, ich fühl's."* She is about to turn the dagger on herself when the three Spirits stop her, and tell her that Tamino still loves her.

In a "wild, rocky place," the two lovers, veiled, are led in by the priests to undergo the ordeal of fire and water. They emerge triumphant, Tamino playing his magic flute, Pamina beside him with her hand on his shoulder. Papageno is next seen in a "small garden," about to hang himself in despair, unless Papagena, his "little wife," comes at his call. Instead, the three Spirits intervene, and tell him to play his chimes. This he does, and the old woman appears, transformed into a beautiful young girl who sings and dances with him in a joyful duet. In a brief scene the Queen, the three ladies and Monostatos enter with torches, seeking to seize Pamina. Suddenly a storm, symbolic of virtue, plunges them into darkness and destroys their power. The opera ends with a chorus of Priests and Priestesses in the Temple of the Sun, Tamino and Pamina standing, consecrated, in their midst.

The Arias with Orchestra

IT WAS an expected part of Mozart's day-by-day life that an aria in the operatic manner could be needed at any time. The Köchel listing of seventy-four for single or grouped voices with orchestra, composed from the age of nine until the last year of his life, tells the tale. He wrote the first for the tenor Ciprandi, as part of a pasticcio in London, the last for Franz Gerl, the first Sarastro. Although he spent much of his time eagerly waiting for a good opera commission, the atmosphere of the theatre was never far removed. Whenever a concert was given, the first attention was for the singer, who must have concert arias, preferably new ones. Mozart knew many singers; he remained in close touch with the opera world even when he was not composing or directing an opera of his own. An aria in or out of opera was the singer's vehicle, and as a matter of course he was most careful to study the singer's voice and intelligence. "I like an aria to fit a singer," he wrote his father apropos of the aging tenor Raaff, "as perfectly as a well made suit of clothes."

He wrote additional numbers for *Idomeneo, Figaro, Don Giovanni, Così fan tutte,* after the first production, with new principal singers in mind. When an opera of another—Anfossi, Piccinni, Cimarosa, Martín—lagged or failed to suit the prima donna or primo uomo, he would provide an aria of his own to suit the singer, to be added or substituted. This without any special consultation with the composer, for it was the singer and the box office, and not the composer that counted. He spent a good deal of his time in Vienna thus helping other people's operas, and even more of his time composing concert arias to oblige singers. Self-interest as well as generosity entered into it, for the success of his own operas to follow would depend on keeping them happy. The singers were invariably delighted with their arias. It does not appear that they rewarded him out of their sometimes vastly greater incomes. This gratuitous expenditure of genius if added up would amount in length to several operas.

The singers were usually avid for coloratura, and though Mozart was impatient with meaningless coloratura as such and once referred to it as "chopped up noodles," he found it his task to oblige with ornamental passages and make them expressive of the text and mood. No singer wanted a *buffo* aria unless it was for a current production. All wanted their concert numbers on a grand scale, to exhibit their vocal power and histrionics. The consequence was that although Mozart did not write an *opera seria* in the ten Vienna years which separated *Idomeneo* and *La clemenza di Tito*, he found himself occupied with fair regularity in that medium.

A concert number of the required pretensions would take the form of a *scena monumentale,* a full and exhaustive (sometimes repetitive) treatment of a heroic text—usually a text from Metastasio which might have been set a dozen or more times by others and would be already familiar to the audience. Actual opera arias would not be suitable for a concert. They were far shorter—properly so on the stage, where they were prepared by what had preceded, the flowering of a mood from a situation already built. A concert *scena* had to start cold, without visual scenic illusion, establish the situation with an expository recitative, and draw the audience into sympathy with a tragic dilemma. The chosen text always depicted an emotional crisis. The character would plunge into a heavy soliloquy, or appeal to the gods for release in death. A long aria with graphic elements of recitative would follow, and lead into a final section in quickened tempo, heightened orchestral sonority, often an almost hysterical vocal climax. Mozart knew that he had to drive his point home.

"Va, dal furor portata," Aria for Tenor, K. 21 (Composed in London, 1765)

This was Mozart's contribution to a pasticcio on Metastasio's *Ezio*. The boy of nine gives a competent accounting, according to pattern, of a wronged father heaping reproach upon his "treacherous" daughter.

"Conservati fedele," Aria for Soprano, K. 23 (Composed in The Hague, October, 1765)

Composed for the Princess von Oranien at a royal concert. The text is from Metastasio's *Artaserse*.

"Tali e cotanti sono" (Recitative: *"Or che il dover"*), Aria for Tenor, K. 36 (Composed in Salzburg, December, 1766)

A *licenza* in praise of the Archbishop Sigismund.

"Sol nascente" (Recitative: *"A Berenice"*), Aria for Soprano, K. 70 (Composed in Salzburg, February, 1769)

A *licenza* which may have been composed for the birthday festivities of the Archbishop.

"Ah, più tremar non voglio," Aria for Tenor, K. 71 (Composed in Salzburg, early 1770?)

This may have been written for the first Italian journey. The text is from Metastasio's *Demofoonte*.

"Non curo l'affetto," Aria for Soprano, K. 74b (Composed in Milan or Pavia, 1771)

The text is from Metastasio's *Demofoonte*.

"Misero pargoletto" (Recitative: *"Misero me"*), Aria for Soprano, K. 77 (Composed in Milan, March, 1770)

The text is from Metastasio's *Demofoonte*.

"Per pietà, bell'idol mio," Aria for Soprano, K. 78 (Composed in Milan, early 1770)

Probably written for a soirée of Count Firmian. The text is from Metastasio's *Artaserse*.

"Per quel paterno amplesso" (Recitative: *"O temerario Arbace"*), Aria for Soprano, K. 79 (Composed in Milan, early 1770)

The text is derived from Metastasio's *Artaserse*. This is the first *scena*, which stops at its climax without resorting to da capo.

"Se ardire, e speranza," Aria for Soprano, K. 82 (Composed in Rome, April, 1770)

The text is from Metastasio's *Demofoonte*. The occasion is unknown.

"Se tutti i mali miei," Aria for Soprano, K. 83 (Composed in Rome, spring, 1770)

The text is from Metastasio's *Demofoonte*. This, and K. 82, may have been written for a singer in Naples, where Mozart went on May 8.

"Fra cento affanni," Aria for Soprano, K. 88 (Composed in Milan, early 1770)

The text is from Metastasio's *Artaserse*. It was intended for a soirée of Count Firmian.

"Der Liebe himmlisches Gefühl," Aria for Soprano, K. 119 (Composed in Vienna, 1782)

The origin of the text is unknown. Saint-Foix has hazarded the period of *Die Entführung*.

"Quaere superna" (Recitative: *"Ergo interest"*), Aria for Soprano, K. 143 (Composed in Milan, February, 1770)

Presumably one of two Latin motets, composed for two young castratos in Milan.

"Kommet her, ihr frechen Sünder," Aria for Soprano, K. 146
(Composed in early 1779, in Salzburg?)

A *"Passionslied,"* in three verses, with accompaniment of strings and organ.

"Si mostra la sorte," Aria for Tenor, K. 209
"Con ossequio, con rispetto," Aria for Tenor, K. 210
(Composed in Salzburg, May, 1775)

Two numbers presumably added to an *opera buffa* in Salzburg, performed by a traveling company.

"Voi avete un cor fedele," Aria for Soprano, K. 217 (Composed in Salzburg, October, 1775)

A substitution in Galuppi's *opera buffa*, *Le nozze*, with altered text.

"Io ti lascio" (Recitative: *"Ombra felice"*), Aria for Contralto,
K. 255 (Composed in Salzburg, September, 1776)

A *scena* for the contralto castrato, Francesco Fortini, of Pietro Rosa's traveling troupe.

"Clarice cara mia sposa," Aria for Tenor, K. 256 (Composed in Salzburg, September, 1776)

Believed to have been written for Piccinni's *opera buffa*, *L'astratto*. It is a patter song "in the tempo of a great chatterbox."

"Ah, t'invola agl'occhi miei" (Recitative: *"Ah, lo previdi"*), Aria for Soprano, K. 272 (Composed in Salzburg, August, 1777)

The text is from Paisiello's *Andromeda*. Mozart wrote this *scena* for Josephine Duscek (who was not an opera singer) when the Duscek couple visited Salzburg from their home in Prague. When Aloysia Lange sang it later, Mozart wrote to her of the importance of due emotional understanding and expression. It is in an incisive dramatic manner, without grandeur or ornament, and would have put to a test the intelligence of the vocalizing Aloysia.

"Non so donde viene" (Recitative: *"Alcandro, lo confesso"*), Aria for Soprano, K. 294 (Composed in Mannheim, February, 1778)

The text is from Metastasio's *Olimpiade*. This was the first number that Mozart wrote especially for Aloysia von Weber, as a would-be fiancé. Its content and brilliant style reflect his estimate (hardly unbiased) of her voice.

"Il cor dolente" (Recitative: *"Se al labbro mio non credi"*), Aria for Tenor, K. 295 (Composed in Mannheim, February, 1778)

When Mozart wrote this aria for Anton Raaff, the destined Idomeneo, the tenor was nearly sixty-four, and had more style than voice. The aria, a love song from Hasse's *Artaserse*, is moderate in range and without fioriture, and greatly pleased the singer. Its expressive vocal style suggests *Idomeneo;* there is life and interest in the orchestral part.

"Io non chiedo, eterni" (Recitative: *"Popoli di Tessaglia"*), Aria for Soprano, K. 316 (Composed in Paris and Munich, 1778-1779)

Gluck's *Alceste* was the topic of Paris when Mozart was there. He set this bravura air from the Italian text by Calzabigi and carried the unfinished manuscript to Munich where his fiancée was singing. On July 30, 1778, the engagement having lapsed, he sent it to her with the words: "I can only say that of all my compositions of this kind—this *scena* is the best I have ever composed." Whether he wished to impress Aloysia or whether he felt the challenge of Gluck's moving setting of Alceste's address to the people of Thessaly, he certainly put his heart into the attempt. The recitative opens in a dark and plaintive C minor, with the characteristic falling half tones to the dominant. The recitative is superb; the aria is broad and fine, while ornate passages and two ascents to high G betray whom he had in mind. Aloysia had every reason to be delighted.

"Sperai vicino al lido" (Recitative: *"Ma che vi fece"*), Aria for Soprano, K. 368 (Composed in Munich, January, 1781)

This may have been intended for Elisabeth Wendling, the wife of the violinist in the Electoral orchestra, and the first Elettra in *Idomeneo*. It is in the ornate, bravura style, and is still another setting from Metastasio's *Demofoonte*.

"Ah, non son' io che parlo" (Scena: *"Misera, dove son?"*), Aria for Soprano, K. 369 (Composed in Munich, March, 1781)

The text is from Metastasio's *Ezio*. The aria was composed for the Gräfin Paumgarten, "favorite" of the Bavarian Elector. It is a characteristic example of a crescendo of emotional intensity, from the Andante in recitative through the melodic eloquence of the aria to a swift and exciting close.

"Or che il cielo a me ti rende" (Recitative: *"A questo sono deh vieni"*), Aria for Soprano, K. 374 (Composed in Vienna, April, 1781)

Written for the castrato Ceccarelli for a concert in Vienna when both composer and singer were under the employ of the Archbishop Hieronymus. The castrato takes the part of a happy wife who anticipates the return of her husband in a bright rondo (Allegretto).

"Nehmt meinen Dank, ihr holden Gönner," Song for Soprano, K. 383 (Composed in Vienna, April, 1782)

Aloysia Lange was Mozart's sister-in-law when he wrote this number for her, probably for a benefit concert, for the singer greets her patrons in a sentimental farewell. The whole is simple and unpretentious.

"Ah non sai qual' pena" (Scena: *"Mia speranza adorata"*) Rondo for Soprano, K. 416 (Composed in Vienna, January, 1783)

Mozart provided this brilliant vocal rondo for Aloysia, for an *"Accademie"* in the *Mehlgrube,* in which they both appeared. Unlike the little German ballad (K. 383), it is a *scena* in the grand style, with expressive recitative, a rondo air exacting emotional understanding, and a swift finale, providing along the way some elaborate vocal passage work.

"Vorrei spiegarvi, o Dio," Aria for Soprano, K. 418
"No, no, che non sei capace," Aria for Soprano, K. 419
"Per pietà, non ricercate," Aria for Tenor, K. 420
(Composed in Vienna, June, 1783)

Mozart wrote these three numbers for Aloysia and for Adamberger, to help their personal success in a current production of Anfossi's *Il curioso indiscreto*. The considerable alteration in the opera aroused some gossip, which Mozart countered by a public statement of his respect for Anfossi, and his sole intent of adapting the score to the particular singers' voices. Adamberger's aria has the effect of a long crescendo of emotion as the Andante is succeeded by a frenzied Allegro assai. Aloysia's arias are more in the sentimental *buffo* manner.

"Aura, che intorno spiri" (Recitative: *"Misero! O sogno!"*), Aria for Tenor, K. 431 (Composed in Vienna, December, 1783)

This might be a "rondo" mentioned in the letters, composed for Adamberger who sang at a benefit concert. The words are those of a prisoner, unjustly, hopelessly shut off from the world. Mozart at no other time wrote music of such gloom (helped by the scoring for the horns), such dark and rebellious violence. It is a curious aberration of the familiar Mozart.

"Aspri rimorsi atroci" (Recitative: *"Così dunque tradisci"*), Aria for Bass, K. 432 (Composed in Vienna, 1783)

The text is from Metastasio's *Temistocle*. The singer who had this aria from Mozart may have been Ludwig Fischer, the first Osmin, whom it would have well suited.

Männer suchen stets zu naschen," Aria for Bass, K. 433
"Müsst ich auch durch tausend Drachen," Aria for Tenor, K. 435
(Composed in Vienna, 1783)

These two comic airs were undoubtedly provided for a *Singspiel* in Vienna; the occasion is not known.

"Ah, non lasciarmi" (Recitative: *Basta, vincesti*), Aria for Soprano, K. 486a (Composed in Mannheim, February, 1778)

The text is from Metastasio's *Didone abbandonata*. Mozart wrote (February 28, 1778) that he had composed this aria for Dorothea Wendling, the wife of the flutist at Mannheim. "She and her daughter are both crazy about it."

"Non temer, amato bene" (Scena: *"Non più, tutto ascoltai"*), Rondo for Soprano, K. 490 (Composed in Vienna, March, 1786)

"Non temer, amato bene" (Scena: *"Ch'io mi scordi di te"*), Rondo for Soprano, K. 505 (Composed in Vienna, December, 1786)

Mozart, anxious to awaken some interest in *Idomeneo* in Vienna, induced his amateur friends Baron Pulini and Graf von Hatzfeld to put on a private performance. He wrote a new opening number for Act II (replacing the lovely aria *"Zeffiretti lusinghieri"*) and rewrote the love duet of Ilia and Idamante in Act III (K. 489). The first *"Non temer, amato bene"* he set with a violin obbligato. Later in the year he rewrote this aria for the voice of Nancy Storace, with a new introduction and a wholly new setting, with a conspicuous piano obbligato. This is a remarkable instance of Mozart's readiness to reset a text with new and fresh power when he could have saved himself the trouble by virtual repetition. Both settings are superb, in both the music is nobly at one with the mood; but the first, more "regular" in its melodic treatment and its obbligato, is also more generally appealing. Both are more advanced than *Idomeneo;* the first has a passing *buffo* touch by the composer of *Figaro*.

"Non so donde viene" (Recitative: *"Alcandro, lo confesso"*), Aria for Bass, K. 512 (Composed in Vienna, March, 1787)

This new and completely different setting of the text used in K. 294 was written for Ludwig Fischer.

"Mentre ti lascio, o figlia," Aria for Bass, K. 513 (Composed in Vienna, March, 1787)

Mozart composed this aria for his friend Gottfried von Jacquin. The text was by Duca Sant' Angioli Morbilli, from Paisiello's *La disfatta di Dario,* and depicts a father's broken heart at the loss of his son. Traits of *Don Giovanni* are discernible in this moving *scena,* as it grows tense in ever-quickening tempo. The orchestral part (including clarinets) has a new fullness of development.

"Resta, o cara" (Scena: *"Bella mia fiamma"*), Aria for Soprano, K. 528 (Composed in Prague, November, 1787)

Before returning to Vienna after *Don Giovanni,* Mozart composed for his friend Josephine Duscek a promised concert aria. If the lady was equal to what he provided she was at least an accomplished dramatic singer. It would have been suitable for the part of Donna Anna if it had been shorter and less frenzied.

"Ah se in ciel, benigne stelle," Aria for Soprano K. 538 (Composed in Vienna, March, 1788)

This bravura air to a text from Metastasio's *L'eroe cinese* was composed for Aloysia Lange. Her brother-in-law accommodated her ambition with a running passage of fifteen bars on one syllable. It was his last contribution to her voice.

"Ein deutsches Kriegslied" (*"Ich möchte wohl der Kaiser sein"*), Song for Baritone, K. 539 (Composed in Vienna, March, 1788)

This "war song" was composed for Friedrich Baumann, a comedian of the Leopoldstadt Theater. A large orchestra is used. The occasion was the Turkish war.

"Un bacio di mano," Arietta for Bass, K. 541 (Composed in Vienna, May, 1788)

An interpolated number for Francesco Albertarelli, for Anfossi's *Le gelosie fortunate.*

"Al desio di chi t'adora," Rondo for Soprano, K. 577 (Composed in Vienna, July, 1789)

This was composed as a substitute for Susanna's *"Deh, vieni, non tardar"* in *Figaro*—an appalling sacrifice! It was written to oblige Mme. Ferrarese del Bene, but by a change in plan Mme. Cavalieri sang it.

"Alma grande e nobil core," Aria for Soprano, K. 578 (Composed in Vienna, August, 1789)

An additional aria provided for Mlle. Luise Villeneuve, the first Dorabella, for Cimarosa's *I due baroni.* It is full of comedy spirit, with a delightful orchestral part.

"Un moto di gioia," Aria for Soprano, K. 579 (Composed in Vienna, August, 1789)

An additional air provided for Mme. Ferrarese del Bene for the part of Susanna in *Figaro.* It is a short and lively number in the tempo of a German dance.

"Schon lacht der holde Frühling," Aria for Soprano, K. 580
(Composed in Vienna, September, 1789)

This was a favor for the sister-in-law Josefa Hofer—an additional number for a German version of Paisiello's *Il barbiere di Siviglia.*

"Chi sà, chi sà, qual sia," Aria for Soprano, K. 582
"Vado, ma dove?," Aria for Soprano, K. 583
(Composed in Vienna, October, 1789)

Mozart wrote these two for Mlle. Villeneuve for Martín's *Dramma giocoso, Il burbero di buon cuore.* The first is light *buffo* with vocal display, the second sentimental *buffo.*

"Rivolgete a lui lo sguardo," Aria for Baritone, K. 584 (Composed in Vienna, December, 1789)

Mozart intended this aria for Guglielmo in the first act of *Così fan tutte,* but on account of its length, wrote the shorter one *"Non siate ritrosi"* (No. 15). Benucci was the singer. The earlier aria is as jocular as the later one, the orchestra sparkles enchantingly. Yet, on the whole, the shorter one is more suitable; nor would any of us willingly give it up.

"Per questa bella mano," Aria for Bass, K. 612 (Composed in Vienna, March, 1791)

Written for Franz Gerl, who sang Sarastro and the contrabass player Pichelberger (there is an obbligato bass part). The aria is a love song with unavoidable sacerdotal associations.

The Songs with Piano

MOZART DID NOT look upon songs with piano accompaniment as important. Large arias with orchestra were for the concert or opera stage, and had full public attention. A song was for home use by a friendly singer, professional or nonprofessional. The composer would sit down and oblige his host or hostess with a song at any time, and often made the family a present of the script, whereby it might find its way into a collection without his name. Of course there was some demand for his songs, which usually came well within amateur abilities. Most of the songs are set strophically, with a melody of twenty bars or so, and a literal repeat of each verse. The texts, usually by minor poets, were sentimentally concerned with the emotions of love. The accompaniments were the lightest and simplest possible, a few chords, without modulation, a few bars of *ritornello* to round off each verse. When Mozart wrote in the style of a popular German street song, he did so quite without conscious intent, for the *"Volkslied"* had not yet become a general cultural pursuit. Indeed the *Lied* in the sense that Schubert was to develop it, an inner union of poetry and music, a true duet with characterization in the piano part such as we meet in *Der Erlkönig* or *Die Forelle,* simply did not exist. In the matter of stylistic development, the strophic songs do not stand apart from a hundred others by contemporaries. They do stand apart as miniatures of exquisite taste and beauty in every note, by the composer who was as capable of turning out a fine melody at any moment as he was incapable of producing a single dull or commonplace one.

The "through-composed" songs usually tapped his powers more deeply. Freed from the necessity of literal repetitions, he could develop the mood, shape the voice to the textual situation, the dramatic summit. He could also mold the accompaniment accordingly, build tension and release, use it descriptively. These ways, needless to say, were operatic ways. Mozart thought instinctively, from constant practice, in terms of opera. The singers for whom he wrote this type of song were also opera-trained. The *durchcomponiert* songs are often operatic airs in reduced length and range.

The earliest of these is *"Ridente la calma"* (K. 152), a glowing depiction of contentment in love and called a "Canzonetta," Italian in vocal style as in text. He composed it in Salzburg, in 1775. In Mannheim, about two years later, he deliberately imitated the French *chanson* in two "ariettes"—

"*Oiseaux, si tous les ans*" and "*Dans un bois solitaire*" (K. 307, 308), for "Gustl," the daughter of his hosts the Wend-lings. "*Dans un bois solitaire*" dramatically depicts the flight of Cupid's arrow to its mark. *Das Veilchen* (K. 476), still a favorite, was composed in Vienna in 1785. An aria in minia-ture, it tells its story with vivid sentiment and an affecting close, in sixty-five bars. Mozart may not even have known that Goethe was the poet, for the poem as he may have found it was published in a collection under another name. The "little violet" hopes to be picked by an approaching maiden, and to have the honor of resting on her bosom. She does not notice it and steps upon it, whereupon it expires with a sigh; at least her foot has been the cause of its end. Mozart adds his personal touch to Goethe's words, in a tiny fermata and cadence: "The poor violet! It was a lovely little violet."

Three songs of 1787 rise from dainty sentiment to strong emotion, delivered with the contained power of the composer of *Don Giovanni*. *Das Lied der Trennung* (K. 519) describes the lover's lingering sentiments after a final separation. The last two of the five verses break away from repetition as his thoughts darken into bitterness. *Abendempfindung* (K. 523) has a broad, almost operatic melody of cumulative intensity. *An Chloe* (K. 524), of similar length and melodic beauty, is a rhapsodic love song, without shadow, simply accom-panied.

The more cut to shape strophic songs yield much special beauty within formal limitations. The bitter *An die Hoffnung* (K. 390) and *An die Einsamkeit* (K. 391) of the year 1780 concentrate the intense feeling of the text within fourteen bars of music. *An die Einsamkeit* is in a weighty G minor. A curiosity is *Die Alte* (K. 517), of 1787. An old woman, singing "slightly through the nose," according to the directions, bemoans the depravity of the modern age, telling how "In *my* time" things were better.

"*Daphne, deine Rosenwangen*" (1768), K. 52
An die Freude (Uz) (1767), K. 53
"*Wie unglücklich bin ich*" (1772), K. 147
"*O heiliges Band*" (1772), K. 148

Die grossmüthige Gelassenheit (J. C. Günther) (1772), K. 149

Geheime Liebe (J. C. Günther) (1772), K. 150

Die Zufriedenheit im niedrigen Stande (F. R. von Canitz) (1772), K. 151

"*Ridente la calma*," Canzonetta (1775?), K. 152

"*Ah, spiegarti, o Dio*," Aria (1772), K. 178

"*Oiseaux, si tous les ans*," Arietta (1777), K. 307

"*Dans un bois solitaire*," Arietta (Houdart de la Motte) (1778), K. 308

Die Zufriedenheit (Johann Martin Miller) (1780 or 1781), K. 349

"*Komm, liebe Zither*," with mandolin (1780 or 1781), K. 351

An die Hoffnung, "Ich würd, auf meinem Pfad" (J. T. Hermes) (1780), K. 390

An die Einsamkeit, "Sei du mein Trost" (J. T. Hermes) (1780), K. 391

"*Verdankt sei es dem Glanz*" (J. T. Hermes) (1780), K. 392

Gesellenreise, "Die ihr einem neuen Grade" (Joseph Franz von Ratschky) (1785), K. 468

Der Zauberer, "Ihr Mädchen, flieht" (C. F. Weisse) (1785), K. 472

Die Zufriedenheit, "Wie sanft" (C. F. Weisse) (1785), K. 473

Die betrogene Welt, "Der reiche Tor" (C. F. Weisse) (1785), K. 474

Das Veilchen (Goethe) (1785), K. 476

Lied der Freiheit, "Wer unter eines Mädchens Hand" (Blumauer) (1786), K. 506

Die Alte, "Zu meiner Zeit" (Friedrich von Hagedorn) (1787), K. 517

Die Verschweigung, "Sobald Damoetas" (C. F. Weisse) (1787), K. 518

Das Lied der Trennung, "Die Engel Gottes weinen" (Klamer Schmidt) (1787), K. 519

Als Luise die Briefe ihres ungetreuen Liebhabers verbrannte, "Erzeugt von heisser Phantasie" (Gabriele von Baumberg) (1787), K. 520

Abendempfindung, "Abend ist's" (Campe) (1787), K. 523

An Chloe (J. G. Jacobi) (1787), K. 524

Des kleinen Friedrichs Geburtstag, "Es war einmal" (Mildheim's *Liederbuch*) (1787), K. 529

Das Traumbild, "Wo bist du, Bild?" (Holty) (1787), K. 530

Die kleine Spinnerin, "Was spinnst du?" (?; extra verses by D. Jäger) (1787), K. 531

Beim Auszug in das Feld, "Dem hohen Kaiser-Worte treu" (1788), K. 552

Sehnsucht nach dem Frühlinge, "Komm, lieber Mai" (C. A. Overbeck (1791), K. 596

Im Frühlingsanfange, "Erwacht zum neuen Leben" (C. C. Sturm) (1791), K. 597

Das Kinderspiel, "Wir Kinder" (C. A. Overbeck) (1791), K. 598

Eine kleine deutsche Kantate, "Die ihr des unermesslichen Weltalls" (F. H. Ziegenhagen) (1791), K. 619

The Canons (unaccompanied)

THE CANONS, all belonging to the Vienna years, were obviously written for friendly gatherings where at least some of those present could read and hold to a musical line. They are mostly for three or four voices, but range from two voices to twelve. The texts of the earlier ones invariably celebrate food, drink, women, and general jollity. The first two of 1788 are on the words *"Alleluja"* and *"Ave Maria."* The rest, in Latin or in broad Viennese dialect, are nonsensical, with uncomplimentary personal allusions, of the composer's making. *"Geh'n ma in'n Prada,"* *"O du eselhafter Martin"* (addressed to Mozart's friendly "impresario," P. J. Martin), and *"Bonna Nox, bist a rechta Ox"* use language unsuitable for any but male society. Their earthy texts are in curious contrast to their immaculate, expressive and wholly delightful counterpoint.

1770

Kyrie for five sopranos (K. 89); Four-voice Canon (K. 89a)

1782

"Sie ist dahin" (Hölty), K. 229; *"Selig, selig, alle"* (Hölty), K. 230; *"Leck mich im Arsch,"* K. 231; *"Leck mir den Arsch fein recht,"* K. 233; *"Bei der Hitz,"* K. 234; *"Lasst uns ziehn,"* K. 347; *"V'amo di core teneramente"* (for three quartets), K. 348

1786

"Heiterkeit und leichtes Blut," K. 507; *"Auf das Wohl aller Freunde,"* K. 508

1787

"Ach, zu kurz ist unsers Lebens Lauf" (Double canon), K. 228; *"Lieber Freistädtler, lieber Gaulimauli"* K. 232

1788

"Alleluja," K. 553; *"Ave Maria,"* K. 554; *"Lacrimoso son io,"* K. 555; *"G'rechtelt's enk,"* K. 556; *"Nascoso è il mio sol,"* K. 557; *"Gehn ma in'n Prada,"* K. 558; *"Difficile lectu mihi,"* K. 559; *"O du eselhafter Martin"* and *"O du eselhafter Peierl,"* K. 560; *"Bona Nox, bist a rechta Ox,"* K. 561; *"Caro bell' idol mio,"* K. 562

The Part Songs for Small Ensembles

"God Is Our Refuge," Motet in four parts, unaccompanied, K. 20 (1765)

"Luci care, luci belle," Notturno for three voices and three basset horns, K. 346 (1783)

"Dir, Seele des Weltalls," for soprano, male chorus and piano, K. 429 (See Cantatas)

"Ecco quel fiero istante" (Metastasio), Notturno for two sopranos and bass, with three basset horns, K. 436 (1783)

"Mi lagnerò tacendo" (Metastasio) Notturno for two sopranos and bass, with two clarinets and one basset horn, K. 437 (1783)

"Se lontan', ben mio tu sei," Notturno for three voices, with two clarinets and basset horn, K. 438 (1783)

"Due pupille amabile," Notturno for two sopranos and bass, with three basset horns, K. 439 (1783)

"In te spero, o sposo" (Metastasio), Aria for soprano and double bass (fragmentary), K. 440 (1782)

Fugue in three voice parts, K. 443 (1782)

"Zerfliesset heut, geliebte Brüder," Song for tenor, chorus and organ, K. 483 (1785)

"Ihr unsre neuen Leiter," Chorus in three parts, with organ, K. 484 (1785)

"Più non si trovano" (Metastasio), Canzonetta for two sopranos and bass, with three basset horns, K. 549 (1788)

"Caro mio, Druck und Schluck," Comic Quartet for soprano, two tenors and bass, with piano, K. 571a (1789)

The Vocal Ensembles with Orchestra

"Welch ängstliches Beben" (intended for *Die Entführung aus dem Serail*), Duet for two tenors and orchestra, K. 389 (1782)

"Del gran regno delle Amazoni," Trio for tenor and two basses, with orchestra, K. 434 (1783)

"Liebes Mandel, wo is's Bandel," Trio for soprano, tenor and bass, with strings, K. 441 (1783)

"Dite almeno" (for Bianchi's *La villanella rapita*), Quartet, K. 479 (1785)

"Mandina amabile" (for *La villanella rapita*), Trio for soprano, tenor and bass, with orchestra, K. 480 (1785)

"Spiegarti, o Dio, non posso" (for *Idomeneo*), Duet for soprano, tenor, and orchestra, K. 489 (1786)

"Grazie agl'inganni tuoi" (for *Idomeneo*), Trio for soprano, tenor and bass, with orchestra, K. 532 (1787)

"Nun, liebes Weibchen" (for Schikaneder's text, *Stein den Weisen*), Comic Duet for soprano and bass, with orchestra, K. 625 (1789) (Doubtful)

The Church Music

THE PROPER style for choral church music in any era has seldom met full accord between its makers and its users. Both want it to glorify the text—a good common ground. But the ministrants of the church will not have the text distorted or obscured. Since every service is before all an act of worship, they cannot welcome distraction in the contemplation of beautiful tones. Because the church before any other institution subsists on tradition, they must be wary of innovation. The composer, on the other hand, lives and feels music as of his own time, as an ineradicable part of his nature as artist, and unless he writes exclusively for the church, his personal style will be largely a lay style. Verdi is an extreme case of this disparity. His *Requiem* sounds like opera because opera was the deepest part of himself. It was because he was also an ardent believer that he could not do less than put his heart into the task and write a great work instead of a faultless but sterile piece in the strict style.

The late eighteenth century had a similar problem. The

Vatican tradition of strict counterpoint persisted, for counterpoint could inspire a sort of impersonal, mystic elevation of interwoven voices, an other-worldly mood which could be disturbed by the intrusion of an emotional solo voice, even if it were not a woman's voice. This remote purity could not have endured because churchly Italy became also operatic Italy. The Masses in the Roman Church could not have withstood that permeation of operatic musical thinking. A *Kyrie* could take the shape of an overture. There were lines in the *Credo* which suggested vivid dramatic treatment. An *Agnus Dei,* an emotional plea, could take on the intensity of an operatic aria; coloratura passages crept in, for coloratura is akin to melisma. A closing *Dona nobis pacem* could sometimes assume the likeness of an operatic finale. It was largely by way of Italy that the whole face of music had become homophonic. Sensuous melody set off by chord accompaniment was the soul of popular Italy. The Roman Church outside of Italy was still more freely colored by lay elements. A compromise could not have been avoided, for counterpoint was entirely outmoded in the lay world.

Mozart, nurtured on the gallant style but also thoroughly equipped in contrapuntal writing, followed the lead of his colleagues in the Cathedral at Salzburg, Ernst Eberlin or Michael Haydn, who quite naturally too made use of both sources. Since the well of Mozart's invention was deeper than his colleagues', the process of blending went further. The alternation of part manipulation and block chords became an opportunity for variety and contrast—a double enrichment. The orchestra, even in the Sunday Masses when he was confined almost entirely to violins, became even more prominent in the functions both of agitating and thematic leading. The Masses show a continual progress in integration until the melodic line controls, lying both in the voices and the instruments. In the last two Masses, written in Vienna, a full orchestra is handled with the maturity of the great symphonist.

In Salzburg, where Mozart wrote almost all of his church music, he was limited in the duration and in the performing forces rather than by any known stylistic objection on the part of either Archbishop. As always, he cheerfully made the most of each assignment. The Sunday Masses, which were his principal duty, had to be short. The nativity, the crucifixion, the resurrection, must each be treated in a few fleeting bars, posing a musical problem of expressiveness, development, unity. An extended fugal treatment would have been frowned upon by Colloredo. The *Kapelle* allowed only violins, with oboes, horns and bass continuo. Violas and cellos were not scored in, and if used at all must simply have doubled the bass. Only for special services could he expand, use ceremonial trumpets and drums, and sometimes trombones to double the choir parts. The litanies allowed more freedom, and seem to have been intended for private services.

In Mozart's church music no less than in the other forms which he used repeatedly through the years, we can follow the gradations of his growth. The vocal counterpoint remains at times strict, but is generally speaking increasingly integrated with the homophonic texture. The instrumental parts become more prominent, sometimes introducing the melodic theme or supplying a coda. A reiterated rhythmic figure tends to bind a movement into a single character; in the later works there is more rhythmic propulsion.

That his religious music has moments of good cheer as well as moments of true and solemn grandeur really proves that his piety was genuine and heartfelt, and not, as with others, a matter for stuffy decorum. His *Exsultate, jubilate* (K. 165) is a flow of high spirits in the boy of seventeen, but it is pure and heart-lifting, anything but irreverent. The *Dona nobis pacem* finales which close his earlier Masses, are like the *Osannas,* pure and light-hearted in the same way. He was not afraid to draw from his operatic style, and he used this style in an entirely pious spirit. He opens the *Agnus Dei* in the "Coronation" Mass with a phrase which is later to appear note for note as "*Dove sono,*" the sorrowing aria of the Countess in *Figaro*. Its treatment is completely different. Objections to these unorthodoxies, and there have been such in the nineteenth century, have been arrived at on unconvincing theoretical grounds rather than after unprejudiced listening. Mozart's faith speaks the more freely and intimately in just these places.

The two Masses which he wrote in Vienna after his church obligations had ended show the fullest development of each of these qualities. They are both much more orchestrally developed. Their melody is more orchestral. They are newly dramatic in sudden dynamic contrast, in crescendo and climax. The C minor Mass has an unprecedented grandeur and brilliance, after its dark opening. The *Requiem* Mass is predominantly somber. It foretells a new Mozart, in orchestral usage similar but in mood at uttermost variance with *The Magic Flute,* from which he had turned for this task. This Mozart was an artist of great solemnity, of affecting pathos, who could turn his back altogether on the cheerful gallant style which had been the keynote of his music.

Perhaps the most astonishing feature of Mozart's church music as a whole is the constant variety, the ever-fresh approach in the repeated treatments of the same text. Certain recurring characteristics are only inessential details. *"Miserére," "Crucifíxus," "In nómine Dómini,"* set countless times, never return as repetition from an earlier work, in spite of the fact that with Mozart, as with Beethoven, syllables fell into natural musical accents, words and music becoming identified in their imaginations.

Mozart's duties in Salzburg could have been dry routine to him. The music speaks to us differently. It confirms the evidence in his letters that his faith was fundamental and unshaken, that he always regarded the church services as worthy of his best powers, and studied counterpoint eagerly through his life in pursuit of this phase of his art.

The Masses

Mozart wrote the first of his Masses which have survived at the age of twelve (K. 49). He is believed to have composed it in Vienna during the visit of 1768, a belief confirmed by the use of violas, instruments not available for the Salzburg services on Sundays. The required brevity permits little more than the introduction of each phrase by a solo singer and its repetition by the quartet. The opening of the *Gloria* and the *Credo* are left to be intoned by the priest, and are not set. The *Agnus Dei* (choral) is sung adagio, in E minor, the *Dona nobis pacem,* as almost invariably later, brings a tranquil close in the major, for Mozart properly looked upon the Mass as a confident, not a lugubrious service.

Missa brevis in D minor, K. 65 (Composed in Salzburg, 1769)

Since this was a Lenten mass, the *Gloria* would not have been sung, but would have been added for use in a different season. The *Christe eleison* as before is briefly incorporated in the *Kyrie,* but here it arrests the attention as the solo voices introduce it, in F major. In the *Credo,* which in the short Mass is always a problem of concentration, unification and expressiveness, the text is in one place overlapped—a short cut usually frowned upon by the Church. The solo voices are treated as a quartet until the *Benedictus,* which is a duet for soprano and alto. The *Agnus Dei,* confined to twelve bars, is followed by a gentle *Dona nobis pacem,* which nevertheless is faithful to the D minor signature.

Mass in C, K. 66 (Composed in Salzburg, 1769)

Mozart had reason to put his heart into his first High Mass, for he wrote it for his friend Cajetan Hagenauer, providing it for Hagenauer's first celebration as priest. The occasion called for orchestral brilliance and included, be it noted, violas. The *Kyrie* is given in a slow introduction and developed at length. Elaborate figures by the violins are resorted to here and later, either for purposes of brilliance or for intensification of feeling. In the Gloria the eight sections become separate movements with use of solo voices. The *Cum Sancto Spiritu* becomes an "amen" fugue. The *Credo,* likewise developed in each part, shows that expressive liberation could bring release. *Et vitam venturi* is likewise fugued. Mozart, aged thirteen, was capable of a *Missa solemnis* of proper grandeur.

Missa brevis in C, K. 115 (Composed in Salzburg, summer, 1773)

Einstein's belief that Mozart wrote this Mass in Salzburg has been disputed. It is a study in compactness, in strict writing relieved by homophonic simplicity. The *Cum Sancto Spiritu* is a double fugue, briefly encompassed. The Mass breaks off at the ninth bar of the *Sanctus.*

Missa brevis in F, K. 116 (Composed in Salzburg, 1768?)

The manuscript consists of a *Kyrie,* and fragmentary notations for a *Gloria* and *Credo.* The autograph has been doubted. The accompaniment is for violins and viola.

Mass in C minor-major, K. 139 (Composed in Vienna, 1768?)

A true Missa solemnis, this work has long been attributed to the winter of 1771-1772, in Salzburg, but Einstein finally accepted the opinion of W. Kurthen that it was indeed the Mass which Mozart wrote in Vienna, in 1768, for the consecration of the Waisenhaus Kirche on the Rennweg, an occasion observed with full pomp in the presence of royalty. The use of four trumpets in the orchestra would make Salzburg doubtful, and the divided violas still more so. It has been found hard to believe that he could write so mature a score at twelve. If he did, the royalty present may well have been impressed. He was to compose the full Mass for Hagenauer in the following year. From the boy who had just written *La finta semplice* anything could be expected.

The Mass bears the C minor signature from its opening bars. It is not a minor mass in spirit, traversing several major keys, touching the minor only at such brief and solemn moments as the *Crucifixus* and the *Agnus Dei.* It ends joyously in C major. It is still ampler than the "Hagenauer" Mass, known as the *"Domenicus"* Mass. The two fugues are more fully worked, there are two duets for soprano and alto (*Laudamus Te* and *Et incarnatus*) a tenor and bass duet (*Domine Deum*), and a long soprano solo for *Quoniam.* In spite of the general air of brilliant ceremony, there are quiet moments of great beauty, such as the hushed *Crucifixus* with muted trumpets, and the *Agnus Dei* with its trombone choir and its agonized *"Miserere."*

Missa in honorem Sanctissimae Trinitatis, in C, K. 167 (Composed in Salzburg, June, 1773)

This is a high Mass in full panoply, a choral and instrumental work, with no solo voices, with a prominent instrumental contingent, including oboes, four trumpets in balanced pairs, and drums. There are instrumental introductions. The violins are brilliantly scored throughout, with rapid figures often pointed by trills. The *Gloria* is treated as a single movement, but the *Credo* is divided into sections, dramatically. The *"descendit"* and *"as-*

cendit" are as graphic as the words imply, and the end an extensive fugue. C major, the key for brilliance, predominates, even in the *Agnus Dei,* and to the final full chords of the *Dona nobis pacem,* music of ceremonial splendor.

Missa brevis in F, K. 192 (Composed in Salzburg, June, 1774)

The use of only strings and organ in the accompaniment does not greatly alter the substance, for the violins are the thematic basis of all the Sunday Masses. The constant alternation of full chorus and solo quartet, which in the *Gloria* here gives the sense of responses, creates an impression very different from that of the "Trinity" Mass which precedes it. The *Credo* gains unity by the recurrence of the word:

Cre - do   cre - do

This is to become the favorite motto of Mozart, and is most familiar as it opens the fugal finale of the "Jupiter" Symphony.* The motto here fits the words *"cru-ci-fix-us," "con-fit-e-or," "A-men,-a-men."* The *Sanctus* is briefly stated, with a ponderous bass, followed by an *Osanna* of open brilliance, which here, as after the quiet *Benedictus,* makes a dramatic effect by its sheer twelve-bar brevity. The *Agnus Dei,* an adagio in D minor with an expressive string subject, is sung by solo voices, each followed by a choral *"miserere."* The close is choral.

Missa brevis in D, K. 194 (Composed in Salzburg, in August, 1774)

The Masses are not only a study in the integration of the contrapuntal and the harmonic Mozart—they show the gradual emergence of his genius in the molding of the rigidity and complexity of the strict style into a fluent texture with clear melodic lines. The *Requiem,* and, in the purely orchestral music, the "Jupiter" Symphony, are ultimate examples. This Mass in D major shows an advance in this direction over its predecessor of

---

* This usable note succession derives, according to Abert, from the third mode of the Roman liturgy. It appears in the religious music of Alessandro Scarlatti and Michael Haydn, and was later used by Mozart in the *Sanctus* of the Mass in C major of 1776 (K. 257), the Symphony in B flat (K. 319) of 1779, the Violin Sonata in E flat (K. 481) of 1785.

two months before. Even the close four-part writing has a clear and strong melodic current, and also a rhythmic current. This Mass is a remarkable combination of concentration and drama —the life of Christ from birth to death, from "*Et incarnatus est*" to "*passus est*" is depicted strikingly in nine bars! The Mass becomes intensely personal in the *Agnus Dei* where, over an agitated accompaniment in B minor, the solo voices in turn sing phrases where a trilled note is like a voice breaking with emotion. The Mass is earnest, dignified in character, with solo phrases (the bass in *Quoniam,* the soprano in *Et incarnatus est*) churchlike rather than operatic. The *Dona* is lightened by a joyous ornamental figure.

Missa brevis in C, K. 220 (Composed in Munich, January, 1775)

Composed in Munich during the preparation of *La finta giardiniera,* this Mass was surely intended for Salzburg, for one of the shortest of his Masses and one of the most elementary would have been his last choice to show a strange community what he could do. The choral portion is in straight chords, entirely without counterpoint, not even in the close of the *Credo,* and the solo voices have nothing more than the simplest imitative coupling. Whether or not this Mass was designed to please the Archbishop, it would probably have been quite to his taste.

Mass in C major, "Credo" Mass, K. 257 (Composed in Salzburg in November, 1776)

Mozart's fourth Mass in C major confirms his fondness for this as the majestic tonality. It has his strongest orchestra to date, with three trombones doubling the lower voices. The trumpets and oboes step forward as independent instruments. The orchestra is no longer an accompaniment but a symphony—it often holds the center of interest, the thematic lead, and introduces the voices. There is little counterpoint, for the score advances on a strong harmonic current, with thematic melody, rhythmic interest. It is called the "*Credo*" Mass because of the many striking elements in the *Credo,* which is in one long movement. The word, repeated in staccato unison, supported by the trombones, sounds abrupt in its bare statement, but as it recurs again and again, varied or thematically combined, it is wonderfully effective. The mystic "*crucifixus*" on fortepiano chords, the *homo factus est* on strong displaced accents, are among many striking details in this extraordinary movement. The *Sanctus* is based on the four-note motive of the "Jupiter" finale. In the *Benedictus,* the chorus does not enter until the orchestra has well established the thematic substance. The *Agnus Dei,* unlike its predecessors as treated by Mozart, is a powerful choral movement (an andante maestoso) in the major tonality, with piano passages and dramatic crescendos.

Missa brevis in C, K. 258 (Composed in Salzburg, in December, 1776)

The so-called "Spaur" Mass is believed to have been provided for the consecration of Friedrich Franz Josef, Count von Spaur, who was to become Dean of the Salzburg Cathedral. This would explain the fortifying use of trumpets and drums. Otherwise it is fairly straightforward, with the solo voices used mostly as an alternating quartet, the violins mostly for supporting figures, the vocal texture only occasionally and briefly departing from a basis of chords.

Missa brevis in C ("Organ" Mass), K. 259 (Composed in Salzburg, in December, 1776)

This Mass in the favored key of C major has the same orchestration as the "Spaur" Mass, and was written in the same month, indicating special use. It was performed at the consecration of the Archbishop of Ölmutz, in Salzburg, in 1778. It is similar in treatment to the earlier Mass, consisting largely of alternate choral and solo quartet passages, and has instrumental interest. The *Benedictus,* which, as in the previous Mass, is the only really developed movement in a work of minimum length, allows the organ to step up momentarily from its purely bass function and provide the principal accompaniment.

Missa longa in C, K. 262 (Composed in Salzburg, May, 1776)

This is one of the longest of the Masses, with a notably developed and extended *Credo.* It calls for oboes and trumpets, and, for the first time in the Masses, horns. The instrumental introduction to the *Kyrie* indicates at once that the orchestra is to have an important part. This Mass has far more choral counterpoint than its companions of the same year, especially in the *Kyrie,* and in the *Credo* with its fully fugued "*Et vitam venturi.*" The *Et in spiritum sanctum* has a long, melodic orchestral introduction and is sung by the tenor, with choral responses. The *Benedictus* breaks precedent as the solo voices in turn deliver the first phrase and the chorus sings *"Osanna in excelsis"* each time as a response. The *Agnus Dei* is a choral movement.

Missa brevis in B flat, K. 275 (Composed in Salzburg, in 1777)

Almost a year had elapsed since the three Masses of 1776, when Mozart wrote this one, shortly before his departure with his mother for Munich, on their long tour. The instruments are simply but none the less expressively confined to violins and bass. The opening words *"Kyrie eleison"* are for a soprano solo which, according to a letter from his father, on December 22, was sung "most excellently" by the castrato, Ceccarelli. Ceccarelli would also have sung the *Benedictus.* The voices are handled with a smooth dovetailing of parts, but the texture is harmonic throughout. It is frankly melodic with a gentle, propulsive bass rhythm. The descriptive episodes in the *Credo* are lovingly and beautifully, rather than dramatically, treated. There is no fugueing, no attempt to be imposing. The *Dona,* with many alternate solo phrases, brings a gentle, somehow a personal, close.

Mass in C, "Coronation," K. 317 (Composed in Salzburg, 1779)

The "Coronation" Mass, the next to last of the Salzburg Masses, is the most orchestral of them all. It has a full quota of oboes, horns, trumpets in pairs, drums, with trombones (according to custom) to double the underlying voices. It was composed for an annual service at the church of Maria Plain, a shrine on the bank of the Salzach near Salzburg, and an object of many pilgrimages. There the coronation of the Virgin was commemorated by a service on the fifth Sunday after Pentecost. Composed two months after Mozart's return to Salzburg from Munich, Mannheim and Paris, this Mass shows a new integration, an eloquence and expressive power of the matured traveler, aged twenty-three. Orchestra, chorus, solo voices are welded into one purpose—a community of noble sound, a combination of splendor and human warmth, a free and open use of the composer's natural musical leanings, but of unquestionable religious sincerity.

The very first notes of the solemn introduction, a *"Ky-ri-e"* with a mighty first chord and two soft chords which follow like a mysterious echo, is a declaration of individual character, found later in sudden contrasts, as in the thunderous motto rhythm of

"*Glor-i-a*" and its soft answer in the violins, forte-piano chords in the *Credo*. The score has some sudden hushed moments, such as the *Et incarnatus est*, where the intoned text is set with a lovely figure for the muted violins. This figure persists until the pianissimo "*Crucifixus*," followed by a full burst of sound in the "*Resurrexit.*" The *Sanctus* is brief, but majestic, with striding chords. The *Benedictus* opens with a sprightly instrumental allegretto which sounds anything but churchly, until with the entrance of the solo quartet, it at once becomes so. An innovation is the return of this quartet, sotto voce, to interrupt the proclamatory *Osanna in excelsis*. The *Agnus Dei* is operatic in character, a soprano solo with an exact initial resemblance to "*Dove sono*," the aria of the Countess in *Figaro*, not to be written until seven years later. This too is an aria, but it is infused with a true religious spirit. The soloist carries her voice into the *Dona nobis pacem*, the solo voices enter, and then the full chorus in a brilliant and joyous close.

Missa solemnis in C, K. 337 (Composed in Salzburg, in March, 1780)

This was Mozart's last Mass as an employee in Salzburg. In the autumn following he would compose *Idomeneo* for Munich and thence make his way to Vienna. It bears the title "*Missa solemnis,*" which would be justified by the full winds used (oboes, bassoons, trumpets, trombones) and a certain formality of treatment, rather than by its general plan, which is concentrated. The free use of the orchestra, the thematic interest, and the beauty of various episodes class it in general with the "Coronation" Mass of the year previous. The strict part-writing of the *Benedictus* is surprising because it is a style which he had largely worked away from. The *Agnus Dei*, like that of the "Coronation" Mass, is a soprano solo. Here the orchestra, which states the melody, is richer, with a full organ part, and an independent use of the oboes and bassoons, over muted violins. The *Dona* is imposing, but ends quietly in the solo voices.

Mass in C minor, K. 427 (Composed in Vienna, in the season 1782-1783)

If proof is needed that music for the church was more for Mozart than the fulfillment of a duty, and held a deep place in his affections as composer, the Mass in C minor would in itself be evidence enough. There were many calls upon his time in Vienna, but none for this kind of music. With no prospect of performance or return, and none of the restrictions which had been imposed on him in Salzburg, he laid out his own concept of what a Mass should be and exceeded anything he had done, both in length and performing forces. He scored it for oboes, bassoons, horns and trumpets in pairs, four trombones (used independently as well as to double the choral parts), strings (including violas) and organ. For only the second time in his life,* and profiting by the example of Handel, he used a double chorus. The length of the Mass if completed would have been at least an hour and a half. Having recently composed *Die Entführung,* the "Haffner" Symphony, the Piano Concertos K. 413, 414, 415, the splendid Serenade for winds, in C minor (K. 388), he drew upon his symphonic and operatic maturity. Having just delved into the music of Bach and Handel, he strongly reflected them both.

An immediate motive of the Mass was his desire to please his bride with effective soprano solos displaying her range, and so to increase his family's respect for her in their planned first visit to Salzburg. He obviously gloried in this, his one opportunity to put into a Mass exactly what he wished, even to the point of making it a "vehicle" for Constanze. The visit was postponed until July, 1783, on account of the crowding concert obligations of Lent, and the completion of the score was no doubt prevented for the same reason. The Mass was performed in the Church of St. Peter in Salzburg, on August 25, 1783, and must have been achieved by the friendly co-operation of singers and players, for the Archbishop would hardly have given his patronage to so expensive a venture, especially on the part of a fallen angel. The missing portions must have been supplied from a previous Mass to fulfill the service. For many years no one bothered to revive this torso of a Mass. In the present century it has been resurrected, notably in Salzburg, where, since 1940, it has often been performed in a version pieced out from the Missa longa in C major (K. 262).† The score consists of the *Kyrie,* the *Gloria,* and the *Sanctus* (including the *Osanna* and the *Benedictus*) complete. The *Credo* is written through the *Et incarnatus est.* The

---

* Mozart used a double chorus in his Offertorium (K. 260).

† Although opening darkly in the key of its signature, the great Mass, traversing many keys, minor and major, scarcely touches again upon C minor.

Agnus Dei and *Dona nobis pacem* are missing altogether. In current performances the music of the *Kyrie* is repeated with the words of this last movement.

The *Kyrie eleison* is an anguished plea for mercy. It has a strong melodic current, both orchestral and choral. The *Christe eleison* enters as an aria-like soprano solo in a gleaming E flat major. The *Gloria* is a great outburst of sound in C major, contrapuntally treated. The influence of Handel is felt, and the words *"in excelsis"* are almost a quotation of the *"alleluias"* from *The Messiah*. The *Laudamus Te* is an extensive and ornate solo for the mezzo-soprano. The *Gratias* is a brief choral adagio, characterized, as are other movements, by a pervading rythmic figure. The *Domine Deus,* a duet between the soprano and the mezzo, to string accompaniment, is a test of vocal range for both, but it is Bach-like and devout in spirit. The *Qui tollis* brings the contrast of full weight, with double chorus and massive orchestra. It could be called the high point of the *Gloria*. The strings maintain throughout a figure of paired chords, undergoing arresting modulations. More than one commentator has been reminded of Christ carrying the cross, bearing the sins of the world. The words *"suscipe"* and *"miserere"* become a plaint, a descending chromatic figure, the whole subsiding to a hushed pianissimo and rising again to power. The *Quoniam,* for three solo voices, is a superlative feat of contrapuntal texture by the composer who has been newly awakened by the music of Bach to further possibilities in the strict style. The *Jesu Christe* again brings in the full orchestra. It is a choral adagio in six measures, an introduction to the *Cum Sancto Spiritu* which brings from the composer a magnificent fugue, the most extensive Mozart ever undertook—a tonal edifice not only resembling Bach but rivaling Bach. The *Sanctus,* for double chorus, is a largo, impressively conceived, the *Osanna* solemnly rather than joyously exultant. The *Benedictus* establishes itself as an orchestral movement before the chorus enters and predominates. The *Credo* is a majestic assertion in C major, the *Et incarnatus est* a soprano solo, both tender and ornate (a cadenza is indicated). To the string accompaniment are added the delicate voices of a solo flute, oboe and bassoon.

Mozart's unfailing judgment cannot be questioned in this fusion of the free and strict styles. Nor will the listener bother his head about rules or ritual, extraneous liberties, before this evidence of sincerity in the young man of twenty-two who loved God as devoutly and reverently as his middle name implied.

Requiem Mass in D minor, K. 626 (Composed in Vienna, December, 1791)

Mozart's only Requiem Mass, the last music he wrote, and the music which death prevented him from finishing, has remained a subject for study and indeterminate speculation as to how much of the music was actually his own. The true mystery which surrounds the score has nothing to do with the fact that an anonymous patron ordered it secretly to be performed privately in memory of his wife and presented as his own composition, but with the particulars of authorship submerged in the transaction.

Constanze, anxious after her husband's death to collect the remainder of the fee and to retain the first payment, labored secretly to present a complete score to Count Walsegg, the *"Unbekannter,"* as she called him. As it stood, the first two numbers—the *Requiem aeternam* and the *Kyrie*—were fully written. The six movements of the "Sequence," from the *Dies Irae* to the *Lacrimosa,* ceased after the ninth bar, the offertorium (the *Domine Jesu Christe* and the *Hostias* existed in the choral parts with figured bass and some indications of the instrumentation). The *Sanctus,* the *Agnus Dei* and the final *Lux aeterna* were missing altogether from the score. Constanze engaged Johann Eyblers, Mozart's pupil, who filled out the missing parts until the opening of the *Lacrimosa,* and at that point, faced with blank pages, gave up. Thereupon Franz Xaver Süssmayr, a pupil who had been close to Mozart both in the preparation of *La clemenza di Tito* and the *Requiem* itself, took up the task. He recopied the revision in order that the "Unknown" should not receive a score in three different handwritings, completed the *Lacrimosa,* filled out the *Offertorium,* composed the *Sanctus, Benedictus* and *Agnus Dei,* supposedly out of his own head (so he wrote to Constanze in 1799), and for the *Lux aeterna* repeated the fugue from the *Kyrie.* The manuscript as delivered to the "Unknown" consisted of the first two movements in Mozart's original script, complete; the remainder in Süssmayr's not too different hand. The Count probably believed that he had Mozart's script until the last three sections. After he had duly presented the Mass in 1793, it had public performances from Constanze's copy of the score. When it became generally known that Mozart was the composer, he would have been too embarrassed to raise his voice. In 1799, Constanze negotiated with Breitkopf and Härtel, in the hope that it might be considered free for publication. The publisher acted promptly, and under the protest of Walsegg as the original owner.

Süssmayr's statement that the *Sanctus, Benedictus* and *Agnus Dei* were entirely supplied by him has been suspected as a false claim, since the *Mass* maintains its character on a level which would postulate clever stylistic imitation, a faithful carrying through from thematic sketches, but hardly a full dependence upon Süssmayr's resources. The *Benedictus,* for example, is hard to credit as the entire invention of the none too original Süssmayr, whose own church compositions are paled to extinction by comparison. The few bars of the *Lacrimosa* gave him the two principal thematic elements and their combination. He carried them through with skill and effect, more briefly than Mozart would have done. He had the good taste not to put in development of his own. Mozart would probably not have repeated the fugue from the *Kyrie* for the close, but this was Süssmayr's best expedient.

The *Requiem Mass* has its own distinctive character, a voice apart from all the music of its composer. It is music of terrible earnestness, of awesome solemnity. Its dark, minor mood prevails, and is only momentarily relieved by the peaceful flowing F major of the *Recordare, Jesu pie,* without brass, and the quiet chords of the *Hostiam et preces,* in E flat. These are interludes in a score otherwise somber and forcefully urgent. Mozart used no woodwinds except the dark colors of basset horns and bassoons; the *Tuba mirum* introduces a solo trombone in passages of doom. A trombone choir is introduced in the *Confutatis* and the *Domine.* He has shaped chorus and orchestra to his special purpose with the craftsmanship of his last works. In the fugal movements he is deliberately archaic, showing the unmistakable influence of Bach. At the very beginning he gives his theme to the basset horns and bassoons, and the string accompaniment in a characteristic syncopation. At *"Te decet hymnus"* by the soprano solo he works in, as purely vocal, a traditional chorale, the psalm melody *"In exitu Israel de Aegypto."* The second movement is a double fugue, in which the *Kyrie eleison* is combined with a *Christe eleison* in continuous sixteenths. The *Dies Irae* is formidable, unrelenting, with a chordal chorus and agitating strings. The *Tuba mirum* opens with a fateful solo for the trombone, the instrument which stood for solemnity with Mozart, and which he used more subtly as a choir, notably in this score and in *The Magic Flute.* The *Rex tremendae majestatis* is all that the words imply, the word *"Rex"* delivered three times to introduce a choral treatment in counterpoint, against an inexorably repeated rhythmic figure in the strings. The gentle ending, "*Salva me,*" brings in the *Recordare*—a fully developed, tranquil movement for the four solo voices, combining with an expressive orchestra conspicuous in the low woodwind color, and without brass—in beautiful and unarrested melody. The *Confutatis maledictus* restores the full orchestra, again a threatening string figure, the male voices alternating with the female voices, who introduce the pleading "*voca me*" in a contrasting *sotto voce*. The last part is a supplication by the combined choir. The *Lacrimosa* continues without break as a quiet choral movement. The few bars which Mozart was able to write establish the mood and furnish the thematic substance—a gently convulsive syncopation, an emotional choral crescendo. It is openly "Romantic," unique in all of Mozart's music. The *Domine Jesu Christe* is music of sudden dramatic contrast between forte and piano, ending in a fully developed fugue ("*Quam olim Abrahae*") to a string figure of leaping intervals which Bach might have written. The *Hostias* is a choral movement, again with a syncopated accompaniment, followed by a repetition of the fugue of "*Abraham.*"

It is with the *Sanctus* that we come upon doubtful territory. Süssmayr stated that from this point the music was his own. It is known that Süssmayr was constantly with his master in the last weeks, going over the score with him. Constanze once intimated that there had been fragmentary sketches, although none were found, and such sketches were rare with Mozart. There have been numerous opinions, pro and con. Nothing can be proved, but the strongest evidence and the ultimate appraisal must be based upon the music itself.

Listening to the debated portion without preconceptions, one does not feel a lapse of the intensity or of the elevated mood which makes the *Requiem* a distinctive work of art. We know that the arranger had the earlier portions as his model for instrumental coloring, rhythmic usage, contrapuntal treatment, alternation of forte and piano. He was wise enough to hold to pattern, and to brevity. It could be called a piece of skillful but justifiable forgery, later confessed. But it is impossible to believe that Süssmayr, faced with entirely blank pages, as Eybler had been, could have produced anything approaching the music we know. The ten bars of the *Sanctus* are conceivable as a clever stylistic imitation, the following fugal *Osanna,* hardly more than an exposition, might have been the work of a composition pupil. The fully developed *Benedictus* is a Mozartean melody set with

Mozartean nobility. The accompanying violin theme in the *Agnus Dei,* the harmonic progressions, the dramatic chorus, the suddenly hushed passages for *"Dona eis requiem,"* all have the aspect of what is called "greatness." If Süssmayr had had nothing to build upon, he might have and probably would have resorted to one of the Salzburg Masses, then quite unknown to the rest of the world.

Single Movements

Kyrie in F, K. 33 (Composed in Paris, June, 1766)

Miserere in A minor, K. 85 (Composed in Bologna, July or August, 1770) (Fragmentary)

Kyrie in G, K. 89, for 5 sopranos (Composed in Rome, May, 1770)

Kyrie in D minor, K. 90 (Composed in Salzburg, summer, 1771) (Fragmentary)

Kyrie in D, K. 91 (Composed in Salzburg, 1774) (Fragmentary)

Kyrie in C, K. 221 (Composed in Salzburg, summer, 1771) (Fragmentary)

Osanna in C, K. 223 (Composed in 1773) (Fragmentary)

Kyrie in E flat, K. 322 (Composed in Mannheim, early 1778) (Fragmentary)

Kyrie in C, K. 323 (Composed in Salzburg, 1779) (Fragmentary)

Kyrie in D minor, K. 341 (Composed in Munich, 1781)

Mozart, aged ten, on his return to Paris from London, made his first attempt at a Mass when he wrote the Kyrie, K. 33. It is short, based on a single melodic phrase, a correct but simple beginning in part-writing. The single movements from Masses which followed from time to time are for the most part fragmentary exercises.

The single and notable exception is the final Kyrie (K. 341). This was the last service Mozart wrote while still under the employ of Hieronymus. He composed it in Munich, and obviously for Munich, in 1781. The use of a full orchestra, including clarinets, which Salzburg did not possess, puts this beyond a doubt. It is an Andante maestoso, a movement of impressive breadth in a solemn key. The tonality of D minor was a flag signal of heavy matters. The eloquence of the orchestra and the matching of vocal and instrumental tone put this definitely among his maturest choral works. It must be a matter of regret that the interest of the Elector was not enough to justify the completion of a Mass shaped to Mannheim abilities by the Mozart of *Idomeneo.*

The Offertories

Offertorium in Festo Sancti Benedicti, in C, K. 34 (Composed in 1767)

The Feast of Saint Benedict (March 21, 1767) was the occasion of Mozart's first offertory. It may have been composed for the Monastery of Seeon at Chiemgau in Bavaria. It consists of an aria for soprano with violins, and a chorus with trumpets and drums added. The story, told by Jahn, is that Mozart was taken for a visit to the monastery, and, hearing the Abbot remark that they had no Offertory for this Feast Day, slipped away from the dinner table and wrote the music on a window ledge in the next room.

Offertorium, Veni sancte spiritus, in C, K. 47 (Composed in Vienna, autumn, 1768)

Leopold Mozart lists this offertory before *Bastien und Bastienne,* which might make it a preparatory exercise for the Missa brevis in G, K. 49, and the full Mass in C minor-major (K. 139), both believed to have been written in and for Vienna. *Veni sancte spiritus* consists of an allegro, with full orchestra and a presto *Alleluia* chorus.

Offertorium pro Festo Sancti Joannis Baptistae, in G, K. 72 (Composed in Salzburg, May or June, 1771)

There is a legend, traceable to Max Keller, organist at Altötting, that Wolfgang, visiting the Monastery of Seeon, was especially fond of a Father Johannes, and had his own melody for him, to the words *"Mein Hanserl, lieb's Hanserl."* For his name day, Mozart wrote this offertory, using his little tune in the long instrumental introduction, and pointedly at the words *"Joanne Baptista."* This work of youthful appeal ends properly with a choral *Alleluia.*

Offertorium pro omni tempore, in C, K. 117 (Composed in Salzburg, 1769)

This *"Benedictus sit Deus"* is believed to have been the offertory sung with the Mass in C major, K. 66, which Mozart composed for the first service of his friend Hagenauer. It is in three sections, a lively Allegro, an Andante (*Introibo domum tuum*) for the soprano, an aria of gentle appeal and some elaboration. The final Allegro consists of a choral *jubilate,* interspersed with phrases of a traditional plain chant, sung by the male voices.

Offertorium, Sub tuum praesidium, in F, K. 198 (Composed in Milan, in early 1773)

This duet for solo soprano and tenor with strings survives only in a copy found in the Monastery of Gottweig, in lower Austria. It is generally considered genuine by its character. Einstein hazards that it may have been written for two principals in *Lucio Silla,* perhaps Rauzzini (the castrato) and Morgnoni.

Offertorium de tempore, Misericordias Domini, in D minor, K. 222 (Composed in Munich, in early 1775)

This was the motet which Mozart wrote in Munich and sent to Padre Martini as an example of his counterpoint. It is an exercise in the methods then current in Salzburg and even borrows a subject from a motet by Eberlin which he had previously copied out. Mozart has divided his exhibitions of *contrappunto osservato* into sections, joined by a chanted "*Misericordias Domini.*" The Padre approved its correctness and commended its skill.

Offertorium de venerabili sacramento, "Venite, populi," K. 260 (Composed in Salzburg, in June, 1776)

This is the only instance except the C minor Mass where Mozart wrote church music for a double chorus. The choir was the most skilled part of the Salzburg *Kapelle,* but neither their numbers nor the cathedral space would have favored anything on this scale. The occasion and place of performance are not known, but Einstein remarks that the service would have been proper for the Feast of the Assumption. The choirs have no support other than the bass and two violin parts *ad libitum.*

Offertorium de Beata Virgine Maria, in F, K. 277 (Composed in Salzburg, in the autumn of 1777)

This is a sort of companion piece to the hymn to the Virgin written in the same autumn (K. 273). The treatment is similar, except that a solo voice introduces each phrase.

The Evening Services

Vesperae de Dominica, in C, K. 321 (Composed in Salzburg, 1779)

This vesper music consists of five psalms: *Dixit Dominus* (110), *Confitebor* (111), *Beatus vis* (112), *Laudate pueri* (113), *Laudate Dominum* (117), followed by the *Magnificat*, the evening canticle of the Virgin Mary. Each part is treated separately without thematic or key relationship. It is therefore not a ritual service, and could be considered as an oratorio. This gave the composer a freedom of treatment which shows particularly in the independent use of the orchestra. After the lightly scored *Laudate pueri*, with its almost a cappella effect, and the *Laudate Dominum*, for soprano solo and strings, the final *Magnificat* for full orchestra with trombones added, the word majestically introduced, gives an impression of grandeur.

Vesperae solemnes de confessore, in C, K. 339 (Composed in Salzburg, 1780)

It could be said of this entire score that the choral writing is smooth and rounded, making beautiful chord progressions, the orchestral accompaniment matching the voices with music in the light *buffo* vein, lending color and charm throughout, providing in the rapid movements a perpetual rhythmic animation. The result is an irresistible product of Mozart's last church music in Salzburg. The choral part is only occasionally contrapuntal, except in the *Laudate pueri*, an involved but smoothly sounding fugue, marked by a descending scale subject matched with the sustained notes of the principal subject, sometimes in a sort of cantus firmus through augmentation. The *Laudate Dominum*, a gentle, fully phrased aria for the soprano, is one of the most beautiful of its sort in all of the church music, although several wonderful examples of the *Agnus Dei* come to mind. How convey in words the beauty of a particular melody? It is enough to say that this one is worthy of the finest vocal melodist that has graced our world.

Dixit and Magnificat, in C, K. 193 (Composed in Salzburg, July, 1774)

This must have been intended for some important vesper service, for the style is strict, the instrumentation brings in trumpets and drums. The *Magnificat* may have been performed separately.

Litaniae de Beata Maria Virgine (Lauretanae), in B flat, K. 109 (Composed in Salzburg, May, 1771)

The litanies were for private as well as church performance. Mozart designed them as concert works, respecting the text but freely injecting lay orchestral or vocal graces. The first of the two litanies to the text from the Marian Chapel of the Casa Santa, in Loreto, is frankly music to delight. It is by far the shortest of Mozart's litanies. It is simply scored for violin accompaniment which often doubles the voices. The *Sancta Maria* is a likable tune divided among the vocal parts; the *Regina angelorum*, a sprightly vivace, instrumental in character, again for the solo quartet; the *Agnus Dei,* another aria with a touching *miserere* coda.

Litaniae de venerabili altaris sacramento, in B flat, K. 125 (Composed in Salzburg, March, 1772)

Mozart's sacramental litanies were by the nature of the subject more impersonal than the litanies to the Virgin. They were written for broad effect, and aimed at grandeur and brilliance. The two which he wrote have a certain similarity in this respect. They call for a full orchestra (the second, K. 243 adds trombones); they are instrumentally conceived and developed; they exploit the abilities of a solo soprano and a tenor. The *Kyrie* of K. 125 has a long instrumental introduction, and after a solemn entrance of the chorus, develops contrasting themes. Solo voices and ritornelli occur in the succeeding movements. The *Panis omnipotentia* is an elaborated tenor solo, the *Pignus futurae* a long and fine fugue, instrumental in voice leading and almost rivaling the magnificent fugue in the same position in the later litany. The *Agnus Dei* is an operatic aria for soprano. Since the litany ends with a *Miserere* instead of *Dona nobis pacem,* a joyous close is precluded. Mozart makes this one a display of brilliance rather than a plea for mercy.

Litaniae Lauretanae, in D, K. 195 (Composed in Salzburg, May, 1774)

The second of the Loreto litanies is more ceremonial, more external than the first. The instrumental parts often indulge in unchurchly flourishes. A soprano (or castrato) and a tenor of considerable skill were evidently on hand when he wrote it, for he gives the first a long and ornate *Sancta Maria* and an *Agnus Dei* with scales and wide skips, the tenor has a likewise elaborate solo in the *Regina angelorum,* a more cheerful than devout movement which opens with a close resemblance to a minuet. The most beautiful portion of the litany is the *Agnus Dei,* a tender and expressive solo melody, echoed by the chorus, moving to a close which fades away in an unusual decrescendo.

Litaniae de venerabili altaris sacramento, in E flat, K. 243 (Composed in Salzburg, March, 1776)

If this were identified as the *"Miserere"* Litany (which it is not), it would be suitably named. Although the response occurs often in this evening service, Mozart has here developed it extensively on each occurrence, with electrifying results. The melody with which the chorus opens and closes the *Kyrie* returns as the final *Miserere* becomes a separate movement. The word permeates the fugal *Pignus* in a way which gives the whole a special chromatic character:

The soprano in the *Dulcissimum convivium* embellishes the word at length, giving as much as eight bars to the third syllable, and the tenor in the *Panis vivus* almost equals her part. It is treated at length in numerous ways in the *Hostias,* notably with forte-piano chords on the first syllable.

This, the last litany, has nine movements, one or two of them unrewarding, some curious, some surpassingly beautiful. The *Panis vivus* is mostly an instrumental movement, favoring the tenor soloist at length with display passages. The *Tremendum,* utilizing a trombone choir and a dramatic violin accompaniment, is a milder forerunner of the corresponding movement in the *Requiem.* The *Viaticum* is a series of chorale phrases sung by the sopranos, to an accompaniment of pizzicato strings in the serenade tradition! The *Pignus* is a remarkable double fugue, instrumentally conceived. After the entrance of the second sub-ject (following a chordal cadence on "*Miserere*"), the fugue becomes a complex, a close-knit thematic flow in which the sense of melody is never obscured. The nearest rival to this movement is the *Agnus Dei,* an ornate but expressive soprano solo, with a part for the instrument Mozart elsewhere neglected for solo uses—the violoncello.

Te Deum, in C, K. 141 (Composed in Salzburg, 1769)

The *Te Deum,* believed to have been composed before the first Italian journey, is scored for string accompaniment, varies in tempo and character according to the text, and concludes with a double fugue. Although a *Te Deum* of 1760 by Michael Haydn was Mozart's obvious model, he made the music very much his own.

Anthems, etc.

"Cibavit eos," Antiphon, K. 44 (Composed in Bologna, autumn, 1770)

This fragment of an *Introitus* is believed by Jahn to have been composed as an exercise for the Padre Martini. It consists of an introductory bass chant and twenty-seven bars of a four-part chorus, with organ.

Quaerite primum regnum Dei, Antiphon, K. 86 (Composed in Bologna, October 9, 1770)

Mozart submitted this Antiphon as his test for admission to the *Accademia Filarmonica* of Bologna. Having gone through the paces of the archaic *contrappunto osservato* with Padre Martini, he was duly locked up in a room with the phrase of a Gregorian chant to which he had to add the three upper voices. The work was judged "sufficient," but no more than that, in spite of the claims of Leopold. It was later corrected by the venerable Padre.

De profundis clamavi, Psalm, in C minor, K. 93 (Composed in Salzburg in the summer of 1771)

This setting of the 129th Psalm is for four-part chorus, with organ bass, in the simplest chordal manner, a brief but moving piece of music which has been compared in character with the *Ave, verum corpus* (K. 618).

Regina Coeli, in C, K. 108 (Composed in Salzburg, May, 1771)
Regina Coeli, in B flat, K. 127 (Composed in Salzburg, May, 1772)
Regina Coeli, in C, K. 276 (Composed in Salzburg, probably May, 1779)

The *Regina Coeli* is a setting of the antiphonal anthem to the Virgin, for use from Holy Saturday to Whitsuntide. Each line is separately treated:

> *Regina coeli, laetare—Alleluia.*
> *Quia quem meruisti portare—Alleluia.*
> *Resurrexit sicut dixit—Alleluia.*
> *Ora pro nobis Deum—Alleluia.*
>
> Bright Queen of heaven! rejoice—Alleluia.
> For He, whom you deserved to bear—Alleluia.
> Is, as he prophesied, arisen—Alleluia.
> Pray for us—Alleluia.

According to Mozart's pattern, the first line is for chorus with full orchestra, the second for the soprano solo with choral *alleluias*. The *Ora pro nobis* is a soprano solo (in the third *Regina Coeli* it is choral). The finale is an *alleluia* chorus with alternate soprano solo parts. There is a similarity of mood in the three works, and of treatment, which is free and symphonic.

Exsultate, jubilate, Motet in F, K. 165 (Composed in Milan, January, 1773)

Mozart was seventeen when he wrote this scena on a religious text for Venanzio Rauzzini, the castrato who had just sung in his *Lucio Silla,* in Milan. It is in three movements, all in the same joyous mood, the slow movement (not really slow) introduced by a short recitative. The solo part is coloratura throughout. Sopranos today have a habit of using the last movement only, a setting of the word *"Alleluia,"* as a show piece. It is an unfortunate deprivation, because although this movement is a glittering delight, the earlier movements are even more beautiful. The melodies, set off in the first by the bright gaiety of oboes in thirds, the second set to a string accompaniment of much charm, sing from a young heart. In none of his music is the innocent exuberance of the boy Mozart more apparent. The music has no odor of incense, but to speak of "irreverence" would be sheer nonsense.

Graduale ad festum, Beatae Mariae Virgines, in F, K. 273 (Composed in Salzburg, September, 1777)

This motet, addressed to the Virgin (*"Sancta Maria, Mater Dei"*) was probably composed and performed as a pious offering in Salzburg before Mozart's departure with his mother on their long journey to Mannheim and Paris, on September 23, 1777. It is scored for chorus with strings, simply and harmonically treated, and has been compared in straightforward simplicity and earnest beauty of expression to the better known *"Ave, verum corpus."*

"Ave, verum corpus," Motet in D, K. 618 (Composed in Baden, June, 1791)

The last works of Mozart, like those of Beethoven, sometimes give us the sense that the utmost in beauty can be the utmost in melodic simplicity. Such beauty needs no adornment; it is a kind of expressive perfection arrived at by a refinement of sensitivity to the detail of the phrase. Mozart had a practical reason for simplicity in this case. He composed the motet for the *Corpus Christi* service of the choir school of Anton Stoll at Baden, near Vienna, where he was a friend and a welcome visitor, and performed as well as wrote music for certain occasions. The simplicity of the choral writing and the string accompaniment would have suited the modest resources of the school and its performers. This adagio of only forty-six bars, played and sung sotto voce, deserves its perennial popularity.

The Hymns: *"Salus infirmorum,"* K. 324 (1779) is doubtful; *"Sancta Maria,"* K. 325 (1779) is doubtful; *"Justum deduxit Dominus,"* K. 326 (1771); *"O Gottes Lamm"* and *"Als aus Aegypten Israel,"* K. 343 (1779?).

K. 326 is fragmentary; K. 324 and K. 325 are doubtful. A *Tantum ergo*, K. 142, and another, K. 197, are doubtful.

The Oratorios and Cantatas

Grabmusik (Passion Cantata), K. 42 (Composed in Salzburg, Holy Week, 1767)

This score is conjectured to be the subject of the anecdote that Daines Barrington, the English scientific investigator of the authenticity of the child Wolfgang's genius, induced the Archbishop at Salzburg to confine him in a locked room for a week with pen and paper. The "Funeral" Cantata consists of a dialogue with alternate arias and a duet between a "soul" (bass) and an "angel" (soprano), with recitatives. The first of these and a closing chorus were added later.

La Betulia liberata, Azione sacra, K. 118 (Composed in Salzburg?, 1771)

An oratorio of this sort was similar to an *opera seria* on a religious subject, sung in concert form in church during Lent, when opera performances were forbidden. This one, with a text by Metastasio, has fifteen arias and choruses.

Judith exhorts the Israelites in the besieged city of Bethulia to have faith in their God and not yield to the Assyrians. She leaves the city and returns with the head of Holofernes.

Dir, Seele des Weltalls, Cantata for two Tenors and Bass, with Orchestra, K. 429 (Composed in Vienna, 1783)

This cantata, uncompleted, and partly in sketch form, has an opening indication for three-part men's chorus, the tenor aria later indicated for a soprano. The text, an address to the "Sun, soul of the universe," would mean a Masonic piece, which however could not have been sung at a closed meeting of the Lodge, since Mozart at that time was not yet a member.

Davidde penitente, Oratorio for two Sopranos, Tenor, and Chorus, with Orchestra, K. 469 (Arranged in Vienna, March, 1785, from the Mass in C minor, K. 427, of 1782-1783)

Mozart recast the movements of his uncompleted Mass, in C minor, and adapted them to a new Italian text, adding an aria for Mme. Cavalieri (No. 8) and one for Adamberger (No. 6). The occasion was a Pension concert for the Music Society of Vienna. The re-use of an earlier large score, a resort unique in Mozart's record, is probably accounted for by haste, by an onerous assignment, and by the fact that his Mass had been written for his own private use, and was unknown in Vienna.

Die Maurerfreude, Cantata for Solo Tenor, Men's Chorus and Orchestra, K. 471 (Composed in Vienna, April, 1785)

Mozart wrote this cantata in honor of Ignaz von Born, the director of his Masonic Lodge. It was performed in the presence of his father, an initiate. The tenor sings an address to his brethren of the Order, and after a recitative of excited anticipation, introduces a rousing song of jubilation, the chorus joining.

Eine kleine Freimaurer—Kantate, for Tenor and Bass solo, Men's Chorus with Orchestra (Text by Schikaneder), K. 623 (Composed in Vienna, November, 1791)

Although this is called a "small" cantata, it is a good deal longer than the earlier one. The chorus opens it in tones of rejoicing. The tenor continues in a long recitative and sings an aria. Finally, the tenor and bass join in a duet, and the chorus bring a hymnlike close. This is music of sincere feeling. The atmosphere of the temple scenes in *The Magic Flute,* with which Mozart had just been occupied, lingers through its warm and solemn measures.

The Symphonies

Mozart's symphonies rival his string quartets as a remarkable phenomenon of musical evolution. The final "Jupiter" Symphony, if placed beside the first, composed by the boy of eight, is hardly recognizable as in the same category. The rudiments of sonata form and movement succession in the First have been in the last enlarged and developed to an entirely different purpose. There are certain traits which Mozart never abandoned, probably because it never occurred to him to question them: tricks of transition, or modulation, intensification by string tremolo, a lingering fondness for ornaments, the ineradicable cadences. Especially conspicuous is his play with sudden contrast of forte and piano, a relic of the concerto grosso with its large and small groups. The very opening bars of the first symphony and of the last (it would be pointless to try to carry a comparison further) indicate that the same composer was at work.

The broad tonic unison in the first, followed abruptly by a piano passage, was a workable combination and became a sort of formula. The "Jupiter" Symphony begins with a crisp triple unison and an immediate soft answer in the strings. But here the assertion by the full orchestra is pregnant with future meaning; the answer is the gentle completion of a melodic phrase. The effect is totally different. Where the boy wished to catch the attention of his audience and hold them with his wit, the mature artist, in four bars, draws us into a special, elevated realm of C major resplendence. A symphony with anything like these proportions, or with its mood—warm, brightly serious, almost mystic—would not only have bewildered a London audience in 1764. It would have been completely incongruous to the time and place. What was then called a "symphony" was a short piece in three parts, often connected, the whole lightly regarded as useful for momentary diversion. The models which fell to the boy Mozart to copy were simply overtures, and usually bore that title. The word "*sinfonia*" gave them no special dignity, for the *sinfonia* was nothing else than the overture to an Italian *opera buffa*. Mozart used four of his so-called symphonies as overtures to his early stage works. An "overture" became the customary opening for a concert, serving to introduce more important matters to come—concertos, arias and the like. It set the mood for a social function, exuding ceremony and light, gentlemanly grace. Anything so serious as an adagio with genuine feeling or so complex as real development or fugato would have been looked upon as worse than bad taste— actually a bore.

Mozart and Haydn were the true leaders in bringing the symphony to the point where, by 1788, it was at the very center of concert importance, three times the length of the early "overture," and many times its measure in subtlety and emotional range. The "Jupiter" was the crown of orchestral development in its century. Mozart would have credited Haydn as his colleague in the symphonic pursuit with a large part of this development, and Haydn freely and warmly admitted his indebtedness to Mozart. There was no particular demand for such a magnification. Both are to be credited with overcoming a considerable audience impermeability by the sheer persuasion of their abundant genius.

There is a striking difference, however, in the progress of each composer in the symphonic cause. The bulk and chronology of the symphonies of each shows vividly how Haydn was favored by circumstance. The total count is not the true measure—Haydn wrote over twice as many because he had many more years at his disposal and more occasions for which to provide them. Haydn spent the greater part of his long life, and Mozart the greater part of his short life, furnishing convenient "overtures" to fill in at concert performances. Thus they each wrote the bulk of their symphonies. Only in the 1780's, when the two were in close communion in Vienna, did each come to the point of enlarging, broadening, intensifying the symphony into the primary orchestral form. Haydn wrote his beautiful symphonies for Paris and made his fame with them in those years. He later added his magnificent twelve for London, but by then Mozart was out of the running. He had died before the first of them was written.

Mozart was far less fortunate than Haydn, for in Vienna there was little or no demand for symphonies from him in the new and larger sense. Through the ten Vienna years that public was simply not interested, and did not require as many as one. A Salzburg symphony that happened to be on hand would do. He wrote the last great five for other uses. A bid came from Linz and one from Prague, and later he was moved to compose his final three without any bid at all. With what a brace of symphonies he might have matched Haydn's dozen if he had lived a little longer! Mozart had occasion to compose only eight symphonies, beginning with No. 33 in B-flat major, of 1779, which can be considered as in the full maturity of the form, and comparable in that sense to Haydn's last twenty. With Mozart the point of maturity in his symphonies came far later than it had in his piano concertos for the simple reason that his audiences, even his Vienna audiences, gave their real attention only to piano concertos in full regalia. Vienna, then, is to be thanked for the profusion of great concertos and blamed for the paucity of great symphonies.

This does not mean that the earlier symphonies are lacking in interest, musical significance, many surpassing beauties. Mozart turned them out with fair regularity through all of his traveling years, when he never entered a city or visited a court without at least one in readiness for a concert. Mozart knew what was expected of him and provided accordingly. He was not the kind to remake audiences or chafe at their obtuseness. It was not because he was more at home with the piano that his concertos matured much earlier than his symphonies. It was because his patrons looked upon him expectantly as a phenomenal pianist, and as a composer only incidentally. The players he was given to deal with were limited in number and organized mostly for purposes of accompaniment. Not until Mannheim did he encounter an orchestra of independent importance. The stimulation of listening in Mannheim added to the stimulation of Haydn and the stimulation of a first-rate orchestra to work with resulted in the "Paris" Symphony of 1778, not the most deeply felt he had composed, but his most deft product of craftsmanship by that time.

The symphonies until then are anything but negligible. They are a barometer of Mozart's musical growth. Even in the earliest, the formula of gallantry is often transformed into natural boyish exuberance. There are fresh thoughts in each; some abound with fascinating forerunners of the Mozart to come. Increasingly, he applies sleight-of-hand in the way of modulations, sudden fancies, dramatic incursions. Mozart was incapable of dry formality. In their course, the symphonies attain smoothness, amplitude, variety. They sometimes forget ceremony and become personal in mood, as when he plunged into the minor. He could provide easy charm in an allegretto, pretty sentiment in an andantino, according to formula, but he could also unexpectedly reveal his heart.

Symphony No. 1, in E flat, K. 16 (Composed in London, 1764)
Symphony No. 4, in D, K. 19* (Composed in London, 1765)
Symphony No. 5, in B flat, K. 22 (Composed in The Hague, 1765)

Wolfgang at the age of eight in London composed his first two symphonies for immediate concert purposes. The boy had been eagerly attentive to the mannerisms of the day, especially to the symphonies of Karl Friedrich Abel and of Johann Christian Bach, both of whom befriended him. He was particularly influenced by the gracefully elegant, simple and pleasing music of Christian Bach. Wolfgang quickly picked up the ways of instrumental and formal treatment around him. He had no difficulty in putting this material together into symphonies entirely acceptable and performable, if somewhat less polished than those of his older colleagues. Mozart's two London symphonies and those he wrote later for Italy show a fondness for a succession of chords changing with each bar under an animated figura-

---

* The Symphonies included in the complete edition as K. 17 and 18, and listed as Nos. 2 and 3, have since been found to be copies by Mozart of symphonies by other composers, No. 3 by Abel. They indicate admiration and close study on the part of the young symphonist.

tion. Tremolo strings are a frequent resort. This sort of writing tends to chordal rather than melodic themes, and development through modulation. Here, Wolfgang was never at a loss. The final presto in his first two symphonies is as animated and sparkling as the current style demanded; mimicry accomplished with adult skill.

The Fifth Symphony, written in The Hague, is much like the London ones, but has a section in G minor in the Andante which is arresting, a personal expression of a London formula.

Symphony No. 6, in F, K. 43 (Composed in Olmütz and Vienna, late 1767)

Symphony No. 7, in D, K. 45 (Composed in Vienna, January, 1768)

Symphony No. 8, in D, K. 48 (Composed in Vienna, December, 1768)

The next three symphonies were composed for the second visit to Vienna, and a minuet is accordingly added after the slow movement, to meet the Viennese taste. The four-movement succession, thus established, was still optional, for in Italy the minuet was often omitted. These symphonies show Mozart, or rather his new public, as opera-minded. The Andante of the Sixth is almost an operatic aria. It could easily have been transformed into one, for the melody given to the first violins is entirely vocal in character. The Finale too is a typical *buffo* finale, with the kind of excitement to ring down a curtain. The Seventh Symphony, its four movements brief and continuous, was actually an operatic overture, and was used to introduce *La finta semplice,* note for note, months later. This symphony and the Eighth are ceremonial, with trumpets and drums. The slow movement in each is a short interlude for strings within a brilliant whole.

The following symphonies are not included in the Breitkopf and Härtel edition: K. 45a, in G, and K. 45b, in B flat (Vienna, 1768); K. 74g, in B flat, K. 75, in F; the last three were probably composed in Salzburg, in 1771. K. 76, in F, is attributed to 1776. K. 81, in D (Rome, 1770), is attributed to Leopold Mozart in the full edition, but this is disputed. K. 95, in D (Rome, 1770), K. 96, in C (Milan, 1771) and K. 97, in D (Rome, 1770) are numbered in the full edition as 45, 46, 47. K. 98, in F (Milan?, 1771) is doubtful. K. 102, in C (Salzburg, 1775), is the presto finale for a symphony or divertimento.

Symphony No. 9, in C, K. 73 (Composed in Salzburg, summer, 1771)

Symphony No. 10, in G, K. 74 (Composed in Milan, December, 1770)

Symphony No. 11, in D, K. 84 (Composed in Milan-Bologna, 1770)

Symphony No. 12, in G, K. 110 (Composed in Salzburg, July, 1771)

Symphony No. 13, in F, K. 112 (Composed in Milan, November, 1771)

These five symphonies were composed either in Milan or for Milan and for other Italian cities. Nos. 10 and 11 belong to the first Italian journey, Nos. 9 and 12 to the summer of 1771 in preparation for the second stay in Milan when *Ascanio in Alba* was produced. No. 13 was an additional one in that city just after the opera. Of these only Nos. 10 and 11 have no minuets written in the score, but those in the others may have been for convenience in case of need. Otherwise, to meet Italian expectations required no notable change in style—all symphonies were then "Italian." Among these, only the Ninth has the starch of trumpets and drums—the rest are for strings with oboes and horns, with flutes and bassoons for special slow movement purposes. The Tenth is in three connected movements, the Andante having a formal suggestion of a slowed-down minuet. In the Finale the young composer for the first time puts formality behind him, opens quietly with a playful theme in "easy" style, and follows his mood to the end. In the Eleventh he goes still further in becoming his cheerful and unceremonious self. The very first cadence is whimsical; trilled figures are gaily thrown in. The Andante develops a melody somehow intimate, and the Finale carries through as if racing violin passages were fun to write. A boy of sixteen must weary of the necessity of providing pompous measures for stiff functions, and especially so when that boy was Mozart, without an ounce of pomposity in his nature. His first movements were still built on chord successions and little developed, his minuets still ballroom pieces; but in his slow movements, the easy, natural melodist increasingly breaks through artificial sentiment, as in the Andante of the Twelfth Symphony, with the coloring of flutes and bassoons and the Andante of the Thirteenth, a melody for strings alone. The finales were completely to Mozart's taste. They cut loose from formality into *buffo* wit, with the stimulation of lively, rhythmic brilliance. The spirited composer through sheer abundance of emotion gave them increasing stature. He could hardly have failed to win even a half-attentive audience.

Symphony No. 14, in A, K. 114 (Composed in Salzburg, December, 1771)

Symphony No. 15, in G, K. 124 (Composed in Salzburg, February, 1772)

Symphony No. 16, in C, K. 128 (Composed in Salzburg, May, 1772)

Symphony No. 17, in G, K. 129 (Composed in Salzburg, May, 1772)

Symphony No. 18, in F, K. 130 (Composed in Salzburg, May, 1772)

Returning to Salzburg from Milan a fortnight before the new year of 1772, Mozart dwelt at home in that year, until his departure for Milan for *Lucio Silla* on October 24, and in those ten months composed, besides much else, eight symphonies.* Since six of them followed the installation of the new Archbishop Colloredo in March, it is likely that (if he heard them) this particular "Holiness" favored such pieces, allowing a modest orchestra of horns and oboes (or flutes) with strings. (Trumpets appear only in the Twentieth Symphony, in July.) If Mozart felt skimped it is not apparent. He seemed to savor the wind color, gave the pairs echoing parts, made his string parts more independent, exacted separate fast scale passages from the basses. The Fourteenth Symphony, written in December, and the four which followed in the spring all have the charm of Mozart's playful mood. He delivers a forte chord or a broad, bustling cadence as if with his tongue in his cheek, for he immediately follows it with light staccato notes or charming trills, making palatable frequent liberties in the way of modulations. These piano portions are longer, they are more sequential, more melodic. Mozart was writing in the popular vein. He already knew how to charm an audience, and lead them unsuspecting into strange by-paths. Providing for humdrum home consumption (although some may have been intended for the winter journey

---

* In addition to K. 120, 121, 161, 163, not among the numbered symphonies, which were movements added to the overtures to *Ascanio in Alba, La finta giardiniera,* and *Il sogno di Scipione,* for symphonic purposes.

to Milan), he might have lapsed into a pattern habit—if he had been anyone other than Mozart. The symphonies continue endlessly to probe new ways. The slow movements tend to fill the formal "andantino" prescription with a glow of inner life, the minuets become more legato, modifying or displacing the bar accent. The finales in this group tend to be more melodic than brilliant. A rondo subject can be shaped from a perfectly conventional chord, but what follows can stray from convention until the hearer is brought back to the safe haven of the recurring start.

The Fourteenth Symphony gives the promise of intimacy, as it opens with no proclamation but a quiet melody for the violins. The Fifteenth, short and modest, is also fluent, melodic, full of playful wit. The Sixteenth is still more daring (wit and daring are one) as the first movement and the last lead us through a procession of keys. Echo effects, previously used, are further resorted to. The Seventeenth is a delightful adventure in G major, with a first movement a continuous animation of short notes and trills, an Andante which is a wonderful melody, unabashedly vocal, and a finale in three-eight time, with a theme which is a fanfare. The Eighteenth Symphony, like its predecessor, has a first movement of ornamented themes built to delightful results. This symphony uses two pairs of horns, largely for sustaining color. The Andantino, calling upon flutes over muted strings is again aria-like. The final Molto allegro in common time, is fully developed, unrushed and melodic in character.

Symphony No. 19, in E flat, K. 132 (Composed in Salzburg, July, 1772)

Symphony No. 20, in D, K. 133 (Composed in Salzburg, July, 1772)

Symphony No. 21, in A, K. 134 (Composed in Salzburg, August, 1772)

The three symphonies composed in the summer season of 1772 show in many details an advance in symphonic integration. The first of them uses (except in the slow movement) low and high horns in its key, E flat, to produce full chords. Here there is a continuous, singing line, quite unbroken by episodes. After writing an andante which may have been too sober for some tastes but which certainly needed no apology, Mozart substituted another slow movement more immediately palatable, an andantino grazioso. There could have been no protest about the finale, nor about the finale of its successor, in D, smoothly worked, developed with delicate stress and emphasis. This symphony (No. 20) shows an added assurance in its long, sequential main theme, and the full development of its opening Allegro. The Andante, with flute obbligato over muted violins and plucked bass, is one more expression of gallantry. The finale, in twelve-eights is neatly turned with contrapuntal matching in the strings, the dominating movement of the four. The Twenty-first Symphony substitutes flutes for oboes, giving a special bright sonority in combination with the horns. It opens without the expected ceremonial chords, but with a graceful, swinging theme, malleable and divisible in development. The finale leaves *buffo* pretension behind and dwells on melodic detail, rhythmic play, echo effects.

Symphony No. 22, in C major, K. 162 (Composed in Salzburg, early in 1773)

Symphony No. 23, in D, K. 181 (Composed in Salzburg, May, 1773)

Symphony No. 24, in B flat, K. 182 (Composed in Salzburg, May or June, 1773)

Mozart was in Salzburg from March, 1773, until July, when he visited Vienna until early October. Before that visit he wrote the symphonies numbered 22, 23, 24, 26, 27. The five are without minuets. They have a lingering tendency in the first and last movements toward proclamatory chords for the full orchestra alternating with light string figures, a style which makes for constant contrasts rather than fluency in development. No. 22 is conspicuous for themes in short rhythmic chords with forte punctuation. The Twenty-third has a dramatic Allegro, and an Andantino where the oboe solo vies with the violins in carrying the melody. The symphony following has still another Andante grazioso, the flutes replacing the oboes, and set over muted violins and a pizzicato bass.

Symphony No. 25,* in G minor, K. 183 (Composed in Salzburg, late in 1773)

Only twice in his life (here and in the more famous G minor Symphony of 1788, did Mozart compose a symphony in the minor mode. G minor must have held a special somber significance for him—the late symphony in that key, the String Quintet (K. 516, 1787) and the Piano Quartet (K. 478, 1785) all show

---

* This Symphony should actually follow No. 28. The numbering is that of the complete edition. It is here retained to avoid confusion.

a strain of pathos unusual at the time. Wyzewa and Saint-Foix stress the "extraordinary analogy" between the early and the late symphonies in G minor. Einstein has remarked that Haydn's "*Trauer*" Symphony appeared about this time. There is repeated reference to the "*Sturm und Drang*" movement, and to Goethe's *Sorrows of Werther*, which had recently appeared. No one may know to what extent Mozart was touched by this first blush of literary Romanticism, or whether music as such released his own strain of pathos. The theme of the first Allegro gives a definitely somber minor cast to the opening, although it is relieved by the tripping countertheme in B-flat major. The development is brief, but agitated and modulatory. Commentators have found brightness and relief from the dark colorings of this symphony in the short, lyric Andante in E-flat major. But if there is a romantic movement in the symphony, it is this one—if the "*Wertherleiden*" found their affecting echo in the sensitive and receptive Mozart, it is surely here. The voice of the violins, muted, is arresting as they give forth their plaintive melody of accented, falling half tones—the symbol of pathos with Mozart. Interwoven are dark thirds of the bassoons, here first heard.

The Minuet brings us back to G minor and the full orchestra. Again in contrast is the G major Trio for the winds only. We imagine a peasant-like German dance, which none but an Austrian could have composed. The Finale is again in sonata form in a brilliant ferocity of G minor, justifying (if it can be justified) the coupling of the two G minor symphonies by the French scholars. The movement scintillates in its progress, displaying the twists and turns of its composer's wit along the way.

Symphony No. 26, in E flat, K. 184 (Composed in Salzburg, early 1773)

This symphony, later used as an overture to a play by Plümicke (*Lanassa*), departs from the formula of cheerful inconsequentiality of its immediate fellows in 1773. It prompts speculation as to what the first occasion may have been. It is composed for a full orchestra. It is a restless symphony, beginning molto presto, with urgent, dramatic, even tragic implications, as sensational as any of Gluck's. The first movement unexpectedly ends pianissimo, and introduces an andante (no andantino now) in a dark C minor, with a theme of short, broken figures. The Finale restores the E-flat major brightness with a folkish, Haydnesque theme, but its course is not unclouded.

Symphony No. 27, in G, K. 199 (Composed in Salzburg, April, 1773)

The Twenty-seventh Symphony restores custom with a sunny G major, a grazioso slow movement, and a final presto which dominates what has preceded in length, importance, boldness. No one could have achieved its play of counterpoint except the young master who would later write the "Jupiter" finale. It even opens with a four-note motto, set against a running figure, subjects for intricate manipulation. Mozart may have had his pending journey to Vienna in mind when he turned out this sample of his skill.

Symphony No. 28, in C, K. 200 (Composed in Salzburg, November, 1773)

The Symphony No. 28, written after the return from Vienna, is particularly full of high spirits. It could be called both formal and informal: informal because of its easy, flowing course, often gently melodic; formal because the composer seems deliberately to choose trills and flourishes in order to make fun of them, and turn them into melody. The trill parody begins in the third bar, returns in the Andante, and touches its highest point, as does the symphony, in the Presto Finale, where again we feel the sleight-of-hand of the master.

Symphony No. 29, in A, K. 201 (Composed in Salzburg, in early 1774)

If the Twenty-eighth Symphony makes fun of pretension, the Twenty-ninth is simply without pretension. It is still a favorite, and naturally so, for it is the most direct and personal symphonic expression of the lad of eighteen, written with the true simplicity and disregard for show which was natural to him. It is really a string symphony lightly colored by oboes and horns, moderate in tempi. There is not a single proclamation. It begins with a quiet string figure:

Allegro Moderato (first Violins)

which builds with a series of sequences to a comfortable forte and proceeds in like vein. The development is close and flowing. The Andante is a delicate song by the muted strings, the Minuet is built on a rhythmic figure, which ends the movement with unexpected suddenness in the winds. This is a symphony of abrupt endings, making concise witty points and having no use for reiterated cadences. The Allegro con spirito moves in a light, rapid six-eight beat, with staccato punctuation to an amusingly sudden end. Mozart leads us to expect a long, dominant-tonic peroration but breaks off and gives us an upsweeping scale and two short chords.* This is the most unceremonious symphony that he ever wrote.

Symphony No. 30, in D, K. 202 (Composed in Salzburg, in May, 1774)

This symphony is the antithesis of the one it shortly followed. It begins with a glitter of full chords, trumpets included, and proceeds accordingly. The score is not without smooth handling and happy detail, for its composer has acquired symphonic growth in this season. The Andantino, for strings, is a graceful melody which does not generate the degree of warmth of the previous A major Symphony. The Presto is permeated by a tattoo rhythm, with a staccato effect until the end. Again, it is the principal movement, with humorous sudden modulations, and a close which quite unexpectedly fades away into nothing.

The Thirtieth Symphony marks the end of a period. No more symphonies seem to have been wanted in Salzburg in the four years to follow, in which time Mozart was busy providing all of the violin concertos, a number of serenades, much church music, and the opera *La finta giardiniera* (for Munich in early 1775). Not until he was called upon in Paris for a symphony in June, 1778, did he return to the form.

It was thus the first thirty symphonies which were written under the impulsion of gallant functions and in the mode of *opera buffa* overtures. The overture requirements linger in the last nine—Nos. 22, 23 and 26 are in three short movements. The form nevertheless grows perceptibly through these nine. The basic oboes and horns, to which trumpets and drums are sometimes added, are more subtly blended, more independently used. The opening movements acquire salient themes which admit of more development. The andantino grazioso of surface elegance still persists but at last gives way to the more serious, more

---

* The joke will be repeated in the final E-flat Symphony.

probing slow movement of the later Mozart. The minuets gradually cease to be rigid dances and become more expressive, more symphonic. The finales become longer, more intricate, freer in personal invention. Mozart, as always, was outwardly conforming while inwardly letting his own imagination take hold. The last three symphonies become altogether more personal, more bold in novelty, until we wonder how their liberties may have been received by conventional audiences. These three are indeed no longer opera overtures. Influenced by Haydn, their composer is on the verge of giving the title its new and important aspect. These symphonies have the charm of youth and the freshness of discovery—qualities which would be less felt in the Mozart of four years later, the worldly experienced and sobered man of twenty-two.

Symphony No. 31, in D, K. 297 (Composed in Paris, June, 1778)

The "Paris" Symphony is a predictable landmark in the succession. Its composer, not called upon for a symphony in Salzburg in the last four years, had been composing other orchestral music, acquiring skill, reaching his artistic manhood. He had recently been listening to new orchestral possibilities at Mannheim, without the opportunity to try them. In Paris the opportunity came to write for the *Concert Spirituel*, for an orchestra in the Mannheim tradition, with the claim, at least, of rival precision. He had a full quota of winds at his disposal, including, for the first time, clarinets. He felt (backed by his father's urging) that his destiny hung on making himself known in Paris, and, failing an opera commission, looked upon this symphony as his best chance to show Paris what he could do. Mozart, when on his mettle, never failed to put forth his best powers. His symphony was designed for the Parisian taste. It had no minuet, no repeats. It met the fashion with music of wit and point, and so catered to the orchestra's pride in polish of ensemble and clean attack by the strings. Mozart began his score in his usual way of broad, forte chords for the full orchestra, followed at once by a light staccato string figure. But his opening chords end in a rapid and brilliant rising octave scale:

The contrasting piano figure is extended into a melodic, eminently workable theme. More elements for string virtuosity cluster about the theme in the dominant. The development is a marvel of adroit manipulation, sudden surprises, modulation with touches of minor, even Mannheim crescendos. The movement did not fail to stimulate the orchestra, which had been sluggish and indifferent in rehearsal, and to impress the first audience, which at one point broke into applause. Legros objected to the slow movement as "too long, and too full of modulations." Mozart wrote to his father that it was on the contrary, "both short and natural," but he obligingly provided another, neither better nor worse, but "of different character." The second, and shorter Andante was published in Paris, but the original one is included in the full Breitkopf and Härtel edition, and is the one which is usually performed. The brilliance of the string writing in the final Allegro, with a neat fugato, the blending of the winds (without solos), the show of skill, presented the Parisians with what some of them may have dimly perceived as a piece of smooth craftsmanship superior to anything they had encountered by Gossec or Sterkel, or any importations from Mannheim by Johann or Karl Stamitz. This symphony has far less warmth than the A major of four years before, but far more polish. For once Mozart met his moment with a "*jeu d'esprit.*"

Symphony ("Overture") No. 32, in G, K. 318 (Composed in Salzburg, April, 1779)

Returning from Mannheim and Paris with a new conception of what an orchestra might be expected to do, Mozart put the more limited Salzburg forces to a test. This Symphony ("Overture") of the spring following is exacting in point and precision. The opening sets the pace for brisk, articulated chords and swift, clean scale passages. There are crescendos. It is a piece for a formal occasion, not calling for warmth, rounded out by the composer's accumulated skill into smooth periods.

Symphony No. 33, in B flat, K. 319 (Composed in Salzburg, July, 1779)

This full-length symphony (the Minuet was added later for performance in Vienna) has nothing more than the oboes, horns and bassoons which Salzburg could provide, but Mozart makes the most of them, giving the wind instruments separate prominence, exploiting their color, freeing the bassoons from their undeserved obscurity as mere supporting bass instruments. The first movement takes a light and merry course in the *buffo* style. It avoids even the stiffness of a chordal opening, for a single forte chord becomes the accent for a light staccato theme in the strings. The "Jupiter" motto is introduced, but unobtrusively as the cadence of a theme. The slow movement opens as a harmonized song in the strings, proceeds with an alternate section in delicate staccato, the strings matched by the wind choir. This is a live, singing melody by the composer who had left smooth, surface elegance behind. The finale is swift, subtly rhythmic, and wholly irresistible. The two-four signature becomes, with recurring passages in triplets, a virtual six-eight. This beautiful work deserves far more attention and more frequent performances than it has had.

Symphony No. 34, in C, K. 338 (Composed in Salzburg, August, 1780)

Mozart composed this symphony a year after the previous one, and shortly before he went to Munich to prepare for *Idomeneo*. It was therefore his last Salzburg symphony. It is the first symphony of full stature, with the most fully developed first movement to date. The opening is buoyant in his favorite march rhythm. He takes new advantage of extension through sequence. On introducing his theme in the dominant, he leads us at length through a placid discourse of much resource and invention; the stress of forte passages comes less frequently and with more effect. In the Andante the grazioso style returns with a delicate, staccato melody, sotto voce, but with new warmth and increased charm. The Finale is another six-eight movement, lightly set forth, with punctuating forte chords. Some conductors, reading that Mozart began to write a minuet and broke off after a few bars, have concluded that another of his minuets should be added. In truth, the composer does not seem to have had any positive preference on the point. In Vienna a minuet was looked for. In Salzburg he had often omitted a minuet; in Paris earlier and in Prague later he did not provide one. In view of the quality of his later symphonic minuets whence the atmosphere of the ballroom had quite departed, it is impossible to believe that he did not take special delight in writing them. They afforded an agreeable intermezzo with their triple beat between the slow movement and the presto finale.

Symphony No. 35, in D, "Haffner," K. 385 (Composed in Vienna, July and August, 1782)

When Siegmund Haffner, Mozart's fellow townsman in Salzburg, needed a serenade for a special festivity, probably the occasion of his ennoblement, he applied to Leopold, who promptly wrote to his son in Vienna urging him to supply one. This was a second commission from the *Burgermeister,* a prosperous first citizen of Salzburg. (The "Siegmund Haffner Strasse" still cuts across the old town.) It is to be hoped that he paid Mozart generously. Mozart had written what later became known as the "Haffner" Serenade as long before as 1776, for the wedding of Haffner's daughter, Elisabeth. He received the request for a new serenade in July, 1782, when he was pressed by duties, not to speak of another preoccupation, his pending marriage. He was hurrying to finish an arrangement of *Die Entführung* for wind orchestra, that opera having been first produced on the sixteenth of the same month. He was at work on his Serenade in C minor for wind octet (the *"Nachtmusique,"* K. 388), but nothing could have been less appropriate for Haffner's party than that somber piece. Mozart, always obliging, stole time to put a new serenade together, sent the first movement, and followed it with a slow movement, two minuets and the finale. There was still a missing number, the march. He managed to send it along on August 7, when he was a bridegroom of three days.

Two years later, needing a popular symphony for Vienna, he asked his father to send back four of the movements (including only one of the minuets), which would pass perfectly well as a symphony. When he received the manuscript in the post he was surprised to find that he had forgotten "every note of it," a remarkable evidence that he could write timeless music even in a state of harassment with other matters and forget it forthwith. He liked his forgotten child on second acquaintance, added clarinet and flute parts, and felt that it would "go well." And so it did—it was loudly applauded in Vienna, and repeated. He had remarked to his father that the first movement should "strike real fire," and that the last should go "as quickly as possible." What he meant was that the first movement had the *"recht feuerig"* grandiloquence to suit a big party—its opening broad proclamation and the quieter notes in march rhythm which complete the phrase furnish most of the movement. The presto was wit through speed. *"So geschwind als es möglich ist"* meant as fast as the Salzburg basses could manage its running figure.

This is party music. The minuet has the old elegance, the slow andante has grazioso qualities in dotted rhythm. Mozart could at any time write to catch the lay ear. Yet this symphony has a right to its title and does not deserve to be condescended to as it sometimes has been. It is a true product of the Mozart of 1782. It is really symphonic, it turns up a profusion of happy musical thoughts. It is fully worthy of the composer of *Die Entführung*.

Symphony No. 36, in C, K. 425 (Composed in Linz, November, 1783)

Except for the "Haffner" Symphony, which was extracted from a suite, Mozart wrote no symphony during his first two years in Vienna. A prodigious score from him would be expected at this point, when at last there was an occasion for one. He writes his father from Linz, on October 31, 1783, that, having arrived the day before, been received and entertained by Count Thun, he has been asked for a symphony for a concert on November 4. He has neglected to bring a symphony with him and he is "up to his neck" in a new one. This great C major Symphony, by the original statement of Niemetschek and by the process of elimination, is generally accepted, difficult as it is to believe, as having been conceived, written down, copied, rehearsed and performed within the space of four days. Since he was caught unawares, and had no prospect of a symphony in Vienna to plan for, this would confound the theory that his greater works must have been put on paper only after secret thought and gestation. There is indeed no accounting for this serious, ground-breaking, elaborately worked score. If the Count's orchestral players were anything less than the best, they would have been hard put to manage it, and especially in so short a time. The winds are treated in choir fashion, where any false intonation would have been ruinous. The violas and cellos have separate parts; the basses in the presto must scramble through running passages in sixteenths. In this movement particularly there is contrapuntal involvement. For the first time, and after the example of Haydn, but differently, he used a slow introduction (he was to do this twice again—in the "Prague" and the last E flat Symphony). There is broad solemnity in the opening bars of this adagio, followed by a gently developed figure which leads to a fortissimo dominant chord. This precludes the need of a proclamatory first theme and enables the composer to begin with a quiet one and proceed at will. The development produces a march rhythm, but mostly quieter, lyric subjects, joined by unconventional transitional passages. The *poco adagio* shows a new ability to ornament a long-phrased melody without obscuring it, to color it with sustained wind chords. A second section turns to the bassoons or the horns or sometimes (in a delicate staccato) to the oboes in combinations as never quite before. The trio of the minuet relies upon the solo bassoon and oboe, and the two together. In the presto, the composer who had long since built up finales beyond all precedent in deftness, variety, cumulative excitement, goes further still.

Symphony No. 37, in G, K. 444 (A symphony by Michael Haydn, the Introduction composed by Mozart in Linz, November, 1783)

This symphony, long considered to have been composed by Mozart during his visit to Linz, is found to have been by Michael Haydn, except for the introductory Adagio maestoso, which is Mozart's own. The manuscript is in his hand as far as the second part of the Andante sostenuto, and is continued in the hand of a copyist. In this and in the "Linz" Symphony, Mozart, plainly influenced by Haydn's brother Joseph, provides for the first time in his symphonies slow introductions. Both are grave and solemn. If he had passed off the symphony itself as his own he would have been merely fulfilling an exchange of favors, for in Salzburg he had obliged Michael Haydn with the two Duos for Violin and Viola (K. 423 and 424), which Haydn had conveniently claimed. Mozart, who both respected his colleague and drew upon him musically, could hardly have been tempted to pre-empt so sorry a companion as this to his own "Linz" Symphony. It is expert and amiable, in a style Mozart had left behind, but without any kindling development or arresting feature.

Symphony No. 38, in D, "Prague," K. 504 (Composed in Vienna, December, 1786)

The symphonies through the Salzburg period are a record of growth from season to season within the cramping limitations of the occasions they were written for. The last six, through the Vienna decade, are a more striking record of growth, not because they are more widely spaced, but because they are quite free of limitations and restraints of performance. The "Linz" Symphony shows no sign of regard for limited abilities, and the

"Prague" Symphony, although presumably addressed to a better orchestra, must have been found mercilessly exacting by the players there. This symphony, like the last three symphonies of two years later, seems to be an idealization by the composer who until then had never been able to break loose from the immediate contingencies of performances. He ranges freely, he indulges his fantasy, finds new musical images. He assigns to the players parts requiring an instant agility, an attack, ensemble, a refinement of phrasing which he must have known they did not possess. Nor did it apparently bother him that most of the fine points of the "Prague" Symphony would surely drift past the ears of its first audience. The "Prague" Symphony, technically speaking, is at last the full symphonic Mozart. The discourse throughout has a new degree of pliancy in chromaticism and modulation, in the combination of motives. The melodic line is continuous, never yielding to episodes or cadences, but rather generating them. Nor is it broken by the constant alternation of strings and winds within a phrase, for they are integrated as never before. The overall color of orchestral sound, the variation of rhythmic stress, the overlapping of parts—these are all the craftsman's devices in presenting a pervasive melodic wealth which only Mozart could conjure up.

Symphony No. 39, in E flat, K. 543 (Composed in Vienna, June, 1788)

The last three symphonies, composed in a summer of acute money shortage, with no prospect of performance, will always remain an enigma. Jahn has hazarded the guess that Mozart may have had a subscription concert in view for the winter. Subscription concerts were no longer wanted from him, and even if there had been a chance for three, works of this length and diffifulty would hardly have been looked for. The three symphonies are an inescapable proof that Mozart's musical thoughts were venturing far beyond the fulfillment of jobs, carrying him out of the environment which kept him bound to the modes of the moment.

The first of the three is the only one with an introduction. It is an adagio at least as serious as those in the "Linz" and "Prague" symphonies, yet all three are light-hearted works. Mozart plainly sought contrast between sections, rather than an integral relationship. This Adagio opens with heavy, fateful chords which subside into a gentle resolution. The ponderous chords return in what at that time would have seemed a piercing dissonance, only to soften again in a murmuring subsidence which Beethoven might have used (and almost did) in *Fidelio*. The movement runs a gentle, lyric course, the composer taking obvious delight in his beloved clarinets, which here he is using for the first time in a symphony (with the exception of the "Paris" and the "Haffner" symphonies). It acquires urgency rather than power, with a dramatic hint from the Adagio in the form of descending scales. The Andante con moto is one of Mozart's longest symphonic movements. It is instrumental melody which sings through a pattern of short notes, at first by the strings, to which the winds are added in the rarest of alternate groupings. The fact that he used a minuet in each of these symphonies confirms his ultimate preference, together with Haydn's, for the four-movement succession. Beethoven's development of a fast scherzo for a third movement would have been precluded for Mozart by his favorite presto finales. A minuet like this one, no longer a dance, alternately staccato and legato, turning the trio into a melody and accompaniment by the two clarinets, fits beautifully into his scheme. The Finale is, like its near fellows, a display of technical manipulation, and of course, much else. He insists on full chordal figures only to give more point to his play of humor as fragments of the principal theme are bandied about among the woodwinds. The same fragment makes fun of the closing cadence, and all closing cadences, by abruptly adding itself at the end.

Symphony No. 40, in G minor, K. 550 (Composed in Vienna, July, 1788)

The G minor Symphony is cast as plainly as any symphony of Mozart in a pervasive mood and style. It is a strongly incisive music which attains its strength by deftness and concentration instead of by massive means.* The special coloring of the G minor Symphony is illustrated by Mendelssohn's retort to a declaration of Liszt that the pianoforte could produce the essential effects of an orchestral score. "Well," said Mendelssohn, "if he can play the beginning of Mozart's G minor Symphony as it sounds in the orchestra, I will believe him." (The symphony

---

* Mozart dispenses altogether with trumpets and timpani, attaining contrasts by delicate adjustment within a limited orchestral plan. The first autograph indicated two oboes but no clarinets; later Mozart wrote out extensive parts for two clarinets, robbing the oboes of many passages and retaining the oboes principally for ensemble, as if to preserve a requisite touch of acidity. Editions are current with clarinets and without.

begins with a delicate piano in the string quartet, the lightly singing violins supported by darkly shaded chords of the divided violas.)

The opening theme shows at once the falling semitone to the dominant, which for generations seems to have been the composers' convention for plaintive sadness. (In Tchaikovsky's Sixth Symphony it reaches a sort of peak.) The melodic phrasing tends to descend, and to move chromatically. The harmonic scheme is also chromatic and modulatory. Conciseness and abruptness are keynotes of the score. The composer states his themes directly without preamble or bridge. The first movement could be said to foreshadow the first movement of Beethoven's C minor Symphony in that it is constructed compactly upon a recurrent germinal figure which is a mere interval; in this case, the falling second. The second theme is conspicuous by a chromatic descent. The development, introduced by two short arbitrary chords which establish the remote key of F-sharp minor, moves by swift and sudden, but deft, transitions. Its strength is the strength of steel rather than iron, the steel of a fencer who commands the situation by an imperceptible subtlety, whose feints and thrusts the eye can scarcely follow. After pages of intensity, the music subsides softly to the last chord of its coda.

The Andante states its theme, as did the first movement, in the strings, the basses giving another chromatic figure. The affecting beauty of the working out has been praised innumerable times, Wagner comparing the gently descending figures in thirty-second notes to "the tender murmuring of angels' voices." Past writers on Mozart have found harshness and tension in the Minuet—all agree that the Trio, in the major tonality, has no single shadow in its gentle and luminous measures. The Finale has a bright and skipping first theme; a second theme which shows once more the plaintive chromatic descent. Like the first movement, the last is compact with a manipulation which draws the hearer swiftly through a long succession of minor tonalities. The development of the movement (which is in sonata form) reaches a high point of fugal interweaving, the impetus carrying to the very end.

Symphony No. 41, in C major ("Jupiter"), K. 551 (Composed in Vienna, August, 1788)

People with pliant imaginations have accepted the title (probably given by J. B. Cramer) as descriptive of the music. Others have strenuously objected. It would probably have amused the composer. It persists as a convenient and ornamental tag name.

The first movement is more than Jovian—it is an extraordinary combination of various elements, conditioning each other in a serene overall equilibrium, with a development prodigious for its time, with a renewing freshness of invention which deserves the word godlike if any music can be so called. The four opening bars at once disclose two of these elements: a strong martial rhythm from the orchestra, answered by a gentle, persuasive phrase from the strings. The martial beat becomes without preamble (there is no preamble in the direct progression of this movement) a full, striding march rhythm. Its character is indisputable—there is no mistaking the military Mozart (compare the snare drum triplets of "*Non più andrai*" in *Figaro* to the triplet figure here suggesting the drumbeat). Yet it need not be pointed out that this military buoyancy, enforcing the other elements, never overbears them. The second subject, in the dominant, opens lyrically, but at once develops a gay rhythm, whereby the composer has two more combinable elements. With these ingredients—martial, tender and gay—Mozart proceeds with his wonderfully unified development through close upon a hundred bars. He is sly and vagrant, but adroit in tonality, resourceful in adding relevant detail.

There is a sense of tragedy in the Andante cantabile (a tempo direction which he had never before used in a symphony). When the first phrase (from the muted violins) is followed by a loud defiant chord, one is reminded, as elsewhere, of the "Eroica." In a second phrase, ornate thirty-second notes increase the emotional expressiveness, and forzando chords in the winds over halting triplets increase the tension. This thesis is developed, there is a fresh treatment of the opening subject matter, bringing the climax of the movement. The coda is magnificent.

The sudden alternation of forcefulness and gentleness, a lifelong characteristic of the instrumental Mozart, in his last symphony acquires a new meaning. In the Minuet it takes the form of alternate eight-bar phrases. It has been remarked that the dotted half notes which open the second part of the trio are a foreshadowing of the motto subject of the finale, immediately to follow (resemblances of this sort should be looked upon as the instinctive outcome of the artist's singleness of purpose rather than as deliberately planned).

The final movement is Mozart's supreme achievement in counterpoint so smooth-flowing and natural, so apparently simple, that the layman may make himself comfortably at home with its surface charm while the student examines the various permutations and inversions of the five themes. The movement is in sonata form with a fugato development and extended coda. So Mozart ended his symphonic works with a fugal peroration, as if to demonstrate for his own satisfaction how he could put counterpoint to symphonic uses. The result was then, and still remains, absolutely supreme in its kind.

The Entertainment Music
(Cassations, Divertimentos, Serenades)

COMMENTATORS STILL break their heads trying to distinguish between these titles. It is far simpler to consider Mozart's party music (*Unterhaltungsmusik*) as one category than to look for three workable definitions. The terms are often interchangeable. If Mozart had written his two cassations (they imply sizable Salzburg functions) at a later date he would probably have called them serenades, somewhat comparable to the "Haffner" Serenade. The titles "divertimento" and "serenade" each apply to night music under a window or in a garden in the warm season, in a ballroom or banquet hall in winter. Each includes works for strings alone, or winds alone, or mixed groups. Each consists of movements from four to ten, with elements from the symphony and the suite. The serenades are sometimes called "*Finalmusik,*" and (like the divertimentos) often opened and closed with a march, as if to start off a party and to bring it to a brilliant conclusion, yet a divertimento could call for a considerable orchestra with brass and drums, especially the earlier ones. K. 187 is labeled "*Tafelmusik oder Festmusik.*" Usually the divertimentos call for a smaller group—a favorite one was a string quartet with two horns. The serenades when strings are involved are always in the convenient key of D major. The music however named was obviously played at intervals through the evening. Mozart gives us examples of the custom in the "Table Music" which accompanies Don Giovanni's aristocratic repast at the end of the opera. An example of "night music" by gentle wind voices is heard in the Second Act of *Così fan tutte,* when the two men approach their ladies. This would probably have been called a serenade, but in divertimentos too a wind *"Harmonie"* was a favorite outdoor choice, sometimes joined with a string trio—or string quartet. When this happened the principal violin more or less took over, became a leading voice, and provided what was in effect the slow movement of a violin concerto. The wind players were given solo passages too, where talent permitted, and were usually treated as a concertante group. The type pattern is six movements—a more or less symphonic allegro and finale, and in between two slow movements and two minuets in alternation. The score is open, transparent, only occasionally leaning toward chamber music texture. For the most part, Mozart used simple means to please his casual listeners, capturing their attention with his wit, attaining distinction with his sensitivity to balance and color, his lively and unfailing imagination.

Popular music in the eighteenth century did not have, as now, a separate category of composers. Mozart was called upon at any moment to provide any music whatsoever, from the most solemn Mass to the lightest stage entertainment; music for concerts, music for dancing. Music by the yard for social functions did not in the least bother him. He provided it with enthusiasm, for he was incapable of turning out music automatically. Taste, resource, skill, enthusiasm never lapsed. He neither wrote above the heads of his audience, nor did he demean his art. He knew the pulse of popularity, in the sense that Johann Strauss in another century, and Offenbach, and Tchaikovsky knew it. Often he gave his patrons not only surface charm, but undying beauty of detail which, even if they were more attentive than social gatherings are now, they must have missed altogether.

Mozart cheerfully wrote down to a society audience, but

did it in such a way that the critic of today who would pass this music by is only revealing academic prejudice. To debase his talent to a job Mozart would have had to do what anyone else would have done—turn out listless, pattern music which would have perfectly well met the occasion—and died with it. This was simply not in his nature. In almost every one of the many movements in his party music there is fresh invention, special charm, inexhaustible melody, as if he had never before composed a minuet or an andantino.

Cassation No. 1, in G ("Divertimento-Finalmusik"), K. 63
Cassation No. 2, in B flat, K. 99 (Composed in Salzburg, 1769)

The origin of the word is undetermined, but there is nothing doubtful about the character of the two which Mozart left. The music bespeaks the best elegance of Salzburg. It is salon music, and would have graced parties in full dress, formal, politely festive. The two cassations are alike in spirit, almost identical in plan. The most accomplished players are the violinists, one of them a first rate soloist, while the parts for oboes and horns, viola and bass, mostly fill in. There are seven movements in each—an opening march and a similar ceremonious close (in the second the march is repeated). The second movement in each is for rapid, showy string playing. There follow two slow movements and two minuets, alternated. The minuets are stiffly elegant, and could have been danced. The slow movements would have required quiet, settled listening, especially the first in each case, for they were played by muted strings; they would also have held the general attention by their immediate charm. The second slow movement in the Cassation in G is an extended violin solo with muted accompaniment. The composer, aged thirteen, knew how to provide exactly what was wanted: music to set the tone of the affair—spirited and romantic by turns, always appealing, and with no particular depth.

Divertimento No. 1, in E flat, K. 113 (Composed in Milan, November, 1771)

In Milan, after the production of his *Ascanio in Alba,* Mozart evidently had at his disposal a far wider choice of wind players than at home, and accordingly wrote for five pairs (clarinets, oboes, English horns, bassoons) with string quartet. The divertimento, in four movements, is concertante in character but without conspicuous solo parts.

Divertimento No. 2, in D, K. 131 (Composed in Salzburg, early June, 1772)

In this divertimento more than any other the solo abilities of the players are extensively exploited. It calls for a single flute, oboe and bassoon, a horn quartet, which is heard alone, and a string quartet, from which the principal violin is particularly prominent in the first adagio. The flute however is the most favored virtuoso. In the minuets the horn quartet have a prominent part to themselves, and in the trios each soloist has his inning. This divertimento, with its high spirits and melodic charm, is one of the most captivating of them all.

Divertimento No. 3, in E flat, K. 166 (Composed in Salzburg, March, 1773)
Divertimento No. 4, in B flat, K. 186 (Composed in Milan, 1773)

Since these two works are each written for ten wind instruments (pairs of oboes, clarinets, English horns, bassoons and French horns), they could not have been performed in Salzburg, and may have been intended for Vienna and Milan respectively. The double reed quality predominates as the oboes and English horns, usually grouped, take the lead. The clarinets, less penetrating, have an occasional alternate function; the horns are mostly for color, the bassoons for a bass in unison.

Divertimento No. 5, in C, K. 187 (Composed in Salzburg, March, 1773)
Divertimento No. 6, in C, K. 188 (Composed in Salzburg, early 1776)

The character of these two, as band music for two flutes with five trumpets ("clarini") and four drums, suggests similar occasions. The first was for the installation of the Archbishop, and Einstein hazards the guess that the second was for an affair at the Riding School under the Mönchsberg in Salzburg. Each is a series of short movements in which the flutes and two trumpets in C have a treble, the remaining trumpets and the drums a supporting function.

The so-called divertimentos in E flat and in B flat (K. 196e and 196f), composed in Munich, 1775, were classed as "doubtful" by Köchel, but have since been supported. The instrumentation, a wind octet, is identical with that of the last two serenades.

Divertimento No. 7, in D, K. 205 (Composed in Vienna, 1773)
Divertimento No. 10, in F, K. 247 (Composed in Salzburg, June, 1776)
Divertimento No. 15, in B flat, K. 287 (Composed in Salzburg, February, 1777)
Divertimento No. 17, in D, K. 334 (Composed in Salzburg, summer, 1779)

Mozart must have had a special fondness for the combination of strings and two horns, for he returned to this grouping in succeeding seasons, as shown by these four works.* The blend of tones is most happy, or at least becomes so with his special delicate handling. The horns are not treated melodically and seldom separately. Nevertheless it is always the horns which give the real touch of beauty to the ensemble. The principal violin is the virtuoso solo instrument in each work.

Mozart opens his Divertimento No. 7 with a sober melody, largo, as if with a straight face, and suddenly at the ninth bar breaks into a boisterous allegro. Again his mood is quiet with a minuet too legato for dancing, and a trio with the gentlest of melodies. There follows a duet (adagio) for violin and viola, with the lightest bass accompaniment. The final presto is as lively and full of sudden turns as the first movement. A march (K. 290) was added for outdoor performances.

The Divertimento in F favors the horns more than its predecessor. It, too, has a separate march (K. 248). Like No. 15, for the same combination, it was written for a party given by the Countess Lodron. The outstanding movement is the Adagio —a real violin concerto movement of emotional appeal. Otherwise, the music skims a glittering surface.

The Divertimento No. 15 is the most familiar today, and probably deserves the attention it gets, because of the sustained quality of all its six movements, and its depth of expressive detail. This one is outstanding in the beautiful thematic blend

---

* A bassoon in No. 7 merely doubles the bass, and therefore does not upset the category.

of horns and strings. Mozart may have made a special effort to please the Countess Lodron, who was a musician, and who is believed to have been the hostess both when this one and the Divertimento of the previous year were performed. The Adagio, for strings only, is one of the finest of the divertimento slow movements and the theme with variations is rivaled only by the variations in the Serenade for thirteen winds (K. 361). The first violin (a solo quartet was used) has a virtuoso part. It introduces the finale with a recitative passage (later repeated) with a sense of serious anticipation, and then, surely as a joke, suddenly breaks into a final swift and carefree allegro, based upon a popular air of the Austrian Tyrol (*"D'Bäuerin hat d'Katz verloren"*), giving the principal violin plenty to do.

No. 17 is also a gem among the divertimenti. The first movement and the last deliberately cultivate a popular touch. It was composed for Mozart's special friend, Sigmund von Robinig. It is almost a string quartet with a shadow of horn bass. The first minuet (a parody of elegance?) has been honored by familiarity through popular arrangements. There are moments, too, such as the variations in an unrelieved D minor, which inject stormy episodes into a presumably festive evening. The two trios of the second minuet, also in D minor, are slow and pensive. K. 288, in F, is also for strings and horns.

Divertimento No. 8, in F, K. 213 (Composed in Salzburg, July, 1775)

Divertimento No. 9, in B flat, K. 240 (Composed in Salzburg, January, 1776)

Divertimento No. 12, in E flat, K. 252 (Composed in Salzburg, January, 1776)

Divertimento No. 13, in F, K. 253 (Composed in Salzburg, August, 1776)

Divertimento No. 14, in B flat, K. 270 (Composed in Salzburg, January, 1777)

Divertimento No. 16, in E flat, K. 289 (Composed in Salzburg, summer, 1777)

No less than six times, probably within the space of three years, Mozart composed a divertimento for a wind sextet, consisting of oboes, horns and bassoons in pairs. Since these instruments were always available in Salzburg, they were the obvious choice. These divertimentos were used either in the festive carnival month of January, or in the summer, and so would have served indoors as well as out. They are mostly in four short movements. They fall into an inevitable pattern— the penetrating oboes take the treble, the melodic part; the horns provide tonal body; and the bassoons, the bass.

Divertimento No. 11, in D, K. 251 (Composed in Salzburg, July, 1776)

This is a septet for string quartet with two horns and oboe solo. It differs at once from those for strings and horns, for the oboe penetrates the ensemble, in this case agreeably, for variety's sake. The oboe disputes the thematic lead with the first violin, and, as it happens, is generally favored. It has been conjectured that Mozart wrote this work for his sister's twenty-fifth birthday. If it was to her taste, Nannerl must have preferred gaiety to sentiment, merrymaking to pretentiousness. It sings throughout, and is more concerned with sparkle than depth. Only the march, to open and close, is pompous, as if to make fun of French ceremony—a *"marcia alla francese."*

Serenade No. 1, in D, K. 100 (Composed in Salzburg, 1769)

The early serenades, and this one unmistakably, are party pieces, in short movements, music simple, tuneful, designed for easy listening. The First, like the Third, is labeled *"Final-musik,"* as if intended to close the festivities. It is probable that the First (written for strings and three pairs of winds) was performed in a garden on a summer evening. The first of its eight movements is an allegro in march time, enlivened by light scale passages. The next three movements introduce solo passages for oboe and horn, as if favoring special available talent. There are three minuets. The second andante would have commanded special attention with its flutes in sixths over muted violins and pizzicato bass.

Serenade No. 2, in F, K. 101 (Composed in Salzburg, 1776)

The Second Serenade, subtitled *"Contredanse,"* was written for the carnival season at Salzburg. It is in four short movements, in duple time, consisting entirely of eight-measure phrases, each repeated. This lightly tossed-off suite was no strain whatever upon the performers, the company, or the composer himself.

Serenade No. 3, in D, K. 185 (Composed in Vienna, July or August, 1773)

The party in Vienna which called for this must have been formal and elaborate. Mozart had the use of a pair of "long trumpets" in D, which would have suited him because D major, a playable string key, was his choice for all of his serenades (except the *"Contredanse,"* and the last three for winds only). There are seven movements, the violin solo introduced in the first Andante and second Allegro.

Serenade No. 4, in D, K. 203 (Composed in Salzburg, August, 1774)

The Salzburg affair which prompted this music must have been as grand as the wealth of that town could afford, for it has as full an orchestra as the previous one for Vienna, and its eight movements come to twice the length. The first movement has a formal introduction (Andante maestoso), and must soon have assured the guests that their attention would not be heavily taxed, for the main allegro is light and tuneful, transparent by the use of short notes and trills. It could be called "tiptoe" music. The first andante of this serenade, a full violin concerto slow movement, is light, graceful and completely captivating.

Serenade No. 5, in D, K. 204 (Composed in Salzburg, August, 1775)

Whatever there is of pomp in this serenade, such as the fanfare-like opening of the second allegro and the rather stiff minuets, is probably intended humorously, for it is promptly dispelled by what follows. This is one of Mozart's most unpretentious serenades from the opening allegro (without introduction), where there is constant contrast of forte and piano phrases and no particular development, to the finale of tunes in the popular style (they would have suited Papageno), where the composer amuses himself by a constant sudden alternation of andante grazioso in two-fourths beat with allegro sections in a merrymaking three-eighths. The solo flute and the solo violin are much favored together in the first andante; the violin, in the third movement; the flute, with oboe and bassoon, in the second andante; and alone in the trio of the second minuet.

Whatever the occasion for this serenade, it would have been high bourgeois rather than aristocratic.

Serenade No. 6, in D (Serenata Notturna), K. 239 (Composed in Salzburg, in January, 1776)

The *"Serenata Notturna"* was composed for two groups: the first consisting of two solo violins, viola and bass; the second, a larger string body, with drums. It is thus an approximation of the traditional concerto grosso, so far as the distribution of instruments is concerned—a concertino and concerto grosso. Their use is different—Mozart never indicated a clavier in this department of his music. One can imagine the two groups placed separately, to give novelty and effect to their dialogue. The group of soloists takes the lead, and the larger group, with the pomp of drums, joins them to complete each phrase. The orchestra is therefore almost never heard alone. The piece is necessarily short, since this scheme excludes development. It consists of a march, a minuet and a rondo.

Serenade No. 7, in D ("Haffner Serenade"), K. 250 (Composed in Salzburg, July, 1776)

Siegmund Haffner was evidently a merchant of means. The wedding of his daughter Elisabeth must have been a large affair to judge by the music Mozart provided for it. The serenade is his longest. The seven movements are each extended, leisurely, often light in sonority, as if the composer enjoyed dwelling on his themes, manipulating them to the utmost. The result, it must be admitted, is sometimes repetitious. The music, with all the repeats, would have lasted more than an hour if it had been played continuously, which of course it was not. How such celebrations were musically spaced is not known. It is to be hoped, in view of the many quiet portions, that there was less music-drowning chatter than there is at wedding receptions today. The serenade would be performed more often now if there were any function, concert or otherwise, which it would in the least suit. It is mostly transparent music, turning up delightful wayward episodes. The first Andante is another violin concerto slow movement, and the Rondo after the first minuet throws a second spotlight on the *violino principale,* who opens with a rapid "perpetual" figure, and by the exactions of the form extensively employed, drives it to the utmost. The three minuets are all in the *galant* manner, and the second of them, labeled

"Menuetto galante" is plainly a parody, with its mincing staccato, its trills and turns. Gallantry, charming from Mozart even when he may have been poking fun at it, persists in the Andante which follows. The finale is an allegro assai in three-eight, developed at length, and characterized by alternate forte and piano sections. The adagio which introduces it is in utter contrast. It is completely serious, contemplative music, as if the couple were to be reminded that matrimony is really a solemn obligation, and then to be reminded by what follows (with a gentle change of mood) that this is after all the moment for the gayest possible front.

Serenade No. 8, in D (Notturno), K. 286 (Composed in Salzburg, December, 1776, or January, 1777)

Four identical orchestras, each having a string quartet with two horns, perform this serenade. There are three short movements (an Andante, Allegretto grazioso and Minuet) which allow little development, for the plan throughout consists of a phrase by the first group, echoed by the three others in turn, linked at the last bar, abbreviated in the process, the fourth group getting the tail end of the phrase. A novel effect would have been obtained by placing the four groups in different parts of a large room, or in adjoining rooms. Only the trio of the Minuet is given to the first orchestra alone.

Serenade No. 9, in D ("Post Horn"), K. 320 (Composed in Salzburg, August, 1779)

This serenade might be performed more often if in its long course there were even one movement which could be dropped without regret. It is rewarding in its variety. It opens with a majestic adagio and breaks into a high-spirited allegro, symphonically developed, and peppered with one of Mozart's jokes. There is another quizzical touch before the cadence of the first minuet. There follow two fine concertante movements (an andante grazioso and a rondo) in which the flute is the prima donna and the oboe the seconda donna, an andantino in a wistful D minor where the violins come to the fore, a second minuet with (in the second trio) a humorous quotation of the four natural notes of the then familiar post horn. The finale is a whirlwind presto. This is indeed a serenade to cherish.

Serenade No. 10, in B flat ("Gran Partita"), K. 361 (Composed in Munich and Vienna, in early 1781)

The Serenade for thirteen winds could not possibly have been performed in Salzburg, for it calls for four clarinets (two of them basset horns). The remaining four pairs of instruments make twelve: oboes, horns in F, low horns in B, bassoons. A contra bassoon (or contrabass) is the thirteenth. This is not the sort of *Unterhaltungsmusik* Mozart could have turned out casually for light and half-attentive social entertainment. There is every sign that he set himself the problem of deriving a great variety of color combinations from the thirteen instruments (each often becomes an individual part). No master has ever handled a large body of wind players with such wondrous results. The basset horns extend the range of the dulcet clarinet tone, which is brightened by the sharper voice of the oboes (flutes, as Mozart used them, would have been intruders in this tonal palette). After the first five movements—the allegro with a slow introduction, a minuet with two trios, an exceptionally beautiful Adagio with a murmuring accompaniment to the singing first oboe, a second Minuet with two trios and a second slow movement, a "Romanza" with an interpolated allegretto —it would seem that the composer had exhausted his color possibilities if not his musical resources. Thereupon he gives us a theme with six variations, each a gem of new variety. The seventh and closing movement is a rondo on the jolliest of themes. No other master could have detained an audience so long in this constricted medium without causing a weary sense of repetition. Mozart's score gives a sense of fresh disclosure to the very end.

Serenade No. 11, in E flat, K. 375 (Composed in Vienna, October, 1781; rearranged for wind octet in July, 1782)

The last two serenades (so listed) are wind octets for oboes, clarinets, horns and bassoons, in pairs. They are therefore similar to the divertimentos for the three pairs of winds to which, since Vienna permitted, Mozart could add clarinet color. This one was first written as a sextet for clarinets, horns and bassoons. A distinction between these and the wind sextets called divertimentos is a matter for quibbling. All were intended for outdoor as well as indoor use, even street use, where no elaborate party would have been involved. If there is a difference between these two works and their Salzburg predecessors it would be in the seriousness of their workmanship, for they have eight independent parts and a true chamber quality. Mozart has enlightened us on this work in a letter to his father (October 15, 1781). He composed the sextet for the sister-in-law of Herr von Hickel, the Court painter, but wrote "rather carefully," because he knew that Herr von Strack, the Emperor's chamberlain, would be present. The "six gentlemen" who played it were so pleased, either with the piece or their own performance of it, that they played it in (or before) three other houses, and gratified the composer by saluting him on the night of his name day (October 31) in his own courtyard.

Serenade No. 12, in C minor ("Nacht Musique"), K. 388 (Composed in Vienna, July, 1782)

Mozart could hardly have intended this, a serenade in a minor key, and, until the close in C major, in a somber mood, for light, sociable entertainment. It argues rather that it was composed for his musician friends in Vienna, whether listeners or players, and these only would have caught the point of a minuet in canon with a trio in reverse canon. His later arrangement of it for string quintet (K. 406, 1787) may have indicated a special fondness for it, but was more likely a matter of a convenient fulfillment, for the piece loses point in the string medium.

Various Orchestral Works

Galimathias musicum (Quodlibet), for Piano, Oboes, Horns, Bassoon and Strings, K. 32 (Composed in The Hague, March, 1766)

A suite of eighteen short numbers (including a fugued finale on the national song *Willem van Nassau.*

Les petits riens, Ballet Music, K. 299b (Composed in Paris, May-June, 1778)

The suite, lost and later found in Parisian archives, consists of an excellent full-length overture for large orchestra (including clarinets) and thirteen dance numbers. It is quite in the style of a ballet suite by a French master at the time, with the crispness and elegance of a Grétry or Gossec, but also the warm and singing themes of Mozart himself. The instrumental writing, with various grouping, oboe solo, flutes in echo, separate strings, etc., is as neat as the "Paris" Symphony. This is *"Unterhaltungsmusik"* masked in Gallic wit.

Gavotte, for two Oboes, two Horns, two Bassoons and Strings, K. 300 (Composed in Paris, May or June, 1778)

Apparently intended for *"Les petits riens,"* but not used.

Finale (for a Symphony), in D, K. 121 (Composed in Salzburg, early 1775)

Masonic Funeral Music, K. 477 (Composed in Vienna, autumn, 1785)

Mozart composed his *Maurerische Trauermusik* upon the death of two fellow Freemasons, the Duke Georg August von Mecklenburg-Strelitz and Franz Count Esterházy von Galantha. It was accordingly played at a memorial service for the two notables on November 17, 1785.*

Mozart cultivates the lower range of the orchestra with three basset horns,† clarinet, two oboes, two horns, contra bassoon, and strings. The mood and coloring of the *Requiem* is already evident. It is an adagio, opening with heavy chords in C minor, music of restrained mourning, more moving and personal than a formal ceremonial might have prompted. At the twenty-fifth bar, the oboes and clarinet (soon to be joined by the wind choir) intone a chorale of somber ritual suggestion, with accompanying chords from the lower strings and a continuing violin filigree:

---

* The work was listed by Mozart as composed "in the month of July, 1785," but his two brother Masons died on November 6 and 7 respectively. Alfred Einstein surmises that Mozart, making a later notation of the score, "simply forgot," being much preoccupied at the time with *Figaro*.

† Two were later replaced by French horns.

Mozart must have known Bach's chorale preludes; the cantus firmus here serves as a slow march. The melody of the introductory part returns to close this gentle slow movement pianissimo.

Ein musikalischer Spass (A Musical Joke), Divertimento in F, for Strings and Horns, K. 522 (Composed in Vienna, June, 1787)

When Mozart wrote his one lampoon of a musical score, he was at work upon *Don Giovanni;* he had composed his great G minor Quintet in the month previous, and would compose *Eine kleine Nachtmusik* in August. An inveterate joker, fond of word play in his letters and in certain unrefined canons of faultless counterpoint, he never, except in this case, distorted music itself. This bit of parody has been published as a *"Dorfmusikanten Sextett,"* but wrongly. Village musicians are not the butt of this joke, but the would-be composer. It is in the form of a divertimento like four others he had written, for string quartet and two horns, with the difference that the smoothest of composers here forces himself, against every instinct, to be ungainly. The harmonies are wrong, the distribution of chords awkward. There are trills on wrong notes. The horns for once refuse to blend with the strings. The opening theme is choppy and ends a bar too soon. If the breaking of musical laws were constant, the point would be lost—Mozart ripples along amiably for a few bars only to trip us up unawares. In the minuet a solo passage for the horns begins dolce, only to go completely awry. In the trio the first violin carries a scale passage to its top and adds a lame extra note. In the "Adagio cantabile" (a direction Mozart rarely permitted himself) the solo violin becomes lost in ornamental passages. His cadenza makes fun of that custom and the ensuing cadence disposes of the impregnable dignity of cadences for once and for all, as if Mozart too were weary of them. The presto leads us on only to spring surprises, traverses a false fugato, and coming to its close, hammers away at the tonic chord, only to end in harmonic confusion.

Eine kleine Nachtmusik, in G, for strings, K. 525 (Composed in Vienna, August, 1787)

This work, written in the mature period of *Don Giovanni,* defies classification. The full Breitkopf and Härtel edition includes it among the string quartets, but it has nothing in common with Mozart's intricate quartet writing at that time. His catalogue indicates "bassi," in the plural, and the score has the indication "violoncello e contrabasso" for this part, which would make it a quintet for an orchestral group. Jahn referred to it merely as an "easy, precisely worked out, occasional piece." Its title would indicate a serenade, and an additional minuet, before the Romanze, has disappeared. But Mozart had written nothing in the nature of serenades or divertimentos since his serenade for wind octet in C minor, in 1782, and that work was in anything but the popular style. This "Night Music," a simple harmonic piece, reverts to earlier days. It was certainly not written for connoisseurs, nor, like the string quartets and string quintets of 1782, was it a project for performance by Mozart's more perceptive colleagues. The transparent style, the elegant, polished phrases of gallantry, he had long since left behind, excepting the dances for the Imperial balls which he wrote in the line of duty. The delicate sonority of the strings unsupported, the very brevity of the piece, would not have suited the usual functions for which serenades and divertimentos were intended. The fact that he had also called his C minor Serenade "Night Music" might suggest that in each case he was composing to please himself, giving his own title to a form which was no longer demanded of him, but which lingered in his heart with a sort of nostalgia. The two works are at opposite poles in character. The C minor Serenade is too somber for any festive occasion—it is musicians' music, a personal score. The *"Kleine Nachtmusik"* is festivity itself, though on a miniature scale. It is reminiscent of Salzburg evenings, designed with the utmost grace and suavity, surface sentiment. One could turn to the early "Divertimento" for Strings, K. 136, and find the two works similar, surprisingly so in view of the fact that the one was the impetuous expression of a boy of seventeen, the other the polished sophistication of a superlative craftsman, aged thirty-one. Einstein has hazarded the guess, and not implausibly, that the "Musical Joke," recently composed, lingered in Mozart's consciousness, his sensitive musical soul, as a violation of every rule of smooth sonority, a jarring contradiction which required compensation in tones of complete correctness, rounded perfection. The ironical outcome of the puzzle is that a piece which Mozart deliberately wrote in an earlier style, perhaps for his own amusement, without thought or prospect of an audience, has become the most popular of his instrumental works, even accepted by some as if it were quite typical of the matured artist.

Marches and Dances for Orchestra

Marches

K. 62, in D, "Cassation" (1769); K. 189, in D (1773); K. 206, in D* (1774); K. 214, in C (1775); K. 215, in D (1775); K. 237, in D (1774); K. 248, in F (1776); K. 249, in D (1776); K. 290, in D (1773); K. 335, Two Marches, in D (1779); K. 362, in G* (1780); K. 408, Three Marches, in C, D, C, (1782); K. 445, in D (1779); K. 544, "*Ein kleiner Marsch,*" in D (1788)

Marches for various occasions have in some cases become separated from divertimentos and serenades which they opened or closed.

Minuets

K. 61g, Two Minuets (1769); K. 61h, Six Minuets (1769); K. 64, Minuet in D (1769); K. 103, Nineteen Minuets (1769); K. 104, Six Minuets (1769); K. 105, Six Minuets (1769); K. 122, E flat (1770); K. 164, Six Minuets (1772); K. 176, Sixteen Minuets (1773); K. 363, Three Minuets (1780); K. 409, Minuet for a Symphony, in C (1782); K. 461, Six Minuets (1784); K. 463, Two Minuets and Two Country Dances (1784); K. 568, Twelve Minuets (1788); K. 585, Twelve Minuets (1789); K. 599, Six Minuets (1791); K. 601, Four Minuets (1791); K. 604, Two Minuets (1791)

The minuet as an instrumental movement and the minuet to be danced become increasingly different through Mozart's works, until the former retains little more than the basic rhythm and the da capo succession. Ballroom minuets, however, were wanted from him even into his last year.

Country Dances (*Contretänze, Contredanses*)

K. 106, Overture and Three Country Dances (1790); K. 123, in B flat (1770); K. 267, Four Country Dances (1777); K. 462, Six Country Dances (1784); K. 463, Two Country Dances, with Minuets (1784); K. 510, Nine Country Dances or Quadrilles (doubtful) (1787); K. 534, "*Das Donnerwetter*" (1788); K. 535, "*La Bataille*" (1788); K. 535a, Three Country

---

* Afterwards used in *Idomeneo*.

Dances (1788); K. 565, Two Country Dances (1788); K. 587, *"Der Sieg vom Helden Koburg"* (1789); K. 603, Two Country Dances (1791); K. 607, in E flat (1791); K. 609, Five Country Dances (1791); K. 610, in G, *"Les filles malicieuses"* (1791)

German Dances *(Deutsche Tänze)*

K. 509, Six German Dances (1787); K. 536, Six German Dances (1788); K. 567, Six German Dances (1788); K. 571, Six German Dances (1789); K. 586, Twelve German Dances (1789); K. 600, Six German Dances (1791); K. 602, Four German Dances (1791); K. 605, Three German Dances (1791); K. 606, Six German Dances (1791); K. 611, in C (1791)

The Piano Concertos

I T COULD almost be said that Mozart created the piano concerto as a form—it is certainly true that he developed it from almost negligible beginnings to great ends. His first direct model was Christian Bach, and this Bach owed much to his older and more exploratory brother, Carl Philip Emanuel. Emanuel Bach's gropings toward the sonata form were still heavily overlaid with the tradition of the concerto grosso—a chamber ensemble in which the keyboard was a supporting continuo instrument. Only exceptionally, as in the father Bach's splendid specimens, had it become a prominent part of the counterpoint, assuming an occasional solo function, not yet an independent, thematic function.

Mozart, the virtuoso perpetually on show, had a lifelong inducement to develop both factors in a concerto. No phase of his art was pressed upon him so persistently as this, and the result was prodigious both in quantity and quality. He achieved the spectacular metamorphosis quite alone and

unaided, not even by the example of Haydn. Haydn's concertos were unprogressive—he readily filled in at the clavier
but never cultivated it as a conspicuous solo performer.

The concerto as Mozart found it was little more than a
harpsichord sonata with a backing of string players. He left
it a full orchestral form, an organization even more complex
than the symphony, in which the two elements of solo and
orchestra each blended or alternated with the other in a
perfect integration. Any one of the later concertos is fully
symphonic—often richer in color, variety and invididual expression than a symphony.

Beethoven, on whom the mantle of successor was to fall,
assumed it with uneasiness, for he had a deep admiration for
Mozart's concertos. With a strengthened piano and orchestral
sonority at his command and a new impulse of dramatic intensity, he could have made the concerto a mere vehicle for
virtuosos. He did not because he was Beethoven, and because
unlike pianistic lions of a still later day to whom the concerto
was to be thrown, he had a healthy respect for Mozart's ideal
—the balancing of both elements for one expressive purpose.
Beethoven's hesitancy to commit his first two concertos to
publication must have come from a sense that in magnification a certain peak of perfection would be destroyed. The
light Mozartean orchestra, the light-toned piano, made a
transparent ensemble in which every detail was luminously
clear, the voices of the individual and the group wonderfully
matched. It was indeed a state of felicity doomed to succumb
to new ways. The sacrifice was organizational too. Mozart
had developed as a personal skill the ordering and reordering
of manifold themes, their changing applicability, their fusion
into a fluent whole. This complex had to go, for new needs
called for new construction.

To appreciate what Mozart did for the piano concerto it
is not enough to compare the first and last—one must compare his very first efforts with the models about him at the
time. As a small boy in London he encountered concertos
by Wagenseil and other composers now forgotten, but particularly the concertos as well as the symphonies of Johann
Christian Bach. This youngest Bach frankly purveyed to

fashionable audiences with gracefully ornamented melodies and elementary accompaniments calculated not to disturb. His earlier concertos were composed for harpsichord and strings, with sometimes a light reinforcement of oboes and horns. The later ones were published for "harpsichord or forte-piano," but the string group was still constricted by the fainter instrument. A typical concerto at the time (there were of course exceptions) began with a principal subject by the string tutti, this later repeated in a series of ritornelli, each followed by a display of passage work from the soloist, to which the orchestra would add a gingerly bass or an occasional short interjection. The result was wooden alternation and thematic repetitiousness, which, when one principal theme was relied upon, became a squirrel cage. The orchestra was the servant to the soloist, bowing him in and out and standing ready with discreet pizzicati or obsequious bass notes where required. The following movements the soloist had even more to himself, carrying in the rondo an almost continuous pattern of running sixteenths. In old Sebastian Bach's concerti grossi, the clavier had been pushed forward from its function of figured bass, and while promoted from its solo duty of providing chord accompaniment, was still a voice in the general texture. The result was beautiful and exciting until counterpoint went out of fashion. As a melodic instrument in the newer regime of Bach's sons, the harpsichord became in concertos a weakling ruler incapable of sustaining any position of tonal eminence.

Mozart thought and worked from the beginning in terms of the sturdier pianoforte. He began at once to treat the orchestra as a respected partner and to break up the sectional block procedure. His first original piano concerto (K. 175), written in Salzburg late in 1773, at once leaves all previous concertos far behind. The scheme of those to follow is already laid out and needs only to be amplified, eased, subtilized. The piano and orchestra proceed like good dancing partners instead of an ill-assorted and stilted pair, each afraid of stepping on the toes of the other. Since the true valuation of any of Mozart's concertos lies in its inner impulse, its buoyancy and invention rather than its anatomy, it need only be said that the very first brought the piano concerto to life as a new apparition in music, and those to follow would range variously according to the adventuring imagination of the growing artist.

A cynical view of the concertos stresses the point that Mozart as a child was initiated in an atmosphere of *galanterie* at its most superficial. Concertos were necessarily made to entertain light-minded audiences. As he grew up he continued to appear before such audiences, to impress them as a remarkable pianist, and was expected to furnish new scores for this plain purpose. It could be said that he was catering to contingencies all along, the limitations of available performers even more than the limitations of his audiences. The more perceptive view is that he brushed aside such annoyances as insufficiency around him and dilettantism before him, and poured into the music, beneath the unruffled surface of the accustomed graceful style, the utmost of his musical nature. The concertos contain something of Mozart's every aspect—the chamber, the symphonic, the operatic composer. We have all of his moods from light playfulness, sheer joyousness, to the somber, the violent. The slow movements are unexcelled elsewhere. The finales in the aggregate are unequaled. They repeat favorite rhythms but treat them in as many fresh ways as there are concertos. Most astonishing of all is the variety of treatment. No concerto is reminiscent of any other either in large plan or small detail. There is even constant variety in patterns of figuration, and this includes the piano parts. Any composer other than Mozart, in the position of perpetually having to dazzle his audiences, could not have avoided, even if he had wished to, the displacement of musical interest in his concertos by sterile bravura. Mozart continued to dazzle, but while doing so, his scales, arpeggios, trills, became at one with the long melodic line, integral to the ensemble.

There are no really weak links in the chain of twenty-seven.* There is no other group of works in the orchestral repertory by any composer where there are so many truly great ones that no conductor or soloist can get around to performing

---

* Only twenty-three are original.

them all. Even an ardent Mozartean is necessarily guilty of important omissions.

Piano Concerto No. 1, in F major, K. 37
Piano Concerto No. 2, in B flat, K. 39
Piano Concerto No. 3, in D major, K. 40
Piano Concerto No. 4, in G major, K. 41
(Composed in Salzburg, in 1767)

These concertos are not original. Mozart had apparently brought back with him from Paris clavier sonatas by Raupach, Honauer, Schobert, Eckardt and C. P. E. Bach, and rewrote movements from them as concertos, both for practice in the form and for performance at home. He also rewrote three clavier sonatas of Johann Christian Bach, in 1765, in London or in Holland, as concertos with string accompaniment (K. 107). They are all apprentice works for the study of his models in style, form, and treatment. The orchestral portions have a light, accompanying function.

Piano Concerto No. 5, in D, K. 175 (Composed in Salzburg, 1773)

This, Mozart's first original piano concerto, was not a preliminary practice in the form but a self-standing work which he would use at home and carry with him to Mannheim and even to Vienna, where in 1781, he played it with a new rondo finale (K. 382). Not only was he far past the stage of reworking the music of others—at this his first attempt, he at once established a new and fresh level for the concerto. The scheme was laid out for all that were to follow. At seventeen he could create themes of complete charm and put them together quite naturally. It should not be held against his ability that the wind parts have a subordinate and almost entirely doubling function. Salzburg probably provided no adequate talent for individual uses. The parts for trumpets and drums may have been added for Mannheim or Vienna. Mozart holds to the gallantry of Christian Bach to give immediate, sensuous pleasure, as if this were also his own impulse. In the principal subject and a second brought in pianissimo, the young composer is already speaking for himself. Already the orchestra and soloist both color the themes in their own ways. The transitions are masterly. The intervening Andante is lightly scored by contrast.

It is built on a melody of sustained sentiment. In the finale he puts to use his new skill in canonic imitation, and does it with ease and grace.

Rondo for Piano and Orchestra, in D, K. 382 (Composed in Vienna, March, 1782)

Mozart composed this rondo as a new finale for the above concerto of nine years previous when he presented it in Vienna, in 1782. Although the original finale is more ingeniously worked, and at the same time delightful, this one is obviously an applause catcher, designed to capture the fancy of any audience to the last man. Its light staccato theme with elegant grace notes is embroidered by the pianist after each repetition rather than developed. It is not in the least surprising that the composer had to repeat it, and, three weeks later, play it again "because it is such a favorite here."

Piano Concerto No. 6, in B flat, K. 238 (Composed in Salzburg, January, 1776)

This Salzburg concerto Mozart also found useful on the road, playing it in Mannheim and Augsburg. The solo is a sleight-of-hand part with delicate running figures, clever turns and surprises. After the "Allegro aperto" which has its "open" brilliance, he invites in the Andante a subdued sentiment with an accompaniment of muted strings, touched by light notes from the horns and flutes (instead of the oboes). It is in E flat, dwelling briefly in C minor. Here the mood of tender dreaming, practiced by the boy Mozart in imitation of the current style, becomes the genuine impulse of the adolescent. The Rondo is particularly effective, for the theme as stated each time (here each time brought back by a fermata indicating a cadenza) can engender fresh episodes, the one factor growing from the other. The rondo (or minuet) had been a favorite form for concerto finales. Never had one been contrived with such variety and resource, so delicately handled.

Concerto No. 7, for Three Pianos, in F, K. 242 (Composed in Salzburg, February, 1776)

The dedication, in Italian, in the father's hand, is to "The incomparable merit of Her *Eccellenza* the *Signora Contessa* Lodron, born *Contessa* d'Arco, and her daughters the *Signor-*

ine Contesse Aloysia and Josepha." The three ladies in flowing satins, perhaps in triangulated placement, can be imagined as a captivating sight. Soundwise, it may have been different. The third part, considerably simplified, would indicate that one of the trio, perhaps the youngest daughter, Josepha, was something less than "incomparable." The solo parts are neatly matched, without involvement. The middle movement is in delicate and excellent taste (Abert calls it music of "sweet dreams"). The rondo is in the style of a conventional minuet. There are no fast tempi, nothing to dismay amateur fingers except perhaps the cadenzas. It is amiable music, pleasing to play, and could not have exacted from its composer much more than his ready facility. Mozart made an alternate arrangement for two pianos (actually an improvement)—probably for performance in Mannheim and Augsburg.

Piano Concerto No. 8, in C, K. 246 (Composed in Salzburg, April, 1776)

The piano part of this concerto, not technically difficult, was written for the Countess Lützow. Since it is especially prominent throughout, and subtly expressive, it is to be hoped that the composer did not have to listen to a performance something less than delicate and discerning on the part of his pupil. There are long orchestral introductions to the opening and the slow movements; otherwise the solo part, illuminated by the orchestra rather than paired with it, discourses courtly elegance. The Andante maintains this aristocratic air, while the miracle of Mozartean warmth comes through the gracefully ornamented measures. The finale, in "Tempo di Menuetto," is really a rondo on a minuet theme in the slow, elegant eighteenth-century *Redouten* style. The piano alone states it on each recurrence and the orchestra gives the formal ritornello. Only after the second return does the composer wander from his strict periods as his fantasy takes hold.

Piano Concerto No. 9, in E flat, K. 271 (Composed in Salzburg, January, 1777)

Mozart wrote this concerto for Mlle. Jeunehomme (or, for Teutonic throats, "Jenomé"), a French pianist who presumably visited Salzburg in 1777. We cannot know whether or not he was moved by the skill of this pianist to extraordinary effort, but the music itself shows a considerable advance over anything he had done in any form. He had already solved the basic problem of the concerto combination, but here it acquired its full stature. He struck out boldly, molded his materials at will in untried ways. The orchestra imposed upon him still consisted of oboes and horns which for the most part must be supported by string doubling. Within these limitations the orchestra becomes newly eloquent, closely fused with the piano to the advantage of both. Einstein compared this "monumental" concerto with Beethoven's "Eroica" Symphony for its "originality and boldness." He could have carried the comparison further. It is in the same key and reaches the unprecedented length of thirty-five minutes. It was the case of a young man who took hold of a polite form and poured into it a flood from an astonishingly abundant imagination in such a way that its profusion throughout is compact with fresh beauty. Like the "Eroica," too, the first movement is built on a complex of themes which merge into a continuous melodic current in development; the slow movement is a deep lament, the finale an outpouring of ebullient strength. It establishes a custom which was to make Mozart the supreme master of the piano concerto— a cluster of six themes in the opening tutti, to be heard from later in varied sequence and manipulation, usually shared with the piano which introduced subjects of its own.

At the very beginning the composer breaks precedent as the orchestra gives out a phrase and the pianist, who should be quietly waiting for his proper entrance much later, completes it. This was a happy *trouvaille* which Mozart did not have occasion ever to repeat. The first part of the principal subject was an orchestral proclamation, its melodic cadence was pianistic, whereby holy matrimony was declared at the outset. As in any ideal union, there is later a congenial interchange of thoughts. The thematic material of the first movement according to current custom could have furnished three. The Andantino is in C minor—the first of Mozart's concerto movements in the minor tonality. Its plaint in the low strings is strongly suggestive of the slow movement of the *Sinfonia concertante* for Violin and Viola (K. 364) to be composed more than two years later. There is even a suggestion of duet in its first statement. The feeling becomes more intense as the orchestra introduces the soloist with a cadential phrase like a singer's recitative, as if emotion were striving for words.* The passage recurs and softly closes the movement, but not before a suspensive pause on the dominant (instead of the usual six-four chord) introduces a cadenza which carries the whole magic, veiled discourse to its true summit. The rondo (presto) is based on an extended theme from the pianist, proposed and carried through with swift brilliance. In place of the third section, Mozart unexpectedly introduces and develops the theme of a slow minuet. This is a long movement, for the young composer had much in his heart. There is a cadenza which becomes a crucial part of the development and brings back the recitative passage as a soft reminiscence before the close. The bridge to the return of the Presto is quite indescribable. It has trappings of elegant grace but with a new and personal meaning. This is a concerto of daring, as if the usually compliant Mozart were suddenly possessed. Every bar supersedes formal gallantry.

Concerto No. 10, in E flat, for Two Pianos, K. 365 (Composed in Salzburg, in early 1779)

Mozart is believed to have composed his two-piano concerto for performance with his sister. In Vienna there was great pressure in the Aurnhammer household for such music to be played by the composer wth his pupil, Fräulein Josephine, and he sent home for this one, added clarinet parts (not included in the full edition), and performed it with success at at least two concerts, together with the four-hand Sonata in D, and the three-piano concerto which he rearranged for two.

The two-piano concerto is a "home" piece in the sense that it is quite without the pretension of bravura. The two solo parts are evenly balanced in the exact echoing of phrases, in unisons, or solos lightly accompanied by the partner. No formidable feats are required, even in the cadenzas to the first and last movements, but rather a perfect unanimity and sensitive exactitude, the ultimate test, as everyone knows, of worthy Mozartean style. The opening forte chord is a mere flourish. As the orchestra proceeds with an exposition of melodic themes, each engendering the next, it becomes apparent that the pianists will be provided in kind. The Andante, in B flat, goes deeper than

---

* One is reminded that Beethoven, whose music this concerto foretells, sometimes used quasi-recitative passages in his sonatas. The Piano Concerto in D of 1772, by C. P. E. Bach, which Mozart may have known, breaks into a long instrumental recitative, which, however, lacks tension and dissipates its effect.

a gentle felicity of matched pianism. When the soloists repeat the melody, delicately pointed with short notes and trills, they more or less take over. A beautiful cadence by the orchestra in descending sixths leads to a second subject by the pianists, and a final repetition of the cadence, ornamented and by themselves. Moments such as these are longest remembered. The Rondo restores the gaiety and sparkle of E flat.

Piano Concerto No. 11, in F, K. 413 (Composed in Vienna, in the season 1782-1783)

This concerto was one of three (K. 413, 414, 415) which Mozart wrote in Vienna between the autumn of 1782 and the new year, in preparation for concerts in Lent. It must be admitted that the Concerto in F has little of the warmth of the great E flat Concerto of three years before, and less of its challenge. Mozart wrote to his father on December 28, while he was at work upon the three: "These concertos are at a happy halfway point between what is too easy and what too difficult; they are very brilliant, pleasing to the ear, and natural, without being empty. Here and there the connoisseurs alone will find satisfaction; but at the same time the less learned cannot fail to be pleased, though without knowing why."

Apparently Mozart already knew his Viennese public well, for the concertos were enthusiastically received. Mozart had his eye on subscription and publication and made his horns and oboes expendable (though not without deprivation) so that the music could be bought for home performance with only string accompaniment. The Concerto in F has much to please the *"Kenner,"* in which posterity might be included, but little to excite them. It is a show piece for the pianist, lightly accompanied. The first movement is engaging it its themes, unusual in its triple beat, but in parts merely fulfills its pattern. The Larghetto is based on a songlike melody. It could have been turned, with its plucked accompaniment, into a delightful serenade in an opera, and in fact is less interesting in its instrumental development than in its quasi-vocal theme. The Rondo is on a minuet subject.

Piano Concerto No. 12, in A, K. 414 (Composed in Vienna, autumn, 1782)

The second concerto of this season in Vienna (which may have been the first in the order of composition) is more fruitful than the one in F major by the attractiveness of its themes, the individual handling of its solo part, and the importance of the orchestra, which not only supports but can take over, interchange, and swell to a climax. In a word, Mozart is more his lively self. The first theme of the orchestral exposition wins us and the second, announced softly (one should always watch for those gentle second themes), is entrancing. The two become the principal, but not the only, subjects of the development. The harmonized theme of the Andante as stated by the piano might have been composed by the early Beethoven (indeed Mozart's piano concertos often point to Beethoven's indebtedness). Its extended pianissimo cadence is magic, and is to be developed later by the soloist through a movement which holds the hearer enthralled. The subject of the final rondo, Allegretto, is one of those sparkling, playful tunes of the kind to be found in the piano sonatas, and this is one of the best of them. Mozart never wrote in a more consistently cheerful A major.

Rondo for Piano and Orchestra, in A, K. 386 (Composed in Vienna, October, 1782)

This is believed to be an alternate finale for the Concerto in A (K. 414). The score, listed by André, was sold, lost sight of, recovered in part, and restored by Einstein. Why Mozart wrote alternate finales for this concerto, and which he may have preferred, is a puzzle, for they are equally "popular." Mozart never wrote two concerto movements more closely alike in style and spirit. Each proceeds upon a graceful, trilled, wholly "eighteenth-century" and wholly delightful "allegretto" subject, with a contour similar to the other but maintaining its own identity. Each is of a "sonata" simplicity in left-hand treatment, each is lightly echoed by the orchestra. The displaced rondo is rather more subtly developed, but, unlike its mate, has no cadenza.

Piano Concerto No. 13, in C, K. 415 (Composed in Vienna, season 1782-1783)

The third concerto of this winter in Vienna shows that Mozart's resource extended to variety as between three concertos as well as within them. (It will be seen later how the concerto was always for him a subject for exploration). Here the orchestra has trumpets and drums, which however are used with the oboes and bassoons only in a doubling function in order that all three works when published would be playable with string accompaniment. The full brilliance therefore is resorted to only in the opening and close of the outside movements and a climax in the development of the first. It is possible to guess which aspects of this concerto were addressed to connoisseurs and which to the "less learned," the *"Unkenner,"* mentioned in Mozart's letter of December 28. The connoisseur would have followed the fugal interplay in the first movement, daring modulations and connecting passages in the first and last. The first movement Mozart could have counted upon to please the dullest ear present. The march rhythm which opens it strides gaily and persistently through the whole, although the piano, which is used with great brilliance, also gives it a lyrical contour. The same military rhythm would also close the First Act of *Figaro* (then still unwritten) where the reluctant Cherubino is about to be marched off to war. Before the close of the movement the piano and then the orchestra heighten the excitement with quasi drum tattoos. The melody of the Andante, one of those which could have been readily turned into an operatic aria, could not have been coldly received by anyone, although the layman might have failed to sense the expressive justice of its subsequent embellishment by the soloist. The finale was surely designed to please both sorts and puzzle both sorts as well. The rondo theme is a jolly tune in six-eight rhythm impossible to resist. But twice its course is suddenly interrupted by adagio sections, suggesting but not repeating the Andante. This was a disturbing innovation, encased in a sugar coating of lively six-eight. Mozart would have had to cope with the layman's impatience at the slowing down, the connoisseur's raised eyebrow. In both the first and last movements there are bravura passages to capture the layman's applause.

Piano Concerto No. 14, in E flat, K. 449 (Composed in Vienna, February, 1784)

In the spring of 1784 Mozart was reaching the summit of his popularity in Vienna as a pianist. He composed four concertos for Lent (K. 449, in E flat; 450, in B flat; 451, in D; 453, in G)— the first and last for his pupil Barbara ("Babette") Ployer—but also, like the others, for his own use. His mastery after a gap of two years shows a marked advance in these four. In a letter to his father (May 26, 1784), Mozart reveals that he was well aware of having lifted the concerto to a new degree of integration and expressive variety. He had never before proudly submitted his latest works to his father and sister for an opinion. He singles out from the four the ones in B flat and D, which he had composed entirely for himself, with no stint upon pianistic brilliance and orchestral freedom: "I really cannot choose between the two of them, but I regard them both as concertos that are bound to make the performer sweat. From the point of view of difficulty the B flat Concerto beats the one in D. Well, I am curious to hear which of the three, the B flat, D, and G, you and my sister prefer. The one in E flat does not belong at all to the same category. It is one of a particular sort, composed rather for a small orchestra than a large one." The E flat Concerto is indeed of a "particular sort," not like any other he wrote. It is as mature as those to follow, but moderate as to difficulty, restrained in pace and volume. It is plainly constructed to the convenience of Barbara Ployer with presumably adjustable oboe and horn parts to permit home performances with string quartet (either multiplied or as single instruments).

After a long exposition by the tutti, piano and orchestra proceed hand in hand, in a duet of close give and take, without flights of unaccompanied bravura from the one or formal ritornelli from the other. The Andantino, a beautiful song, placid in B flat and F, is finely treated by the combined piano and strings, developed as well as embellished. Its charm is sealed by a pianissimo close. The finale is the most venturesome of the three movements, the most arresting, for it has no counterpart in all his works. It is a quasi-rondo, so adroitly handled that formal sections are hardly discernible. Its combination of themes becomes a remarkable contrapuntal integration. They stand in separate clarity by the contrast of staccato and legato, of note values rather than imitation. Mozart builds in his own way without recourse to fugal formula, and attains his own smooth and flowing results. If this concerto yielded more display and exacted less of musicianly understanding it might be performed as often as it deserves.

Piano Concerto No. 15, in B flat, K. 450 (Composed in Vienna, March, 1784)

When Mozart made the remark, which was quoted above, that this concerto and the one in D following, were "bound to make the performer sweat," he meant that the pianist dominates throughout with every sort of running figure. Here, in much of the first movement, the orchestra supports him with light chords; in the finale, his part is still more brilliant, but it must be added that the brilliance is really due to the fired imagination, the bold incursions of the composer rather than to the purpose of dexterity as such. Nor is the orchestra really subordinate, for Mozart exploits its colors as never before in the concertos. None had sounded so symphonic. At the very opening he rejoices in separate treatment of the wind choir, alternating with the strings. In the finale, a flute is added to the oboes, bassoons and horns to give a bright edge to the sonority. Flute and oboes have solo passages, and the "hunting horns," hitherto used mostly for soft, sustained notes, come into their own. The Andante consists of an air in E flat, in triple beat, which is varied. It seems to open the way to Beethoven as ornamental running figures in thirty-second notes cease to be decorative and become moving melodic expression. The finale, on another romping six-eight theme, rises from light exuberance to one of the richest of all Mozart's rondos, with endless surprises in transition, contrast, chromatic manipulation.

Piano Concerto No. 16, in D, K. 451 (Composed in Vienna, March, 1784)

Mozart dated this concerto in his thematic notebook as of March 22, 1784, seven days later than the Concerto in B flat, K. 450. It is one more proof, if proof is needed, that under pressure his workmanship was at its best. The result does not suggest a pondered concerto, but a spontaneous one. It has orchestral brilliance, with trumpets and drums, full pianistic display in the first and last movements. The opening Allegro assai strides like a jaunty march, with rhythms established in the long orchestral exposition. The Andante is simple and placid by contrast. Mozart's sister objected to the bareness of the eight-measure phrase at the fifty-third bar, whereby the present performer has a choice of a completely simple and an elaborated version of the melody at this point. It is a matter of taste, but the player should bear in mind that Mozart often cultivated simplicity with a purpose. The finale is for show and designed to please any social gathering. Before anyone puts the outside movements down as surface music he should listen carefully to the development sections in each.

Piano Concerto No. 17, in G, K. 453 (Composed in Vienna, April, 1784)

"Tomorrow," wrote Mozart on June 9, 1784, "Herr Ployer, the agent, is giving a concert in the country at Döbling, where Fräulein Babette is playing the new Concerto in G, and I am performing the Quintet [K. 452]; we are both to play the Sonata for two claviers [K. 448]. I am taking Paisiello in my carriage, as I want him to hear both my pupil and my compositions."

It would be interesting to know what Paisiello, who was an Italian and exclusively operatic, thought of the new compositions, and what he thought of the daughter of his host. Ployer had obviously engaged good wind players for the Döbling concert, essential no less for the wind quintet than the concerto, which called for a separate wind group and their solo voices. Mozart must have thought well of his pupil thus to show her off, for not only does it have difficult solo passages, particularly in the last movement—it is an intensely individual, an emotionally searching work, and exacts an unusual musical intelligence in its performer. Although the G major Concerto opens softly and never attempts to stun with virtuosity, it ranges far through a great variety of moods and treatment. The exposition is a profusion of themes, gay, singing, at moments even darkly dramatic, which become symphonic with the separate use of the winds, and grow upon the hearer as the piano develops them in close conjunction with the orchestra. The Andante is a true symphonic slow movement in variation form, where the concertante woodwinds build to a climax of emotion. The final Allegretto presents more variations, quite free of any traditional pattern on another theme, which would have well suited Papageno. After seven variations, through which the development becomes passingly tender, almost serious, the composer seems to feel that the time has come to round off the whole with swift gaiety, and he does so with a presto which could easily have served for a *buffo* finale. It creeps in pianissimo with soft fanfares, picks up a sort of "final curtain" excitement and ends with the return of the main theme.

Since the excelling qualities of any of the concertos lie in the beauty of their themes and their particular note-for-note manipulation, matters not to be conveyed in words, any description of them becomes a mere signpost, nothing more demonstrable than a personal preference. The G major Concerto holds a special place in the hearts of all Mozarteans—but so too do many others in this astonishing phase of his art.

Piano Concerto No. 18, in B flat, K. 456 (Composed in Vienna, September, 1784)

This was almost certainly the concerto which moved Leopold to tears of delight when, visiting Vienna, he heard it in 1785, and was charmed by the "interplay of instruments." He wrote to his daughter that Mozart had composed it "for Paradis for Paris." Maria Theresa Paradis was a blind pianist of Vienna, who toured Europe in 1784, but could hardly have received the score in time for performance in Paris. It is neither one of the most difficult nor one of the most showy of the concertos, but its charms are many. The march rhythm of the opening bar

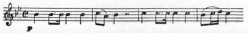

was a favorite with the composer. He had used it in martial guise in his earlier Concerto in C (K. 415). It appears again to open the concertos preceding and following this one and written in the same year (K. 453 and 459). It is interesting to note that Mozart, who never repeated himself in his concertos, could think of one rhythmic pattern in at least four completely different ways (we shall meet it again in the D minor Concerto (K. 466). In the case in hand the rhythm is freshly developed and at last dismissed with an especially delightful coda. The slow movement, hovering around G minor, has been compared with the plaintive little cavatina of Barbarina which opens the third act of *Figaro*. Barbarina's naïve dismay (rather than deep sorrow) at the loss of a pin entrusted to her is somehow anticipated in this Andante, until the discourse becomes closely orchestral and leads into a section in the tonic major which puts her for the time being out of mind. The rondo-sonata finale in six-eight meter is expectedly cheerful with a certain restraint and repose, until a stressful and apparently extraneous episode in B minor interrupts it. Did the composer wish to strike a sort of balance by a serious episode in a gay movement as against an optimistic major episode in the previous gloomy movement? There is no point in trying to reason or justify, since Mozart surely did not. Enough that he was moved at the moment to lead us afield with a magic transition, convince us, and lead us back again.

Piano Concerto No. 19, in F, K. 459 (Composed in Vienna, December, 1784)

This is the fourth consecutive concerto which opens with an identical rhythmic pattern. It might have settled again into a march, as in K. 415, but here it takes a totally different aspect. Not only is the rhythm not exhausted on its fourth incipit—it pervades the movement both as a theme and as a motto, as freshly as if Mozart had come upon the rhythm for the first time. The unfoldment is ever self-renewing. A newly pliable symphonic development pervades each movement. If there is a single criterion for the measure of an instrumental composer, it is his resource in development, and that resource is the combined depth and quality of the well of his tonal imagination. By this criterion only two are supreme—Mozart and Beethoven.

This concerto shows that Mozart was always working toward a closer inter-identification of piano and orchestra. They are heard together most of the time, in pursuit of a single musical purpose. That purpose subordinates bravura as inessential. Even the cadenzas, and particularly the one in the finale, are no longer an interpolation, but a continuation. This is an entirely cheerful concerto, and without a true slow movement. For the second movement Mozart gives us a C major Allegretto in six-eight. Instead of a strophic song we have a theme divisible into segments and correspondingly useful for integral development. The development is in binary sonata form, without a middle section. The theme of the final Allegro assai is also segmentary, and for the same reason. Its development and the contrapuntal episodes—the most considerable excursion into fugato in all of Mozart's concertos—confirm this one as in its way his most symphonic to date. It is the choice for a performer who loves Mozart at least as much as his own prowess in glittering cascades.

Piano Concerto No. 20, in D minor, K. 466 (Composed in Vienna, February, 1785)

The first of Mozart's two concertos in the minor is unique in character among them all. Nor does it in the least resemble the piano concertos of Emanuel Bach in the minor mode. (Mozart had written two of his string quartets in D minor, the early K. 173 and K. 421 in 1783, the second of the Haydn set.) Quartets were for musicians who knew, concertos a bid for general applause from hearers who expected to be pleasantly entertained. Yet there is no record of protest over this one. It was bound to appeal to the nineteenth century for it had what the nineteenth century sought—open pathos, dynamic range, conflict of mood, sudden contrast. There is no note for note similarity with Beethoven—there are no parts Beethoven could have written. But the Beethoven of the stormy piano sonatas may have been stirred by it—we know that he was fond of this concerto, for he supplied his own cadenzas.

The orchestral prelude opens softly but ominously, and accumulates power in this portentous mood to a climax in the same "march" rhythm which had opened four previous concertos (K. 415, 451, 456, 459), but here it becomes sinister. A theme in plaintive descending appoggiatura by the oboes is swept aside. The pianist enters with a new theme, gentle and pleading, setting up a struggle between this and the orchestral threat of violence. The piano makes the orchestral mood more stormy by swelling the sonority with agitated figures. No mere by-play of scales and arpeggios here. The movement ends darkly. The thesis of irreconcilability sits strangely on this composer. The middle movement is based on a placid, strophic melody in B flat major, as if the troubled discourse must be relieved by "romance." On the other hand, whether to make the whole work congruous or to maintain its duality, the composer interrupts his idyl with a section as stormy as the first movement, although thematically different. The finale is less tragic, but the D minor persists, the orchestra developing into sudden threatening chords through chromatic modulation, the piano again serving both to restore tranquillity and to dispel it. At last a joyous D major is established, the trumpets and horns which had served to strengthen dark chords now gleam forth with their more usual bright orchestral colors.

Piano Concerto No. 21, in C, K. 467 (Composed in March, 1785)

When Mozart composed this concerto just a month after the "serious" one in D minor (K. 466), he may have felt the urge for relaxed gaiety in C major, or he may have felt that this would be a welcome restitution of high spirits on the part of his public (he was then at the peak of his popularity as the first pianist in Vienna). In any case, he produced his most carefree concerto. Its opening of light, short notes prophesies delicate, lyrical intertwining, and the prophecy is fulfilled. At this advanced stage of his development one has come to expect a profusion of entrancing Mozartean themes in every concerto, wonderfully ordered, linked, combined, varied. Analysis cannot probe its surface. Dissection, being intended for skeletons or cadavers, is useless when living flesh and blood is in question. The music lives only in sound. A scribe can say that this concerto is to him enchanting throughout, but his statement proves nothing and can be no more than backed up by the opinion of others. An attempt to convey the flavor of a melody such as that of the Andante with a flood of verbal images is equally futile. Let it be enough to note that the melody is first divulged by muted strings over diaphanous string chords, in a murmuring twelve-eight, that the pianist varies it while the solo voices of the winds add their charm, that the total effect is "glamorous," in the pristine, unabased sense of the word. The finale is an adventure in modulation, surprises, happy invention.

Piano Concerto No. 22, in E flat, K. 482 (Composed in Vienna, December, 1785)

Three concertos (K. 482, 488 and 491) interrupted Mozart's work upon *Figaro* in this winter. In this, the first of them, he allowed the *buffo* spirit to creep into the fast movements. They have a theatrical externality of treatment, a play for attention, and this externality includes a showy part for the soloist. He approaches the close with growing momentum to a brilliant curtain. This does not mean that the music is superficial in any unfavorable sense, unless *Figaro* is to be called superficial. Mozart did not have to be deep to be great. Melody, by-play, subtle changes, are not wanting. Indeed the concerto becomes serious in its Andante. He gives us another of his great melodies, at first by the strings, con sordino. He has at his command a full and competent wind section, and he proceeds to make the most of it. After the piano has expatiated upon the melody—the *"harmonie"*—by itself, flute, clarinets (for the first time in his piano concertos) bassoons and horns take over. Later the flute and first bassoon join the strings in true concertante fashion. The finale offers still another of Mozart's lively rondo tunes in six-eight time. The hilarity is interrupted by a short Andantino cantabile where the woodwind choir affords new delights before the swift close.

Piano Concerto No. 23, in A, K. 488 (Composed in Vienna, March, 1786)

The first movement of this concerto is relatively simple and unpretentious. Its themes join into a continuous, melodic flow. The orchestral prelude gives the not unusual impression of a symphonic score until the piano, entering upon the opening subject, proceeds to make the themes its own as well, exchanging emphasis with the orchestra in their combined development, making no long solo excursions until the cadenza. The bright A major gives way to the relative F sharp minor in the slow movement. The manuscript heads this movement as "Adagio," an inexplicable tempo since Mozart himself was opposed to dragged-out slow movements where a piano was concerned, and otherwise always labeled the middle movements of his piano concertos "Andante," "Andantino," or "Larghetto." Certainly the subject accompanied by a six-eight barcarolle rhythm, asks for a singing motion in the "Andante" sense, and is so indicated in the Breitkopf and Härtel edition. Its mood could be called veiled sorrow, restrained yet eloquently expressive. It is certainly to be included in Mozart's profusion of "great" slow melodies, specifically where it follows the piano statement with an orchestra of interwoven phrases by the flute, clarinets and bassoons. The movement continues to divulge new beauty. The tender mood is swept aside by a swift and gay rondo, again inexhaustible in invention.

Piano Concerto No. 24, in C minor, K. 491 (Composed in Vienna, March, 1786)

This is the third concerto of the *Figaro* season, composed with the production of the opera just five weeks off. Einstein wrote that Mozart here "evidently needed to indulge in an explosion of dark, tragic, passionate emotion." The composer's motive is of course pure conjecture. The plain and astonishing fact is that Mozart, tied up with many duties, absorbed in the preparations of his opera, turned out not a casual piece in the entertainment pattern, but what is generally considered his most independent and challenging, his most prodigious work in this form. It is his ultimate venture, his furthest exploration of the piano concerto, for the three which were to follow were to be a further refinement on what he had done. If Mozart could be said ever to have ignored his public in a concerto and followed completely his own inner promptings, it was here. The first audience must have been dismayed when instead of the usual diatonic opening subject they were presented with a tortuous, chromatic succession of phrases with upward skips of diminished sevenths. This was a new and strange tonal world, and not a gracious one. Their dismay would not have been lessened when the whole orchestra proclaimed the theme with dire emphasis. A soft theme introduced by the woodwinds gives only momentary relief, for the first theme sweeps it away. The piano enters with a new theme, still in C minor, but is drawn into the ubiquitous theme, adding an octave to the wide interval. The theme dominates the movement, the soloist (as in the D minor Concerto) adding to the excitement with agitating scale pasages. It is a less stormy opening movement than that of the D minor Concerto, but it is more vivid, more subtle, and more deeply felt. Although the cadenza brings a long coda, ending pianissimo, there is no assuagement, and the serenity of a major mode is imperative. Nothing could be more serene than the melody of the Larghetto. Certain pedants have been disturbed by the "over-simplicity" of the cadence of the first phrase:

Mozart, whose taste could be relied upon, knew how to be simple with a difference. The three elements—piano, strings and winds —are combined each way with wondrous results. In treating the wind choir, the composer obviously gloried in having a full quota, clarinets and oboes included, and he made the most of them (the trumpets and drums had no place here but are mustered in the other movements). The final Allegretto brings no happy ending as the finale of the D minor does. It begins and ends in C minor, traversing many keys. It is a series of variations on two subjects, the second of which opens the way for astonishing chromatic development—a chromaticism which serves for thematic individualization, modulation and transition equal in skill to the manipulations in the G minor Symphony which would come two years later. These variations defy description— they are surely one of Mozart's highest achievements in the form.

This concerto combines range, intensive direction and extraordinary adventurousness. It speaks to the nineteenth century, and was a favorite with Beethoven. Under the immediate spell of a performance, one is strongly moved to give it some sort of crown, the crown, let us say, for the ultimate point, as Mozart through his life sought to bring the orchestra and his own instrument into ever closer communion.

Piano Concerto No. 25, in C major, K. 503 (Composed in Vienna, December, 1786)

This was the last concerto of the great succession of fifteen composed for public performance in Vienna. The two which followed, after a space of two and four years respectively, were for other uses.* The last of the C major concertos is a splendid close to the Vienna series. It is also the complete antithesis of its predecessor, the C minor Concerto. It is expansive, unruffled in its sunny key. Dr. Friedrich Blume, in his preface to the Eulenberg minature score, relates it to *Figaro,* which it followed, "both in conception and time of origin." There is an occasional chance echo, such as the theme introduced in the fiftieth bar:

where the gaiety of the second act finale bobs up. It has the special elevation of mood of *The Magic Flute,* or indeed the "Jupiter" Symphony, where C major becomes for Mozart a realm of special, effulgent purity, not without nobility of sentiment. Indeed this concerto could as readily be called "Olympian" as the final symphony, and, associated with that province of Mozart's art as its complement, the C minor Concerto might be associated with the G minor Symphony.

The last C major concerto unfolds itself broadly and amply throughout. The tempi are unhurried from the well-titled "Allegro maestoso" through the placid course of the Allegretto finale. The piano is well occupied with running figures, which however are never meaningless and serve to amplify the extended melodic line of the score. The "majestic" first movement dwells in broad chord successions and unhurried cadences. The composer prevents it from becoming static by leading us with clever transitions through a number of keys. The theme of the Andante, in F major, is calm and unarresting, until the development engenders

---

* There is no record of a performance of the "Coronation" Concerto of 1788 in Vienna while he lived; the last one, in B flat, was privately commissioned.

delicate episodes. The principal subject of the last movement is rather innocuous, but here again the skill of the mature Mozart leads us through fine if leisurely musical vistas. The fourth of his concertos in the key of C major is the most serene of them all.

Piano Concerto No. 26, in D ("Coronation"), K. 537 (Composed in Vienna, February, 1788)

The so-called Coronation Concerto has the amplitude, the leisurely tempi of its predecessor, indeed it is one of the longest, lasting a full half-hour. It has much to commend it, with themes which persuade and win us. It was one of the most popular and most performed in the nineteenth century. And yet it has little of the special elevation of its predecessor—its place is lower on the slopes of Parnassus. It was given its title, "Coronation," by André, not because there is anything especially regal about it, but because Mozart took it to Frankfort in October, 1790, and performed it during the coronation festivities of Leopold II. Mozart had also played it in Dresden, on April 14 of the year previous. Its special popularity then and later is hard for us to understand now. Among the wealth of the concertos a pianist now might choose it for the limpid beauty of the solo part, which completely avoids the empty glitter of passage work; a conductor would pass it by for a concerto of more orchestral interest, which here is almost entirely lacking. Except for the full tutti of openings and closes, or an occasional ritornello, the winds are not used at all, and the piano is supported only by a light filling in from the strings. The concerto could have been written for some house performance where only a piano (or harpsichord) and string quartet were available. Mozart may have hastily added the full orchestral contingent for Dresden or Frankfort, in separate parts without rewriting. This is nevertheless a concerto of much melodic charm with themes to cherish. The melody of the Larghetto, and indeed the whole movement, creates its own atmospheric spell of dreaming.

Piano Concerto No. 27, in B flat, K. 595 (Composed in Vienna, January, 1791)

Composed at the beginning of Mozart's last year, with his concertos for public performance three years behind him, this one has been called his "farewell" to the magnificent series. It was not an emotional or an observably conscious farewell on the composer's part. He had simply turned from a form which

Vienna no longer asked for and occupied himself, among other prodigious matters, with his four greatest operas. No one can say with assurance that he returned to this favorite form in a nostalgic mood. He wrote it for Joseph Bähr to be played by himself in the concert hall of the Court Caterer Jahn in Lent (March 4, 1791). The solo part is correspondingly prominent, the orchestra moderated to circumstances. It is neither a deeply probing concerto nor a joyfully brilliant one. The composer proceeds in an even-tempered mood, with assured mastery. The themes as we first meet them in the opening movement are characteristic and agreeable rather than striking. Only as he develops them, does his invention seem really to take hold. The Larghetto, too, increases in beauty in the telling. The opening refrain is in the by now familiar mood of romantic musing. The melodies which grow from it (the movement is a rondo) increase to ardor and breathless beauty. The piano dominates and continues to do so in the final Allegro—still another rondo in the familiar six-eight beat, and his last in that rhythm. The theme however is mildly cheerful rather than hilarious. The rondo is rich in invention as the orchestra comes to the fore. The composer brings to a close his last piano concerto in good spirits and with the superb craftsmanship of his last year.

The Concertos
with String Instruments

IN THE YEAR 1775 between April and December, in Salzburg, Mozart composed his five bona fide violin concertos. Two years before, he had written the "Concertone" for Two Violins, and four years later, also in Salzburg, he wrote the *Sinfonia concertante* for Violin and Viola. Since the two later violin concertos, attributed to 1777 and 1780, exist only in copies, and at best may have been filled out by later hands from fragmentary sketches, it could be said that Mozart gave his full attention to violin concertos in only one season of his career. Whether he intended these works for his own use in Salzburg is not known, but he was then Concertmaster, and would have been expected, though reluctant, to step forward as soloist. He did play one or another of them on occasion elswhere. He was often called upon to compose music for violin solo in Salzburg, probably for Gaetano Brunetti, and notably in the divertimentos and serenades where a slow movement which would have served for a violin concerto was called for. The "Haffner" Serenade is in effect a violin concerto pieced out with orchestral movements. Outside of Salzburg he never had occasion to write for violin solo, although he sometimes played one of his concertos, usually at private gatherings. He may have been wary of the popular tendency to fasten upon a musician as a virtuoso and ignore all else but his tricks—a tendency which required his best wit as pianist to counter.

One thing is certain from the evidence of the music. The composer who could write with such consummate skill for the violin as a chamber or orchestral instrument could also favor its fullest advantage for solo melody or solo display. The violin concertos, or at least the best of them, have a firm and enduring place in the heart of every violinist who puts music as an art above music as a personal opportunity.

Concertone, with Two Solo Violins, Oboe and Cello, in C, K. 190
(Composed in Salzburg, May, 1773)

The title may have been coined by Mozart, who could not have correctly called the piece a "concerto grosso," then an obsolescent form. Later he would have called it a sinfonia concertante, and properly, for the orchestra is symphonic, and the soloists are in grouped alternation. They consist of two "principal" violins, an oboe and (in a brief token appearance in the finale) a cello. The orchestra is the center of interest, and propounds the substance of each movement before the soloists detach themselves. The two violins sometimes engage with the body of violins in a sort of duet. The Concertone is unusually advanced for its date, which precedes the violin concertos by two years, and the *Sinfonia concertante* for Violin and Viola by six.

There is far more to the Concertone than surface gallantry, particularly in the long and beautiful slow movement. Mozart took the score with him to Mannheim and Paris.

Violin Concerto No. 1, in B flat, K. 207 (Composed in Salzburg, April, 1775)

It is evident at once in Mozart's first attempt at a solo violin concerto that he considered it in the class of "entertainment music." Its course is simple, open, relies on melodic charm, and in doing so keeps the soloist always to the fore. The orchestra provides for the most part a light chordal accompaniment or an echoing ritornello. A great melodist, though a young one, speaks, and in the Adagio warms to sentiment. The Presto, the only swift movement in these concertos, is a runaway exhibition for the soloist, abetted by the orchestral violins. It is also sparkling, clever and irresistible. This is the only concerto which did not end with a rondo, and Mozart later substituted for the Presto a rondo finale (K. 269).

Violin Concerto No. 2, in D, K. 211 (Composed in Salzburg, June, 1775)

The Second Concerto is an advance over the First in the orchestral portion, which has a more independent life, more contributive variety. The solo part, too, becomes free of merely violinistic figures, becomes ornamental with triplets and trills in the first movement, which indeed Mozart would later have simplified. There is again a ready melodic abundance. The Andante has at least the incandescence of the previous Adagio. The final "Rondeau" is deliberate French elegance, taken not too seriously.

Violin Concerto No. 3, in G, K. 216 (Composed in Salzburg, September, 1775)

The spectacle of Mozart, aged nineteen, growing in musical stature from month to month in the succession of violin concertos becomes miraculous in his Third, as the orchestra takes on a new inner life, while the soloist has a constant, pliant singing line, until passage work becomes thematically beautiful. The Adagio attains a new height as, under its cantilena, the orchestra, in muted triplets, with pizzicato bass, supersedes the rather straightforward accompaniment of the earlier slow movements. The Rondo, in an elegant minuet tempo, is interrupted in casual fashion by an andante which seems to make fun of courtliness, and an Allegretto which is nothing more than a setting of a simple folk song.

Violin Concerto No. 4, in D, K. 218 (Composed in Salzburg, October, 1775)

The Fourth Concerto continues the mounting succession, with ampler periods, consistently greater invention, further integration of solo and tutti forces into a single discourse. This concerto rivals the Fifth in popularity. It seems to have been preferred by Mozart himself, for he refers to it in the letters as the "Strasbourg" concerto, probably on account of a popular tune drawn from that city, and mentions having played it with success in Augsburg. The Andante cantabile is a great instrumental aria. The "Rondeau" is again light and humorous as if its composer delighted in sudden switches of subject and meter. It begins in a mincing French style as an Andante grazioso, which gives way twice to a brighter Allegro in six-eight, then to a little gavotte, and a peasant dance to a droning oboe. The six-eight tempo ends the piece, but rather quietly, as if Mozart enjoyed depriving the virtuoso of the expected brilliant conclusion, or, if he himself were to be the soloist, fooling his audience. The Fifth Concerto, which also indulges in some amusing episodes in its finale, likewise ends with a whimsical bit of nothing.

Violin Concerto No. 5, in A, K. 219 (Composed in Salzburg, December, 1775)

The A major Concerto has the most broad and expansive opening movement of them all. The direction "Allegro aperto," a favorite one with Mozart, is here justified by the brilliance freedom and amplitude of the music, with a solo part of bold attack, wide skips, soaring range. The soloist does not in the least deprive the orchestra of its importance, nor is the orchestra ever a mere provider of chords. The orchestral exposition proceeds as engrossingly as if no soloist were to be involved or needed, but the soloist is given an impressive entry with a special adagio section and a start upon the "open" allegro tempo with a true brio theme. The Adagio, in amply phrased periods, still finds its true life in the orchestra. Many would name this the peak of all slow movements to date. However deeply in earnest Mozart may have been in dreaming out his superb Adagio, he is quite ready to resume his spoofing manner with another "Rondeau" *à la Française,* again in minuet tempo. The light-stepping decorum of the ballroom is suddenly invaded by a juggernaut of a Turkish march, in which the thumping upon a bass drum is clearly imagined. A joke of this sort by any other could become clumsy and pointless. With Mozart controlling there is sheer delight in every bar.

Violin Concerto No. 6, in E flat, K. 268 (Composed in Salzburg-Munich, 1780?)

Violin Concerto No. 7, in D, K. 271a (Composed in Salzburg, July, 1777?)

Unlike the masterly five violin concertos of 1775, these two posthumous ones have been given by most experts the damning label *"zweifelhaft."** These "dubious" scores have survived in unauthenticated copies which were presumably made by the early collector of Mozartiana, Aloys Fuchs (1799-1853), and eventually acquired by the *Staatsbibliotek* in Berlin, where they were left to lie little regarded for many years.

The Concerto in E flat was in Einstein's opinion given by Mozart to the violinist of Munich, Johann Friedrich Eck, as a fragmentary sketch which he had cast aside, and which Eck filled out and passed along as Mozart's. By Einstein's estimate only the first movement and the opening of the last have elements of the true Mozart. The middle movement, he has concluded, "is certainly a crude forgery." Professor Rudolf Gerber, in a preface to an Eulenberg score, with scholarly caution calls the concerto "more or less not genuine." In the last analysis the music itself must plead its own worthiness to be called Mozart's. The orchestral opening at once rings true, its themes are characteristic and presented with the assurance of mastery. With the development one's confidence ceases. The solo part is bustling and often empty, the accompaniment a mere trickle of filling in. The Poco adagio is a warm cantilena over an accompaniment

---

* The so-called Adelaide Concerto, attributed to Mozart's childhood visit to Paris, was swallowed whole when "discovered" in 1933 by Henri Casadesus, a gentleman with a special sense of humor, but is now universally repudiated.

of strings only. If this is a forgery it is a smooth and impudent rather than a "crude" one. The Rondo has the authentic Mozart ring, and only here and there has barren stretches, as if the composer had again left the counterfeiter to subside into his impotence.

The Concerto in D stands in better repute, and has raised doubts principally on account of the un-Mozartean technique of certain solo passages. If the original manuscript was a sketch with full indications, the result could be a fundamentally true but slightly doctored Mozart. Georges de Saint-Foix stoutly supports the piece and does not even admit the intrusion of another hand. Two bits of discovery have indicated its authenticity and pointed to Paris as its source. A theme of the final Rondo:

Solo violin

almost matches the second phrase of the *Gavotte joyeux* (No 6) in the ballet, *Les petits riens,* which Mozart wrote in Paris in 1778, and which lay in the library of the Paris opera, forgotten, until 1872. In the early part of the last century, F. A. Habeneck, the conductor of the Paris Conservatory Orchestra, let it be known that he possessed the manuscript of an unknown concerto of Mozart—whether the original or a copy is not clear. In 1837, this manuscript mysteriously "disappeared," but not before Eugène Sauzay, a pupil of the violin virtuoso Baillot, had made a copy for his teacher. Sauzay's son inherited it and held it close. Eventually the copy was compared with the copy by Fuchs in the State Library in Berlin. The two were so close that they must have come from the same source. Unless one copy had been made from the other, which seemed unlikely, the case was strong. The concerto was published by Breitkopf and Härtel in 1907, has been much played, but also much disputed. The concerto abounds with Mozart's musical "fingerprints": his favorite martial rhythm as the basis of the first movement, mincing gallantry in the Andante, a typical and delightful rondo theme and its usual treatment. This music could have plausibly preceded the great five of 1775. There is inscribed on both of the copies: *"Salisburgo—li 16 di Luglio, 1777."* (Why the composer should have carefully dated a sketch he was about to discard is not clear.) Mozart never progressed backwards. That he could have composed this work in the year of the "Jeunehomme" Piano Concerto is hard to believe.

Sinfonia concertante ("Konzertante Sinfonie") for Violin and Viola, in E flat, K. 364 (Composed in Salzburg, summer, 1779)

The viola plays a subordinate part in the great bulk of Mozart's music, with the magnificent exception of his later orchestral and chamber music, particularly of course the string quintets. Twice in his life he exploited it to the full as a solo instrument, paired with the violin—the two duos for violin and viola unaccompanied (K. 423, 424) for Michael Haydn, in 1783, and in 1779 the Sinfonia concertante for the two instruments. The occasion, and whether he played the viola part, is not known.

If this work is considered as a sort of appendage to the violin concertos it must be at their expense. Since the first five violin concertos of 1775, he had been in Mannheim and Paris, and grown considerably in orchestral skill. The accompaniment is richer in development than those of the violin concertos, both because he was branching away from concerto practice, and because of what he had learned in the interim. He was limited, as before, to oboes, horns and strings, but his use of them is in this case so distinctive, so advanced, that the limitation is hardly noticed by the hearer.

The long orchestral exposition before the two soloists enter independently indeed justifies the symphonic character of the title. Their entrance on a high, sustained E flat is at once commanding, and the commanding position is never to lapse. The two play in unison, thirds, or alternation, often not in exact echo. The cadenzas are carefully provided with equal apportionment. The Andante, in C minor, is the outstanding movement, for it has a pathetic utterance more like the nineteenth century than any other slow movements he had written. The soloists are more subtly, more variously matched than in the first movement. The violin first sings the long two-phrased melody, and yields to the viola, which repeats it with striking effect in the intensity of the dark register. The melody in development is a song inconceivable by any voices other than these. The final Presto sweeps gloomy sobriety aside with the gay return of E flat.

Adagio for a Violin Concerto, in E, K. 261 (Composed in Salzburg, late 1776)

According to a remark by Mozart to his father in 1777, he wrote this Adagio at the request of Brunetti as a substitute slow movement for the Fifth Concerto, Brunetti having found the original one *"zu studiert."* "Too studied" would have meant too worked out, too developed and imaginative, either for his own taste or for popular consumption. The superb original slow movement is actually crystal clear, appealing in every contour. It has more orchestral interest. The substitute one needs no apology nevertheless. It is a fine movement with a sustained melody, eminently violinistic, over muted violins, a violin aria. It makes entirely worthy company for the great concerto slow movements of 1775.

Rondo concertante for a Violin Concerto, in B flat, K. 269 (Composed in Salzburg, late 1776)

If, as is supposed, this Rondo was substituted for the Presto finale of the First Concerto to accommodate Brunetti, the implication would be that the Presto was too rapid for his fingers. The earlier movement should have pleased a virtuoso, being principally a display piece. The later one has a richer orchestral score and a closer working of orchestra and soloist. Mozart was not only complacent about such requests—he readily gave them his best.

Rondo for a Violin Concerto, in C, K. 373 (Composed in Vienna, April, 1781)

Brunetti was again responsible for an additional rondo. When Mozart, and Brunetti too, visited Vienna under the employ of their Archbishop, a concert was arranged in the home of the father of Hieronymus, on April 8. Brunetti evidently asked for a new rondo, probably as a separate piece, for none of the earlier concertos of Mozart was in the key of C. It is an Allegretto grazioso of much charm, built around the soloist, but with a quiet ending.

The Concertos
with Wind Instruments

Mozart's close understanding of each wind instrument, its best notes and phrasing, its color and blending possibilities, is evident enough in all his later orchestral and concertante writing. This understanding well bears the virtuoso test of the concertos. He composed them in each case for a special player, and exacted the utmost from the player and the instrument in its state of development at the time. The most important as full-rounded orchestral scores are the *Sinfonia concertante* with four winds (the one composed in Paris) and those of the Vienna years—the horn concertos and the Clarinet Concerto of 1791. Those which have survived from the Mannheim-Paris journey, for bassoon, for flute and for flute and harp, are lightly scored, music of more charm than depth.

Concerto for Bassoon, in B flat, K. 191 (Composed in Salzburg, June, 1774)

This concerto, like three others which have not survived, was probably composed for Freiherr Thadaeus von Dürnitz, an amateur bassoonist. The original manuscript, once in the possession of André, is lost.* The tonal allurements of the instrument, its best leaps and turns, its guttural velvet, are skillfully brought forth. Mozart puts the instrument most gracefully through its paces, with a light accompaniment for strings alone. In the

---

* Another concerto in the same key was restored from copied manuscript parts and published in the edition of Max Seiffert in 1934. This concerto is listed in the appendix of the Köchel Catalog as number 230, under the heading of "Doubtful Works."

Andante the strings are muted, resulting in one of the young Mozart's special movements of tender sentiment.

Concerto for Flute, in G, K. 313 (Composed in Mannheim, early 1778)

Andante for Flute, in C, K. 315 (Composed in Mannheim, early 1778)

Concerto for Flute, in D, K. 314 (Composed in Mannheim, early 1778)

Mozart's hard words about the flute in his letters to his father from Mannheim may have been prompted by the then still uncertain intonation of the instrument in lesser hands than those of his friend J. B. Wendling. It was more likely prompted by his impatience at the task of composing a set of "short and easy" flute concertos and quartets for the amateur De Jean who was to pay him 200 gulden, and paid him less than half of that amount, when his funds were at their lowest. The resulting scores, two concertos with an alternate Andante for the first, and three quartets, were neither short nor easy. They were a handsome contribution all the same for value not received. Their composer could not have been as indifferent to the flute as he claimed to be and yet written for it with such gusto, such obvious delight in its limpid color. The Adagio of the first concerto seems not to have pleased the client, for Mozart provided another movement, the Andante (K. 315). This is more conventional in melody and treatment, simpler in its accompaniment, though still a gravely beautiful movement. The displaced Adagio may not have been beyond the patron's abilities, but would have been beyond his comprehension. It is more personal music, more intricately detailed in the accompaniment of muted strings, too delicate for the uninitiated. The first movement, designed for light pleasure, the pupil would surely have approved, and also the final Rondo in minuet tempo. The second concerto, with a less serious Andante, with tuneful themes delightfully treated, must surely have pleased its owner. The theme of the finale is nothing else than the joyous air of Blondchen, *"Welche Wonne, welche Lust,"* which he would compose for *Die Entführung* three years later. This concerto is believed to have been a rearrangement of an oboe concerto which Mozart wrote for Giuseppe Ferlendis in Salzburg the year before, and which is lost. It is sometimes so performed.

Concerto for Flute and Harp, in C, K. 299 (Composed in Paris, April, 1778)

The combination falls into an inevitable pattern—since the harp at the time lacked the modulating and other mechanical conveniences of the modern chromatic instrument, its use became largely a simple melody and accompaniment, mostly in the middle register, in something resembling a keyboard part. The sustaining flute with its correspondingly light tone naturally takes over the treble melody. The orchestral accompaniment is necessarily of the lightest. The Andantino is graceful French salon music, the Rondo a treatment of a French gavotte.

Sinfonia concertante in E flat, for Oboe, Clarinet, Horn, Bassoon, with Orchestra, K. 297b, Appendix No. 9 (Composed in Paris, April, 1778)

This music is the very definition of the title (which is more accurate than *"Konzertantes Quartett"* as it was first published). Like the *Sinfonia concertante* for Violin and Viola (K. 364), it is symphonic in its expanse, in the character of the development. At the same time it derives from the concerto grosso by the setting of the solo quartet, which is a sort of concertino against the orchestral tutti. The quartet is a unified group rather than a succession of soloists—a *Harmoniemusik,* where the individual voices are alternated, blended, interlaced, backed by the accompanying orchestra or relieved by the predominant string tone of the tutti. Only in the adagio, where the melodic line is lengthened in time, does each soloist have his extended phrase while accompanied by his fellows.

The first movement, which is the longest, is thematically rich and tends to prolong the development by the varied possibilities of color combination and alternation which the composer has given himself. The long "cadenza" before the close is not used for virtuoso display but is a sort of coda where the group as a group demands the sole attention. The slow movement is an andante rather than an adagio. The solo players carry the melody in turn, the bassoon providing in one place a sort of dulcet "Alberti bass" to the higher instruments.

The variation finale naturally permits solo virtuosity to come to the fore, but always in a musically integrated way. The ten variations give special solo opportunities to the oboe or clarinet, or the two together. The second variation brings the bassoon to prominence, and the eighth provides a duet by a melodic bassoon and an ornamental oboe on arpeggios. The horn has no extensive solos, but its function is by no means subordinated. Each variation is rounded off by a recurring refrain from the tutti. At last there is an adagio passage and an allegro coda in a lively six-eight rhythm.

The score disappeared in Paris, without performance, but it is believed that Mozart rewrote it from memory, for a copy was posthumously found in the State Library in Berlin. (The original had an oboe instead of a clarinet.) The essential gold of the music precludes any doubt as to its authenticity.

Concerto for French Horn, in D, K. 412 (Composed in Vienna, 1782)

Concerto for French Horn, in E flat, K. 417 (Composed in Vienna, May, 1783)

Concerto for French Horn, in E flat, K. 447 (Composed in Vienna, 1783)

Concerto for French Horn, in E flat, K. 495 (Composed in Vienna, 1786)

These concertos may all have been written for Ignatz Leitgeb, once solo hornist of the *Kapelle* Orchestra in Salzburg. Leitgeb was apparently a "*musikant*" of more proficiency than culture. He opened a cheesemonger's shop in a suburb of Vienna with money borrowed from Mozart's father, but evidently continued to play the horn. Mozart seems to have enjoyed poking fun at him in the way of good-natured insults. The concerto, K. 417, bears the inscription "Wolfgang Amadeus Mozart has taken pity on Leitgeb, the ass, the ox, the fool." The Rondo of K. 412 carries remarks at various points in the score: "*Signor asino—su via—da bravo—Coraggio—bestia—Oh che stonatura—Ahi!*" As if to confuse him, Mozart wrote the horn part for the last concerto in a variety of colored inks—blue, red, black, green. It is inscribed in his personal notebook: "*Ein Waldhorn für den Leitgeb.*"

All four concertos end with a rondo in six-eight time, built on the natural notes, hunting-horn fashion. All four rondos are completely engaging. The second has touches of humor, and the last, like the whole last concerto, is a superior score, reflecting its year. It was characteristic of the Mozart of 1786 to revise this one in the year of its writing, giving added life and interest to the developments of the first and last movements. The first has no slow movement, and indeed its two movements may not have belonged together.

Concerto for Clarinet, in A, K. 622 (Composed in Vienna, October, 1791)

Mozart's last concerto for any instrument is certainly his greatest in the wind category. He composed it for his fellow Mason, Anton Stadler, together with the Clarinet Quintet. Stadler had much improved the instrument, and Mozart was plainly eager to exploit its color. Both works show this, for in both he draws upon its dulcet beauty of tone and never debases it as a thing for vain show. There is no provision for a cadenza in either work. The similarity extends further, for the concerto, using a string accompaniment exclusively with the soloist, becomes in effect another "quintet" in a felicitous blending of reed tone with the string tone of quartet writing. At the same time the concerto is symphonic, for the tutti add flutes, bassoons and horns, and become an important part of the whole, as in the long orchestral exposition. The ritornellos thus provide a delightful alternation with the more delicate combination.

The String Quartets

THE FULL Breitkopf and Härtel edition, here followed as to order, lists twenty-three string quartets; three so-called divertimentos which are early, unclassifiable, and consist of four string parts; and the Adagio and Fugue which Mozart arranged for string quartet.

Mozart had occasion to write string quartets at two periods in his life: in the season 1772-1773, and later as the matured artist in Vienna between 1783 and 1790. They are therefore the early and the late Mozart, separated by a significant gap of about nine years. Actually he wrote his first quartet on the first Italian journey of 1770, and it was two years later that he wrote six, mostly in Milan. In Italy both string quartets and symphonies were in demand for gentlemanly concerts, and the sixteen-year-old Wolfgang kept a good store of both in readiness. They did not greatly differ—a symphony at that time was usually a quartet multiplied, with pairs of oboes and horns added. In the following year (1773) during his stay in Vienna, he found a similar demand, and wrote six more. By then the extraordinary and finely matured string quartets of Haydn, Op. 20, had just appeared, and these with the earlier six of Op. 17 stimulated Mozart to imitate this fresh and exciting concept of chamber music instead of continuing in the simpler gallant style of accompanied violin melody.

After these he did not touch the form again through nine important years of growth—the years which produced the first great symphonies and piano concertos, *Idomeneo* and *Die Entführung*. Neither Salzburg nor Western Europe seems to have cultivated string quartets sufficiently to look for them from Mozart at that time.

In 1783, established in Vienna, and a close companion of Haydn, he was more than ready to take full advantage of the older man's innovations in making the quartet an advanced chamber form as inspiringly set forth in Haydn's six quartets, Op. 33, which had appeared in 1781. The ten great quartets of Mozart's last years draw upon Haydn in extending the themes and their development into a continuous melodic discourse, the elements integrated in development, the leading and subsidiary voices finely adjusted, the fluctuations smoothly shaped to the form.

Mozart composed at fairly regular intervals the six which he dedicated to Haydn, and four more—one for the publisher Hoffmeister and three for the King of Prussia. These ten are the great ones, the superb specimens of chamber music in its fullest flowering to date. With them must be classed the string quintets, notably the last four, the one in E flat (K. 614) following the last quartet. The quintets are nothing other than quartets with an added third inner voice, and are in no way inferior to the quartets.

Haydn and Mozart are both rightly credited with the "creation" of the string quartet. Haydn was the pioneer who showed the way. He had begun writing quartets in their rudimentary form shortly before Mozart was born. By 1782, when he and Mozart became close friends, he had composed at least thirty-six, including his then recent six of Op. 33, and had developed in all its essentials the quartet as we still know it. Mozart and Haydn together from that point strove mightily in the cause of a perfectly balanced chamber group, each composer a strong stimulation to the other. Haydn wrote twelve (Op. 50 and 51) in the course of Mozart's last ten. It so worked out that whereas Haydn wrote his greatest symphonies after Mozart's death, he also wrote more string quartets but could hardly advance the form. It was as if the last word in eighteenth-century chamber music had been spoken by the two together.

As in the case of the symphony, Mozart and Haydn had developed the string quartet from nondescript beginnings to great ends. The quartet owed something to the traditional baroque trio sonata, where two violins had the melodic burden, supported by a string bass and keyboard continuó. When four string players assembled to make music, the violins still carried the melody and the lower instruments—the viola and cello—fell into the homophonic style and simply made accompanying chords as the harpsichord had done. The movements also derived from the suite and had a purpose of light entertainment. The earliest quartets of Haydn were sometimes called "*cassationi*" or "*divertimenti*," and had two minuets. This was the sort of music that the small Wolfgang, traveling in Italy, was called upon to provide. The aged Milanese Sammartini then became his model.

The early quartets of both Mozart and Haydn suggest lightminded listening. When Haydn began to work the four parts as four balanced and independent voices, the most important transformation had already taken place. Four voices so treated mean a complex beyond dilettante listening, and lead to "learned" writing. When Haydn wrote fugued finales to two of his quartets of Op. 20, he was no longer favoring a casual pleasure-seeking assemblage, but taking advantage of his growing position of authority to compose for the edification of the colleagues who would play them with him. When, somewhat later, he would go to the house of Mozart to try a new quartet by his friend or himself, the group including Haydn as first violin, Dittersdorf as second, Mozart as viola, Vanhall as cello, we may be quite sure that the manuscript on their stands was designed for their own pleasure, their own taste and musical understanding rather than any popular applause. The battle cry might have been equal rights and fair representation for all strings. This was "musicians' music."

As at no other time in his life, Mozart was freed from the necessity of catering to the popular musical appetite. As in no other phase of his music, he wrote quite as his fantasy prompted, with texture quite as intricate as his heart desired. The consequence was music more daring, more finely and subtly wrought than any other that came from his pen.

Haydn, who had opened the way, was outdistanced, not in technical mastery, but in sheer altitude. The emotional range of Mozart's quartets is wider, their moods more various. They are richer in detail, with a sense of tone combination which in the later quartets is even uncanny. Still, Haydn the pioneer nobly held his own. There never was a happier association to a double fruitfulness.

The seven "Italian" Quartets, composed mostly for Milan, but also for those other centers which required a concert number, have without exception surface charm and wit. They are all in three movements, usually avoiding minuets, according to Italian taste. They fall into a comfortable, sure-to-please pattern of smooth-flowing, melodic violins over an agreeably cushioning bass. The cello has the velvety ground notes and the viola, or the two inner parts, have often arpeggio chords. Where a gentle agitation or urgency of tempo is wanted, a constant repetition of chords in eighth notes is used. These are only recurring devices. Mozart often divides his voices into pairs, in various combinations; sometimes he gives the cello or viola a bit of the theme, which he could not have done in a symphony at that time. Occasionally there is a touch of four-part juggling. Obviously he could have done a great deal more of voice weaving if he had not been restricted by circumstances to a simple, easily assimilable homophonic style. The young boy, the *"tedesco"* on exhibition, is constrained to please, and not expected to mystify.

String Quartet No. 1, in G, K. 80 (Composed in Lodi, March, 1770)

The First Quartet, written in the coach on the way to Lodi on the first Italian journey, takes its own movement order—an Adagio, an Allegro and a Minuetto, to which he added a "Rondeau" four years later for performance in Vienna. For a first attempt by a boy of fourteen it is remarkably assured and well-turned.

String Quartet No. 2, in D, K. 155 (Composed in Bozen, October, 1772?)

The Second Quartet is more experimental; there is a bit of part-writing in the first movement, as much perhaps as the boy felt he would be allowed, an Andante elegant with trills, and a brief finale of youthful charm. Here and throughout the Italian quartets, Mozart toys with gallantry, avoids effusion of sentiment, and is generally light and entertaining as no other could be. These early quartets are among the better "juvenilia," where the flow of distinctive melody, the freshness of young invention, beckon in every work, every movement.

String Quartet No. 3, in G, K. 156 (Composed in Milan, late 1772)

The Third Quartet has a waltz-like Presto, an eloquent pairing of voices in the Adagio, and a Minuet with a trio of special, delicate beauty. Another Adagio was later substituted for the original one. It becomes a duet between the first violin and the cello.

String Quartet No. 4, in C, K. 157 (Composed in Milan, late 1772 or early 1773)

The Fourth Quartet is continuous melody. The Andante (in three-eight) lends enchantment with its bass, and the Presto is built on a theme with displaced accents which in its time may have bewildered the layman.

String Quartet No. 5, in F, K. 158 (Composed in Milan, early 1773)

The Fifth Quartet is an excursion into the whimsical, opening with a "sudden" triplet figure interspersed with rests and justifying itself in development. The Andante, "un poco allegretto," alternates staccato and legato with special effect. The final Minuet again indulges in triplets and rests, but differently.

String Quartet No. 6, in B flat, K. 159 (Composed in Milan, early 1773)

The Sixth Quartet is notable for its middle movement, an Allegro in G minor in three-quarter time, long, chromatic, cleverly handled. The opening is an Andante, the close a Rondo in grazioso style, with shades of minor.

String Quartet No. 7, in E flat, K. 160 (Composed in Milan, early 1773)

The last quartet of the Italian journey begins with the theme Mozart used in the "Divertimento" for String Quartet in D, K. 136, composed shortly before and a plain evidence of consanguinity. It is as spirited as its predecessors, and closes with a Presto introduced by the composer's favorite march rhythm.

Although the six quartets which Mozart composed in the autumn of 1773 during his stay in Vienna follow his "Italian" ones by less than a year, they show a sudden and considerable change in his point of view. The earlier quartets had been a complacent fulfillment of audience expectations—confections of melody and wit, more appealing in the intimacy of the form than the current symphonies which they closely resembled. In Vienna, Mozart evidently experienced an awakening when he encountered the recent quartets of Haydn—the six of Op. 17 and the six of Op. 20 (The "Sun" Quartets) which had appeared in 1771 and 1772. Haydn was an older and more experienced hand at this form—he had been composing quartets for seventeen years or more, and by then had composed thirty-six. He had the authority of his forty years, and a considerable reputation, against the obscurity of a mere boy of sixteen. Mozart was obviously much struck to find that the older man had transformed a light salon style into a true chamber style of exciting potentialities.

For the only time in his life, Mozart was confronted with musical possibilities beyond his ability to make the most of them. In 1773 he had yet to develop his symphonies, chamber music, concertos, operas to a point of true maturity. In the quartets he imitated Haydn's innovations without always finding for them an expressive purpose of his own. They are experimental, and not always successfully so. A good deal of the ease and grace, the fresh bloom of the recent Italian quartets, is lost in thematic irregularities and the desire to be "learned." These quartets were not looked upon with favor by the connoisseurs when they were circulated in manuscript copies in 1785, after some of his later, great ones had appeared.

String Quartet No. 8, in F, K. 168 (Composed in Vienna, August, 1773)

The first quartet of the early Vienna series opens with a lively, swinging theme and proceeds with a freer manipulation of the four voices. Thus, the old sparkle is enhanced. The device of reiterated eighth notes in the bass has for the time being disappeared. The Andante, in F minor, muted, is sinuous in voice leading, concordant, wholly captivating. The finale is a quasi fugue, not a worked-in fugato, and obviously takes a direction from the three fugue finales in Haydn's Op. 20. It is a smooth piece of work, but as a quartet finale not wholly appropriate. Mozart would try it once more in the D minor Quartet of this year, but never again.

String Quartet No. 9, in A, K. 169 (Composed in Vienna, August, 1773)

The Quartet in A takes an agitated course and courts sonority. The Andante is an extended melody, Haydnesque in contour and Haydnesque in its achievement of tension by a persistent accompaniment of ostinato chords, as in *The Seven Last Words*. The Minuet, trying to find a new interest, sacrifices lightness and grace, which however is recaptured in the Trio. The Rondeau, built on a singular theme of descending tenths, is brief, like most of the closing movements in this set, and unlike the finales of Mozart's contemporary symphonies.

String Quartet No. 10, in C, K. 170 (Composed in Vienna, August, 1773)

The opening movement produces, for the first time in the quartets, a theme with variations. The Un poco adagio, which follows the minuet, is based on a fine, full-phrased melody, which in the development is given to the four voices in turn. There is a syncopated accompaniment. The Rondo is unusual in theme and humorous in treatment.

String Quartet No. 11, in E flat, K. 171 (Composed in Vienna, August, 1773)

The first movement opens with a grave Adagio of fourteen bars, and closes in a similar vein. The main body is also serious —an exercise in fugato. The Andante opens in C minor, forte but muted. It is a contrapuntally worked movement on a curious chromatic theme which gives a special character to the whole— a foretaste of the fugued *Pignus* in the last sacramental litany (K. 243).

String Quartet No. 12, in B flat, K. 172 (Composed in Vienna, September, 1773)

The opening movement falls back into the old accompaniment pattern, but the Adagio finds, and overpersists in a new accompaniment pattern, with little development. Again it is a forte movement, with a melody Haydn might have written. The Minuet has a trio of old-time charm. The finale again reverts to monodic ways, with a forte theme recalling the early "Divertimento," K. 136. The development however is brought contrapuntally up-to-date.

String Quartet No. 13, in D minor, K. 173 (Composed in Vienna, September, 1773)

This and the Quartet in F (K. 168) are perhaps the gems of the six. Each cultivates the old grace—with a difference, each is not afraid to be simple—and each ends with a fugue. Perhaps the composer is eager to prove himself as "modern" as Haydn after three movements in an earlier style. Perhaps each fugue is a sort of declaration of independence. The outside movements in this last quartet are the D minor movements. They have the strong assertion and the concentration of chromaticism. The two middle movements, an Andantino grazioso in D major and a Minuet, are cheerful and unblushingly gallant.

String Quartet No. 14, in G, K. 387 (Composed in Vienna, December 31, 1782)

The first quartet of the six dedicated to Haydn shows Mozart in full command of the form. To single out any from this magnificent succession becomes entirely a matter of personal choice.

The G major Quartet opens with an eight-bar phrase, fluent, pregnant with possibilities for organic development, already bearing fruit before the dominant subject brings in as many more possibilities. The ever expanding and renewing imagination of the development, the resiliency in the chromatic handling, establishes at once the superiority of Haydn's young colleague, always capable of great melodies but now newly capable of malleable ones, always an instinctive formalist, but now the new master of period, suspense, dramatic point. The Minuet has no reminder of the ballroom other than the rhythmic signature and a few trilled accents. In the chromatic opening Mozart throws the beat as if to make it quite undanceable and to declare himself rhythmically nonconformist:

Minuetto - Allegro (violin I)

The Andante cantabile gathers in the course of its development an intensity that Haydn never quite reached. The expansive movement of the voices, the roving bass, the mysterious transition as the theme returns, the subtle harmonic coloring, the unison for power at the end—these qualities make a slow movement unprecedented in the quartets, the first of a great succession of slow movements. In using the fugato style for his finale, Mozart discards his former adherence to strict counterpoint. He fully realizes that contrapuntal texture and harmonic simplicity are most effective in alternation, each active as a foil to the other—the obvious solution in chamber finales, as it had been in his Masses.

String Quartet No. 15, in D minor, K. 421 (Composed in Vienna, June, 1783)

Mozart's only quartet in the minor among the last ten is not only outstanding—it is one of his most sharply arresting and ferociously earnest works. Each movement starts with a deceptive thematic simplicity, but the subsequent treatment is anything but orthodox. The Andante opens in F major—a typical vocal air with a simple cadence. The trio of the Minuet is made of short notes in the gallant style with plucked accompaniment. The Finale is a graceful, six-eight theme, quasi-allegretto. But the very naïveté is misleading.

Here as elsewhere, he seems to fall casually into a subject in his early manner, as if by habit, and at once to take hold of it with fresh and unprecedented imaginative vigor. He proceeds with a restless chromaticism, always tending to become urgent and tense. The first movement is a masterpiece of manipulation as he multiplies a trilled turn from the second bar and builds it into a dramatic structure. The final Allegro ma non troppo, in the form of variations, transforms the custom of decorative passages into a new and fresh vitality in every bar. It closes (as it opened) in D minor. The theme returns at the end, and by the simple process of developing a triplet figure becomes wildly challenging, tragic in the highest degree.

String Quartet No. 16, in E flat, K. 428 (Composed in Vienna, July, 1783)

In his opening theme, Mozart leaves his early custom of the simple tonic chord completely behind:

The intervals at once open possibilities for development, and indeed the long exposition lays out variety before the development proper begins. There is a new sense of power, of equilibrium, in the rhythmic stresses, the interweaving of parts, the formal whole. The Andante con moto is based on a melody with an undulant accompaniment (in six-eight) which is an inextricable part of it; with its shifting accidentals it becomes a sort of adult and arresting version of the basic and over-used Alberti bass. Chromaticism develops a yearning figure which is a startling premonition of the "desire" motive in *Tristan:*

The minuet has a second section of forty-two bars. As if to banish all dance associations, it starts emphatically on an offbeat. The Trio, traversing C minor and G minor, is plaintive in character. The Allegro vivace is a rondo on an abrupt theme, which germinates excitement, attains beauty and significance in development.

String Quartet No. 17, in B flat, K. 458 (Composed in Vienna, November, 1784)

The fourth quartet of the Haydn set has acquired the identification "The Hunt" on account of its opening theme, in a rollicking six-eight rhythm, and a fresh, fanfare-like theme which opens the development. If the themes are traditional in contour they are certainly individual in life and character. They are still more spirited in the development, which surrounds them with an innumerable sprinkling of a gay figure in sixteenth notes. The Minuet is more gallant than its immediate predecessors, but at least equal in appeal. The slow movement is a true Adagio, as "soul-searching" as Beethoven, as Romantic as the best of the Romantics. This was more than Mozart could have learned from Haydn, and such music could have given more to Beethoven than Haydn did. Any attempt to describe such music is an impertinence. The finale is an Allegro assai which gains its impetus by its close-packed wit—a fitting close for one of the most superb of the quartets, and deservedly one of the most loved.

String Quartet No. 18, in A, K. 464 (Composed in Vienna, January, 1785)

Mozart ventures further in this quartet in the manipulation of themes, sequential, modulatory, transitional. The Minuet (again a long one) is in the chamber style at its best. The Andante is a set of variations which at first are decorative, but soon become engrossed in new thoughts. The last variations are built on a figure in a delightful tattoo rhythm, with an inning for each instrument. The final Allegro is again a fully developed movement, neat, resourceful, rich in episodes.

String Quartet No. 19, in C ("Dissonant"), K. 465 (Composed in Vienna, January, 1785)

This quartet is the last of the set of six which Mozart dedicated to his "very celebrated and most dear friend," Joseph Haydn. It has been labeled the "Dissonant" Quartet on account of the introductory Adagio. The twenty-one bars seem today poignant but musically logical; when the quartet first appeared they caused no end of perplexity. Haydn, who was the only man while Mozart lived who had an adequate sense of his friend's true greatness, remarked serenely on this point: "Since Mozart wrote it this way, he must have had a good reason to do so." That reason may have been a conscious tribute to Haydn, a serious personal message at the head of a joyous movement. It may also have been a compliment to Haydn's fondness for slow introductions, particularly in his symphonies. (Mozart wrote such an introduction to his "Haffner," "Prague" and final E flat symphonies, but never elsewhere in his symphonies or later quartets.) This could also be a pledge of courage, of the personal freedom and independence the two composers could enjoy in their quartets.

After this introductory Adagio, and as a relief in complete contrast, Mozart gives us a smooth and elementary diatonic theme in C major, over the tonic assurance of repeated eighth notes. The theme is to dominate the movement in an abundance of guises, whereby simplicity becomes endlessly various and intriguing. The Andante cantabile, in F, fulfills the promise of its designation. A brief motto, at first bandied between the principal violin and the cello, suffuses the whole, makes a large part of its charm, and even persists through the last diminuendo of the coda—which is sheer magic. The rather brisk minuet has a fine swaying trio. The final Allegro is long and varied. It begins a light course, develops climaxes which are witty and incisive but never ponderous, traverses contrapuntal episodes, shows passages for the first violin. An appropriate climax for the six!

String Quartet No. 20, in D, K. 499 (Composed in Vienna, August 19, 1786)

Mozart wrote this quartet for the publisher Hoffmeister, and in a probable effort to please him, planned it on conventional lines. The movements open mildly enough, with "understandable" themes, but the composer's imagination gives them a subtler vitality. Even if the date of the quartet were not positively known, there would be no mistaking it for an earlier one. The quartet begins Allegretto, with a straightforward, diatonic theme, which, with those that follow, leads a circuitous course. The development begins with a staccato figure in the middle voices which accompanies to the very end many transmutations of the first

theme. The Minuet has a deceptive air of gallantry which conceals intricate inner working, and the Adagio, at first promising
an extended air, couched in fioriture, develops broadly into an
impassioned discourse as the lower voices add harmonic as well
as "horizontal" richness. The rapid concluding Allegro is by no
means for "beginners." It has incisiveness and thrust, develops
a passing resemblance to the scherzos of a later century as the
two-four signature is abandoned in a runaway six-eight.

String Quartet No. 21, in D, K. 575 (Composed in Vienna, June, 1789)

This quartet and the two to follow were composed with an
intended dedication to King William of Prussia. The King was a
cellist and had chamber music at court. With this in mind, Mozart gave the cello part special emphasis in the development of
the first movement, an important solo in the slow movement
which is concertante between the cello and violin, and another in
the Trio of the Minuet. Like its predecessor, the Quartet in D cultivates an outwardly elementary style but is treated with the
intricacy of the supreme craft of its year. The Minuet is a rapid
Allegretto of scherzo suggestion, and the final Allegretto (surprisingly in a similar tempo) is the most fanciful of all his
quartet movements. Haydn's occasional humorous touches, not
unmixed with counterpoint, are outdone with sudden runs in
triplets, choppy or trilled figures.

String Quartet No. 22, in B flat, K. 589 (Composed in Vienna, May, 1790)

The second of the quartets for the King of Prussia is even
simpler than the first in its opening. The theme, the bass in
repeated eighth notes, the light, descending short notes, all hark
back to the very early days. Mozart never quite abandoned the
musical tricks of his childhood. He ultimately used them more
sparingly and more subtly. The cello, not forgotten, introduces
the theme in the dominant, opens the Larghetto, and is most
prominent in that movement. If the Larghetto does not reach
the incandescence of certain slow movements in the "Haydn"
Quartets, it is superbly wrought, nevertheless. The Minuet, an
elaboration of gallantry, is conspicuous by its long and striking
Trio, with a curious staccato accompaniment. The Allegro assai
is built on an elementary theme in six-eight, a theme entertain-

ingly handled, decorated with rapid scales, taken through surprising keys, broken and juggled.

String Quartet No. 23, in F, K. 590 (Composed in Vienna, June,
1790)

Mozart's last quartet makes an exciting culmination to them
all in his most mature handling of the style. It begins deceptively
with a simple do-mi-sol and a descending scale, but he at once
proceeds to use the tonic triad to plant himself unequivocally in
a constant succession of keys. From the end of the second phrase
he derives this workable figure:

Only the composer of the great G minor Symphony could have
done such a piece of motto weaving in such a chromatically
clever movement. The cello part is simple, but pivotal and truly
regal. The remaining movements are simple as to themes, but
full of enlivening animation, even daring, in their development.
This is particularly true of the finale on a typical Mozartean
rondo subject. Through the thematic repetition which the form
requires there is inexhaustible freshness of invention and treatment. The composer ends his adventures in the string quartet at
the very top of his bent.

Three Divertimentos for String Quartet
    In D (No. 24), K. 136
    In B flat (No. 25), K. 137
    In F (No. 26), K. 138
    (Composed in Salzburg, January, 1772)

The full edition includes these three early works at the end of
the string quartets. It is doubtful whether the composer gave
them the title "Divertimento," for they are each in three movements (like his "Italian" quartets) instead of the usual minimum
of six, nor was he often asked for divertimentos in Italy. Only once
did he use the title for a piece for strings only—the string trio
of 1788 (K. 563), whose six movements have little in common
with the early divertimentos. These three are very close in character to the string quartets which followed them, in the same year.
Except that the part-writing implies a larger group than four,
they could be considered as among the string quartets for Italy.

Einstein has concluded that they were intended for symphonies on tour, perhaps at the house of Count Firmian in Milan, and could easily have been transformed into symphonies by the simple addition of oboes and horns as doubling instruments. Nevertheless, as string pieces they have their particular charm. The first, in D major, is a good sample of the alternate exuberance and tenderness of Wolfgang just turning sixteen. The remaining two give some justification of the title "divertimento" by the prominence of the first violin part, although it is not separated as "*principale*." The one in B flat has an Andante, followed by two Allegro movements. These, like the Allegro and the Presto of the third, are gay and festive in mood. The Presto, which ends the first and also the third, has a touch of counterpoint. The last was the kind of music which must have given the boy sheer fun in the writing.

The String Quintets

Mozart's string quintets as a pure and developed form, an amplification of the mature string quartets, are four in number. The one in C major was written in 1787; the last, in E flat, in April, 1791, after his last quartet. They can be considered from their character as having sprung from an entirely personal and individual impulse. There is no particular evidence of "influences" in them, either from Boccherini —who had the monopoly of the combination, leaving 125— from Michael Haydn, whose ventures were earlier and rudimentary, or from his illustrious brother who did not compose so many as one. Mozart's impulse is understandable. Having developed his quartets to a supreme point of rich four-part writing, the next challenge was to handle five voices with equal mastery. Mozart did not use a second cello, as Boccherini did, or as Schubert would later in his C major masterpiece, but preferred two violas. The opening of the first of the four reveals his purpose: an outstanding, melodic part by the cello as bass, a first violin part complementing it, duet fashion, and a substantial supporting body of tone in the three middle voices. The dark, almost nasal quality of the two violas gives a special, often somber color to the quintets in general. Sometimes the composer divides his group into antiphonal trios—two violins and first viola against the two violas and cello, the first viola thus serving in both. This kind of division was not possible in a quartet, where any breakdown resolves into individual voices. Here the first viola as leader of the lower group takes an important melodic function to balance the first violin. The second viola does not simply double the cello, but is more often an additional inner voice. Generally speaking, a single melodic voice, wherever it may be, is assured a balanced four-part harmony. The combined five voices can give a tonal amplitude approaching chamber orchestra sonority. That it is richer than a quartet sonority does not mean that it is preferable. A certain clarity, a structural transparency in the quartet, a sense of every individual voice, is sometimes sacrificed. It is a matter of choice between works of equal beauty at the ripest point of Mozart's chamber style. The quintets are far too infrequently performed in public for the obvious reason that a professional quartet group can far more easily choose from the wealth of the ten last quartets than go to the trouble of finding an extra violist who will play in their style, and with them adjust the difficult new balance.

The full edition lists nine string quintets, five of which for various reasons are not completely in the category. Mozart wrote his first in 1773, with a considerable doubling of parts, and in the style of a divertimento. The Quintet in C minor, K. 406, is simply an arrangement of the wind octet (K. 388). The Quintets K. 407 and K. 581 are for horn and clarinet respectively, with string quartet—a quartet plus. *Eine kleine Nachtmusik* is an unclassifiable string piece in four parts with an indication for doubling the bass.

String Quintet in B flat, K. 174 (Composed in Salzburg, 1773)

Mozart's first essay in the combination of five string instruments coincides with his quartets of 1773. It is simpler even than these in part-writing, for he is obviously providing music for an audience with other than chamber taste. The slow movement is an adagio in his best divertimento style, muted, courting sentiment, truly beautiful music in the earlier manner. If there is a real resemblance with the later quintets it is in the way he divides the melody between the first violin and the first viola in this movement. The Minuet and the final Allegro are square-cut and peasant-like rather than gallant.

String Quintet in C, K. 515 (Composed in Vienna, April, 1787)

The Allegro in the first of the great quintets begins with an ascending arpeggio by the cello, the first violin completing the phrase to repeated chords of restless eighth notes, a pattern of melodic top and bottom and accompaniment in between. The thematic triad invites constant and unequivocal modulation. It also gives way to many new thoughts in the dominant tonality. The Andante becomes a duo for first violin and first viola, with echoes, concertante fashion, exploiting the two instruments much in the fashion of the great *Sinfonia concertante*. The final rondo is built on a theme which would be sure to delight the untutored listener. The movement develops some fugato working and some amusing episodes. After a certain sobriety in the earlier movements it stands out as utterly gay.

String Quintet in G minor, K. 516 (Composed in Vienna, May, 1787)

The G minor Quintet is often compared with the great symphony in the same key which followed it a year later. There is certainly a similarity of mood and manner in the opening Allegro of each as the motto figure in the first bars, bearing the minor stamp, runs through the movement, closely and constantly woven into the texture, becoming incisive through chromaticism, the development becoming drama increasingly intense. The Minuet of the quintet maintains the minor mode (though major in the Trio) with broad and sudden chords on the third beat, as if this were music of defiance behind the external courtly style. With the Adagio the resemblance to the symphony ceases, for this is far more probing, more emotional than any other slow movement in all of Mozart's music. The movement opens and closes in E flat major, and is veiled by the use of mutes throughout, but its urgency is not diminished. Short broken notes with dramatic pauses, descending phrases which fall away from a sforzando note, tensions gathering and threatening to break, make this music an expression of grief as poignant (within the bounds of taste) as anything to be found among the Romantics. It is Mozart's "*Pathétique*," and who shall say that Tchaikovsky did not learn from it? Indeed, Tchaikovsky worshipped Mozart before all other composers. He wrote to Mme. von Meck: "In his chamber music Mozart charms me by his purity and distinction of style and his exquisite handling of the parts. Here too are things which can bring tears to our eyes. I will only mention the Adagio of the D minor [G minor] String Quintet. No one else has ever known as well how to interpret so exquisitely in music the sense of resigned and unconsolable sorrow."

After this Adagio, with its breathless pianissimo ending, the sudden breaking in of the final Allegro in G major, in six-eight, would be an unpardonable intrusion. Until this moment Mozart had had little concern with movement succession except with contrast as a principle. Now he prepares us for the change, as Beethoven would later. Another superb adagio, without mutes, is heavily tragic, as if sorrow were no longer personal, but were brought out into the open. The finale, despite its gay rhythm, has both thrust and challenge in its course.

String Quintet in D, K. 593 (Composed in Vienna, December, 1790)

As in the case of the Quintet in C major, this one opens portentously with the cello, the phrase smoothly finished by the first violin. Here we have a larghetto introduction, mysteriously quiet save for the deep rinforzando cello notes introducing unexpected keys. The main allegro is rather elegant in character until in development it gathers strength and complexity. Before the close there is a reminiscence of the introduction, a precedent for Beethoven surely, but with a greater contrast of mood. The Adagio is one of the longest and one of the most beautiful of Mozart's slow movements, chamber or otherwise. It is great by the manifold results of voice leading, by a trilled figure from the cello which becomes structural, by almost mystic divagations. The Minuet leans characteristically on the third beat of the measure and provides a featherweight trio. The Finale is made on a bright six-eight subject which through accidentals is constantly changed and put through contrapuntal and other paces. Never was a simple tune more variously turned about.

String Quintet in E flat, K. 614 (Composed in Vienna, April, 1791)

If this is Mozart's farewell to his chamber music for strings, it is a light-hearted one. The opening theme has a trilled figure which as a prodigiously multiplied fragment makes a trilled movement, but a wonderfully various one. The Andante is in free variation form, recalling the air of Belmonte, *"Wenn der Freude Tränen fliessen"* from *Die Entführung*. The theme of the final Allegro in other hands could be a pleasant commonplace. Under Mozart's alert imagination and incredible skill it becomes an exciting play of tonal wit.

The Piano Sonatas

U NLIKE THE PIANO concertos, the solo sonatas do not give a picture of Mozart's gradual development as an expressive artist. Sixteen complete ones have survived, and all but the last three fall into two periods—the first five were composed in Salzburg in 1774, at the end of which year Mozart, aged eighteen, went to Munich to produce *La finta giardiniera* (and there wrote a sixth). At that time he had hardly begun his succession of piano concertos, but he had composed thirty symphonies and thirteen string quartets. On his journey to Mannheim and Paris in 1778, he composed two sonatas for Mannheim and five for Paris. They are as subtly contrived as the other music of that fruitful year of musical awakening, and can be justly compared with that milestone of pianistic advance, the "Jeunehomme" Piano Concerto in E flat (K. 271), of the year previous. The great Fantasia in C minor and the sonata with which it is linked are the magnificent product of the later Viennese Mozart of 1784, the Mozart of the finest piano concertos and the quartets for Haydn. At that time there seems to have been little demand for new sonatas. Two more, the "Sonatina" in C and the final one in D revert to an earlier, more elementary style, and were obviously intended for pupils. For other piano music of an earlier date, we must look to the Sonatas for Piano with Violin. They are thirty-five in number and have a much fuller time spread. They were a popular household as well as a concert combination, and were more sought by publishers. They extend from the first engraved music of the eight-year-old boy until 1788. This does not mean that Mozart in the earliest years was without solo sonatas of his own to perform at any moment. He was never far from the instrument which from his babyhood was a part of himself, a means of expression as natural as his first words. He improvised constantly, in private and in public—variations, dances, allegros, slow aria-like pieces. Apparently his father saw no necessity for putting these on paper. When at length Wolfgang saw fit to do so, he was an easy and accomplished master of the sonata. He had only to formalize his improvisations with the proper thematic recurrence and the proportion of considered notation. When he did write them out, it was for home performance rather than publication. He sent manuscript copies from Mannheim and Paris to his sister, who was always eager for them.

The music for piano solo was the most direct, the most sensitive of all to his tonal thoughts. The keyboard was his closest confidant. It responded as instantaneously to his fingertips as his fingers responded to the animation of his tonal moods. There was no barrier whatever between thought and deed, there were no clumsy performers, rehearsals, copyists, audience ceremony, money-minded publishers. The sonatas are an immediate, a personal emanation. Their style is the utter simplicity of melody lightly supported. Mozart uses the elementary Alberti bass with intent, and only under an extended melodic phrase; it is no more than a shadow in a murmuring pianissimo—an ideal setting for the jewel of melody. He cultivates the middle register, and only the lighter dynamics. He saves his bravura, his more intricate texture for elsewhere. He conveys songlike slow movements which at their best are more affecting, give a more sustained sense of melodic line than his contemporary symphonic or concerto slow movements. The finales never drive home their point with force, but with light and sometimes swift dexterity. They can take fanciful turns in transition, modulation, dissonance, accent, but the texture never thickens. Mozartean simplicity here most clearly proves its worth. Mozart remarked that his sonatas were easier than the concertos. Pianists know to their dismay that they are in fact more difficult. Players are unable to take cover under brilliant passage work, for anything short of utter delicacy of control, sensitivity to phrasing, is mercilessly exposed.

Mozart wrote for the piano and not the harpsichord. His pianos were limited in resonance, dull and dry by modern standards, but they were the best of his time. It is certainly a mistake to deaden the modern instrument while playing his music, for Mozart was plainly eager for any improvement, and would certainly have welcomed a warmer coloration, a better sustaining pedal, if he could have had those aids to melodic expression.

Whether he would have welcomed the greater range and power of tone in the instruments which came to Beethoven, is another matter. In a letter to his father, in 1882, after his pianistic encounter with Clementi, he pronounced Clementi "too mechanical," and "lacking in taste and feeling." Clementi's way pointed to the grandeur of the generation to follow, the style which would obliterate the Mozartean esthetic in the sonatas. Only the C minor Fantasia of three years later challenges this esthetic and indicates a search toward dramatic forcefulness.

Piano Sonata in C, K. 279
Piano Sonata in F, K. 280
Piano Sonata in B flat, K. 281
Piano Sonata in E flat, K. 282
Piano Sonata in G, K. 283
Piano Sonata in D, K. 284

The first five piano sonatas, composed in Salzburg in 1774, are the full pattern of the form, not to be altered later, but on occasion deepened and subtilized. There would be no transformation, no expansion, for Mozart instinctively kept their simplicity of style as a personal communication.

The five are as various as their key signatures. The first of them could well have originated as an improvisation, in the Allegro and Andante especially, where a basic succession of harmonies engenders melody as if on the instant under the agile fingers of the player. The second, in F, has a more constructive plan. The three opening chords become a motto in conscious development. The Adagio, a tempo which Mozart here used with a particular significance, for he believed in flowing animation on the keyboard, is the outstanding movement. It begins in F minor, the theme repeated upon itself, duet-wise, growing into a song of increasing fervor. This quality particularly applies to the whole Sonata, with the full melodic phrases of its two principal themes, the extended phrasing of its adagio, which attains its legato through veritable festoons of sixteenths and thirty-second notes, the finale which sings through its right-hand passage work. The Sonata in B flat seems to embrace simplicity of style, as if its composer were wary of elaboration, determined never to force or cloud the light interplay of his two hands. Within that moderate range there is increasing chromatic subtlety, a fresh figuration, a free use of the left hand.

This sonata depends more than the first two on scale passages and grace notes to connect and accentuate the melodic part. In the slow movement particularly they become a means of intensified expressiveness which may well have given a hint to Beethoven and found later echoes in such Romantics as Chopin. Mozart labeled the slow movement "Andante amoroso," an unusual but appropriate title, which would have been even more appropriate for the slow movements of the two to follow, for in each case we have a truly romantic love song, a mood piece with its captivating spell. The Adagio of the E flat Sonata, in particular, is music with an unmistakable message of veiled melancholy, a nostalgia. This sonata shares the unusual movement order of the "Alla Turca" Sonata for Paris, a slow movement, minuet, and finale. Yet no two among them all could be more different—this one is not, like the other, a frank bid for applause. The Adagio which opens the E flat Sonata (it is not an introduction) is far more deeply felt, the minuets (a second minuet in place of a trio) more delicate and legato, the final allegro light and whimsical save for a stormy episode in D minor. The last sonata of the Salzburg series also has a whimsical finale, a presto which departs delightfully from the beaten track with such surprises as unexpected forte punctuations.

Mozart wrote a sixth sonata in the following spring for the

Count Dürnitz, in Munich. Since this amateur was slow in payment, we can forgive Mozart for giving rather less of his time and heart for this score than usual, for much of it is more formal than warm. The slow movement is a *Rondeau en Polonaise,* the finale a theme with twelve variations.

Piano Sonata in C, K. 309
Piano Sonata in D, K. 311

These two sonatas were a result of Mozart's visit to Mannheim, and were composed in 1777 and 1778. Being particularly anxious to show his skill, he opened each with an Allegro con spirito. The remaining movements are more outstanding. The final Rondo of the first is an Allegretto grazioso, of the second an Allegro of greater length and ambition. Both are light and fanciful. The second introduces the last return of the rondo theme with a slow quasi-cadenza. The slow movements of each are particularly beautiful. Mozart wrote home that the Sonata in C was a great favorite in the household of the Cannabichs, the family who became his greatest friends in Mannheim. Mozart took the youngest daughter, Rosa, aged thirteen, in hand as his pupil and taught her to play it. (He had already played "all six" of his previous sonatas for that musically avid family.) The Andante of the new sonata he composed with Rosa in mind, and wrote that it was "exactly like her." The music would indicate that she was warm-natured, affectionate, and given to sudden capricious impulses. The fact that she played the whole sonata as a farewell to her teacher and almost moved him to tears would also indicate that the youngest member of the family was well imbued with its musical tradition. The Andante of the Sonata in D is at least as "amoroso" as the Andante of K. 281, for it is one of the most ardent slow movements of them all. When Mozart indicated "Andante con espressione" he meant this as his immediate intention but not his only style, as would have been more or less the case in the later century of all-pervasive "expression."

Piano Sonata in A minor, K. 310
Piano Sonata in C, K. 330
Piano Sonata in A ("Alla Turca"), K. 331
Piano Sonata in F, K. 332
Piano Sonata in B flat, K. 333

When Mozart wrote these five sonatas in Paris, in 1778, he may not have had a public performance in mind (there is no record of such an opportunity) nor any immediate prospect of publication. He may have played one or two of them in a private house in his search for pupils. A more likely inducement was an occasional musical gathering of his Mannheim friends in Paris. His father's letters reproach him for "wasting" his time in this way, when he should have been earning. This would account for the quiet, unostentatious, musically probing character of these five—with the exception of one, the Sonata in A major. This one is an applause catcher, as plainly designed for a general audience as some of his party music. Its three movements—variations, minuet and rondo "*alla Turca*"—do not admit of any sonata-form development. As usual when Mozart becomes deliberately "popular," he is quite irresistible. He can give popular tunes, such as the varied theme and the Turkish march, appeal to last through many generations. The other four sonatas are musically subtler and richer in content. The first of them (also his first sonata in the minor) is stormy in its opening Allegro, with dissonant chords and a dramatic bass. The Andante cantabile opens in F major, but shades into minor, and in its middle section becomes dramatic, as nearly convulsive as could be expected of Mozart at his keyboard. The Presto is the most adroit to date in light and shade, major and minor alternation, gossamer texture.

The Sonata in C, which follows, has a relieving, unruffled surface of gaiety, save in the slow movement (another "Andante cantabile"), a sustained and affecting song, with a second strain in F minor. The Allegretto finale has the quality to be found increasingly in these and all of the later works—the shaping of every element: scales, arpeggios, grace notes, into a continuous melodic current.

Fantasia for Piano, in C minor, K. 475
Piano Sonata in C minor, K. 457
  (The sonata was composed in October, 1784,
    the Fantasia in May, 1785)

The Sonata in C minor and the introductory Fantasy with which Mozart himself coupled it stand apart from all his piano works, indeed from all his instrumental works. The two, which must be considered as one, for they are at one in character, have no trace of the gaiety of style which was Mozart's heritage and his custom through his life. The Fantasia is not only music of greater range than before, with its sometimes thunderous bass —it is music of direct challenge, of somber earnestness, of restlessness and questioning. No other music of Mozart so unmistakably points the way to Beethoven, and no other so plainly proves that had he lived only a few years longer, he could have become a very different composer indeed, even an artistic companion of Beethoven. The Fantasy has been described as an "improvisation," and it is true that like most works of that character it is exploratory, unconfined by formal procedure. The word nevertheless would be completely misleading. This is not the music which would come to the pianist on the instant, seated at his keyboard, allowing his tonal images to drift through his fingers. This Fantasy, unlike the others he composed, is heavily charged, explosive, compact with accumulated emotion. It should be remembered that he wrote the Fantasy several months after the sonata it introduces. Like Beethoven he seems to have pondered an earlier musical thought until its concept gained in intensity and force and overrode all precedent.

The Fantasy opens with an Adagio which is to modulate constantly:

The heavy octave unison, the ominous, whispering notes that follow, and the quizzical, broken chord resolutions give the character of the whole work and the sonata to come—mysterious, indeterminate searching, sudden forte interruptions. There is a section in a serene D major, broken by a stormy allegro, another calm melody, in F major, and a lyrical Andantino, but each of these gathers urgency and is lost in the restless, tempestuous mood.

The sonata opens with a phrase similar in character to the opening of the Fantasy and proceeds similarly. That it is less concentrated, less dramatic, may be because it was composed earlier. The middle movement is an extended Adagio in a tranquil E flat, disturbed occasionally by sudden forte chords. The Allegro assai is an oppressive return to C minor. It gains force in speed, but no release from the heavy mood of the whole. Even the subsidiary theme, in E flat, is troubled and plaintive.

Piano Sonata ("Sonatina") in C, K. 545
Piano Sonata in F, K. 547a (K.54)
Piano Sonata in D, K. 576

Mozart composed two of these sonatas in June, 1788; the last in July, 1789. They cannot be associated with those ripe years except as a throwback to an earlier style. They were designed for less expert hands. The Sonata in D was the only one composed of an intended six for the Princess Friedericke of Prussia. It can be said of all three, but especially of the third, that the superlative Mozart of those late years has been careful to indicate in their simpler lines the utmost expressive subtlety in inflection, in grace or dotted notes. When Mozart marked the last two for "beginners," for *"Anfänger,"* he must have known that violation would result. The second movement of the Sonata in F (a score with many corrections) is a set of variations on the rondo theme of the Sonata in C. The Sonata in B flat, K. 570, is also of 1789.

The Variations for Piano Solo

SINCE VARIATIONS were the favorite form for improvisation, Mozart must have composed a far larger number than were written down or published. The form is constricted by the necessity of repeating and embellishing rather than developing the theme, which being borrowed is usually below Mozart's level. In the later ones, the theme itself is heightened by transforming touches as well as by the expressiveness of its embellishment. The variation pattern is the most invariable of any in Mozart's music. The final plan is adherence to the theme until the slow variation in the tonic minor, later an adagio extended by ornate scale passages, followed by a final allegro variation with an altered rhythmic signature, and at last a literal repetition of the original theme.

8 Variations on a Dutch song, in G, K. 24 (Composed in The Hague, 1766)
7 Variations on "Willem van Nassau," in D, K. 25 (Composed in Amsterdam, February, 1766)

Of these two sets of variations composed in Holland, the first on "*Laat ons juichen*" was published as a specimen of what the nine-year-old composer could do. It was composed for the ceremony of the installation of Willem V, Prince of Orange. It is sparsely notated, on the principle of gradually increasing elaboration and a corresponding shortening of note values. Each hand is given for the most part a simple line, with a result clear, poised, and in excellent taste. The variations on the popular national song, "*Willem van Nassau*," have more display passages.

6 Variations on Salieri's "Mio caro Adone," in G, K. 180 (Composed in Vienna, autumn, 1773)
12 Variations on a Minuet by Fischer, in C, K. 179 (Composed in Salzburg, 1774)

The passage of years and the experience of Vienna have produced a more advanced style. The Variations on a Minuet by Johann Christian Fischer (an oboist of London) are music for the display of skill, with equal interchange and crossing of hands, double octave passages or staccato brilliance. In both sets the theme, in minuet tempo, becomes a point of departure rather than a subject for mere decorated repetition. In each there is an extended, improvisatory adagio before the end, a custom Mozart would continue to cultivate. The theme is transformed in development; Salieri's minuet (taken from his opera *La fiera di Venezia,* which Mozart may have heard in Vienna) becomes at last an allegretto in two-four beat.

9 Variations on Dezède's "Lison dormait," in C, K. 264 (Composed in Paris, 1778)

Four sets of variations are a result of Mozart's sojourn in Paris, in 1778. All are on airs presumably popular in France at the time. Nicolas Dezède, whose operas were then much sought at the Comédie-Italienne, may have been the composer of "*Je suis Lindor*," in Beaumarchais' play with music, *Le barbier de Séville.* His "*Lison dormait*," was from *Julie.* He may also have been the author of the nursery song "*Ah, vous dirai-je, maman,*" which with its "do-mi-sol" simplicity has so often since been found useful for variation building.

The *"Lison dormait"* variations are frankly a display piece, with daring and adventure in its course. The second part of the theme has a rising scale to a fermata on G major, which results in a heavy pause wherever it is to recur. The Adagio is long and elaborate, with runs, trills and grace notes. It gives way to a final variation in triple beat, a cadenza and a bare return to the original theme to close.

12 Variations on "Ah, vous dirai-je, maman," in C, K. 265
(Composed in Paris, 1778)

"Ah, vous dirai-je, maman" proceeds with droll touches of naïveté, takes on a subtle inflection in the fifth variation, becomes adult in the eighth (in the minor), gives way to a cadenza-like adagio, and is quite lost in a conclusion in three-eight time.

12 Variations on "La belle Françoise," in E flat, K. 353 (Composed in Paris, summer, 1778)

"La belle Françoise" is a particularly lovable set of variations. It seems to suggest a French coquette. It begins with a demure and entirely engaging theme in six-eight, mezza voce, but the first variation and the second are suddenly pert. The fourth is gentle again, the fifth and sixth are in a dreamy legato; the seventh is capricious, forte and piano, but there follows romance, moving into the minor. A short adagio, courting sentiment, is suddenly brushed away by a vivacious presto in two-four. A final repetition of the original mezza voce theme, with a "calando" cadence, seems to establish a tender stability in "Françoise" after all.

"La belle Françoise" has been traced by Saint-Foix to an air by a Mme. Kamermann, depicting the farewell of the Duke of Marlborough to his French lady.

12 Variations on "Je suis Lindor" (Beaumarchais' Le barbier de Séville, composer unknown), in E flat, K. 354 (Composed in Paris, 1778)

"Je suis Lindor" is the most brilliant of the sets of variations for Paris and not without substance. It is the most elaborate in trilled or octave passages, and other suggestions of concerto

bravura. There is musical interest in the seventh variation of broad chords and scales ("maestoso"), the variation in the minor, the contrasting major return, the broad "molto adagio," the final transformation into minuet tempo, and the closing cadenza, with the direction "caprice."

8 Variations on Grétry's March ("Les Mariages samnites"), in F, K. 352 (Composed in Vienna, June, 1781)

The march theme is light-footed, with grace notes, whereby the character of the whole work is set at once. The theme and the style of its variations suggest the variation movement of the Sonata "*alla Turca*" of three years before, but these variations are more subtly worked, more resourceful, and in the minor and the adagio variations, more emotional.

6 Variations on Paisiello's "Salve tu, Domine," in F, K. 398 (Composed in Vienna, March, 1783)

The basic sectionalism and thematic rigidity of the form is much modified in this set of variations. Mozart develops fragments of the theme, sonata fashion. From the fourth variation, in the minor, the music takes on the character of improvisation, with cadenza-like bridge passages, extended trills (Variation 5), finally a ranging cadenza and a whimsical close. Effective piano-figurations by the then industrious composer of concertos give great impetus to the third and sixth.

10 Variations on Gluck's "Unser dummer Pöbel meint," in G, K. 455 (Composed in Vienna, August, 1784)

Gluck's light opera, *Die Pilgrimme von Mecca*, a German version of *Le Rencontre imprévu*, was put on in Vienna shortly before *Die Entführung*, an attempt at a *Singspiel* on an oriental subject which was far less successful, needless to say, than Mozart's. According to the text, a monk is amused at the thought that the stupid public are giving him credit for leading an abstemious life. The theme, in common time, has a thumping *buffo* suggestion, which Mozart emphasizes by carrying it into the bass and otherwise making fun of it. The second variation brings in the semblance of a bass drum, Turkish fashion. Interspersed are sections with serious musical development.

8 Variations on Sarti's "Come un agnello," in A, K. 460 (Composed in Vienna, June, 1784)

Mozart complimented Sarti by making variations on this theme from *Fra due litiganti,* then successful at the Vienna opera, and by introducing it into the supper scene of *Don Giovanni.* The tune, which is anything but striking, had more attention than it deserved, but Mozart had the magic touch. He treats it caressingly, in legato fashion at first, but works up excitement with bravura. The minor is briefly introduced within the adagio.

12 Variations on an Allegretto Theme, in B flat, K. 500 (Composed in Vienna, September, 1786)

The custom of improvising variations on a favorite tune by a fellow composer was doubly useful because it complimented the composer, who might be present, and gave the audience a comforting sense of familiarity. In following this custom, Mozart was careful to choose an air of elementary simplicity, because being diatonic and in regular beat made it a prime skeleton for tonal adornment. There was the disadvantage that if the tune was really insipid, it would tend to pall on the hearer, however subtly treated (K. 455 and 460 are cases in point). For once, as seems probable, Mozart contrived his own theme, an allegretto with trilled phrases, giving it interest and character even before it was developed. It was then his task to subtilize further with trills, broken rhythms, chromatic treatment. The variations are short and to the point, modest in range, refreshing in the absence of any extended decoration.

9 Variations on a Minuet by Duport, in D, K. 573 (Composed in Potsdam, April, 1789)

The little waltz-like tune is what Beethoven, as when referring to Diabelli's, would have called a "cobbler's patch." Mozart, who had no great respect for Kaiser Friedrich's right-hand man, probably wrote the variations as a polite compliment, and merely decorated the tune in his own inimitable way, without attempting to make much of it, in the Adagio and final Allegro leaving it pretty well behind.

6 Variations on Schack's Song, "Ein Weib ist das herrlichste Ding," in F, K. 613 (Composed in Vienna, March, 1791)

As with the "Duport" Variations, Mozart keeps the theme more to the fore than its quality can stand. The theme consists of an introductory eight bars before the regular two phrases, the second pausing on the dominant before the return of the first. He treats the "introduction" differently and separately and then forgets it until the very end. When in the last two variations he takes his own course, the whole acquires a new stature. The theme came from the opera *Der dumme Gärtner* by Benedikt Schack and Franz Gerl, which had been produced by Schikaneder in Vienna two years before.

The Fantasias for Piano Solo

Fantasia and Fugue, in C, K. 394 (Composed in Vienna, April, 1782)

Fantasia in D minor, K. 397 (Composed in Vienna, 1782)

Fantasia in C minor, K. 475 (Composed in Vienna, May, 1785)

Fantasias and variations, the popular forms for improvisation both before and after Mozart, were expected of him at every concert—the few fantasias that are extant in print must be a negligible number as compared to those that were played before an audience and promptly forgotten. The first of the fantasies that have survived opens with an adagio, as if the composer's hands were wandering over the keyboard in arpeggios and scales, dwelling on a chord, a figure, never quite crystallizing a melody. He introduces a fugue, another of his improvisational forms. In the fantasia that follows he opens in the minor, his mode for meditation and exploration. The Fantasia in D minor finds melodies and variety in its brief duration, the changes introduced by free cadenzas. Thus a somber adagio theme and another in anguished staccato notes give way to a brighter allegretto in the tonic major. The great C minor Fantasia of 1785 is a more powerful emergence on a similar plan with a more extended treatment. It thunders and storms in its course, has bass notes to tax any Mozart piano, has lighter moments, but ends as inexorably as it began. While listening, one knows where Beethoven's pianistic imagination was first fired. This Fantasia is discussed in connection with the C minor Piano Sonata (K. 457) with which it belongs. The Fantasia in C minor, K. 396, is an arrangement for piano solo by Abt Stadler of a fragmentary sonata movement for piano and violin.

Various Works for Piano Solo

Minuets

K. 1, in G, 1761 or 1762; K. 2, in F, K. 4, in F, K. 5, in F, 1762; K. 94, in D, 1770; K. 315a, 8 minuets, 1779; K. 355, in D, 1790

Rondos

K. 485, in D, 1786; K. 494, in F, 1786; K. 511, in A minor, 1787

Allegros

K. 3, in B flat, 1762; K. 9a, in C, 1763; K. 312, in G minor, 1774; K. 400, in B flat, 1781; K. 533 (Allegro and Andante) in F, 1788

Andante, in B flat, K. 9b, 1763
Andantino, in E flat, K. 236, 1790
Capriccio, in C, K. 395, 1778
Adagio, in B minor, K. 540, 1788
Gigue ("Eine kleine Gigue"), in G minor, K. 574, 1789
Suite for Piano, in C (Overture, Allegro, Allemande, Courante), K. 399, 1782
Fugue, in G Minor, K. 401, 1782

A miscellany of small piano pieces, most of them probably intended as parts of sonatas, have survived in publication. They extend from Wolfgang's first piece, the minuet he composed at six (or perhaps not quite six), to *"Eine kleine Gigue"* of the year 1789, the last a striking example of the simplest form treated with the utmost maturity. These are not lesser odds and ends— nothing could be further from the truth. Some of them might rather be looked upon as vivid entities which did not fit in any sonata succession, but seemed to belong apart. One such is the Rondo in A minor (K. 511), a study in gentle pathos which in its quiet gravity would not do at all to end a sonata, or the Adagio in B minor (K. 540), with its solemn chords, softly resolved, its phrases in falling half tones. Although it ends with an unexpected, magic brightening into the major, it might have been too much for salon sensibilities. The Allegro in G minor (K. 312) is not disturbing in spite of an ominous opening. It could have stood confidently at the head of any sonata at that earlier time. The Gigue in G minor (K. 574) and the Minuet in D (K. 355) are brief adventures into dissonant intervals, the Gigue a study in equivocal rhythm. Mozart wrote it in the album of Herr Engel, the organist at Leipzig. It opens in three voices, as a tribute to the contrapuntal Bach.

The Works for Piano (or Two Pianos), Four Hands

THE NUMBER of piano duets that appeared in early publication indicates that although cultivated in some homes they were far less popular than pieces for piano solo, also that sonatas for players on two pianos were as good as unwanted. If parlors contained two instruments and two players, those players would have been more comfortable side by side where each could watch the other's hands. Mozart could no doubt handle a two-keyboard piece beautifully with his evidently able pupil, Josephine Aurnhammer. He would have preferred to compose some of his duets for two pianos instead of one if his publisher had given him any encouragement. The difference in possibilities between the two forms is immense. At a single keyboard each player has to side-step the other, keep within his own territory, unless the hands are crossed. With two instruments the players are at an absolute equality. They can be made to double, interchange, weave their parts in a close texture. Greater brilliance, greater variety are possible.

Only one sonata for two pianos has survived. The four-part Fugue in C minor, probably written for home performance and home study of the form, naturally requires two keyboards, where again the texture is close, the voices intermingled.

(A sonata for four hands, in C (K. 19d), is believed to have been composed in London, in 1765, and so would have been Mozart's first venture in this form. The autograph is lost. A four-hand sonata in B flat, K. 358, exists in the handwriting of Marianne and may have been a copy of her brother's score. It was composed in Salzburg in the spring of 1774.)

Piano Sonata for Four Hands, in G, K. 357 (Composed in Vienna, in 1786) (Fragmentary)

This sonata consists of an Allegro and an Andante (a quasi-allegretto), both movements unfinished. The movements are thematically charming, the Allegro having unusual skips which would go with its late date, as the otherwise elementary procedure would not. The Andante, a light staccato movement, is a regular turnabout between the two players until the bass is relegated to perpetual arpeggios.

Piano Sonata for Four Hands, in D, K. 381 (Composed in Salzburg?, early 1772)

Piano Sonata for Four Hands, in B flat, K. 358 (Composed in Salzburg, May, 1774)

These two sonatas were composed for home performance by Mozart and his sister. He could surely have made them more taxing to skill if he had felt inclined. Both are what could have been called "for beginners." The finale of K. 358 is labeled "Molto presto," a movement for effect through speed, but the composer is careful to make his short notes lie under the hand, and to avoid difficult scale passages altogether. The final Allegro molto of the K. 381 is also within easy reach.

Piano Sonata for Four Hands, in F, K. 497 (Composed in Vienna, August, 1786)

This sonata and the one that follows are among Mozart's finest works. The fact that he was writing for a makeshift home and not a professional concert combination did not in the least deter him from pouring his utmost into sonatas which stand with the solo sonatas of the same years and even surpass them. They have the same sort of simplicity which sets off distinction and delicacy of treatment. There is an Adagio introduction to the Sonata in F, not grave as in his usual introductions, but full of gentle fervor. The following swift Allegro is a contrast more in tempo than mood, for the movement is one of meltingly beautiful amiability. The Andante in its development draws the two parts into a duo which is not echoing or imitating but mating as with a double strand. The final rondo, in six-eight, has the special allure of a simple melody withdrawn from all commonplace by the imaginative use of accidentals, the play of light humor. Before such music the verbal rhapsodist subsides into shamed silence.

Piano Sonata for Four Hands, in C, K. 521 (Composed in Vienna, May, 1787)

The last among the duet sonatas is a particular gem—a gem indeed among the sonatas *in toto*. The melodic discourse of the first movement, delicate and fanciful, is smoothly couched in scale passages. The Andante theme quite captivates even in its first statement and before it is varied. It attains strength and breadth in elaboration, as the theme moves sturdily into the bass and a fragment of it is worked into the treble as a manifold motto. The Allegretto turns up a perfect example of a Mozartean rondo theme combining immediate appeal with distinctive subdivision in its working. Episodic development uncovers perpetually new vitality, becomes stormy, and ends with the headlong festive mood of an *opera buffa* finale.

Andante with Five Variations, for Piano, Four Hands, in G, K. 501 (Composed in Vienna, November, 1786)

Except in certain details, such as the variation in the minor, this work could have had an earlier date. It follows the custom of increasing elaboration in passage work.

Sonata for Two Pianos, in D, K. 448 (Composed in Vienna, November, 1781)

Listening to the Sonata for Two Pianos causes keen regret that Mozart did not write more, or that more did not survive in publication, for to compare this to the piano duet sonatas is to be struck by the freedom, the expressive resource which the two keyboards give. When he wrote this two-piano work in 1781 for performance with Josephine von Aurnhammer, he exacted much from her and put her strictly on a level with himself. The sonata is gay throughout—there is not even a momentary cloud on the surface of the Andante. The Allegro con spirito opens rhythmically and smartly with a full unison, whereby double power is attained. It is a movement of scales similarly reinforced, or delightfully echoed in the same range, of a close or spread texture, as the composer wills. The final Allegro molto is swift, for show, and for delight.

Fugue for Two Pianos, in C minor, K. 426 (Composed in Vienna, December, 1783)

This fugue was very likely intended for the sessions of the Baron van Swieten in pursuit of Bach. Mozart had used fugal treatment in many of his works, particularly his Masses, and improvised fugues often on the piano or organ, but not until recently had he written out a strict fugue as such. Later (in 1788) he rescored it for string quartet or string orchestra, with an introduction (K. 546).

The Sonatas for Piano and Violin

THE FIRST music by the small Mozart to be given to the engraver by his father was a set of three "Sonatas for clavier which may be played with violin accompaniment." They were dedicated to three ladies of the royal family at Versailles, in 1764. There, as in many polite houses, the keyboard was cultivated, and up to a certain point, the more difficult violin. A sonata which could be performed with or without a second player was therefore most in demand. Consequently, sonatas evenly matched, in which the singing instrument would have its just and obvious privilege, were yet to be developed. In the earlier day of Sebastian Bach it had been different. The violin had been the dominating, the harpsichord largely a supporting, continuo instrument. Johann Christian Bach in London followed a newer custom when he wrote sonatas for harpsichord or piano with an added and entirely dispensable violin part, which he treated on a doubling or filling-in basis. Christian Bach was the model of the boy Mozart in this form as well as in piano concertos and symphonies. Wolfgang composed for publication no less than sixteen sonatas of this sort during his long tour with his family from his eighth to his tenth year. They antedate all of his published music with a few fragmentary exceptions, and are mostly of historical interest as childhood exercises. They would have little reward for a violinist today.*

It was in Mannheim, twelve years later, that Mozart, an artist accomplished in each department of chamber music, again became interested in sonatas for this combination. He

---

* Sonatas (1762-1766) in C, K. 6; D, K. 7; B flat, K. 8; G, K. 9; B flat, K. 10; G, K. 11; A, K. 12; F, K. 13; C, K. 14; B flat, K. 15 (K. 10-15 were published as trios, having also a cello part); E flat, K. 26; G, K. 27; C, K. 28; D, K. 29; F, K. 30; B flat, K. 31.

wrote to his father from Munich on his way to Mannheim, on October 6, 1777, that he had found and "often played" a set of "six duets for clavicembelo and violin by Schuster. . . . I shall write six myself in the same style."

This would not mean that Mozart, who knew a thing or two about both instruments and had by that time written five concertos for each, had never thought of combining them as chamber music to their mutual advantage. It means rather that such a combination had been proven by this enterprising gentleman by the name of Schuster to be marketable ("Popular" was Mozart's word). In any case Mozart took immediate advantage of the opportunity and wrote seven violin sonatas on his Mannheim journey, five more in the summer of 1781, his first year in Vienna, where he evidently found a call for them. Artaria promptly published the first three Vienna sonatas (K. 376, 377, 378), together with K. 296 of the Mannheim series. Mozart sent these to Salzburg, where Marianne and her father would have eagerly received and enjoyed playing them (the Sonata in B flat, K. 378, was actually begun in Salzburg). Three more, composed in Vienna in the ensuing years (K. 454, in B flat, in 1784; K. 481, in E flat, in 1785; and K. 526, in A major, in 1787) became duo sonatas in the fullest sense, and reflected his ripest abilities. One more sonata, in F, K. 547, composed in 1788, was for amateur uses, and has an expendable violin part. To these thirty-two should be added two sets of variations and three sonatas which were not completed.*

Sonata for Piano and Violin, in C, K. 296

This, the first of the sonatas of Mannheim, Mozart wrote for his pupil, Theresa Pierron Serrarius. Theresa was no great pianist, but her teacher was obliging, and had reason to be. He was received as lodger and boarder, together with his mother, when their funds were at rock bottom. In return, he taught Theresa, allowed her to play in two of his concertos at a grand musical evening, and composed for her this violin sonata. He never wrote one more gay than this, more dressed

---

* Six more (K. 55-60) have been found doubtful or spurious. K. 61 is by Raupach.

up in the first movement with frills in the way of grace notes. The Andante is a song of dreamy sentiment which would have charmed a romantic Fräulein of fifteen. He actually owed the melody to Johann Christian Bach. The Rondo is full of high spirits, and would have been a success at any party.

Sonata for Piano and Violin, in G, K. 301
Sonata for Piano and Violin, in E flat, K. 302
Sonata for Piano and Violin, in C, K. 303
Sonata for Piano and Violin, in E minor, K. 304
Sonata for Piano and Violin, in A, K. 305
Sonata for Piano and Violin, in D, K. 306

These six sonatas were composed in Mannheim and Paris, in 1778, and dedicated to Maria Elisabeth, wife of Carl Theodor, Elector of the Palatinate. Each is in two movements except the last, which is broader in design, and has three—two brilliant, virtuoso movements, and between them an Andante cantabile which unfolds sotto voce, an appealing song in the mood of a nocturne. De Saint-Foix believed, from indications in the manuscripts of the first and from the character of the violin part in the third, that Mozart may have originally intended these two as flute sonatas for the amateur player, De Jean, who had engaged him to write a group of flute pieces, much against his inclination. The one in G ends with a set of variations in which the piano has little more than an accompanying function. The other, in C, has a closing sonata movement in minuet tempo, with flute-like runs. The intervening Sonata in E flat, on the other hand, has for its second movement a Rondo, Andante grazioso, in which the violinist does little more than dance attendance. The Sonata in E minor stands out strongly from the rest. It is emphatically a violinist's piece, with full-throated, violinistic themes in both movements. The Allegro is bold and dramatic, the short finale is in variation form, again in minuet tempo. The Sonata in A is a cheerful, party piece, gay in every measure. It opens in Mozart's best six-eight style, developing in its course a crescendo in the true Mannheim manner, and closes in his best grazioso style, with variations of neat, clipped elegance, on a whistleable tune, traversing a staccato variation, favoring the violinist, and ending in a transformation into three-eight rhythm. This sonata vies with K. 296, the first Mannheim sonata, as music of sheer, sparkling, inconsequential entertainment.

Sonata for Piano and Violin, in F, K. 376
Sonata for Piano and Violin, in F, K. 377
Sonata for Piano and Violin, in B flat, K. 378
Sonata for Piano and Violin, in G, K. 379
Sonata for Piano and Violin, in E flat, K. 380

Five sonatas were completed in Vienna in 1781. They would have won the composer many new friends and new general listeners, for he found fresh and happy combinations for the two instruments, beyond current practice, so far as the violin is concerned, and a most agreeable way of presenting them. The first of the two Sonatas in F by no means neglects the violinist, and yet the themes are generally pianistic, the interest centering on the piano. The Rondo (Allegretto grazioso) is on still another tune of the Papageno variety. There are touches of humor, a suggestion of drum tattoos, and, before the last return of the theme, broken chords as if the whole thing were about to expire.

The second Sonata in F takes a light, rippling course, with running passages (in twelve-eight) for both instruments. The variations are on a piquant Andante theme which bears such fruit as a Siciliana and a developed Tempo di Menuetto. Indeed it is one of the best of Mozart's many sets of variations. This sonata is a gem in the group, but so is the next, in B flat. This one (K. 378) has a long and finely developed Allegro, and an Andantino sostenuto e cantabile which could have become a violinist's concerto movement.

The Sonata in G, K. 379, (the main allegro opens in G minor) begins with an Adagio where both instruments show their best singing properties, proceeds in an equally happy pairing, and traverses variations where each has his turn. The first section of the theme is repeated before the coda. The Sonata in E flat is more brilliant in character, has an Andante con moto with chromatic boldness, traversing G minor, and a Rondo on another lively six-eight theme.

Sonata for Piano and Violin, in B flat, K. 454

Violinists seek out this sonata, and with reason. It was composed in 1784 for Regina Strinasecchi, a young and celebrated violinist from Mantua. It is therefore not surprising that Mozart went out of his way to favor her, and indeed she was very well served. The introductory Largo and the main body of the first movement are music in a nobly serious vein, with themes conceived for the violin, full-breathed and expressively phrased. The Andante too is pre-eminently violinistic—a cantilena string melody which could have served for a concerto or a divertimento. The Allegretto is more serious than most of the sonata finales—the grazioso style is for the moment forgotten. The pianist is brought more to the fore than previously, but only for a closer matching and the enhancement of the two as a pair.

Sonata for Piano and Violin, E flat, K. 481

This sonata, of 1785, is a pleasant work which tends to allow the violin its singing function and to spare it the humiliation of obtrusive accompanying figures. The first movement develops in sequence the composer's favorite four-note motto usually identified with the "Jupiter" Symphony finale. The Adagio seeks to apportion the two players fairly and without competition by giving each an extended subject of his own. This is Romantic nineteenth-century music before its time. At last the two are paired in a sonorous duet, the pianist providing a free-ranging bass. The finale consists of six variations on a typical allegretto theme, which is at last transformed from a duple into a six-eight beat.

Sonata for Piano and Violin, in A, K. 526

In depth and workmanship the last of the sonatas in the full style is surely the finest of them all, and can stand with those works, such as the G minor Quintet which it followed by three months (it is dated August 24, 1787), which bespeak a new and serious Mozart in his last years. That autumn saw the completion of *Don Giovanni*. The magnificent Sonata in A was plainly composed for musicians of professional taste and skill, nor could the casual sort who looked for a simplified violin part in their sonatas have managed the swift scale passages in the Presto finale, exacting alike to both players. There is a minimum of harmonic filling in by the string player, or mere doubling, or literal echoing. The two instruments are more closely alternated within a phrase, and when combined have often independent thematic parts. The smooth and sober grace of the style almost completely supersedes the gallantry of a lifetime (it is curious fact that *Eine kleine Nachtmusik* was written just fourteen days before this sonata, as Mozart's careful catalogue shows). It is a "legato" sonata from the flowing opening theme to the smooth conclusion of the Presto. The harmonic treatment is "advanced," the counterpoint subtle and concealed. The Andante is based on a gently sinuous legato theme which is almost Brahmsian. Here the two players have eloquent solos but with combined intent—it is a duet in the ideal sense. The Presto is Mozartean light-winged virtuosity at its best.

"Sonatina" for Piano and Violin, in F, K. 547

Composed in 1788, and inscribed "A Little Clavier Sonata for Beginners with a Violin," this work has every aspect of a piece for piano solo, and was so arranged by the composer. Only the opening Andante cantabile is anything like a proper duet. The following two movements, an Allegro and a set of variations, simply make room for the second instrument.

6 Variations on "Hélas, j'ai perdu mon amant," K. 360
12 Variations on "La Bergère celimène," for Piano and Violin, K. 359

These two sets of variations on French themes were composed (probably) in 1781. The first was composed for the Countess Rumbeck, a piano pupil. Both are in the gallant style and both could be played with a minimum of alteration by a pianist alone.

Three uncompleted sonatas date from 1782. One (K. 402) consists of an Andante in A major, and the beginning of a Fugue in A minor, completed for publication by Maximilian Stadler. Mozart intended it for Constanze who was something of a pianist and had expressed a (sincere?) interest in fugues then newly studied by her husband. Mozart may have lost interest in what was an unsuitable combination for a fugue. Two sonatas in C (K. 403 and 404) and an Adagio (K. 396) are fragmentary. K. 403 was completed by Abt Stadler.

The Piano Trios

"E in Terzett" was Mozart's title for each of his trios for piano, violin and cello, except for the early one in B flat, which he called a "divertimento," a strange designation, since it differs in no way from the pattern of the rest. The piano always predominates. If the early duo sonatas are really piano sonatas with the treble slightly reinforced and varied by the violin, the *"terzetts"* are really duo sonatas with the bass even more slightly reinforced and varied by the cello. They are piano solos agreeably encased in string tone. In the first trio and the last (a made-over piano sonata) the string parts could be dropped altogether with little alteration. Otherwise, the trios are fine products of the maturest years—two in 1786 and two in 1788. These have nothing of the bold innovation to be found in other works of those years, such as the C minor Piano Fantasia or the Violin Sonata in A, K. 526, or the orchestral works. They remain polite, salon pieces, as do in general the piano sonatas. At the same time they are examples of their composer's finest workmanship, a proof that Mozart's late works in the style of his time can be as treasurable as his late scores of bolder innovation.

Piano Trio ("Divertimento") in B. flat, K. 254 (Composed in Salzburg, August, 1776)

Since the bass function is fulfilled by the pianist's left hand, and is merely doubled by the cello, this trio could perfectly well be played as a violin sonata. This does not mean that it would be as beautiful, for the gentle permeation of the cello bass and its chords with the violin add considerably to the charm of the whole. First and last, this is a polite work, but warm and appealing in the melodies of the allegro assai, the development of the rondo in minuet style. The Adagio in the middle is a particularly fine one, with a long breathed opening melody conceived for the violin, another suited to the piano, and a mating of the two.

Piano Trio in G, K. 496, (Composed in Vienna, July, 1786)

The first of the two trios in G major is much in the style of its predecessor, light and elegant. The cello has more privileges, alternation, melodic independence, while the violin echoes or doubles; nevertheless, this is a piano sonata by the nature of its material. The Andante is mere surface grace when compared to the Adagio of the B flat Trio. The Allegretto is a typical one on a theme in staccato notes, subjected to a series of variations in which the piano, even when its role is ornamental, holds the interest.

Piano Trio in B flat, K. 502 (Composed in Vienna, November, 1786)

The flow of melodious themes, their more smoothly adjusted treatment by piano and violin alone and together in a real duet, the delicate ensemble wherein the cello steps forward, make this a luminous and singing trio from beginning to end. Here again is subtlety applied to simplicity. The serene course of the Larghetto, built on two extended melodies, and the light grace of the Allegretto where there is refined animation and no thought of brilliance, leave the listener with the feeling that this style, intimate, subject to the fleck of fancy, is the ideal way for chamber music.

Piano Trio in E major, K. 542 (Composed in Vienna, January, 1788)

This could be called the last of the great trios. It was composed at the beginning of the year which was to bring the final three symphonies. Mozart presumably found it useful—he played it in Dresden in the following year, and sent it to his sister at St. Gilgen. Perhaps for his own purposes of performance he gave the music more substance than its predecessor of two years earlier, brilliance in the piano part which nevertheless was never allowed to harden into glitter. The balance of the three instruments gives the cello an occasional thematic part and a closer chordal blending with the violin. This trio avoids all heavy thoughts and gives us a truly gallant Andante grazioso of studied and self-conscious grace. The theme of the final Allegro might be called sophisticated naïveté, with touches that keep it clear of the commonplace in a fully developed movement.

Piano Trio in C, K. 548 (Composed in Vienna, July, 1788)
Piano Trio in G, K. 564 (Composed in Vienna, October, 1788)

The last two trios must be called "potboilers," because Mozart obviously wrote them under hard pressure for money. It was in this year that he wrote the Piano Sonata in C (K. 545), the "Sonatina" for Piano and Violin (K. 547), designed to provide "beginners" and to bring himself some immediate thalers. This was also the year of the three great symphonies (the Trio in C was composed between the E flat and G minor symphonies), the Divertimento for String Trio, and indeed the Piano Trio in E, which he wrote in January. *Don Giovanni* was his latest opera. The wide gap is plain enough between those works which commanded his full attention and his highest powers, and those which were the easy products of his facility. This is not to imply that the latter were in the least dull or pedestrian. Beethoven could be that when a commission came his way, Mozart never. The themes could not fail to charm the "beginner," the notes fall comfortably under his (or her) hands; the music is not only elegant, faultless, in exquisite taste —it is also engagingly animated. It never really soars or fills us with wonderment for the good reason that such miracles were for the moment not called for.

Only details of workmanship mark these two trios as "late." They were made for pianists, with pianistic themes. The violin and the cello too are dutifully allowed to echo the phrases stated by the piano, but with the striking out of these bars and a few slight touches each would become a sonata for piano solo. Even the variations (Andante) of the Trio in G are interesting for their piano embroidery rather than the mere repetition of the theme by the strings.

The Piano Quartets

Piano Quartet in G minor, K. 478 (Composed in Vienna, October, 1785)

Piano Quartet in E flat, K. 493 (Composed in Vienna, June, 1786)

Mozart wrote the first of his piano quartets in the same month in which he began to work upon *Figaro* and wrote the second, two months after the completion of his opera. The combination of violin, viola and cello with piano was his own invention, for it had no real precedent. These two works do not resemble the piano trios which were shortly to follow, for the addition of a viola makes all the difference between a duet of individual string players and a group. They have no resemblance to the piano concertos for they are not in the least orchestral, and the piano parts while prominent and difficult are not in the open virtuoso vein. This is really chamber music, with four concertante parts in a chamber texture. It is significant that the publisher Hoffmeister ordered three, and having received and published the first, in G minor, found that it had no sale, being too difficult for amateurs, and was ready to withdraw from the agreement. Mozart wrote a second and Artaria published it, but no third was forthcoming. Artaria may have done better with the E flat Quartet, for it is gay and directly appealing for the most part. It is no easier for the players, nor, at times, for the listener. The G minor Quartet opens darkly with a challenge in octave unison, a theme which dominates the movement. One is led to expect the serious and intense earnestness which the minor mode usually meant to Mozart, as in the D minor Quartet and the G minor Quintet. The mood is dispelled, for the final Rondo, like the Rondo of the companion Quartet in E flat, is built on a subject of the utmost lightness and charm. Both finales are rich in episodes, fully worthy of the composer of *Figaro* with imagination alight and skill sharpened. A gem of a tune in D major at the sixtieth bar of the Rondo in the G minor Quartet is a *trouvaille* thrown away, for it is not repeated. The composer later remembered his profligacy when he used it again for a piano rondo three months later (K. 485).

The Quartets and Quintets for Winds and Strings

Quartet for Flute and Strings, in D, K. 285 (Composed in Mannheim, December, 1777)

Whether or not Mozart's flute-playing pupil De Jean was satisfied with the partial fulfillment of his order for flute concertos and quartets, he had every reason to be pleased with this one among the three quartets provided. In length it is almost equal to the other two combined. The first movement, essentially a string quartet with a leading flute instead of a violin part, gains quartet character in the development. The Adagio is not a developed slow movement but an introduction to the finale, a true flute melody of great beauty set off to perfection by a pizzicato accompaniment. The theme of the Rondo, and indeed the leading theme of the opening movement, are sheer delight. The composer's thesis seems to be that the flute is the prime instrument for unalloyed gaiety.

Quartet for Flute and Strings, in C, K. 285b (Composed in Mannheim, early 1778)

The quartet is in two movements, in the manner of Christian Bach, the Allegro consisting mostly of solo melody over repeated accompanying chords. The Andantino is a curiosity and a puzzle, for it is a close version of the superb variations in the Serenade for thirteen winds (K. 361), composed in Vienna in 1781. It is hard to believe that Mozart first conceived the delicately wrought woodwind music in the terms of this nonblending combination, which almost makes a travesty of it.

Perhaps Mozart made this as a sort of sketch, with the later use in mind, and put it in his quartet as a convenient way to dispose of a commission. Strangest of all, the flute is the one woodwind instrument sternly excluded from the Serenade.

Quartet for Flute and Strings, in A, K. 298 (Composed in Paris, summer, 1778)

This quartet has been the cause of indeterminate dispute. The music is "early" in character—it consists of three movements, little developed, lasting ten minutes. The first is a set of four eight-bar variations on a melody which sounds like a borrowed folk tune. There follows a conventional minuet, and a Rondo grazioso on a rather insipid theme, likewise obviously borrowed. Saint-Foix summons evidence to prove that it could not have been written before 1786, when Paisiello's Opera buffa *Le gare generose,* containing almost precisely this rondo theme, was first heard. He accounts for the late date of a work hardly believable as of 1786 by calling it a "parody," and quotes Mozart's humorous inscription over the Rondo: "Not too fast, but also not too slow—so-so—with much elegance and expression."* Mozart was more in the mood for parody in Paris, in 1778, when he was impatient with French elegance in general, the flute and his client De Jean in particular. The issue is not clarified by the inscription by Mosel on the manuscript— "composed in Paris, in 1778. Manuscript received from the Baron Jacquin." Yet Jacquin was Mozart's friend much later, a participant in musical evenings in Vienna and Prague. Einstein has adhered to the Paris date, but with admitted misgivings. Abert has argued himself into the implausible solution that Paisiello got the theme from Mozart! In any case, Mozart reverted to a formality earlier even than Mannheim and Paris. There are gay moments only because he was incapable of being really dull.

Quartet for Oboe and Strings, in F, K. 370 (Composed in Munich, early 1781)

Mozart wrote his oboe quartet for his friend Friedrich Ramm, the famous virtuoso of the electoral orchestra, while *Idomeneo* was in course of preparation. He obviously put his best efforts

---

* "*Allegretto grazioso, mà non troppo presto, pèro non troppo adagio—così-così—molto garbo ed Espressione.*"

into it, for he both expected a first-rate performance and valued Ramm's regard for his own abilities. The score puts the soloist through his paces, as in the last movement where the oboe plays rapid runs to four beats in six-eight measures. The string writing shows that Mozart had not forgotten how to write string quartets although he had long left them untouched. The string trio has no mere accompanying function with an occasional echo of the soloist—it is a concertante partner throughout, but especially in the short Adagio. The theme of the "Rondeau," in six-eight beat, was plainly conceived for the bright, clipped style of the reed instrument.

The beauty of this work makes oboists regret the loss of the oboe concerto which Mozart wrote for Ramm, and in which Ramm took special delight. In default of this, they sometimes play an arrangement of the Flute Concerto in D (K. 314), which in itself may have been Mozart's arrangement of the lost concerto.

Quintet for Horn and Strings, in E flat, K. 407 (Composed in Vienna, late 1782)

This preceded the horn concertos which Mozart wrote for Leutgeb. It is not a quintet in the sense of the Clarinet Quintet —a true string quartet with an added instrument—nor does it resemble the divertimentos for strings with two horns, which are almost orchestral music. Here the quartet is for a single violin, two violas and cello, probably because the composer treats the horn as akin to the cello (the horn part is indicated as optional for a second cello). The violin and the horn are often matched as dueting instruments, particularly in the Andante. The opening and closing movements, which are not ambitious, favor the soloist with such inherent felicities as fanfare-like chords and octave drops.

Quintet for Clarinet and Strings, in A, K. 581 (Composed in Vienna, September, 1789)

There are several reasons why the "Stadler Quintet," so referred to by Mozart, should far exceed anything he had composed in a wind and strings chamber combination: the clarinet was his special love, Stadler had his esteem as a musician, friend and fellow Mason, but most important of all, he had reached one of his ripest composing years, had brought the string quartet to its highest point, and saw his way to combine the clarinet and the quartet to the exceeding advantage of each. The result is not a virtuoso work with string accompaniment, for the quartet is often more important, more engrossing than the soloist; nor is it a quartet with clarinet obbligato, for the clarinet is often the melodic center of attention. It is rather a string quartet and a clarinet matched in a complementary and blending function in a way that had never before been thought of. This shares the distinction with the Serenade for thirteen winds (K. 361) of being the longest of the chamber works, and for the same reason—the composer was full of his subject. There are four movements, as in a string quartet. Each is fully developed. The Minuet has two trios, the finale is an extended set of variations. Mozart often treats the quartet separately (in the first trio the clarinet is silent). More often than not the quartet proposes a theme or section, and when the clarinet carries the melody, the center of interest is still below. This is particularly true in the Larghetto, where the muted strings in the after phrases capture the hearer. This work proves that no other wind instrument (not even the horn) blends with the string texture as does this one.

The Chamber Works for Various Combinations

7 Minuets for Two Violins and Bass, K. 65a (Composed in Salzburg, January, 1769)

Sonata for Bassoon and Cello, in B flat, K. 292 (Composed in Munich, early 1775)

Trio for Two Violins and Bass, in B flat, K. 266 (Composed in Salzburg, 1777)

Adagio in Canon, for Two Basset Horns and Bassoon, in F, K. 410 (Composed in Vienna, 1783)

Adagio for Two Clarinets and Three Basset Horns, in F, K. 411
(Composed in Vienna, 1783)
12 Duets for Two Horns (Basset Horns?), K. 487 (Composed in
Vienna, July, 1786)

Duo for Violin and Viola, in G, K. 423
Duo for Violin and Viola, in B flat, K. 424
(Composed in Salzburg, 1783)

Mozart composed his two duos for string instruments for
Michael Haydn during his last visit to Salzburg. According to
the account of two of Haydn's pupils, Haydn was sick and unable
to complete the order by the Archbishop for six such pieces,
having composed four. Mozart obliged his friend and allowed
him to present them as his own. These duos are in the category
of string quartets reduced to two voices, whereby the composer's ingenuity is taxed to imply the fuller texture. Mozart was
indeed quartet conscious at the time; he had recently written
the first three of the six for Michael's illustrious brother. Each
is in three movements, the second a short slow movement. The
first Duo ends with a "Rondeau," the second with a theme and
six variations. The second is bolder, freer, more "advanced" in
style, more exacting to the performers. There is a fine introduction (Adagio). The viola in the Allegro has a thematic, a complementary as well as a bass, function. In the Andante cantabile the violin is the free-ranging melodic instrument, while
the viola provides chords. The set of variations is richer in
concept than two voices would suggest. There is the illusion of
more, while the paired equilibrium is still sensed. Here as elsewhere, Mozart needed only to dip briefly into an untried medium
to leave a masterpiece.

Quintet in E flat, for Piano, Oboe, Clarinet, Horn and Bassoon,
K. 452 (Composed in Vienna, March, 1784)

It is not really surprising that Mozart, who was never inclined
to speak vaingloriously about his own music, should have
described his quintet in a letter to his father: "I consider it the
best work I have so far written in my life." Since he had written
two magnificent piano concertos for the same concert, the
statement is not to be taken too literally. Let us say that he
still lingered in the glow of warmth, the enthusiasm which
obviously went into its writing. Nothing he had done showed

more loving care in the handling. The piece thematically speaking is more agreeable than striking, although beautiful in its own unassuming way. The magic lies in the extraordinarily perceptive mating of the instruments. As a concertante group from which individual voices emerge and combine, the score becomes one of the special jewels of the music for wind instruments, to be placed beside the *"Gran partita"* (K. 361).

Trio for Piano, Clarinet and Viola, in E flat, K. 498 (Composed in Vienna, August, 1786)

Mozart wrote this trio for his pupil Francisca Gottfried von Jacquin. She would have played the piano part, Mozart the viola, and Stadler the clarinet. The later title, *"Kegelstatt Trio,"* came from the unlikely story that he composed it during a game of ninepins. The character of the music implies anything but haste—rather loving care in the combined treatment of the three instruments, which are beautifully matched, and the highest regard for his two musician friends. It consists of an andante which is the principal movement, a minuet and a fully developed "Rondeau." The gentle and glowing qualities of the viola and the clarinet give a special color to this particular ensemble.

Divertimento for Violin, Viola and Cello, in E flat, K. 563 (Composed in Vienna, September, 1788)

Among Mozart's works this one is unique in combined form and character, and quite unclassifiable. Composing it for Michael Puchberg, his fellow Mason and benefactor, he may have felt that since Puchberg was nothing special as a musician, something in the way of "entertainment music" would best suit him. But the composer who had just finished his last three symphonies had long since left divertimentos behind. The early ones for string trio with horns obbligato are not in the least comparable. Perhaps his impulse was to give full divertimento measure with a second slow movement and a second minuet (this with a second trio). If so, he became more absorbed in the music than mindful of the recipient, for the result is a true chamber work, largely in the "learned" style. Many of the themes, notably that of the Andante with its variations, and the completely cheerful six-eight subject of the finale are as light and engaging as any he wrote for the Salzburg divertimentos. Their treatment is the fine workmanship of 1788. The first movement and the Adagio are definitely "serious." It would be completely misleading to consider this quartet as minus a second violin, like a wagon with a wheel missing. It necessarily lacks chordal sonority, but the three voices find a new, delicate balance, permitting a new, individual prominence to a single end.

The Organ Works

Mozart's interest in the organ began when, as a small boy, he was taken by his father to a church or a monastery during his travels, and would play the organ, standing in order to reach the pedals.* He played the organ for the services in Salzburg as part of his duties. He had less occasion for playing the organ during his Vienna years, but visiting Leipzig he went to the Thomaskirche, drawn by Bach's organ and Bach's music.

Unfortunately he was never called upon to compose for the organ proper other than the *sonate da chiesa* for the Salzburg services. The music he composed for a mechanical organ in the last two years of his life had a grandeur of design totally inappropriate for that contrivance. A chance and rather ridiculous commission released a sample of what he might have done for the proper instrument if he had been asked.

---

* E. Power Biggs, the organist, making a pilgrimage to the various churches and monasteries of German, Austrian and North Italian towns where Mozart had visited and played, found that many of the organs have been preserved through the years.

SONATAS FOR ORGAN AND ORCHESTRA

No. 1, in E flat, K. 67 (1767)	No. 8, in A, K. 225 (1776)
No. 2, in B flat, K. 68 (1767)	No. 9, in F, K. 224 (1776)
No. 3, in D, K. 69 (1767)	No. 10, in D, K. 245 (1776)
No. 4, in D, K. 144 (1772)	No. 11, in G, K. 274 (1777)
No. 5, in F, K. 145 (1772)	No. 12, in C, K. 278 (1777)
No. 6, in B flat, K. 212	No. 13, in C, K. 328 (1779)
(1775)	No. 14, in C, K. 329 (1779)
No. 7, in F, K. 224 (1776)	No. 15, in C, K. 336 (1780)

(Sonatas in G, K. 241, 1776 and C, K. 263, 1776, the latter calling for trumpets, are unpublished.)

As organist at Salzburg, Mozart was required to furnish accompaniments in the *Kapelle* services, and to provide a sonata as instrumental interlude between the epistle and the gospel. These sonatas are short, one-movement pieces, lightly scored and unpretentious. They are quite cheerful, and with no particular religious suggestion. All seventeen are in the major. All but the Tenth and the last three have simply two violin parts and a string bass, the organ serving entirely a bass function and sometimes written in as a continuo. The Twelfth adds oboes, trumpets and timpani, and the Fourteenth further adds horns to these. The Fourteenth and Fifteenth give the organ an alternate solo part, as if in a concerto.

MECHANICAL ORGAN

Adagio and Allegro, in F minor, K. 594 (Composed in Frankfort and Vienna, 1790)

Fantasia, in F minor, K. 608 (Composed in Vienna, March, 1791)

Andante, in F, K. 616 (Composed in Vienna, May, 1791)

There was a great vogue in the eighteenth century for "musical clocks," organs operated by revolving cylinders. Count Josef Deym (his real name was Müller) had a collection of these. Mozart accepted commissions from him, and fulfilled the first on his Frankfort journey. He wrote to his wife of his effort to overcome his boredom and keep at the task. The assignment must have seemed the more absurd to him because he was to write appropriate music of mourning to be played in front of a wax effigy of the late Field Marshal Laudon (the Field Marshal had died in the July previous, and was thus honored in Deym's waxworks). The Adagio is heavily somber, with a middle section in the tonic major, broad and ceremonious in character. The music goes far beyond the limitations of the instrument and its immediate function. It is suitable for a humanly controlled organ and is so accepted. The Fantasy in the same key is still grander in conception. If Mozart took suggestions from Handel's organ sonatas in the earlier work, the Fantasia shows even more plainly that he had been studying and absorbing the organ music of Sebastian Bach and his fantasias. A short prelude of ample, Bachian chords recurs to introduce each section and close the whole. There is a fine fugue on a flowing theme, a slow movement at first simple in character, building with multiple strands to a climax. The fugue returns, more fully manipulated, but brief. No "organ in a clock" could have produced more than a travesty of this piece in the grand style calling for the fullest instrumental forces. The Andante in F major would have been far more appropriate to Deym's mechanical oddity. It is written in the upper register, a rondo developed in the style of variations, on a tune of popular character.

GLASS HARMONICA

Adagio for Harmonica, in C, K. 356 (Composed in Vienna, early 1791)

Adagio and Rondo, for Harmonica with Flute, Oboe, Viola and Cello, in C minor, K. 617 (Composed in Vienna, May, 1791)

These pieces were ordered by Marianne Kirchgessner, a blind virtuoso on the instrument developed by her teacher, J. A. Schmittbauer, who in turn had refined upon the invention of Benjamin Franklin. It consisted of glass bowls of graduated size, partly filled with water, and rotated by pedal action, the notes produced by the touch of the finger on the rotating edge. The tones were high, tenuous and bell-like, with a quality which was admired as "ethereal." The adagio tempo would best suit the instrument; the Rondo, Allegretto, would have taxed the agility of the player without a special keyboard contrivance. In this work, Mozart gently supports the faint tones with strings and varies it with high woodwinds. There is a certain "music box" charm in the result.

Appendices

Appendices

Eighteenth-Century Money Values

Monetary standards in Mozart's day varied in Europe according to time and place, gold and silver. A thaler in Austria or the German States was the rough equivalent of the early American dollar. A gulden was worth about a half dollar. A ducat, the common gold coin, was equal to $2.25, a friedrich d'or, $4. Thus, when Hieronymus paid Mozart a salary of 150 gulden for his duties at Salzburg, it was the equivalent of about $75; when Mozart signed an agreement to pay his fiancée Constanze an annuity of 300 gulden if he should change his mind about marrying her, he pledged $150. A florin, according to one of Mozart's letters to his father from Paris, was about a third of a thaler, or 33 cents.

A zecchino (sequin) was the Italian equivalent of a ducat, a scudo was worth a dollar. When in *Così fan tutte* the wager of 100 zecchini is laid, $225 is at stake; when Don Alfonso bribes the servant Despina with 70 scudi, he is giving her $70, a handsome amount for the time.

The French livre was about equal to the later franc. The louis d'or (22 livres) was equal to the British pound or guinea: about $4.80. When Mozart decided not to take the position of court organist at Versailles for 2,000 livres a year, he figured the sum as equal to 915 German florins, because of the deteriorating French currency. His salary would have been a little over 300 thalers, or approximately that equivalent in dollars.

APPENDIX 2

Cadenzas in the Piano Concertos

Mozart did not need to write cadenzas for his own use, but for friends or pupils. In some concertos, original cadenzas exist for all three movements; in some, for two or one; in some, there are alternate cadenzas for the same movement. Unfortunately, none survive for the three great concertos of 1785 (K. 466, 467, 482), nor for the subsequent ones, with two exceptions: the A major Concerto (K. 488) of which there is a cadenza for the opening movement, and the final concerto (K. 595), for which there is one cadenza for the first movement and one for each fermata of the last.

Mozart also wrote cadenzas for concertos by J. C. Bach, Honauer, and Schroeter. Beethoven wrote cadenzas for the Concerto in D minor, K. 466 (first and last movements).

The numbers in the following list (which is taken from Köchel's Catalog, K. 624) indicate original cadenzas, if any, for those movements:

Movements:	1st	2nd	3rd
K. 175, in D	2	2	–
K. 238, in B flat	–	–	–
K. 242, in F (3 Pianos)	1	1	–
K. 246, in C	2	3	–
K. 271, in E flat	2	2	3
K. 365, in E flat (2 Pianos)	1	–	1
K. 382, in D (Rondo movement)	1		
K. 413, in F	1	1	–
K. 414, in A	2	3	3
K. 415, in C	1	1	1
K. 449, in E flat	1	–	–
K. 450, in B flat	1	–	2
K. 451, in D	1	–	1
K. 453, in G	2	2	–
K. 456, in B flat	2	–	1
K. 459, in F	1	–	1
K. 466, in D minor	–	–	–

Movements:	1st	2nd	3rd
K. 467, in C	–	–	–
K. 482, in E flat	–	–	–
K. 488, in A	1	–	–
K. 491, in C minor	–	–	–
K. 503, in C	–	–	–
K. 537, in D ("Coronation")	–	–	–
K. 595, in B flat	1	–	2

APPENDIX 3

The Köchel Chronology

The numbering of the works generally used for reference, to avoid confusion, is that of Köchel's Thematic Catalogue before the revision and renumbering by Alfred Einstein in 1937 in the light of later research. The dates however are here corrected according to Einstein, and therefore occasionally appear in altered sequence (some dates remain conjectural). Those who wish to pursue further "fragmentary," "copied," "doubtful," "spurious" or "lost" items are referred to the exhaustive (and scholarly) Köchel-Einstein appendix. *The numerals in heavy type indicate the principal page reference.*

KÖCHEL NO.	COMPOSED	PLACE	TITLE AND PAGE REFERENCE
K. 1	1761 or 1762	Salzburg	Minuet and Trio for Piano, in G, **383**
K. 2	1762	"	Minuet for Piano, in F, **383**
K. 3	"	"	Allegro for Piano, in B flat, **383**
K. 4	"	"	Minuet for Piano, in F, **383**
K. 5	"	"	Minuet for Piano, in F, **383**
K. 6	1764	Paris	Sonata for Piano and Violin, in C, **388n.**, 25
K. 7	"	"	Sonata for Piano and Violin, in D, **388n.**, 25
K. 8	"	"	Sonata for Piano and Violin, in B flat, **388n.**, 25
K. 9	"	"	Sonata for Piano and Violin, in G, **388n.**, 25
K. 9a	1763	Salzburg	Allegro for Piano, in C, **383**
K. 9b	"	"	Andante for Piano, in B flat, **383**
K. 10-15	1764	London	6 Sonatas for Piano, Violin (or Flute) and Cello, **383n.**, 31

414 · Appendix 3

KÖCHEL NO.	COMPOSED	PLACE	TITLE AND PAGE REFERENCE
K. 40	1767	Salzburg	Piano Concerto No. 3, in D (arrangement), **321**
K. 41	"	"	Piano Concerto No. 4, in G (arrangement), **321**
K. 42	"	"	*Grabmusik* ("Passion Cantata"), **277,** 36
K. 43	"	Olmütz and Vienna	Symphony No. 6, in F, **283**
K. 44	1770	Bologna	Antiphon (Introitus), *"Cibavit eos,"* **274**
K. 45	1768	Vienna	Symphony No. 7, in D, **283**
K. 45a	"	"	Symphony in G, **283**
K. 45b	"	"	Symphony in B flat, **283**
K. 46			Quintet (spurious—copy of K. 361)
K. 47	1768	Vienna	Offertory in C, *"Veni sancte spiritus,"* **269,** 41
K. 48	"	"	Symphony No. 8, in D, **283**
K. 49	"	"	Missa brevis in G, **255,** 269
K. 50	"	"	*Bastien und Bastienne,* **210,** 41
K. 51	"	"	*La finta semplice, Opera buffa,* **211,** 39-42, 209
K. 52	"	"	*"Daphne, deine Rosenwangen,"* Song with Piano, **247**
K. 53	1767	Olmütz	*An die Freude,* Song with Piano, **247**
K. 54	1788	Vienna	Piano Sonata in F (See K. 547a)
K. 55-60	"	"	6 Sonatas for Piano and Violin (doubtful), **389n.**
K. 61			Sonata for Piano and Violin (by Raupach), **389n.**
K. 61g	1769	Salzburg	2 Minuets (one for Orchestra, one for Piano), **316**
K. 61h	"	"	6 Minuets for Orchestra, **316**
K. 62	"	"	March in D, **316**

KÖCHEL NO.	COMPOSED	PLACE	TITLE AND PAGE REFERENCE
K. 63	1769	Salzburg	Divertimento (Finalmusik) in G, **303**, 42
K. 64	"	"	Minuet for Orchestra, in D, **316**
K. 65	"	"	Missa brevis in D minor, **256**, 42
K. 65a	"	"	7 Minuets for Strings, **40**
K. 66	"	"	Mass in C (*"Dominicus"*), **255**, 42
K. 67-69	1767	"	3 Church Sonatas for Organ and Strings, **405**
K. 70	1769	"	Recitative (*"A Berenice"*) and Aria, (*"Sol nascente"*) for Soprano (Licenza), **237**, 42
K. 71	1770?	"	Aria for Tenor (*"Ah, più tremar non voglio"*) **237**
K. 72	1771	"	Offertory (for the Feast of John the Baptist), in G, **269**
K. 73	"	"	Symphony No. 9, in C, **284**
K. 74	1770	Milan	Symphony No. 10, in G, **284**
K. 74b	1771	Milan or Pavia	Aria for Soprano (*"Non curo l'affetto"*) **237**
K. 74g	"	Salzburg	Symphony in B flat, **283**
K. 75	"	"	Symphony in F, **283**
K. 76	1767	Vienna	Symphony in F, **283**
K. 77	1770	Milan	Recitative (*"Misero me"*) and Aria (*"Misero pargoletto"*), for Soprano, **238**, 51
K. 78	"	"	Aria for Soprano (*"Per pietà, bell' idol mio"*), **238**
K. 79	"	"	Aria for Soprano (*"Per quel paterno"*) **238**
K. 80	"	Lodi	Quartet for Strings, No. 1, in G, **356**, 47
K. 81	"	Rome	Symphony in D, **283**, 49, 51
K. 82	"	"	Aria for Soprano (*"Se ardire"*), **238**, 49

KÖCHEL NO.	COMPOSED	PLACE	TITLE AND PAGE REFERENCE
K. 83	1770	Rome	Aria for Soprano (*"Se tutti i mali miei"*), **238**
K. 84	"	Milan-Bologna	Symphony No. 11, in D, **284**, 51, 52
K. 85	"	Bologna	*Miserere*, **268**
K. 86	"	"	Antiphon (*"Quaerite primum regnum Dei"*), **275**
K. 87	"	Milan	*Mitridate, rè di Ponto, Opera seria*, **211**
K. 88	"	"	Aria for Soprano (*"Fra cento affani"*), **238**, 51
K. 89	"	Rome	Kyrie in G, for 5 Sopranos, **250**, 268
K. 89a	"	"	Canon for 4 Voices, **250**
K. 90	1771	Salzburg	Kyrie in D minor, **268**
K. 91	1774		Kyrie in D (fragmentary), **268**
K. 92	1769?		Salve Regina (doubtful)
K. 93	1771	Salzburg	Psalm, *"De profundis clamavi,"* **275**
K. 94	1770	Bologna or Rome?	Minuet for Piano (?), in D, **383**
K. 95	"	Rome	Symphony in D, **283**, 49, 51, 52
K. 96	1771	Milan	Symphony in C, **283**
K. 97	1770	Rome	Symphony in D, **283**
K. 98	1771	Milan?	Symphony in F (doubtful), **283**
K. 99	1769	Salzburg	Cassation in B flat, **303**, 42
K. 100	"	"	Serenade No. 1 (*Finalmusik*) in D, **307**
K. 101	1776	"	Serenade No. 2, in F, **307**
K. 102	1775	"	Finale of a Symphony in C, **283**
K. 103	1769	"	19 Minuets for Orchestra, **316**, 42
K. 104	"	"	6 Minuets for Orchestra, **316**
K. 105	"	"	6 Minuets for Orchestra, **316**

KÖCHEL NO.	COMPOSED	PLACE	TITLE AND PAGE REFERENCE
K. 106	1790	Vienna	Overture and 3 Contredanses, **316**
K. 107	1765	London or The Hague	3 Concertos after J. C. Bach, **31**
K. 108	1771	Salzburg	*Regina Coeli,* in C, **275**
K. 109	"	"	*Litaniae de Beata Maria Virgine (Lauretanae),* **272**
K. 110	"	"	Symphony No. 12, in G, **284**
K. 111	"	Milan	*Ascanio in Alba, Serenata teatrale,* **212**
K. 112	"	"	Symphony No. 13, in F, **284**
K. 113	"	"	Divertimento No. 1, in E flat, **303**
K. 114	"	Salzburg	Symphony No. 14, in A, **285**
K. 115	1773	"	Missa brevis in C, **256**
K. 116	1771	"	Missa brevis in F, **257**
K. 117	1769	"	Offertory in C, **269**
K. 118	1771	Italy or Salzburg	*La Betulia liberata,* Oratorio, **277**
K. 119	1782	Vienna	Aria for Soprano (*"Der Liebe himmlisches Gefühl"*), **238**
K. 120	1771	Milan	Finale of a Symphony in D, **285n.**
K. 121	1775	Salzburg	Finale of a Symphony in D, **313**, 285n.
K. 122	1770	Bologna	Minuet for Orchestra, in E flat, **316**
K. 123	"	Rome	Contredanse for Orchestra, in B flat, **316**
K. 124	1772	Salzburg	Symphony No. 15, in G, **285**, 55
K. 125	"	"	*Litaniae de venerabili altaris sacramento,* **272**, 55
K. 126	"	"	*Il sogno di Scipione, Serenata drammatica,* **212**, 55
K. 127	"	"	*Regina Coeli,* in B flat, **275**, 55
K. 128	"	"	Symphony No. 16, in C, **285**, 55
K. 129	"	"	Symphony No. 17, in G, **285**, 55

KÖCHEL NO.	COM- POSED	PLACE	TITLE AND PAGE REFERENCE
K. 130	1772	Salzburg	Symphony No. 18, in F, **285,** 55
K. 131	"	"	Divertimento No. 2, in D, **304, 55**
K. 132	"	"	Symphony No. 19, in E flat, **286,** 55
K. 133	"	"	Symphony No. 20, in D, **286,** 55
K. 134	"	"	Symphony No. 21, in A, **286,** 55
K. 135	"	Salzburg- Milan	*Lucio Silla, Opera seria,* **212,** 55
K. 136	"	Salzburg	Divertimento in D, **365,** 55
K. 137	"	"	Divertimento in B flat, **365,** 55
K. 138	"	"	Divertimento in F, **365,** 55
K. 139	1768?	"	Missa (solemnis), in C minor-major, **257,** 41, 269
K. 140	1771-72	"	Missa brevis in G (doubtful)
K. 141	1769	"	*Te Deum,* in C, **274**
K. 142			*Tantum ergo,* in B flat, **277**
K. 143	1770	Milan	Aria for Soprano (*"Ergo interest"*) **238,** 51
K. 144	1772	Salzburg	Church Sonata in D, **405**
K. 145	"	"	Church Sonata in F, **405**
K. 146	1779	"	Aria for Soprano (*"Kommet her, ihr frechen Sünder"*), **239**
K. 147	1772	"	*"Wie unglücklich bin ich nit,"* Song with Piano, **247**
K. 148	"	"	*"O heiliges Band,"* Song with Piano, **247**
K. 149	"	"	*Die grossmütige Gelassenheit* (*Ich hab es längst"*), Song with Piano, **248**
K. 150	"	"	*Geheime Liebe* (*"Was ich in Gedanken küsse"*), Song with Piano, **248**
K. 151	"	"	*Die Zufriedenheit in niedrigen Stande* (*"Ich trachte nicht"*), Song with Piano, **248**

KÖCHEL NO.	COMPOSED	PLACE	TITLE AND PAGE REFERENCE
K. 152	1775	Salzburg?	Canzonetta (*"Ridente la calma"*), **248,** 246
K. 153	1782	Vienna	Fugue for Piano, in E flat (fragmentary)
K. 154			Fugue for Piano, in G minor (fragmentary)
K. 154a			Two Little Fugues (Piano or organ) (fragmentary)
K. 155	1772?	Bozen	Quartet for Strings, No. 2, in D, **356,** 55, 56
K. 156	1772	Milan	Quartet for Strings, No. 3, in G, **356,** 55, 56
K. 157	1772 or 1773	"	Quartet for Strings, No. 4, in C, **356,** 55, 56
K. 158	1773	"	Quartet for Strings, No. 5, in F, **356,** 55, 56
K. 159	"	"	Quartet for Strings, No. 6, in B flat, **357,** 55, 56
K. 160	"	Milan	Quartet for Strings, No. 7, in E flat, **357,** 55, 56
K. 161	1772	Salzburg (and Milan)	Symphony in D (Overture to K. 126), **285n.**
K. 162	1773	Salzburg	Symphony No. 22, in C, **287**
K. 163	1772	Milan	Finale of the Symphony in D, K. 161, **285n.**
K. 164	"	Salzburg	6 Minuets for Orchestra, **316**
K. 165	1773	Milan	Motet for Soprano (*"Exsultate, jubilate"*), **276,** 56, 254
K. 166	"	Salzburg	Divertimento No. 3, in E flat, **304**
K. 167	"	"	Mass (Trinity), in C, **257**
K. 168	"	Vienna	Quartet for Strings, No. 8, in F, **358,** 57
K. 169	"	"	Quartet for Strings, No. 9, in A, **358,** 57

KÖCHEL NO.	COMPOSED	PLACE	TITLE AND PAGE REFERENCE
K. 170	1773	Vienna	Quartet for Strings, No. 10, in C, **358**, 57
K. 171	"	"	Quartet for Strings, No. 11, in E flat, **359**, 57
K. 172	"	"	Quartet for Strings, No. 12, in B flat, **359**, 57
K. 173	"	"	Quartet for Strings, No. 13, in D minor, **359** 57, 133
K. 174	"	Salzburg	Quintet for Strings, in B flat, **367**
K. 175	"	"	Concerto for Piano No. 5, in D, **321**, 138, 319
K. 176	"	"	16 Minuets for Orchestra, **316**
K. 177			Offertorium *Sub expositio venerabili* (By Leopold Mozart)
K. 178	1772	Salzburg	Aria for Soprano (*"Ah, spiegarti, oh Dio"*), **248**
K. 179	1774	"	12 Variations for Piano, in C, **378**
K. 180	1773	Vienna	6 Variations for Piano, in G, **378**
K. 181	"	Salzburg	Symphony No. 23, in D, **287**
K. 182	"	"	Symphony No. 24, in B flat, **287**, 138
K. 183	"	"	Symphony No. 25, in G minor, **287**, 138
K. 184	"	"	Symphony No. 26 (Overture), in E flat, **288**, 287
K. 185	"	Vienna	Serenade No. 3 (*Finalmusik*), in D, **308**, 57
K. 186	"	Milan	Divertimento No. 4, in B flat, **304**, 56
K. 187	"?	Salzburg?	Divertimento No. 5, in C, **304**, 301
K. 188	1776	Salzburg	Divertimento No. 6, in C, **304**
K. 189	1773	Vienna	March in D (Orchestra), **316**
K. 190	"	Salzburg	Concertone in C, **341**, 340
K. 191	1774	"	Bassoon Concerto in B flat, **348**

KÖCHEL NO.	COM-POSED	PLACE	TITLE AND PAGE REFERENCE
K. 192	1774	Salzburg	Missa brevis in F, **258**
K. 193	"	"	*"Dixit"* and *"Magnificat,"* in C, **271**
K. 194	"	"	Missa brevis in D, **258**
K. 195	"	"	*Litaniae Lauretanae,* in D, **272**
K. 196	1774-1775	Salzburg-Munich	*La finta giardiniera, Opera buffa,* **213**, 58, 59, 60, 67, 107, 109, 209, 290
K. 196e	1775	Munich	Divertimento in E flat, **305**
K. 196f	"	"	Divertimento in B flat, **305**
K. 197			*"Tantum ergo"* (dubious), **277**
K. 198	1773	Milan	Offertorium *"Sub tuum praesidium,"* **270**
K. 199	"	Salzburg	Symphony No. 27, in G, **289**, 287
K. 200	"	"	Symphony No. 28, in C, **289**
K. 201	1774	Salzburg	Symphony No. 29, in A, **289**, 138
K. 202	"	"	Symphony No. 30, in D, **290**
K. 203	"	"	Serenade No. 4, in D, **308**
K. 204	1775	"	Serenade No. 5, in D, **308**, 138
K. 205	1773	Vienna	Divertimento No. 7, in D, **305**
K. 206	1774	"	March in D (*Idomeneo*) **316**
K. 207	1775	Salzburg	Concerto for Violin, No. 1, in B flat, **342**, 58, 205, 347
K. 208	"	"	*Il rè pastore, Dramma per musica,* **213**, 58
K. 209	"	"	Aria for Tenor (*"Si mostra la sorte"*), **239**
K. 210	"	"	Aria for Tenor (*"Con ossequio, con rispetto"*), **239**
K. 211	"	"	Concerto for Violin, No. 2, in D, **342**, 58, 205
K. 212	"	"	Church Sonata in B flat, **405**
K. 213	"	"	Divertimento No. 8, in F, **306**

KÖCHEL NO.	COM-POSED	PLACE	TITLE AND PAGE REFERENCE
K. 214	1775	Salzburg	March in C (Orchestra), **316**
K. 215	"	"	March in D (Orchestra), **316**
K. 216	"	"	Concerto for Violin, No. 3, in G, **342**, 58, 205
K. 217	"	"	Aria for Soprano ("*Voi avete un cor fedele*"), **239**
K. 218	"	"	Concerto for Violin, No. 4, in D, **343**, 58, 73, 205
K. 219	"	"	Concerto for Violin, No. 5, in A, **343**, 58, 205
K. 220	"	Munich	Missa brevis in C, **259**
K. 221	1771	Salzburg	Kyrie in C, **268**
K. 222	1775	Munich	Offertorium *de tempore* ("*Misericordias Domini*"), in D minor, **270**, 60
K. 223	1773		Osanna in C (fragmentary), **268**
K. 224	1776	Salzburg	Church Sonata in F, **405**
K. 225	"	"	Church Sonata in A, **405**
K. 226			Canon ("*O Schwestern traut dem Amor nicht*") (spurious)
K. 227			Canon ("*O wunderschön ist gottes Erde*"—Byrd) (spurious)
K. 228	1787	Vienna	Double Canon ("*Ach, zu kurz*"), **250**
K. 229	1782	"	Canon ("*Sie ist dahin*"), **250**
K. 230	"	"	Canon ("*Selig, selig alle*"), **250**
K. 231	"	"	Canon ("*Leck mich im Arsch*"), **250**
K. 232	1787	"	Canon ("*Lieber Freistädtler, lieber Gaulimauli*"), **250**
K. 233	1782	"	Canon ("*Leck mir den Arsch fein recht*"), **250**
K. 234	"	"	Canon ("*Bei der Hitz*"), **250**
K. 235			Canon for Piano (P. E. Bach)
K. 236	1790	Vienna	Andantino for Piano, in E flat, **383**

KÖCHEL NO.	COM- POSED	PLACE	TITLE AND PAGE REFERENCE
K. 237	1774	Salzburg	March in D (Orchestra), **316**
K. 238	1776	"	Concerto for Piano, No. 6, in B flat, **322**
K. 239	"	"	Serenade No. 6, for Two Orchestras, in D, **309**, 61
K. 240	"	"	Divertimento No. 9, in B flat, **306**
K. 241	"	"	Church Sonata in G, **405**
K. 242	"	"	Concerto for Three Pianos, No. 7, in F, **322,** 61
K. 243	"	"	*Litaniae de venerabili altaris sacramento,* **273**, 60, 272
K. 244	"	"	Church Sonata in F, **405**
K. 245	"	"	Church Sonata in D, **405**
K. 246	"	"	Concerto for Piano, No. 8, in C, **323,** 61
K. 247	"	"	Divertimento No. 10, in F, **305**
K. 248	"	"	March in F (Orchestra), **316**, 305
K. 249	"	"	March in D (for "Haffner" Serenade), **316**, 61, 301
K. 250	"	"	Serenade No. 7, in D ("Haffner"), **309**, 61, 294, 341
K. 251	"	"	Divertimento No. 11, in D, **307**, 61
K. 252	"	"	Divertimento No. 12, in E flat, **306**
K. 253	"	"	Divertimento No. 13, in F, **379**
K. 254	"	"	Divertimento (Trio for Piano, Violin, Cello) in B flat, **394**
K. 255	"	"	Recitative and Aria for Alto (*"Ombra felice"*), **239**
K. 256	"	"	Aria for Tenor (*"Clarice cara mia sposa"*), **239**
K. 257	1776	Salzburg	Missa (Credo Mass) in C, **259,** 60
K. 258	"	"	Missa brevis (Spaur Mass) in C, **260,** 60

KÖCHEL NO.	COM- POSED	PLACE	TITLE AND PAGE REFERENCE
K. 259	1776	Salzburg	Missa brevis (*"Organ Solo"*) in C, **260**, 60
K. 260	"	"	Offertorium (*"Venite, populi"*), **270**, 60, 260
K. 261	"	"	Adagio in E (for the Violin Concerto, K. 219), **347**
K. 262	"	"	Missa longa in C, **262**, 60, 263
K. 263	"	"	Church Sonata in C, **405**
K. 264	1778	Paris	9 Variations for Piano (*"Lison dormait"*), **378**
K. 265	"	"	12 Variations for Piano (*"Ah, vous dirai-je, maman"*), **379**
K. 266	1777	Salzburg	Trio (*Nachtmusik*) for Two Violins and Bass, in B flat, **401**
K. 267	"	"	4 Contredanses, **316**
K. 268	1780?	Salzburg-Munich	Concerto for Violin, No. 6, in E flat (doubtful), **344**
K. 269	1776	Salzburg	Rondo concertante for Violin and Orchestra, in B flat, **347**
K. 270	1777	"	Divertimento No. 14, in B flat, **306**
K. 271	"	"	Concerto for Piano, No. 9 (*"Jeune-homme"*), in E flat, **323**, 61, 205, 370
K. 271a	1777?	"	Concerto for Violin, No. 7, in D (doubtful), **344**
K. 272	1777	"	Recitative and Aria for Soprano (*"Ah, lo previdi"*), **239**
K. 273	"	"	Gradual (*"Sancta Maria"*), **276**, 60, 270
K. 274	"	"	Church Sonata in G, **405**
K. 275	"	"	Missa brevis in B flat, **261**, 60
K. 276	1779	"	*Regina Coeli*, in C, **275**

KÖCHEL NO.	COM- POSED	PLACE	TITLE AND PAGE REFERENCE
K. 277	1777	Salzburg	Offertory (*"Alma Dei creatoris"*), 270
K. 278	"	"	Church Sonata in C, 405
K. 279	1774	"	Sonata for Piano, in C, 372
K. 280	"	"	Sonata for Piano, in F, 372
K. 281	"	"	Sonata for Piano, in B flat, 372, 374
K. 282	"	"	Sonata for Piano, in E flat, 372, 322
K. 283	"	"	Sonata for Piano, in G, 372
K. 284	1775	Munich	Sonata for Piano, in D, 372
K. 285	1777	Mannheim	Quartet for Flute and Strings, in D, 398
K. 285a	1778	"	Quartet for Flute and Strings, in G (lost)
K. 285b	"	"	Quartet for Flute and Strings, in C, 398
K. 286	1776 or 1777	Salzburg	*Notturno* (Serenade No. 8), for Four Orchestras, in D, 310
K. 287	1777	"	Divertimento No. 15, in B flat, 305, 67
K. 288	"	"	Divertimento in F, 306
K. 289	"	"	Divertimento No. 16, in E flat, 306
K. 290	1773	Vienna	March in D (Two Horns and Strings), 316, 305
K. 291			Fugue for Orchestra (Michael Haydn)
K. 292	1775	Munich	Sonata for Bassoon and Cello, in B flat, 401
K. 293	1783	Vienna	Concerto for Oboe, in F (fragmentary)
K. 294	1778	Mannheim	Recitative and Aria for Soprano (*"Alcandro, lo confesso"*), 240
K. 295	"	"	Aria for Tenor (*"Se al labbro mio non credi"*), 240

KÖCHEL NO.	COMPOSED	PLACE	TITLE AND PAGE REFERENCE
K. 296	1778	Mannheim	Sonata for Piano and Violin, in C, 389
K. 297	"	Paris	Symphony No. 31 ("Paris"), in D, 291, 97, 205, 282, 298
K. 297a	"	"	(App. 1) 8 numbers to a Miserere by Holzbauer (lost)
K. 297b	"	"	(App. 9) *Sinfonia concertante* in E flat, 350, 94
K. 298	"	"	Quartet for Flute and Strings, in A, 399
K. 299	"	"	Concerto for Flute and Harp, in C, 350, 95
K. 299b	"	"	(App. 10) Ballet Music, *"Les petits riens,"* 312, 97, 345
K. 300	"	"	Gavotte for Orchestra, in B flat, 313
K. 301	"	Mannheim	Sonata for Piano and Violin, in G, 390
K. 302	"	"	Sonata for Piano and Violin, in E flat, 390
K. 303	"	"	Sonata for Piano and Violin, in C, 390
K. 304	"	Paris	Sonata for Piano and Violin, in E minor, 390
K. 305	"	"	Sonata for Piano and Violin, in A, 390
K. 306	1778	Paris	Sonata for Piano and Violin, in D, 390
K. 307	1777	Mannheim	Arietta (*"Oiseaux, si tous les ans"*), 248, 79, 247
K. 308	1778	"	Arietta (*"Dans un bois solitaire"*), 248, 79, 247
K. 309	1777	"	Sonata for Piano, in C, 374, 79
K. 310	1778	Paris	Sonata for Piano, in A minor, 374
K. 311	1777	Mannheim	Sonata for Piano, in D, 374

KÖCHEL NO.	COM- POSED	PLACE	TITLE AND PAGE REFERENCE
K. 311a	1778	Paris	(App. 8) Overture in B flat (doubt- ful)
K. 312	1774	Salzburg	Allegro of a Piano Sonata, in G minor, **383**
K. 313	1778	Mannheim	Concerto for Flute, in G, **349**
K. 314	”	”	Concerto for Flute (or Oboe), in D, **349**
K. 315	”	”	Andante for Flute and Orchestra, in C, **349**
K. 315a	1779	Salzburg	8 Minuets, **383**
K. 316	1778	Paris	Recitative and Aria for Soprano (*"Popoli di Tessaglia"*), **240**, 103
K. 317	1779	Salzburg	Mass ("Coronation") in C, **261**, 105 254
K. 318	”	”	Symphony No. 32 (Overture), in G, **292**, 105
K. 319	”	”	Symphony No. 33, in B flat, **292**, 105, 281
K. 320	”	”	Serenade No. 9, in D ("Post Horn"), **310**, 105, 138
K. 321	”	”	*Vesperae de Dominica*, in C, **271**, 105
K. 322	1778	Mannheim	Kyrie in E flat (fragment), **268**
K. 323	1779	Salzburg	Kyrie in C (fragment), **268**
K. 324	”	?	Hymn, *"Salus infirmorum"* (doubt- ful), **277**
K. 325	”	?	Hymn, *"Sancta Maria, ora pro nobis"* (doubtful), **277**
K. 326	1771	Salzburg	Hymn, *"Justum deduxit Dominus,"* **277**
K. 327			Hymn, *"Adoramus te"* (Gasparini)
K. 328	1779	Salzburg	Church Sonata in C, **405**, 105
K. 329	”	”	Church Sonata in C, **405**, 105
K. 330	1778	Paris	Sonata for Piano, in C, **374**

KÖCHEL NO.	COM- POSED	PLACE	TITLE AND PAGE REFERENCE
K. 331	1778	Paris	Sonata for Piano, in A ("Alla Turca"), **374, 373, 380**
K. 332	"	"	Sonata for Piano, in F, **374**
K. 333	1778	Paris	Sonata for Piano, in B flat, **374**
K. 334	1779	Salzburg	Divertimento No. 17 in D, **305**
K. 335	"	"	2 Marches in D (Orchestra), **316**
K. 336	1780	"	Church Sonata in C, **405**, 105
K. 337	"	"	Missa solemnis in C, **262**, 105
K. 338	"	"	Symphony No. 34, in C, **293**, 105, 138
K. 339	"	"	*Vesperae solemnes de confessore,* in C, **271**, 105
K. 340	"		Kyrie (lost; dubious)
K. 341	1781	Munich	Kyrie in D minor, **268**, 205
K. 342			Offertorium, *"Benedicite angeli"* (Leopold Mozart)
K. 343	1779?	Salzburg	2 German Church Songs, **277**
K. 344	1779	"	*Zaïde, Singspiel* (incomplete), **215**
K. 345	"	"	Choruses and Interludes for *"König Thamos,"* **214**, 106
K. 346	1783	Vienna	Notturno (*"Luci care, luci belle"*) for 3 Voices, with 3 Basset Horns, **250**
K. 347	1782	"	Canon (*"Lasst uns ziehn"*), **250**
K. 348	"	"	Canon (*"V'amo di core teneramente"*), **250**
K. 349	1780 or 1781	Munich	Song with Piano, *Die Zufriedenheit* (*"Was frag ich"*), **248**
K. 350			Song with Piano (*"Schlafe mein Prinzchen"*—Bernhard Flies), **248**
K. 351	1780 or 1781	Munich	Song with Mandolin (*"Komm, liebe Zither"*), **248**
K. 352	1781	Vienna	8 Variations for Piano (*"Les Mariages Samnites"*), **380**

KÖCHEL NO.	COM-POSED	PLACE	TITLE AND PAGE REFERENCE
K. 353	1778	Paris	12 Variations for Piano (*"La belle Françoise"*), **379**
K. 354	"	"	12 Variations for Piano (*"Je suis Lindor"*), **379**
K. 355	1790	Vienna	Minuet for Piano, in D, **383, 384**
K. 356	1791	"	Adagio for Glass Harmonica, in C, **406**
K. 357	1786	"	Piano Sonata for Four Hands, in G (fragment), **385**
K. 358	1774	Salzburg	Piano Sonata for Four Hands, in B flat, **385**
K. 359	1781	Vienna	12 Variations for Piano and Violin (*"La Bergère Célimène"*), **393**
K. 360	"	"	6 Variations for Piano and Violin (*"Hélas, j'ai perdu mon amant"*), **393**
K. 361	"	Munich and Vienna	Serenade No. 10, for Winds, in B flat, **311, 398, 401**
K. 362	1780		March (*Idomeneo*), **316**
K. 363	"	Salzburg	3 Minuets, **316**
K. 364	1779	"	*Sinfonia concertante* for Violin and Viola, in E flat, **346**, 105, 340, 346, 350
K. 365	"	"	Concerto for Two Pianos, No. 10, in E flat, **325**, 105, 138
K. 366	1780-1781	Salzburg and Munich	*Idomeneo, rè di Creta, Opera seria,* **216f.**, 95, 107-114, 138, 140, 150, 196, 205, 209, 236
K. 367	1781	Munich	Ballet Music to *Idomeneo*
K. 368	"	"	Recitative and Aria for Soprano (*"Ma, che vi fece, o stelle"*), **240**
K. 369	"	"	Scena and Aria for Soprano (*"Misera, dove son!"*), **241**
K. 370	"	"	Quartet for Oboe and Strings, in F, **399**

KÖCHEL NO.	COM- POSED	PLACE	TITLE AND PAGE REFERENCE
K. 371	1781	Vienna	Rondo for Horn and Orchestra, in E flat (sketch)
K. 372	"	"	Allegro of a Sonata for Piano and Violin, in B flat (fragmentary)
K. 373	"	"	Rondo for a Violin Concerto, in C, 347
K. 374	"	"	Recitative and Aria (*"Or che il cielo"*), for Soprano, 241
K. 375	"	"	Serenade No. 11, for Winds, in E flat, 311
K. 376	"	"	Sonata for Piano and Violin, in F, 391, 389
K. 377	"	"	Sonata for Piano and Violin, in F, 391, 389
K. 378	1779	Salzburg	Sonata for Piano and Violin, in B flat, 391, 389
K. 379	1781	Vienna	Sonata for Piano and Violin, in G, 391
K. 380	"	"	Sonata for Piano and Violin, in E flat, 391
K. 381	1772	Salzburg?	Piano Sonata for 4 Hands, in D, 385
K. 382	1782	Vienna	Rondo for Piano and Orchestra, in D, 322, 138
K. 383	"	"	Aria for Soprano (*"Nehmt meinen Dank"*), 241
K. 384	1781- 1782	"	*Die Entführung aus dem Serail,* Singspiel, 218 f., 122, 123, 128-133, 136, 163, 177, 193-194, 209, 263, 294, 349
K. 385	1782	Vienna	Symphony No. 35 ("Haffner"), in D, 294, 138, 298
K. 386	"	"	Rondo for Piano and Orchestra, in A, 327
K. 386d	"	"	(App. 25) Recitative (*"O Calpe"*) (fragmentary)

KÖCHEL NO.	COMPOSED	PLACE	TITLE AND PAGE REFERENCE
K. 387	1782	Vienna	Quartet for Strings, No. 14, in G, **359**, 142
K. 388	"	"	Serenade No. 12, for Winds, in C minor, **312**, 263, 294, 367
K. 389	"	"	Duet (*"Welch ängstliches Beben"*) (*Die Entführung*), **251**
K. 390	1780	Salzburg	Song with Piano (*"Ich würd auf meinem Pfad"*), **247**
K. 391	"	"	Song with Piano (*"Sei du mein Trost"*), **248**
K. 392	"	"	Song with Piano (*"Verdankt sei es dem Glanz"*), **248**
K. 393	1782	Vienna	Solfeggi, for Soprano
K. 394	"	"	Fantasia and Fugue for Piano, in C, **382**
K. 395	1778	Paris	Capriccio for Piano, in C, **383**
K. 396	1782	Vienna	Adagio for Piano and Violin, in C minor (fragmentary), **393**, 382
K. 397	"	"	Fantasia for Piano, in D minor, **382**
K. 398	1783	"	6 Variations for Piano (*"Salve tu, Domine"*), **380**, 147
K. 399	1782	"	Suite for Piano, in C, **383**
K. 400	1781	"	Allegro of a Sonata for Piano, in B flat, **383**
K. 401	1782	"	Fugue for Piano, in G minor, **383**
K. 402	"	"	Sonata for Piano and Violin, in A (fragmentary), **393**
K. 403	"	"	Sonata for Piano and Violin, in C (fragmentary), **393**
K. 404	"	"	Andante and Allegretto for Piano and Violin, in C (fragmentary), **393**
K. 404a	1782	"	6 Preludes to Fugues by J. S. and W. F. Bach, for String Trio

KÖCHEL NO.	COM- POSED	PLACE	TITLE AND PAGE REFERENCE
K. 405	"	"	5 Fugues by Bach arranged for String Quartet
K. 406	1787	"	Quintet for Strings arranged from K. 388, in C minor, **367**
K. 407	1782	"	Quintet for Horn and Strings, in E flat, **400**
K. 408	1782	"	3 Marches for Orchestra, **316**
K. 409	"	"	Minuet to a Symphony, in C, **316**
K. 410	1783	"	Adagio for 2 Basset Horns and Bassoon, in F, **401**
K. 411	"	"	Adagio for 2 Clarinets and 3 Basset Horns, in F, **402**
K. 412	1782	Vienna	Concerto for Horn, in D, **351**
K. 413	1782- 1783	"	Concerto for Piano, No. 11, in F, **326**, 159, 263
K. 414	1782	"	Concerto for Piano, No. 12, in A, **326**, 159, 263
K. 415	1782- 1783	"	Concerto for Piano, No. 13, in C, **327**, 138, 159, 263, 326, 332, 334
K. 416	1783	"	Scena and Rondo for Soprano (*"Mia speranza adorata"*), **241**
K. 417	"	"	Concerto for Horn, in E flat, **351**
K. 418	"	"	Aria for Soprano (*"Vorrei spiegarvi, oh Dio"*), **241**
K. 419	"	"	Aria for Soprano (*"No, no, che non sei capace"*), **241**
K. 420	"	"	Aria for Tenor (*"Per pietà, non ricercate"*), **241**
K. 421	"	"	Quartet for Strings, No. 15, in D minor, **360**, 142, 333
K. 422	"	Salzburg	*L'oca del Cairo*, Opera buffa (fragmentary), **220**, 140, 151
K. 423	"	"	Duo for Violin and Viola, in G, **402**, 140, 296, 346

KÖCHEL NO.	COMPOSED	PLACE	TITLE AND PAGE REFERENCE
K. 424	1783	Salzburg	Duo for Violin and Viola, in B flat, **402**, 140, 296, 346
K. 425	"	Linz	Symphony No. 36, in C, **295**, 296
K. 426	"	Vienna	Fugue for 2 Pianos, in C minor, **387**
K. 427	1782-1783	"	Mass in C minor, **262**, 135, 140, 161, 166, 255
K. 428	1783	"	Quartet for Strings, No. 16, in E flat, **361**, 142-146
K. 429	"	"	Cantata (*"Dir, Seele des Weltalls"*), **278**
K. 429a	"	"	Cantata (*"Dir, Seele des Weltalls"*) with Piano, **251**
K. 430	"	Salzburg	*Lo sposo deluso, Opera buffa* (fragment), **221**, 151
K. 431	"	Vienna	Recitative and Aria for Tenor (*"Misero! o sogno!"*), **242**
K. 432	"	"	Recitative and Aria for Bass (*"Così dunque tradisci"*), **242**
K. 433	"	"	Arietta for Bass (*"Männer suchen stets"*), **242**
K. 434	"	Salzburg	Terzetto (*"Del gran regno delle Amazoni"*), **251**
K. 435	"	Vienna	Aria for Tenor (*"Müsst' ich auch"*), **242**
K. 436	"	"	Notturno for 2 Sopranos and Bass (*"Ecco quel fiero istante"*), **251**
K. 437	"	"	Notturno for 2 Sopranos and Bass (*"Mi lagnerò tacendo"*), **251**
K. 438	"	"	Notturno for 3 Voices (*"Se lontan ben mio, tu sei"*), **251**
K. 439	"	"	Notturno for 2 Sopranos and Bass (*"Due pupille amabile"*), **251**
K. 440	1782	"	Aria for Soprano (*"In te spero o sposo"*), **251**

KÖCHEL NO.	COMPOSED	PLACE	TITLE AND PAGE REFERENCE
K. 441	1783	Vienna	Terzetto (*"Liebes Mandel, wo is's Bandel?"*), **251**
K. 442	"	"	Trio for Piano, Violin and Violoncello, in D minor (incomplete), **403**
K. 443	1782	"	Fugue, in 3 vocal parts (fragmentary), **251**
K. 444	1783	Linz	Introduction, in G, to a Symphony (No. 37) of Michael Haydn, **296**
K. 445	1779	Salzburg	March in D (Orchestra), **316**
K. 446	1783	Vienna	Music to a Pantomime (fragmentary)
K. 447	"	"	Concerto for Horn, in E flat, **351**
K. 448	1781	"	Sonata for 2 Pianos, in D, **387**, 331
K. 449	1784	"	Concerto for Piano, No. 14, in E flat, **328**, 140-141
K. 450	"	"	Concerto for Piano, No. 15, in B flat, **329**, 140-141, 328
K. 451	"	"	Concerto for Piano, No. 16, in D, **330**, 140-141, 328, 332
K. 452	"	"	Quintet for Piano and Winds, in E flat, **402**, 141, 331
K. 453	"	"	Concerto for Piano, No. 17, in G, **330**, 140-141, 328, 332
K. 454	"	"	Sonata for Piano and Violin, in B flat, **391**, 389
K. 455	"	"	10 Variations for Piano (*"Unser dummer Pöbel meint"*), **380**
K. 456	"	"	Concerto for Piano, No. 18, in B flat, **331**, 140, 141n., 143, 334
K. 457	"	"	Sonata for Piano, in C minor, **375**, 382
K. 458	"	"	Quartet for Strings, No. 17 ("Hunt"), in B flat, **362**, 142-146

KÖCHEL NO.	COM-POSED	PLACE	TITLE AND PAGE REFERENCE
K. 459	1784	Vienna	Concerto for Piano, No. 19, in F, **332**, 141n., 186, 332, 334
K. 460	”	”	8 Variations for Piano (*"Come un agnello"*), **381**, 147
K. 461	”	Vienna	6 Minuets for Orchestra, **316**
K. 462	”	”	6 Contredanses for Orchestra, **316**
K. 463	”	”	2 Contredanses with minuets, for Orchestra, **316**
K. 464	1785	”	Quartet for Strings, No. 18, in A, **362**, 142-146
K. 465	”	”	Quartet for Strings, No. 19, in C (*"Dissonant"*), **362**, 142-146
K. 466	”	”	Concerto for Piano, No. 20, in D minor, **333**, 142-146, 332, 334, 337
K. 467	”	”	Concerto for Piano, No. 21, in C, **334**, 144
K. 468	”	”	Song with Piano (*"Die ihr einem neuen Grade"*), **248**
K. 469	”	”	*Davidde penitente*, Oratorio, **278**
K. 470	”	”	Andante to a Violin Concerto of Viotti (lost)
K. 471	”	”	Cantata (*"Die Maurerfreude"*), **278**
K. 472	”	”	Song with Piano (*"Ihr Mädchen, flieht"*), **248**
K. 473	”	”	Song with Piano (*"Wie Sanft, wie ruhig"*), **248**
K. 474	”	”	Song with Piano (*"Der reiche Tor"*), **248**
K. 475	”	”	Fantasia for Piano, in C minor, **375**, 206, 382
K. 476	”	”	Song with Piano (*"Das Veilchen"*), **248**, 247
K. 477	”	”	*Maurerische Trauermusik*, **313**

KÖCHEL NO.	COM-POSED	PLACE	TITLE AND PAGE REFERENCE
K. 478	1785	Vienna	Quartet for Piano and Strings, in G minor, **397**, 287
K. 479	"	"	Quartet (*"Dite almeno"*), **252**
K. 480	"	"	Terzet (*"Mandina amabile"*), **252**
K. 481	"	"	Sonata for Piano and Violin, in E flat, **392**
K. 482	"	"	Concerto for Piano, No. 22, in E flat, **335**, 157
K. 483	"	"	Song with Chorus (*"Zerfliesset heut, geliebte Brüder"*), **251**
K. 484	"	"	Chorus (*"Ihr unsre neuen Leiter"*), **251**
K. 485	1786	"	Rondo for Piano, in D, **383**, 398
K. 486	"	"	*Der Schauspieldirektor, Singspiel,* **221**
K. 486a	1778	Mannheim	Recitative and Aria for Soprano (*"Basta, vincesti"*), **242**, 79
K. 487	1786	Vienna	12 Duets for 2 Horns (Basset?), **402**
K. 488	"	"	Concerto for Piano, No. 23, in A, **335**, 157
K. 489	"	"	Duet for Soprano and Tenor (*"Spiegarti, oh Dio, non posso"*), **252**
K. 490	"	"	Scena and Rondo for Soprano (*"Non più, tutto"*), **242**
K. 491	"	"	Concerto for Piano, No. 24, in C minor, **336**, 157, 335
K. 492	1785-1786	"	*Le nozze di Figaro, Opera buffa,* **222f.**, 148, 151-161, 163-164, 166-169, 172-173, 182-183, 186, 209, 236, 254, 328, 332, 335, 338, 397
K. 493	1786	"	Quartet for Piano and Strings, in E flat, **397**, 162
K. 494	"	"	Rondo for Piano, in F, **383**
K. 495	"	"	Concerto for Horn, in E flat, **351**, 162

KÖCHEL NO.	COMPOSED	PLACE	TITLE AND PAGE REFERENCE
K. 530	1787	Prague	Song with Piano (*"Wo bist du, Bild?"*), **249**
K. 531	"	Vienna	Song with Piano, *Die kleine Spinnerin* (*"Was spinnst' du"*), **249**
K. 532	"	"	Terzetto (*"Grazie agl'inganni tuoi"*) (sketch), **252**
K. 533	1788	"	Allegro and Andante for Piano, in F, **383**
K. 534	"	"	Contredanse for Orchestra, **316**
K. 535	"	"	Contredanse (*"La Bataille"*) for Orchestra, **316**
K. 535a	"	"	3 Contredanses for Orchestra, **316**
K. 536	"	"	6 German Dances for Orchestra, **317**
K. 537	"	"	Concerto for Piano, No. 26 ("Coronation"), in D, **339**, 160, 174, 186, 338
K. 538	"	"	Aria for Soprano (*"Ah se in ciel"*), **244**
K. 539	"	"	Song (*"Ich möchte wohl"*), **244**
K. 540	"	"	Adagio for Piano, in B minor, **383**, 384
K. 541	"	"	Arietta for Bass (*"Un bacio di mano"*), **244**
K. 542	"	"	Trio for Piano, Violin and Cello, in E, **395**, 176
K. 543	"	"	Symphony No. 39, in E flat, **297**, 174-175, 198, 290
K. 544	"	"	*Ein kleiner Marsch*, in D (lost), **316**
K. 545	"	"	Sonata for Piano, in C ("Sonatina"), **377**
K. 546	"	"	Adagio and Fugue for Strings, in C minor (originally for 2 Pianos), **385**

KÖCHEL NO.	COMPOSED	PLACE	TITLE AND PAGE REFERENCE
K. 547	1788	Vienna	"Sonatina" for Piano and Violin, in F, **393**, 389
K. 547a	"	"	Sonata for Piano, in F, **377**
K. 548	"	"	Trio for Piano, Violin and Cello, in C, **396**, 176
K. 549	"	"	Canzonetta for 2 Sopranos and Bass (*"Più non si trovano"*), **251**
K. 550	"	"	Symphony No. 40, in G minor, **298**, 174, 198, 206, 337
K. 551	"	"	Symphony No. 41 ("Jupiter"), in C, **299**, 174, 198, 279, 338.
K. 552	"	"	Song with Piano, *Beim Auszug in das Feld* (*"Dem hohen Kaiser-Worte treu"*), **249**
K. 553	"	"	Canon (*"Alleluja"*), **250**
K. 554	"	"	Canon (*"Ave Maria"*), **250**
K. 555	"	"	Canon (*"Lacrimoso son io"*), **250**
K. 556	"	"	Canon (*"G'rechtelt's enk"*), **250**
K. 557	"	"	Canon (*"Nascoso è il mio sol"*), **250**
K. 558	"	"	Canon (*"Gehn ma in'n Prada"*), **250**
K. 559	"	"	Canon (*"Difficile lectu mihi"*), **250**
K. 560	"	"	Canons (*"O du eselhafter Martin"*— *"O du eselhafter Peierl"*), **250**
K. 561	"	"	Canon (*"Bona nox, bist a rechta Ox"*), **250**
K. 562	"	"	Canon (*"Caro, bell' idol mio"*) **250**
K. 562e	"	"	(App. 66) Trio for Violin, Viola and Violoncello, in G (fragment)
K. 563	"	"	Divertimento for String Trio, in E flat, **403**, 365
K. 564	"	"	Trio for Piano, Violin and Violoncello, in G, **396**, 176
K. 565	"	"	2 Contredanses for Orchestra, **316**

KÖCHEL NO.	COMPOSED	PLACE	TITLE AND PAGE REFERENCE
K. 566	1788	Vienna	Instrumentation of Handel's *Acis and Galatea*
K. 567	"	"	6 German Dances for Orchestra, **317**
K. 568	"	"	12 Minuets for Orchestra, **316**
K. 569	1789	"	Aria (*"Ohne Zwang"*) (*lost*)
K. 570	"	"	Sonata for Piano, in B flat, **377**
K. 571	"	"	6 German Dances for Orchestra, **317**
K. 571a	"	"	Comic Quartet, *"Caro mio, Druck und Schluck,"* **251**
K. 572	"	"	Instrumentation of Handel's *The Messiah*
K. 573	"	Potsdam	9 Variations for Piano (Duport), in D, **381**
K. 574	"	Leipzig	Gigue for Piano, in G minor, **383**, **384**
K. 575	"	Vienna	Quartet for Strings, No. 21, in D, **364**, **178**
K. 576	"	"	Sonata for Piano, in D, **377**
K. 577	"	"	Rondo for Soprano (*"Al desio"*), **244**
K. 578	"	"	Aria for Soprano (*"Alma grande"*), **244**
K. 579	"	"	Aria for Soprano (*"Un moto di gioia"*), **244**
K. 580	"	"	Aria for Soprano (*"Schon lacht der holde Frühling"*), **245**
K. 581	"	"	Quintet for Clarinet and Strings, in A, **400**
K. 582	"	"	Aria for Soprano (*"Chi sà, chi sà, qual sia"*), **245**
K. 583	"	"	Aria for Soprano (*"Vado, ma dove?"*), **245**
K. 584	"	"	Aria for Bass (*"Rivolgete a lui lo sguardo"*), **245**
K. 585	"	"	12 Minuets for Orchestra, **316**

KÖCHEL NO.	COM-POSED	PLACE	TITLE AND PAGE REFERENCE
K. 586	1789	Vienna	12 German Dances for Orchestra, **317**
K. 587	"	"	Contredanse for Orchestra, **316**
K. 588	1790	"	*Così fan tutte, Opera buffa,* **229 f.,** 154, 176, 182-185, 188, 208, 236, 302
K. 589	"	"	Quartet for Strings, No. 22, in B flat, **364**, 176, 178
K. 590	"	"	Quartet for Strings, No. 23, in F, **365**, 176, 178
K. 591	"	"	Instrumentation of Handel's *Alexander's Feast*
K. 592	"	"	Instrumentation of Handel's *Ode to Saint Cecilia*
K. 593	"	"	Quintet for Strings, in D, **369**, 176, 187
K. 594	"	Frankfort-Vienna	Adagio and Allegro for a Mechanical Organ, in F minor, **406**
K. 595	1791	Vienna	Concerto for Piano, No. 27, in B flat, **339**, 160, 176, 187
K. 596	"	"	Song with Piano (*"Komm, lieber Mai"*), **249**
K. 597	"	"	Song with Piano (*"Erwacht zum neuen Leben"*), **249**
K. 598	"	"	Song with Piano (*"Wir Kinder"*), **249**
K. 599	"	"	6 Minuets for Orchestra, **316**
K. 600	"	"	6 German Dances for Orchestra, **317**
K. 601	"	"	4 Minuets for Orchestra, **316**
K. 602	"	"	4 German Dances for Orchestra, **317**
K. 603	"	"	2 Contredanses for Orchestra, **316**
K. 604	"	"	2 Minuets for Orchestra, **316**
K. 605	"	"	3 German Dances for Orchestra, **317**
K. 606	"	"	6 German Dances for Orchestra, **317**

KÖCHEL NO.	COMPOSED	PLACE	TITLE AND PAGE REFERENCE
K. 607	1791	Vienna	Contredanse for Orchestra, **316**
K. 608	"	"	Fantasia for a Mechanical Organ, in F minor, **406**
K. 609	"	"	5 Contredanses for Orchestra, **316**
K. 610	"	"	Contredanse for Orchestra, **316**
K. 611	"	"	A German Dance, **317**
K. 612	"	"	Aria for Bass (*"Per questa bella mano"*), **245**
K. 613	"	"	6 Variations for Piano (*"Ein Weib ist das herrlichste Ding"*), **381**
K. 614	"	"	Quintet for Strings, in E flat, **370**, 176, 187
K. 615	"	"	Chorus (*"Viviamo felici"*) (*lost*)
K. 616	"	"	Andante for a Small Mechanical Organ, in F, **406**
K. 617	"	"	Adagio and Rondo for Glass Harmonica, Flute, Oboe, Viola and Cello, in C minor, **406**
K. 618	"	Baden	Motet (*"Ave, verum corpus"*), **276**, 275
K. 619	"	Vienna	Cantata (*"Die ihr des unermesslichen Weltalls"*), **249**
K. 620	"	"	*Die Zauberflöte, Grosse Oper*, **232 f.**, vii, 112, 166, 188-189, 209, 255, 278, 338
K. 621	"	Vienna and Prague	*La clemenza di Tito, Opera seria*, **230 f.**, 192, 209, 236
K. 622	"	Vienna	Concerto for Clarinet, in A, **352**, 198
K. 623	"	"	Cantata (*"Eine kleine Freimaurer-Kantate"*), **278**, 198, 200
K. 624	1768-1791		Cadenzas to Piano Concertos (See Appendix 2)

Index of Names

Index of Names

A

Abel, Karl Friedrich, 29, 36, 282
Abert, Hermann, 258n., 399
Adamberger, J. V., 129, 130, 138, 241, 242, 278
Adélaïde, Princess, 25
Adlgasser, Anton Cajetan, 4, 36, 80, 101, 210
Affligio, Giuseppe, 40
Agujari, Lucrezia, 47
Albertarelli, Francesco, 174, 244
Allegri, Gregorio, 47n.
Amalie, Princess of Prussia, 22
Amicis, Maria Anna de, 55
Anderson, Emily, 75
André, Johann, 106, 215, 348
Anfossi, Pasquale, 59, 236, 241, 244
Angerbauer, Johann Ulrich, 116
Arco, Count Karl, 118
Artaria (Publ.), 159, 389, 397
Attwood, Thomas, 147
Aurnhammer, Herr, 125, 325
Aurnhammer, Josephine, 119n., 138, 325, 387

B

Bach, Carl Philip Emanuel, 26, 29, 317, 325n., 333

Bach, Johann Christian, 29, 36, 100, 282, 317, 318, 321, 388
Bach, Johann Sebastian, 29, 36, 134, 135, 177, 201, 263, 264, 384, 388, 406
Bähr, Joseph, 340
Barisani, Dr. Sylvester von, 74
Barrington, Daines, 32, 277
Bassi, Luigi, 169
Beaumarchais, Pierre Augustin, 151, 152, 154n., 155, 156, 157n., 173, 183, 222, 379
Beethoven, Ludwig van, x, 74, 76, 121, 146, 164, 298-300, 318, 324, 325n., 327, 330, 333, 362, 369, 373, 376, 396
Benucci, Francesco, 158, 245
Bernasconi, Antonia, 50, 51
Bertati, Giovanni, 168
Biggs, E. Power, 404
Blume, Friedrich, 338
Böhm, Johannes, 106, 214
Bonaparte, Napoleon, 155
Bondini, Caterina, 169
Bondini, Pasquale, 166, 168
Bonno, Giuseppe, 114
Bretzner, Christoph Friedrich, 122, 130, 133n.
Brunetti, Gaetano, 62, 115, 116, 347